HUMANIZING PEDAGOGY
THROUGH HIV AND AIDS PREVENTION

Series in Critical Narrative
Edited by Donaldo Macedo
University of Massachusetts Boston

Now in print
The Hegemony of English
    by Donaldo Macedo, Bessie Dendrinos, and
    Panayota Gounari (2003)
Letters from Lexington: Reflections on Propaganda
    New Updated Edition
    by Noam Chomsky (2004)
Pedogogy of Indignation
    by Paulo Freire (2004)
Howard Zinn on Democratic Education
    by Howard Zinn with Donaldo Macedo (2005)
Critical Literacy: What Every American Ought to Know
    by Eugene F. Provenzo, Jr. (2005)
How Children Learn: Getting Beyond the Deficit Myth
    by Terese Fayden (2005)
The Globalization of Racism
    edited by Donaldo Macedo and Panayota Gounari (2006)
Humanizing Pedagogy Through HIV and AIDS Prevention:
    Transforming Teacher Knowledge
    coordinated by the American Association of Colleges for
    Teacher Education with Carl A. Grant and
    Liane M. Summerfield (2006)

Forthcoming in the series
Science, Truth, and Ideology
    by Stanley Aronowitz (2006)
Pedogogy of Dreaming
    by Paulo Freire (2006)
Dear Paulo: Letters from Teachers
    by Sonia Nieto (2006)

HUMANIZING PEDAGOGY
THROUGH HIV AND AIDS PREVENTION
TRANSFORMING TEACHER KNOWLEDGE

COORDINATED BY THE

AMERICAN ASSOCIATION OF COLLEGES FOR TEACHER EDUCATION

Serving Learners

WITH

CARL A. GRANT AND LIANE M. SUMMERFIELD

Paradigm Publishers

Boulder • London

The American Association of Colleges for Teacher Education is a national voluntary association of colleges and universities with undergraduate or graduate programs to prepare professional educators. The association supports programs in data gathering, equity, leadership development, networking, policy analysis, professional issues, and scholarship.

The opinions, conclusions, and recommendations expressed in this publication do not necessarily reflect the views or opinions of the American Association of Colleges for Teacher Education. AACTE does not endorse or warrant this information. AACTE is publishing this document to stimulate discussion, study, and experimentation among educators. The reader must evaluate this information in light of the unique circumstances of any particular situation and must determine independently the applicability of this information thereto.

Published in the United States by Paradigm Publishers, 3360 Mitchell Lane, Suite E, Boulder, Colorado 80301 USA.

Paradigm Publishers is the trade name of Birkenkamp & Company, LLC, Dean Birkenkamp, President and Publisher.

Library of Congress Cataloging-in-Publication Data has been applied for.

ISBN-13: 978-1-59451-259-9
ISBN-10: 1-59451-259-0 (hc)

Printed and bound in the United States of America on acid-free paper that meets the standards of the American National Standard for Permanence of Paper for Printed Library Materials.

Designed and Typeset by Straight Creek Bookmakers.

10 09 08 07 06
1   2   3   4   5

CONTENTS

Contents

Contents

FOREWORD
AIDS AND HUMAN DIGNITY

⤙

The global pattern of AIDS death—2.4 million in sub-Saharan Africa last year, out of 3 million worldwide; only 20,000 in North America but most in minority communities—also evokes the racial order of old South Africa. To date, access to life-saving medicines and care for people living with HIV and AIDS have been largely determined by race, class, gender, and geography.[1]

The uprising in France among North African and Arab youths, the unveiling by Hurricane Katrina of the grotesque poverty delimited by race in New Orleans, and the HIV/AIDS pandemic in many African countries demonstrate, once more, the challenges we are facing as we enter the twenty-first century. No longer can we afford to address the enormity of world problems through the reductionistic lens of science alone—an approach to the world that has too often precluded understanding of how the interaction among critical factors such as race, class, gender, and sexual orientation produce human misery and despair.

The authors of *Humanizing Pedagogy Through HIV/AIDS Prevention* make a convincing argument that, although rigorous scientific intervention is needed to address the current HIV/AIDS pandemic worldwide, this intervention must take place within a global understanding of the material conditions that produce specific manifestations of human misery—conditions of racism and exclusion that make it easier to exploit other human beings. For example, although scientists have made important inroads in better understanding the underlying biological factors inherent in HIV/AIDS, drug company executives, through their monopoly on the market, not only exploit those who have the least means to access HIV/AIDS treatment but they also exclude millions of

HIV-infected individuals from treatment so they can guarantee themselves obscene profit. Thus, the chapters of this important and timely book correctly point out that the current xenophobia and homophobia throughout the world coupled with economic dislocation of tsunami proportions have produced unacceptable discriminatory practices that create fertile terrain for the unchecked spread of HIV/AIDS. These authors passionately and compassionately argue for a new pedagogy based on the moral conviction that we must humanize HIV/AIDS education by eliminating prejudicial and hostile attitudes toward those who are already suffering and are confronting insurmountable obstacles to recapturing their health, their dignity, and their humanity.

Imagine that in a sudden burst of moral rectitude, President Bush uses his bully pulpit to summon the U.S. citizenry to mobilize against a global terror that is claiming approximately 8,219 victims every day who die of AIDS. Imagine that President Bush severely censures Congress for the paltry $400 million it now spends to fight the AIDS terror and challenges all congressmembers to put partisanship aside and rise to the occasion by appropriating $60 billion (to match what they spent rescuing the airline industry after September 11, compensating the corporate world for its financial losses, and helping New York City rebuild from the ashes of Ground Zero). Imagine that President Bush aggressively urges the citizens to be patriotic and make sacrifices, for the war on AIDS terror requires patience, vigilance, and courage since "there are other terrorists who threaten America and our friends, and there are other nations willing to sponsor them. We will not be secure as a nation until all of these threats are defeated," as he said in the aftermath of 9/11.

Imagine that President Bush announces to the nation the appointment of a homeland AIDS czar to coordinate research, education, and services, all designed to eradicate the AIDS terror that not only represents "the most numerically lethal pandemic in 650 years," but is also "an attack on civilization itself."[2] Imagine that President Bush uses his bully pulpit to marshal charity agencies to organize their forces, expertise, and resources against the AIDS terror, which has targeted 40 million people for death, approximately the population of New York and Texas combined.[3] Imagine that President Bush, in a cowboy tone, takes his war on AIDS international by cautioning those leaders who harbor cells that give rise to this terrifying and lethal virus, such as traffickers in children and women and drug dens that contribute to the spread of AIDS, that they will be held responsible for providing sanctuary to the AIDS terrorists and will face swift retribution, including military intervention that will surely put an end to their leadership.

Imagine that President Bush draws the line by telling world leaders that in this war against AIDS terror "you are either with us or you are against us." Imagine that President Bush uses his moral stature to enlist religious leaders, including the Vatican, to use their power and influence to spread the word for safe sex; for example, to require use of condoms and provide sex education in all of the schools and institutions they control. Imagine that Pope Benedict XVI, Reverend Pat Robertson, and Reverend Jerry Falwell, among others, join President Bush in his global crusade against the AIDS terror, which is crippling economic growth because some "countries will lose 20 percent of their GDP by 2020" and therefore threatening democracy as we know it.[4]

Most Americans would cringe at the thought of having to sacrifice for such a large-scale humanitarian war, and point out that President Bush is probably psychologically unstable. Conservative fundamentalists would aggressively mobilize to impeach him. The thought of spending our tax dollars to the tune of $60 billion to rescue people who, according to the conservatives, are responsible for their own misery, smacks of anti-Americanism. Most would argue against the magnitude of such economic waste in trying to educate and change the promiscuity of third world people, African Americans, Latino/a Americans, and homosexuals. Some would also add that, after all, most of these people are genetically predisposed toward promiscuity and there is no amount of money or education that could change this sad but true fact.

Against the backdrop of selective respect for human life, I want to argue in this foreword that in any attempt to launch effective and humane AIDS education in this country and abroad, educators must acknowledge that, in our highly discriminatory and racist democracy, not all human lives are equally worthy, as public outpouring of sorrow over the despicable and tragic loss of September 11 reminds us. The genuine empathy displayed toward the victims of September 11 is diametrically opposed to our complacency, if not complicity, with a far greater tragedy (at least numerically) that most of the civilized world chooses to ignore. Perhaps if the media would also carry pictures and short biographies of the 8,219 lives cut too short daily by the AIDS epidemic, as most newspapers published of the victims of September 11, we would probably begin to put a human face on these tragic statistics. Then perhaps our collective conscience would force us to develop empathy toward those who, by virtue of their poverty, race, ethnicity, sexual orientation, and historical accident, have fallen prey to the lethal HIV/AIDS virus.

Since AIDS is increasingly and incorrectly associated with third world countries, African Americans, Latino/a Americans, and homosexuals, any pedagogy that purports to level the playing field in AIDS education must necessarily acknowledge the sociocultural and socioeconomic reality of those who are targeted to receive AIDS assistance. In other words, it is a lost opportunity to conceive of AIDS education only in terms of technologies and methodologies (in other words, the do's and don't's of avoiding HIV contraction). In order to create effective pedagogical spaces for AIDS education, educators must necessarily deconstruct the intricate interplay of race, ethics, and ideology—a practice that teacher preparation programs, by and large, fail to take on rigorously. Courses that deal with ethical questions such as "What is the responsibility of society in fighting this epidemic?" and "How do we, as conscious human beings, construct our world so as to ignore that 8,219 innocent people, including children, die every day of the disease?" are almost always absent from teacher-preparation curricula. This serious omission is, by its very nature, ideological, and constitutes the foundation for complicity with the discriminatory practices designed to devalue, dehumanize, and demonize people living with HIV/AIDS. How else can we reconcile our democratic ideals and humanitarian values with our implicit or explicit complicity with the deaths of 8,219 people every day because of our willful participation in social structures that generate human misery and disease?

The challenge for AIDS educators is not only to prevent the spread of the HIV virus but also to create pedagogical spaces where students can arm themselves with critical tools to develop a deeper understanding of the material conditions of racism, homophobia, and the systematic negation and devaluation with which most AIDS victims must live. An AIDS education program that only generates technical awareness of the disease will invariably fail if it is disarticulated from the sociocultural and socioeconomic reality within which the victims of AIDS are situated. For example, an AIDS education program designed to prevent the spread of the HIV virus must factor in the conditions faced by people in their communities, as described by Jonathan Kozol:

Crack-cocaine addiction and the intravenous use of heroin, which children
I have met here call "the needle drug," are woven into the texture of existence in Mott Haven. Nearly 4,000 heroin injectors, many of whom are
HIV-infected, live here. Virtually every child at St. Ann's knows someone,
a relative or neighbor, who has died of AIDS, and most children here know
many others who are dying now of the disease. One quarter of the women
of Mott Haven who are tested in obstetric wards are positive for HIV. Rates
of pediatric AIDS, therefore, are high.

Depression is common among children in Mott Haven. Many cry a great
deal but cannot explain exactly why.

Fear and anxiety are common. Many cannot sleep.

The houses in which these children live, two thirds of which are owned
by the City of New York, are often as squalid as the houses of the poorest
children I have visited in rural Mississippi, but there is none of the greenness
and the healing sweetness of the Mississippi countryside outside their win-
dows, which are often barred and bolted as protection against thieves.[5]

What Kozol's description of Mott Haven makes clear is that any honest attempt to develop meaningful AIDS education programs for the
oppressed class cannot be disconnected from the conditions that create, shape, and maintain human misery in the first place. An AIDS
program disarticulated from such sociocultural and socioeconomic
material conditions will only feed into the practice of blaming the AIDS
victims for their own misery by rationalizing the genetic predisposition
for promiscuity with which third world people, African Americans,
Latino/a Americans, and homosexuals are stereotyped. This will lead
to the failure of AIDS prevention and treatment programs.

The inability to link AIDS education programs to larger critical
and social issues often prevents educators not only from engaging in a
general critique of the social mission of their own enterprise but also
from acknowledging their roles as gatekeepers who reproduce the values
of the dominant social (dis)order. This disarticulation of knowledge
anesthetizes consciousness, without which one can never develop a
clear sense of reality. As suggested by Frei Betto, clarity requires that a
person transcend "the perception of life as a pure biological process to
arrive at a perception of life as 'a clothesline of information.' ... On the
clothesline we may have a flux of information and yet remain unable to
link one piece of information with another. A politicized person is one
who can sort out the different and often fragmented pieces contained

in flux."[6] Apprehension of reality concerning the AIDS epidemic requires a high level of political clarity, which can be achieved by sifting through the flux of information and relating each piece to another so as to gain a global comprehension of the facts and their *raison d'etre*. This means, for example, that the pharmaceutical companies that pride themselves on having contributed a great deal toward the technological advancement of AIDS medicine should acknowledge their hypocrisy when they go to court to prevent governments in the third world from making AIDS drugs affordable.

It is important that an AIDS education program develops an analysis of capitalism to demonstrate how, almost always, capitalist enterprises put profit before human lives. Ample materials are available, for example, regarding the AIDS crisis in South Africa and the decision of the Brazilian government to violate the patent rules in order to address the health needs of its poorest citizens. By deconstructing corporate greed, educators and their students will be able to more easily unveil the capitalist ideology inherent in seemingly progressive AIDS projects. Take, for instance, the Benetton advertisement created to promote AIDS awareness, which, in the end, was primarily developed to sell Benetton products. The Benetton AIDS advertisement not only reproduces the existing assumptions that AIDS patients are disfigured, debilitated, and on their deathbeds but it also conveys a sense of hopelessness about the prospects of curing AIDS. An AIDS education program should promote hope by providing students with critical tools to rupture the structure that positions them as mere spectators, so that they can become agents in their world and transform it.

In addition to linking the AIDS epidemic with its economic causes, I believe that a comprehensive AIDS education program must be immersed in the ethnic and cultural reality of students so that issues of how racism informs education in general, and AIDS education in particular, can be analyzed. In short, it is important to highlight that "[t]here is no way to fight HIV and AIDS at the same time without addressing the issue of poverty."[7] I would add that there is also no way to intervene pedagogically to fight HIV and AIDS without addressing the issues of culture, race, and ethnicity.

RACIAL AND ETHNIC IDENTITIES AS PRIVATE LIABILITIES

A central challenge for AIDS educators is the development of awareness concerning the fallacy of becoming "accustomed to thinking of AIDS as someone else's problem. It is not about us, it's about them."[8] AIDS educators need to point out that reducing the problem to the binary of "us" versus "them" makes it possible for human beings with a conscience to fall prey to the social construction of the "other," enabling them to ignore the AIDS pandemic. Unfortunately, the comfort zone that creates the illusion that AIDS has little or nothing to do with us allows us to conveniently neglect the fact that "[o]n this planet, we are all dependent on each other, and nothing that we do or refrain from doing is indifferent to the fate of everyone else. From the ethical point of view, this makes us all responsible for each other. Responsibility is there, put firmly in place by the global network of interdependency—whether we recognize its presence or not and whether we take it up or not."[9]

Given the interdependency that informs our existence, an AIDS education project must necessarily interrogate the creation of a "deviant" otherness designed to measure the lack of worth of those human beings who are not like us. With respect to AIDS victims, this notion of deviance makes it easier to relegate the AIDS epidemic to a private sphere where the human misery connected with the disease is the sole problem and responsibility of the victims. In addition, by straitjacketing the AIDS issue within the sphere of individual pathology, there is no general need for a public debate or call for collective responsibility. Hence, the fact that "AIDS is the leading cause of death among young African-American women [and that] African-American and Hispanic women, 21 percent of the female population, account for 77 percent of new cases" of AIDS is not a cause for alarm for the general (white) public.[10] On the contrary, AIDS as an illness of the "other," is perceived as threatening our individual health and safety. AIDS reminds us of our own mortality as human beings and our transience on this earth. In other words, it reminds us of a temporality that we prefer to forget instead of making it the basis for intervention in the world.

The reduction of the AIDS epidemic to a narrow private sphere makes it substantively easier to typecast AIDS victims along lines of race, ethnicity, and sexual orientation. This typecasting becomes part and parcel of a politics in which, according to Zygmunt Bauman, "the bridges between the private and public life are dismantled or were never built to start with."[11] The direct consequence of dismantling public life is a reality where "grievances aired in public are a sackful of private agonies and anxieties which, however, do not turn into public issues just for being on public display."[12] That is to say, because there is some coverage in the media of people living with AIDS, it does not necessarily translate into a public issue in that no substantive discussion takes place, and the public does not collectively take on the responsibility of addressing this devastating epidemic. Here, again, we see how the attribution of AIDS to third world people, African Americans, Latino/a Americans, and homosexuals leaves the "real" Americans (read: middle- and upper-class white Americans) untouched. As a result, even the more promising and progressive AIDS education projects will invariably fail if they prevent private trouble from being translated into public concern, responsibility, and, therefore, action toward the eradication of HIV/AIDS.

Given the dismantling of public life and the overcelebration of a misguided individualism that calls for more isolation and private space, AIDS educators must learn to work in solidarity with their students to find ways to fracture the ideology that generates, shapes, and maintains private spaces while contracting public spheres. That is, AIDS educators must embrace Zygmunt Bauman's notion of the "agora"—"the space neither private, nor public, but more exactly private and public at the same time. The space where private problems meet in a meaningful way—that is, not just to draw narcissistic pleasures or in search of some therapy through display, but to seek collectively managed levers powerful enough to lift individuals from their privately suffered misery; the space where such ideas may be born and take shape as the 'public good,' the 'just society,, or 'shared values.'"[13]

This kind of deconstruction also involves a critical comprehension of how to denude the racist discourse that "pretends that we live in a color-blind society where individuals are treated according to the American ethic [that] has always held that individual effort and achievement are valued and rewarded."[14] The separation of the individual from the collective consciousness is part of a dominant ideology that makes it easier for individuals to accept the lie that we live in a raceless and color-blind society. The disregard for and neglect of AIDS victims must be understood within the context of the current assault on immigration, multiculturalism, and affirmative action. An AIDS project that fails to link these issues will inevitably reject Derrick Bell's call for a "continuing quest for new directions in our struggle for racial justice, a struggle we must continue even if . . . racism is an integral, permanent, and indestructible component of this society."[15]

Because racism is an integral component of our society, we enter a permanent dance with bigotry through which subordinated groups are constantly demonized. The demonization of these groups is very much a part of the public discourse where racial, cultural, and ethnic identities are often devalued. For example, David Duke, a Republican candidate in the 1990 presidential primaries, minced no words when he stated: "America is being invaded by hordes of dusty third world peoples, and with each passing hour our economic well being, cultural heritage, freedom, and racial roots are being battered into oblivion."[16] He continues his demonization of the "other" cultural and ethnic subjects, stating: "It's them! They're what's wrong with America! They're taking your job, soaking up your tax dollars, living off food stamps, drinking cheap wine, and making babies at our expense."[17] These racist sentiments are not lost in the proliferation of conservative radio talk shows like Rush Limbaugh's. The tenor of such shows is apparent in a local talk show broadcast in Brockton, Massachusetts, in which a caller remarked: "Why should we be supporting these bilinguals? We should take care of our own first. The problem with Brockton is the Haitians, the Hispanics, the Cape Verdeans that are ruining our neighborhood."[18]

It would be unrealistic to expect a bigoted society to spend resources to address the AIDS epidemic when the dominant race of the society views AIDS as mostly affecting the very populations it so readily demonizes. Although these examples point to racism at the level of language, the relationship between racist statements and the effects on people's lives is direct. For example, as California Governor Pete Wilson and other politicians made speeches demonizing so-called "illegal" immigrants, the actual experience of racism became immeasurably worse with the passage of Proposition 187. In fact, Proposition 187 can be viewed as a precursor to the assault on subordinated groups with the passage in November 1996 of Proposition 209, which ended affirmative action in California. These laws have had the effect of licensing institutional discrimination whereby both legal and illegal immigrants experience the loss of their dignity, the denial of their human citizenship, and, in many cases, outright brutality by those institutions responsible for implementing the law. According to Human Rights Watch/Americas: "The politically charged drive to curb illegal immigration may be coming at a serious price: beatings, shootings, rapes, and death of aliens at the hands of the U.S. Border Patrol."[19]

As anti-immigrant sentiment grows stronger, the Immigration and Naturalization Service (INS) plans to increase its force from 4,200 to 7,000 by 2006, with few safeguards in place to ensure that the new hires will not continue to increase the human rights abuses perpetrated along the U.S. Mexican border. As Allyson Collins of Human Rights Watch/Americas notes, the "anti-immigrant sentiment dims the hope of safeguarding aliens as the United States fortifies its border. These are very unpopular victims."[20] Not only is there no guarantee that the INS will protect the rights of human beings who have already been dehumanized as "aliens" or "illegals," but this process has been met by a disturbing silence, even among liberals.

This is not entirely surprising, given the liberals' paradoxical posture with respect to race issues. Liberals often progressively idealize "principles of liberty, equality, and fraternity [while insisting] upon the moral irrelevance of race. Race is irrelevant, but all is race."[21] Some liberals do accept the notion of difference and call for to tolerance of difference, a paternalistic term. For example, there is a rapid increase in textbooks ostensibly designed to teach tolerance for racial and multicultural diversity. But, what these texts in fact do is hide the asymmetrical distribution of power and cultural capital. Missing from this posture is the ethical position that calls for racial and cultural solidarity that leads to a more egalitarian balance of power. As David Goldberg argues, tolerance "presupposes that its object is morally repugnant, that it really needs to be reformed, that is, altered."[22] Accordingly, racial and cultural tolerance practiced by the dominant sectors within U.S. society may be a process through which they are permitted to think, or at least hope, that the intolerable features that characterize the different "other" will be eliminated or repressed. Thus, Goldberg points out that

> liberals are moved to overcome the racial differences they tolerate and have been so instrumental in fabricating by diluting them, by bleaching them out through assimilation or integration. The liberal would assume away the difference in otherness, maintaining thereby the dominance of a presumed sameness, the universally imposed similarity in identity. The paradox is perpetrated: the commitment to tolerance turns only on modernity's natural inclination to intolerance; acceptance of otherness presupposes as it at once necessitates delegitimization of the other.[23]

Tolerance for different racial and ethnic groups as proposed by some white liberals not only constitutes a veil behind which they hide their racism, it also puts them in a compromising racial position. Although they call for racial tolerance, they often maintain the privilege that is complicit with the dominant ideology. In other words, the call for tolerance never questions the asymmetrical power relations that give them their privilege. Many white liberals are reluctant to confront issues of inequality, power, ethics, race, and ethnicity in a way that could actually lead to social transformation that would make society more democratic and humane and less racist and discriminatory. This form of racism is readily understood by its victims, as observed by Carol Swain, an African American professor at Princeton University: "White liberals are among the most racist people I know; they're so patronizing towards blacks."[24] In short, the racism and xenophobia we are witnessing in our society today are not isolated acts of individuals on the fringe.

It is against this mean-spirited and racist backdrop that we should conceive of an AIDS education project where students are encouraged to link their cultural, racial, and ethnic reality with the AIDS epidemic. By developing a deeper understanding of the association of AIDS with mostly subordinated groups, students can begin to understand our society's disregard of strategies for the eradication of the HIV virus and AIDS. By learning about the sociocultural and socioeconomic factors that frame oppressed people as the cause of the AIDS problem, students will be better able to understand that its eradication would require a profound social transformation that goes beyond mere slogans of "Safe Sex" and "Just Say No" to casual sex. Given the exponential increase in AIDS mortality, we have to admit that that these slogans have not been very effective tools in our war on AIDS.

AIDS EDUCATION AS A PEDAGOGY OF HOPE

AIDS educators must become cultural workers who have the courage and ethical integrity to denounce any and all attempts to actively dehumanize the very people from whom they make a living as AIDS educators. We need to say to conservative ideologues that no human being deserves to be victim of the lethal AIDS virus. Rather than the superficial and destructive binary of "us versus them" called for by conservative ideologues, what we need in AIDS education is a process through which we forge cultural and racial unity. The real challenge for AIDS educators is how to make their schools brokers of this cultural unification process, or, in other words, how educators can fashion cultural unity through diversity.

I conclude by reiterating the need for a humanizing pedagogy called for in this important book—a pedagogy that is informed by respect and solidarity; a pedagogy that rejects the social construction of AIDS victims as debilitated, emaciated, disfigured, and dehumanized "others"; a pedagogy that teaches us that by dehumanizing the "other," we become dehumanized ourselves. A humanizing pedagogy will teach us that the social construction of otherness, in its ideological makeup, constitutes the *raison d'etre* for aggression or the rationalization of aggression. In creating the social and cultural separateness that demonizes so-called "deviant other," for example, the dominant group creates a distance from them that engenders an ignorance that borders on stupidification.[25] The creation of "otherness" not only fosters more ignorance on the part of those in power, but also fails to provide the dominant group with the necessary tools to empathize with the demonized "other." By creating rigid borders, either by building or maintaining walls between people or nations, we inevitably end up with the same reality where things lose their fluidity while generating more tensions and conflicts.

In short, we need a humanizing pedagogy that guides us toward the critical road of truth, rather than myths and lies, toward reclaiming our dignity and our humanity. A humanizing pedagogy will point us toward a world that is more harmonious and more humane, less discriminatory, and more just. A humanizing pedagogy will reject the dominant society's policies of hatred, bigotry, and division, and will celebrate diversity within unity. In other words, a humanizing pedagogy will point to the "path through which men and women can become conscious about their presence in the world ... [t]he way they act and think when they develop all their capacities, taking into consideration their needs, but also the needs and aspirations of others." [26] A humanizing pedagogy will also point out to conservative ideologues that they could learn a great deal from those human beings who, by virtue of their place of birth, race, or ethnicity, have been reduced to the nonstatus of "other." A humanizing pedagogy will embrace Carlos Fuentes' words of wisdom when he wrote that "people and their cultures perish in isolation, but they are born or reborn in contact with other men and women, with men and women of another culture, another creed, another race. If we do not recognize our humanity in others, we shall not recognize it in ourselves.[27]

A humanizing pedagogy will teach us that it is necessary to dare, to say no to the bureaucratization of the mind to which we are exposed daily—that it is necessary to dare to say that racism is a curable disease—that it is necessary to dare to speak of difference as a value and to say that it is possible to find unity in diversity. It is necessary to dare to abandon the pernicious labels such as "other" and "alien," among others, in order to avoid the coldness of the heart that further endangers our humanity as succinctly captured by Zygmunt Bauman:

> Cold are the people who have long forgotten how warm human togetherness may be; how much consolation, comfort, encouragement, and just ordinary pleasure one may derive from sharing one's own lot and one's hopes with others—"others like me," or more exactly, others who are "like me" precisely for the reason of sharing my plight, my misery and my dream of happiness; and even more so for the fact of my concern with their plight, their misery, and their dream of happiness."[28]

Donaldo Macedo
University of Massachusetts Boston

NOTES

1. Salih Booker and William Minter, "Global Apartheid," *The Nation,* July 9, 2001.

2. Amir Attaran, "A Good Start to Help Fight Global AIDS," *Boston Globe,* December 20, 2001, p.A23.

3. Salih Booker and William Minter, "Global Apartheid," *The Nation,* July 9, 2001.

4. Amir Attaran, "A Good Start to Help Fight Global AIDS," *Boston Globe,* December 20, 2001, p.A23.

5. Jonathan Kozol, *Amazing Grace: The Lines and the Conscience of a Nation* (New York: Harper Perennial, 1996), p. 4.

6. As cited in Paulo Freire and Donaldo Macedo, *Literacy: Reading the Word and the World* (South Hadley, MA: Bergin and Garvey, 1987), p. 130.

7. Thomas Gagen, "Front Line in the AIDS War," *Boston Globe,* December 26, 2001.

8. Thoraid Obaid, "Africa Is Ground Zero in Fight against AIDS," Boston Globe, June 22, 2001, p. A19.

9. Zygmunt Bauman, "Global Solidarity" *Tikkun* 17, no.1 (2002): 14.

10. Thoraid Obaid, "Africa Is Ground Zero in Fight against AIDS," Boston Globe, June 22, 2001, p. A19.

11. Zygmunt Bauman, *In Search of Politics* (California: Stanford University Press, 1999), p. 2.

12. Ibid, p. 3.

13. Ibid, p. 3.

14. bell hooks, Gloria Steinem, Urvashi Vaid, and Naomi Wolf, "Let's Get Real About Feminism: The Backlash, the Myths, the Movement," *Ms.*, September/October 1993, p. 39.

15. Derrick D. Bell, *Faces at the Bottom of the Well: The Performance of Racism* (New York: Basic Books, 1992), p. xiii.

16. David Nyhan, "David Duke Sent 'Em a Scare But Now He Faces the Old Pro," *Boston Globe*, October 24, 1991, p. 13.

17. Ibid, p. 13.

18. Bill Alex Talk Radio Show, WBET, Brockton, Massachusetts, March 17, 1994.

19. "Trouble on the Mexican Border," *U.S. News and World Report*, April 24, 1995, p. 10.

20. Ibid, p. 10.

21. David T. Goldberg, *Racist Culture* (Oxford, UK: Blackwell, 1993), p. 6.

22. Ibid, p. 7.

23. Ibid, p. 7.

24. Peter Applebone, "Goals Unmet: Duke Reveals the Perils in Effort to Increase Black Faculty," *New York Times*, September 19, 1993, p. 1.

25. Victor J. Rodrigues, *A Nova Ordem Estupidológica* (Lisboa: Livros Horizonte, 1995), p. 18.

26. Paulo Freire and Frei Betto, *Esta Escola Chamada Vida* (Sao Paulo, Brazil: Editora Scipione, 1989), p. 32.

27. Carlos Fuentes, "The Mirror of the Other," *The Nation*, March 30, 1992, p. 411.

28. Zygmunt Bauman, *In Search of Politics* (California: Stanford University Press, 1999), p. 53.

PREFACE

Courageously humane teaching—borne of a commitment not only to transfer specific and meaningful academic knowledge but to further the overall wellness of human beings—is needed by all students. This need to address the whole learner can be gleaned from the eyes of young people. It is explicitly presented here as a call for educators—as they go about their school-based work—to promote behaviors that prevent the devastating effects of the Human Immunodeficiency Virus (HIV) and Acquired Immunodeficiency Syndrome (AIDS).

The logic for teachers' serving as prevention agents is fairly simple. While the global scientific community works earnestly to develop a vaccine against HIV and AIDS, one effective prevention strategy is readily agreed upon across geographic and professional boundaries: safe behavior. People who learn and then practice safe behavior for disease prevention *do prevent the spread of HIV/AIDS.* This universal truth presents a potent opportunity for teachers, both in the United States and abroad. Because teachers are a source of information and education that most young people access, educators are well poised to inform and inspire young people to practice safe behaviors that prevent disease. The issue of HIV/AIDS prevention may then function as an agent for professional transformation, compelling educators to convey not only information and skill but also health and well-being.

Humanizing Pedagogy Through HIV/AIDS Prevention asserts that by attending to the HIV/AIDS health issue, teachers increase their capacity to see and attend to the complete child. This publication identifies critical HIV/AIDS information and prevention skills that all teachers should know so they can serve as catalysts for humanizing pedagogy throughout the world.

This volume was inspired by AACTE's Build a Future Without AIDS project, a 10-year initiative that began in 1995 with funding from the Centers for Disease Control and Prevention (CDC). During the last four years of the project, a consensus panel of teacher education scholars and health education experts was convened to develop a knowledge base for HIV/AIDS prevention for teacher education. The panel produced a report, reviewed by CDC, on what teachers should know about HIV and AIDS prevention (see http://www.aacte.org/Programs/Research/without_aids.htm).

Unlike the CDC report, *Humanizing Pedagogy Through HIV/AIDS Prevention* (an independent publication) considers a broader sociopolitical context for preparing teachers to prevent HIV and AIDS. It reflects the vigor of intellectual engagement, connecting HIV/AIDS prevention to a wide range of issues that influence human conditions associated with teaching and learning. This volume is intended to stimulate discussion, study, and experimentation among educators that will ultimately improve teacher practice.

Humanizing Pedagogy Through HIV/AIDS Prevention reflects AACTE's commitment to preparing teachers for a changing world. Issues pertaining to HIV and AIDS, such as implications of poverty and gender, require those who prepare prekindergarten through grade twelve teachers to challenge pedagogical paradigms that focus solely on the teacher's transference of academic information to the learner. Attending to AIDS prevention compels teachers—and the responsive institutions that prepare them—to partner with the people and institutions that comprise and serve the learner's community. Parental engagement, for example, must become common practice for the teacher prepared to address HIV and AIDS prevention, as must collaboration with health care practitioners, social service providers, and other professionals.

The efforts of the consensus panel also signal change at AACTE consistent with the association's renewed commitment to establishing consensus on what constitutes state-of-the-art teaching. As the organization commences its work to achieve professionally led reform based on unity of purpose, publications that reflect the work of consensus panels take on a new significance. Although AACTE does not singularly endorse the content of each chapter, we fully support the use of this volume as the framework for an essential conversation.

Humanizing Pedagogy Through HIV/AIDS Prevention reflects AACTE's commitment to the creation of a powerful vanguard of responsive teachers. It is our hope that this volume will guide the conversations and subsequent actions that produce such teachers, and in that way serve as a pathfinder for excellence in teacher preparation. We invite each reader to join us in this effort—as a full, consensus-building partner, working toward the systematic preparation of teachers committed to educating learners *and* preventing HIV and AIDS.

Mwangaza Michael-Bandele
Senior Director, Research and Policy
AACTE

INTRODUCTION

⊷

The purpose of *Humanizing Pedagogy Through HIV and AIDS Prevention: Transforming Teacher Knowledge* is to provide educators in the United States and abroad—especially teacher educators, classroom teachers, and teacher candidates—useful material for learning and teaching about HIV/AIDS. This material should help them engage this topic in a holistic manner, taking into account implications for a range of effects from professional efficacy to community well-being.

To develop the content for this volume, a consensus panel was convened by the American Association of Colleges for Teacher Education (AACTE). The panel identified core knowledge and skills to frame the knowledge base for preparing educators to deliver HIV/AIDS prevention education. The knowledge and skills are based on scientific research and grounded in the human dimension of teaching and learning. The resulting knowledge base aims to equip educators to attend to both the academic and human needs of *all* students being served.

This book has several purposes:

- To inform educators that the idea that the AIDS epidemic is over, or at least under control, is a lie. According to the CDC (2003), fewer people died from AIDS in 2003 than 1999, but the number of AIDS cases rose 4 percent during that time; more than 1 million people in the United States are infected with HIV. Almost 40 million people in the world are living with HIV/AIDS, including 2 million children (Joint United Nations Programme on HIV/AIDS, 2004).
- To inform educators that children who have HIV or AIDS face health and educational challenges.
- To inform educators that they can be a source of knowledge about safe practices for disease prevention and that they are appropriately

positioned to inform and inspire students to practice behaviors that prevent HIV/AIDS.

- To provide educators with a knowledge base that will enable them to better deal with controversy surrounding HIV/AIDS—and that could also make them more attractive employees to school districts.
- To provide teachers with information and support for planning instruction about HIV/AIDS.

Humanizing Pedagogy Through HIV and AIDS Prevention: Transforming Teacher Knowledge is organized into five sections. In Part I: Humanizing Pedagogy, those affected by HIV/AIDS are given a face, and the section provides information to empower teachers who respond to the academic and social needs of students. Part II: The Science and Skill of HIV and AIDS Prevention focuses on biological, immunological, and general science information essential to understanding and preventing HIV/AIDS. Part III: Diversity in Teaching and Learning points out that, because HIV/AIDS affects all people, teaching and learning how to prevent it requires an understanding of the varied ways it impacts different groups. In Part IV: International Dimensions of Prevention, the global community's engagement in HIV/AIDS prevention, including common elements of content and teaching strategies, is highlighted. Finally, Part V: Transformative Praxis in School and Community addresses educators as agents of change working in the public interest of their communities and of the larger society.

Serving as editors for *Humanizing Pedagogy Through HIV and AIDS Prevention: Transforming Teacher Knowledge* has been challenging, informative, and inspiring for us. We are challenged to capture content and context that is accessible, instructive, and relevant to all readers. Critical and thoughtful questions faced the part editors, chapter authors, consensus panel members, general editors, and sponsoring organizations: What knowledge and support do teachers need in order to plan curriculum and instruction to teach about HIV/AIDS? How do we help teachers to understand the many different kinds of contexts in which HIV/AIDS is situated—for example, crisis, community activism, science, humanity, and internationalism? What knowledge and support do teachers and other educators need in order to teach children who could themselves have the disease about HIV? How should teachers deal with the cultural, political, and social manifestations of HIV/AIDS? What are teachers' attitudes about teaching about HIV/AIDS, and what will be the effect of teachers' attitudes on students in their class who have HIV infection? We are also challenged (even frightened) by the statistical data that show many young people are at risk of contracting HIV/AIDS; our fervent hope is that this volume will be welcomed by teacher educators, teachers, and teacher candidates as a resource to help them learn about how to deal—personally and professionally—with this issue.

This project has been immensely informative to all participants. Several members of the consensus panel were so supportive of the project that they became editors. All involved spoke about how much they were taking away intellectually and attitudinally because of their participation. They developed a deeper personal knowledge base about HIV/AIDS and a more sincere and caring attitude about the epidemic as a national and global problem. In addition, they saw firsthand how different organizations and agencies are working together in this battle. It was professionally gratifying to see these partnerships taking place at such a high level. On a more practical level, it was instructive to see that material can be developed that responds to the needs and dispositions of the multiple audiences involved in the HIV/AIDS battle. Further, it was exciting to develop material that specifically addresses teacher education and prepares teachers to join in the work of HIV/AIDS prevention education and perhaps work with HIV-positive students.

Health professionals and educators alike are inspired as they see their patients, students, colleagues, and others benefiting from their efforts; this is why they do the work they do. The creation of this book permitted a diverse group of educators, health professionals, and national association members to be inspired by each other's contributions.

Finally, we wish to thank those at our institutions who helped in numerous ways, and we owe special thanks to Mwangaza Michael-Bandele, director of AACTE's Build a Future Without AIDS project and senior director of research and policy at AACTE, for serving as the major shepherd of this project.

Liane M. Summerfield
Associate Dean, School of Health Professions,
Marymount University, Arlington, Virginia

Carl A. Grant
Hoefs-Bascom Professor, University of Wisconsin–Madison

REFERENCES

Centers for Disease Control and Prevention. (2003). *HIV/AIDS surveillance report*. Atlanta, GA: Author. Retrieved September 27, 2005, from http://www.cdc.gov/hiv/stats/2003surveillancereport.pdf.

Joint United Nations Programme on HIV/AIDS. (2004). *AIDS epidemic update*. Retrieved September 27, 2005, from http://www.unaids.org/wad2004/report.html.

PART I
HUMANIZING PEDAGOGY

Overview, Jerry Rosiek

꘍

Preparing teachers to respond to the HIV/AIDS crisis requires addressing the full human context in which the disease takes on meaning for students. It will require teaching them not just about the biology of the disease, but also the way our emotional and cultural responses to the disease can dehumanize its victims. This first section of the book examines what a humanizing pedagogy about HIV/AIDS for teachers would look like.

The section opens with "HIV/AIDS and Current Conceptions of Teacher Education" by Jerry Rosiek, which situates the question of how to prepare teachers to respond to HIV/AIDS issues in the classroom within contemporary scholarship on the practical knowledge that enables good teaching. Rosiek argues that a commitment to preparing teachers for the practical work of responding to the HIV/AIDS crisis calls for broadening teacher education curriculum mandates beyond narrow subject matter learning objectives. In addition to subject expertise, an effective response will also require knowledge of the religious and cultural discourses of students' home communities and how those discourses frame the significance of the disease as well as an interrogation of the teachers' own discourse communities and the pre-existing conceptions they have about HIV-positive persons.

This piece is followed by a classic essay by Paulo Freire, "On the Indispensable Qualities of Progressive Teachers for Their Better Performance." This chapter takes a step back to lay a foundation for both the section and the book by asserting that being prepared to teach means far more than acquiring technical skills. Freire argues that it also means cultivating a political understanding of the work of teaching, seeing

1

oneself as a cultural worker, and finding personal joy in the often challenging work of pedagogy.

Nirmala Erevelles approaches the topic through the lens of contemporary disability studies in her chapter, "Disability Studies as Insight: Deploying Enabling Pedagogies in HIV/AIDS Education." Erevelles reviews the way our conception of "normal" bodies leads us to create learning environments that ignore, exclude, and are hostile to persons whose bodies do not fit within that conception of normality. She argues that the challenge to serve students with HIV/AIDS in our schools has many similarities to the challenge to serve disabled students. Erevelles concludes that a comprehensive strategy for making our schools truly inclusive of all forms of humanity is needed if we are to prepare teachers to respond humanely to the HIV/AIDS crisis.

In the final essay in this section, James Mitchell offers pedagogical strategies for dealing with the emotional response students can have to the controversial topic of HIV/AIDS. In his essay, "Building Trust Through Cooperation in the AIDS Education Classroom," Mitchell describes a general approach to building trust in the classroom through conflict resolution called *academic controversy*. He then illustrates how this cooperative learning strategy can be effectively applied to discussions about the topic of HIV/AIDS in the classroom in a way that students' fears about the disease are surfaced, respectfully listened to, and transformed into more constructive responses to the disease.

I

HIV/AIDS AND CURRENT CONCEPTIONS OF TEACHER EDUCATION

Jerry Rosiek

☙

The threat posed by HIV/AIDS has been a source of considerable scholarly, cultural, and political struggle for the last three decades. At one level, there has been the scientific challenge of identifying the cause of this disease, searching for a cure and ways to prevent its transmission. At another level, there has been the cultural challenge of educating the public about a disease that traverses regions of human experience often considered taboo and unfit for public discussion. Finally, there has been the struggle to mobilize political support to combat a disease that is perceived by many to affect only gay men and drug users. The imperative to address the HIV/AIDS epidemic in teacher education curriculum reaches us as one of the products of this multidimensional struggle.

During this same time period, the field of teacher education has also been a site of struggle, one focused on identifying the proper ends and appropriate means of teacher education. Debating the epistemology of teacher knowledge, scholars have asked, "What is the nature of the knowledge that enables good teaching practice?" Depending on the answer to that question, methodological questions have followed, such as "How can teacher knowledge be best documented and disseminated to other teachers?" Finally, there has been an effort at the level of public policy to create working conditions that would improve teaching practice. There have been many disagreements about what such conditions would look like.

These recent struggles in teacher education have given rise to two major conceptions of educational improvement—conceptions that occasionally complement one another but that are often in conflict. One conception attempts to limit the knowledge that enables teaching to the relatively technical work of delivering specific subject matter content to students. Thirty years ago, this conception of teaching was forwarded through a program of educational improvement known as the "effective teaching" movement. This movement was driven by a set of epistemic and methodological assumptions that put a premium on precisely tracking relationships between discreet teaching practices and specific learning outcomes (Gage, 1972, 1978; McEwan, 2002; Mohan and Hull, 1975; Muijs and Reynolds, 2001; Sarason, 1999; Shulman, 1992). Researchers employed "process–product" approaches to identify measurable positive effects that could be correlated with measurable interventions, which in turn became a requirement for justifying educational changes.

Today, we see a similar effort to narrowly prescribe the work of teaching in what is loosely termed the "accountability movement." Again the focus for policy makers, at least in the United States, has turned to measurable educational outcomes. The U.S. Department of Education has issued guidelines for identifying "scientifically based practices" that are eligible for federal support. These guidelines insist on what has been called the gold standard in research: randomized field trials with experimental controls (Brookings Institution, 1999). The accountability movement shares with the effective teaching movement a focus on narrowly defined and measurable educational outcomes; the former differs from the latter in the rhetoric used to justify it. The effective teaching movement was driven by epistemic and methodological concerns. It was, first and foremost, a research movement. The scientifically based practice movement is being driven by a political concern for accountability, and research methods are a means to that goal.

Whatever the inspiration for these approaches to educational improvement, their implications for teacher education have been largely the same. Where they hold sway, conceptions of teacher preparation are restricted, some would say trivialized (Shulman, 1987) or even dehumanized (Macedo and Bartolome, 2001). Focus is limited to pedagogical technique and methods of assessing the cognitive impact of these techniques. The broader personal and political context of teaching are largely ignored, as are the holistic, tacit, and biographical sources of teachers' knowledge.

The other predominant conception of educational improvement in the last three decades has attempted to broaden conceptions of the knowledge that enables good teaching. Manifested variously as an emphasis on teacher professionalization, teacher inquiry, teacher research, action research, reflective practice, the wisdom of practice, the scholarship of teaching, craft knowledge, practical knowledge, and personal practical knowledge, a body of scholarship known as *teacher knowledge research* has emerged that argues that effective teaching cannot be promoted as a set of discreet practices. Instead, this literature offers that good teaching is grounded in context-bound knowledge, acquired through reflecting on the practical work of teaching. Surfacing this knowledge requires open-ended approaches to inquiry and narrative modes of representation to adequately disseminate (Shulman, 1987, 1992, 2000; Clandinin and Connelly, 1996, 2000). Advocates of this conception of teacher education maintain that teachers need to be prepared as professional decision makers who understand their subject matter as well as the personal, social, cultural, and political context in which their students live and in which they practice.

Such preparation, advocates argue, cannot focus only on general theoretical knowledge about teaching. It also needs to address the practical dimension of teaching. Some scholars have argued that teachers' practical knowledge should be documented—usually in the form of case studies narratives—so that a general knowledge base of practical insights can be established for use in teacher education programs (Shulman, 1987, 2000). Others, citing the radically context-dependent nature of teachers' practice, are skeptical about the possibility of establishing such a general knowledge base. They recommend instead preparing teachers to conduct research on their own practice (Clandinin and Connelly, 2000; Cochran-Smith and Lytle, 1993, 1999; Noffke, 1997). Where teacher assessment is a concern, efforts have been made to develop forms of evaluation that assess not only teachers' knowledge of subject matter and general pedagogical theory but also their ability to problem-solve the challenge of teaching specific subject matter content in specific settings (Tell, 2001).

The imperative to address the AIDS crisis in teacher education curriculum must be negotiated in the midst of this broader struggle in the field. This chapter portrays the HIV/AIDS epidemic as a cultural, political, and personal phenomenon as well as a biological phenomenon. Understanding how communities respond or do not respond to it requires understanding the multiple contexts in which information about the disease is encountered. Therefore, it seems that a broad conception of teacher education, one that addresses the many human contexts in which teaching takes place, is needed for this purpose.

ADDRESSING HIV/AIDS IN TEACHER EDUCATION

The purpose of any program of education about a communicable disease is to slow the vector of that disease by educating citizens about how they can avoid infection. The cooperation of an informed public is essential to slowing the spread of a disease. An HIV/AIDS prevention curriculum for teachers would therefore have two distinct purposes: to influence teaching practice directly and to enable teachers to educate others, primarily their students, about prevention.

Regarding the first aim, education that would inform teachers' practice directly, the curriculum would need to address many things, including, but not limited to, the following:

- How HIV/AIDS is and is not communicated
- How to respond to the situations that involve risk of transmission, such as a student bleeding in class, to minimize possible exposure to the pathogen
- Laws about discrimination against children with HIV/AIDS
- Laws and ethical standards regarding confidentiality about infected children

Regarding the second aim, enabling teachers to educate others, the curriculum would need to address many things (Centers for Disease Control and Prevention, 1988, 1992), including, but not limited to, the following:

- How to educate students to reduce their risk of infection
- How to educate parents of children with HIV/AIDS
- How to educate other parents about disease prevention
- How to educate other teachers about disease prevention

So how might such a curriculum be developed and implemented? Education of this sort requires more than providing information; it requires helping teachers integrate information and imperatives for action into their existing patterns of professional practice. Changing teachers' practice means that the motivation to change will need to be addressed (Fullan, 2001; Hargreaves, 2000). Building motivation entails connecting with an audience at an emotional as well as at a cognitive level (Hargreaves, 2000; Bandura, 1997). Changing practice also means dealing with the context in which that practice occurs (Fullan, 2001; Dufour and Eaker, 1998; Clandinin and Connelly, 1999). Among other things, this context includes the influence of culture (Cochran-Smith and Lytle, 1993; Dilworth, 1998; Chang and Rosiek, 2004; Zeichner and Liston, 1996), economics (Willis, 1971; Apple, 2001), race (Delpit, 1995; Ladson-Billings, 1995; Sconiers and Rosiek, 2000), language (Igoa, 1995; Cazden, 2001), and gender (Hollingsworth and Cody, 1994).

Some might object that the kind of considerations just listed do not always apply to all teacher education objectives. Whether or not such an analysis applies generally, a brief consideration of some of the educational aims listed above illustrates how at the very least, they apply to teacher education about HIV/AIDS.

TEACHERS RESPONDING TO HIV/AIDS

Educating teachers about how HIV/AIDS is communicated involves providing teachers with accurate information about the pathogen. Such information, however, is not delivered to an audience innocent of preconceptions about this disease. Misinformation about HIV/AIDS is widespread and built into the discourses in which teachers live and work. This misinformation is often mixed with fear for personal safety, homophobia, classism, racism, and other prejudices (Gay, Lesbian, and Straight Education Network, 2002). Helping teachers understand and *believe* accurate information about when they are and are not at risk will require, in addition to accurate information, a pedagogy that intervenes in the discursive production of fearful and bigoted responses to persons with HIV/AIDS.

The necessity of treating the issue of HIV/AIDS in more than an informational manner becomes even clearer when considering how to help teachers respond properly to a situation in which exposure to the pathogen is possible, such as when a student in a school setting is bleeding. A proper response requires discrete information about procedures and standard safety equipment (the use of prophylactic gloves, how to stop the bleeding, whom to notify, and so forth). This curricular element in particular, however, is likely to surface teachers' fears for their personal safety. Preparing teachers to deal with such a situation practically means addressing the real emotions that may arise in that situation. This preparation may involve modeling ways to stay focused in such a situation as well as exploring the practical and professional consequences of indulging the fear and responding inappropriately (American Association of Colleges for Teacher Education and WILL Interactive, 2000).

The ethical issues raised by the possible presence of a HIV-positive child in the classroom are profound and could easily serve as the curriculum for a whole course on ethics and schooling. These issues cross all levels of the schooling process (Bennett and Erin, 1999; Office of National AIDS Policy, 2000; National School Boards Association, 1990; Fisher, 1997; Eng and Butler, 1997). How should a teacher weigh her own risk against the needs of a child? The risk of all students against the needs of a single child? When does caution become unjust prejudice? Do children with HIV/AIDS have a right to know they are infected if parents haven't told them? Do other parents have the right to know an HIV-positive student is in the classroom? What are the ethical dimensions of confidentiality issues? These are critical issues that teachers will approach using the moral frameworks they use to guide their lives generally. These moral frameworks are often tied to teachers' professional identity and to their sense of self more generally (Clandinin and Connelly, 1996, 2000). A curriculum that addresses the ethics of dealing with HIV/AIDS in the classroom will therefore need to relate the associated ethical imperatives to teachers' self-concepts and their broader sense of right and wrong.

The legal dimension of this kind of teacher education curriculum might seem to be the most uncomplicated aspect of an HIV/AIDS prevention curriculum. Teachers need to know what the law is and to work within the law. Even here, however, motivation, context, and practicality matter. The law is framed in general terms and is often unclear in its application to specific circumstances. Additionally, teachers' respect for the law as it applies to schooling cannot be assumed. My own work in U.S. schools has revealed that teachers are continually informed about new laws and new state and district mandates and that many of these laws and mandates are routinely ignored. Laws that are frequently ignored or only nominally observed include maximum class size, wheel chair accessibility, Title IX mandates about school funding, the prohibition on prayer in schools, overly ambitious curricular mandates, individual educational plans for mainstreamed students with learning disabilities, excessive documentation requirements, prohibitions against mandatory extracurricular service, prohibitions against using teachers in their preparation periods to cover classes instead of calling a substitute, and more.

Teachers are in the habit of filtering state laws and mandates and responding to them selectively. The consequence is a school culture that regards the law somewhat loosely. The implication for a HIV/AIDS prevention curriculum for teachers is that even education about the legal dimensions of HIV/AIDS needs to take into account the practical context in which teachers work. It will not be enough to inform teachers of a law; they need to be persuaded of its merit and relevance to their own work.

TEACHERS EDUCATING OTHERS ABOUT HIV/AIDS

The practical challenges just outlined are redoubled when we consider preparing teachers to educate others about HIV/AIDS. Teachers must have accurate information if they are to provide it to others. They also need to be prepared to deal with the emotional responses, stereotypes, taboos, and prejudices that frame the popular understanding of this disease. According to DiClemente, writing in the *Journal of the American Medical Association,* "Prevention scientists have acknowledged the importance of tailoring behavioral interventions to be developmentally, culturally, and gender appropriate" (1998, p. 1574). This kind of tailoring will require that teachers not only confront their own privileges, prejudices, and fears, but also learn about how others are likely to respond to the issue.

Unless teachers will be working in completely homogenous communities (a reactionary fantasy more than a real possibility), this work will require them to develop an understanding of the values and experiences of communities other than their own—the unique histories of and daily practical pressures in those communities. Whereas most preservice and in-service teacher education programs provide some "multicultural education" curriculum (Dilworth, 1998; Sleeter and Grant, 1999; Banks, 2000), programs with an HIV prevention agenda will not be able to rely on existing multicultural curricula to accomplish their aims. For the most part, these curricula are too general in their focus. More important, much of their focus is superficial and dwells on those cultural differences that are the least uncomfortable to discuss (Sleeter and Grant, 1999; Scheurich, 2002; Dilworth, 1998; Gay, 2000). HIV/AIDS education, by way of contrast, requires teachers to appreciate, respect, and engage not just differences in history and holidays, or even in learning styles. It will also surface cultural differences about understandings of the body, health, death, gender, sexuality, children's sexuality, and religious beliefs.

THE CHALLENGE

In light of such considerations, it is clear that an information-processing conception of teacher education will be inadequate for the task of developing an effective HIV/AIDS prevention curriculum. If such a curriculum is to be successful in influencing teachers' practice and in enabling them to genuinely influence the behavior of others, it will need to address the complex social and practical realities of teaching this subject matter.

Documenting and communicating these many and multifaceted realities may seem to be a sprawling responsibility. This challenge reveals itself as more manageable if the task is broken down into smaller steps.

1. Determining specific content for the curriculum. Once the basic information that teachers need to know is identified, what aspects of their practical experience need to be addressed in the curriculum to be developed? Where are the key intersection points between an HIV/AIDS prevention curriculum for teachers and issues of context, culture, emotion, race, class, gender, religion, sexuality, and language?

2. Choosing an appropriate mode of representation. Once the kind of situations teachers will face and will need help navigating have been identified, what mode of representing the relevant insights will be most useful? Case studies of real situations? Hypothetical case studies? Clinical prose, or first-person narratives? Biographical narratives? Videographic representations? Web page hypertext? Should these be interactive?

3. Finding the optimal mode of delivery for this curriculum. Is this curriculum best provided in preservice teacher education programs or in in-service curriculum? Can teachers read and encounter the material alone, or do they need to process it in groups?

What is entailed in integrating the new insights into practice, and how long does it take? How can the contextualized insights be presented in a way that promotes further dialogue and inquiry?

BUILDING ON EXISTING STRENGTHS:
TEACHER KNOWLEDGE RESEARCH

Fortunately, theories about and methods for analyzing the complex practical dimension of teaching already exist. They can be found in the teacher knowledge research literature. What follows is a brief review of the ideas in that literature that relate to each of the three steps described above, respectively.

Determining Specific Content for the Curriculum

This step involves both policy decisions and research tailored to the task at hand. Initially, broad goals and specific behaviors need to be identified for teaching practices that contribute to the prevention of the spread of HIV/AIDS. Once such goals and behaviors are identified, then the way these goals and behaviors intersect with emotional, cultural, and local practical realities of teachers work need to be documented and analyzed for insights into how to best accomplish the specified ends. In the best of situations, these two processes—goal setting and the research on practice—would be ongoing and dialectically related. The overarching goals would guide research on teachers' practice, which in turn influences the overall goals of the educational project.

Research on the practical aspects of teaching has been part of the mainstream of educational scholarship for more than a decade (Shulman, 1987, 2000; Grossman, 1990; Grossman and Stodolsky, 1995; Clandinin and Connelly, 1996, 2000; Cochran-Smith and Lytle, 1993, 1999). In his widely cited 1987 *Harvard Education Review* article, "Knowledge and Teaching: Foundations of the New Reform," Shulman wrote

One of the frustrations of teaching as an occupation and profession is its extensive and collective amnesia, the consistency with which the best creations of its practitioners are lost to both contemporary and future peers .... We have concluded from our research with teachers at all levels of experience that the potentially codifiable knowledge that can be gleaned from the wisdom of practice is extensive. Practitioners simply know a great deal that they have

11

never even tried to articulate. A major portion of the educational agenda for the coming decades will be to collect, collate, and interpret the practical knowledge of teachers for the purpose of establishing a case literature and codifying its principles, precedents, and parables. (p. 8)

Although Shulman was speaking about teachers' knowledge of how to teach more traditional subject matter, the lessons he learned apply to the topic at hand as well. Documentation of teachers' practical insights about how to respond to HIV/AIDS in the classroom and how to educate others about it can be an important source of insight and material for an effective HIV/AIDS prevention curriculum.

What is entailed in the documentation of teachers' practical knowledge? Increasingly calls are made to bridge the gap between theory and practice, or between policy and practice, by conducting research on teaching practice *collaboratively* with teachers. Darling-Hammond in her 1996 American Educational Research Association presidential address articulated the rationale for collaboration as it relates to traditional educational objectives:

> What kinds of teaching practices support learning that enables higher levels of performance and understanding for different kinds of learners? ... How can this be done in ways that also build greater cross-cultural understanding and cooperative possibilities across individuals and groups? ... These are central questions for the contemporary reinvention of democratic education. Their answers rest in part, I believe, on our growing ability to produce knowledge *for* and *with* educators and policy makers in ways that provide a foundation for a more complex form of teaching practice. (p. 8)

Darling-Hammond's observation also applies to the development of HIV/AIDS prevention curriculum for teachers. Documenting the practical terrain in which such a curriculum would be enacted requires collaborating with teachers in a practitioner research process. Case studies could be developed in collaboration with teachers who have or may have had HIV-positive children in their classrooms. Close attention would need to be paid to confidentiality issues, of course, in any such research project.

Choosing an Appropriate Mode of Representation

Once the necessary practical knowledge has been identified, further decisions will need to be made about the appropriate mode of representation for these insights. In the above quote, Shulman (1987) mentioned the development of a case study literature of teachers' "wisdom of practice." For the reasons that have been outlined, some form of case study curriculum, in addition to curriculum materials that provide the scientific and policy information teachers need, seems appropriate for an HIV/AIDS prevention teacher education curriculum.

The idea of a case literature will be familiar to those who have had medical training. Medical training involves the study of the science of medicine as well as the study of cases from the practice of medicine. Knowing the microbiology of a disease is not the same as knowing how that disease is likely to present itself, or how a patient unschooled in the art and science of medicine is likely to report on the symptoms. These are the practical human realities of medical practice that doctors need to understand in order to provide their service effectively. Case studies, with their focus on context-bound particulars of health issues, make an education about this aspect of medical practice possible. Similarly, where teaching is concerned, discussing case studies of teaching episodes in which HIV/AIDS issues are addressed will help teachers connect the information and theory they receive from the medical community with the teaching practice they live.

There are many different styles and approaches to case study development and writing. On one hand, Shulman (1987, 2000), Ball (1996), Grossman and Stodolsky (1995), and Wilson and Wineburg (1993) approach case study writing conservatively. Cases developed by these scholars most frequently focus primarily, if not solely, on the cognitive aspect of teaching specific subject matter concepts. Issues of emotion and culture are rarely featured. Case studies are written in the third person, most often providing facts and analysis in a dispassionate clinical prose. On the other end of the spectrum is the more holistic approach of scholars such as Clandinin and Connelly (1996, 2000), Delpit (1995), and Cochran-Smith and Lytle (1993, 1999). Clandinin and Connelly have emphasized the biographical sources of teachers' practical knowledge in their work, and they work with teachers to develop narratives about their teaching that explore the roots of their practical understanding of the classroom in the broad range of their life experiences. Delpit (1995) has explicitly critiqued Shulman's subject-matter-centered approach to teachers' practical knowledge, suggesting that it ignores what teachers need to know practically about the cultural and sociohistorical dimension of students' lives. Cochran-Smith and Lytle (1999) have argued against the development of a general case study literature altogether, suggesting instead that teachers' practical knowledge is so context bound that it is preferable to prepare teachers to be researchers on their own practice.

Somewhere nearer to the middle of this continuum is the work of scholars that seeks to identify connections between specific curricular elements and the broader cultural, social, and moral context of teaching (Ladson-Billings, 1995; Barone, 2000; Sconiers and Rosiek, 2000; Chang and Rosiek, in press). Ladson-Billings (1995) has used cross-case analysis to identify some of the characteristics of mathematics teachers who are particularly successful at teaching African American students. Others (Barone, 2001; Chang and Rosiek, 2004; Sconiers and Rosiek, 2000) have generated first-person, artistically crafted narratives about teaching practice that explore what teachers know (and do not know) about the intersection of the subject matter and the broader context of students' lives. The purpose of these stylized narratives has been to communicate the phenomenological, emotional, and ideological, as well as conceptual, content of teachers' practical knowledge. Additionally, although most case studies to date of teachers' practical knowledge have been in written form, increasingly we see video case studies (Ball, 1996), Web site presentations of teacher knowledge (e.g., Carnegie Foundation for the Advancement of Teaching, 2005), and interactive CD-ROM presentations of hypothetical case studies. The CD-ROM *Everything You Wanted to Know About HIV/AIDS in the Classroom but Were Afraid to Ask* (American Association of Colleges for Teacher Education and WILL Interactive, 2000) is an exemplary model of the latter kind of teacher education curriculum.

For an HIV/AIDS prevention curriculum, it would seem that case studies (in whatever medium) that fall somewhere near the center of the continuum just outlined would be needed. On the one hand, there is a specific subject matter focus for the curriculum under consideration: the policies and practices that will help slow the spread of HIV/AIDS. Therefore, an approach that does not digress too far from that focus is in order. On the other hand, because of the nature of this topic, it will inevitably intersect with emotional, cultural, economic, religious, moral, and other dimensions of teachers' lives. For this reason, a method and style of case study development that documents and accurately represents these intersections will be needed. In order to better evoke and represent the moral and emotional drama of the issues that can accompany dealing with HIV/AIDS in the classroom, a first-person style of writing could be warranted in these case studies, as well as close attention to the style of the narrative.

Finding the Optimal Mode of Delivery for this Curriculum

Once the content and mode of representation for the HIV/AIDS curriculum is established, a way of delivering it to teachers needs to be developed. For a teacher education curriculum that employs case studies (text or video based) on the practical dimension of teaching, the objective is internalization through extended discussion of the case materials. The value of cases and their ability to represent the complexity of teaching practice is not in the one-time reading of those cases, but in the way they precipitate in-depth conversation by and among teachers about their practice.

Where preservice teacher education is concerned, this kind of curriculum would probably find its most natural home in multicultural education courses and in courses dealing with the health and physical safety of children. Preservice teacher education programs have the advantage of involving teachers in discussions of their practice for extended periods of time, which enables issues to be raised, discussed, and revisited over weeks or even months.

In-service teacher education that used the case study curriculum materials for maximum benefit would need to be designed such that teachers had time to reflect on the cases, discuss them with peers, and relate them to their own practice. It would be preferable if this was done with whole school communities, so that the cases became a part of the vocabulary of the local school culture.

Assessing the Results

As with all such interventions, the ground for summative assessment needs to be behavior—first that of teachers, then that of their students. Are teachers changing their behavior when dealing with situations that involve the risk of transmitting blood-born pathogens? Are teachers responding in a more informed and ethical manner to HIV-positive children? Are they practicing within the law? Are they educating children more frequently and effectively? Are children's risk behaviors changing?

Formative assessments of progress being made toward these goals should include monitoring the content of teacher and student discussions as well as changes in their knowledge base. Are teachers having professional discussions about HIV/AIDS prevention with their colleagues? Are they citing the case studies and other curricular material in such discussions? Do they, in fact, know more than they did before about HIV/AIDS prevention? Do students know more? Do they discuss it with friends?

We already know that education about sexual abstinence, condom use, and other means of disease prevention results in lowered exposure to risk for children (DiClemente, 1998). However, our understanding of what teacher knowledge and attitudes enable and enhance teaching HIV/AIDS prevention remains thin. Certainly giving teachers accurate information about HIV/AIDS is the right place to begin, but that information must travel a considerable distance, across different discourses, in order to influence teachers' and students' behavior. It must be integrated into a context with many competing moral imperatives, legal imperatives, cultural narratives about the disease, and demands on teacher time. It is in this practical integration that the struggle against the HIV epidemic in our schools will be won or lost. As such, an HIV/AIDS teacher education curriculum will need to address the practical dimension of teaching substantively and thoroughly.

CLOSING THOUGHTS: HUMANIZING TEACHER EDUCATION

The primary purpose of this chapter has been to highlight how contemporary teacher education research and scholarship might help with the development of an HIV/AIDS prevention teacher education curriculum. I would like, as a closing thought, to turn the trajectory of this analysis around for a moment and look at the way addressing the HIV/AIDS crisis can have a salutary influence on the field of teacher education.

We live in an era in which the widespread use of high-stakes, mandatory, standardized tests—frequently of poor design—threatens to trivialize teaching practice (Shulman, 1987; Madaus and Clarke, 2001; McNeil, 2000; Meier, 2000; Orfield and Wald, 2000). Teaching is increasingly conceptualized by some state- and national-level policy makers as dealing with only those activities most explicitly linked to subject matter learning. The effect of this pressure to narrow the focus of teaching is being felt in teacher education programs.

The problem with reducing teacher education to the exclusive discussion of subject matter teaching is that such narrowing of focus affects teachers' relationships with children (Delpit, 1995; Noddings, 1992, 2002, 2004). And those relationships are an essential component of all the subject-matter- and non-subject-matter-related teaching we need teachers to do. Teaching is far more than preparing students for exams. The teacher education research community has been at the forefront of making this case to national, state, and local policy makers.

The need to develop an HIV/AIDS prevention curriculum for teachers provides an excellent illustration of why an overly narrow conception of teacher education is unrealistic. We are practically and morally compelled to prepare teachers to deal with HIV/AIDS in the classroom, despite the fact that such preparation might take time away from preparation to teach academic content. Dealing with this disease means addressing fears of the disease; it will require confronting stereotypes about persons who are HIV positive; it will mean transgressing taboos about discussing human bodies and human sexuality; it will require addressing economic differences that create stratified access to education and health care; it will inevitably involve discussing tragedy and death with students; and it will mean struggling alongside teacher education students to find hope in sometimes hopeless situations. In short, the necessity of dealing with this deadly virus provides a perfect case illustration of why teachers need to be prepared to deal with children's whole lives, not just their test scores. A poignant irony thus emerges as we take seriously the need to address the HIV/AIDS crisis in teacher education programs. It may be that the need to effectively address a violently antihuman disease will provide one of the clearest reasons for fully humanizing teacher education curriculum.

REFERENCES

American Association of Colleges for Teacher Education and WILL Interactive. (2000). *Everything you wanted to know about HIV/AIDS in the classroom but were afraid to ask: A teacher's interactive journey* (CD-ROM). Potomac, MD: American Association of Colleges for Teacher Education.

Apple, M. (2001). *Educating the "right" way: Markets, standards, God, and inequality.* New York: Routledge-Falmer.

Ball, D. L. (1996). Teacher learning and the mathematics reforms: What we think we know and what we need to learn. *Phi Delta Kappan* 77(7): 500–508.

Bandura, A. (1997). *Self-efficacy in changing societies.* Cambridge, UK: Cambridge University Press.

Banks, J. (2000). *Cultural diversity and education: Foundations, curriculum, and teaching.* New York: Allyn and Bacon.

Barone, T. (2000). *Aesthetics, politics, educational inquiries: Essays and examples.* New York: Peter Lang.

Barone, T. (2001). *Touching eternity: The enduring outcomes of teaching.* New York: Teachers College Press.

Bennett, R., and Erin, C. (1999). *HIV and AIDS: Testing, screening, and confidentiality.* New York: Oxford University Press.

Brookings Institution, Brown Center on Education Policy. (1999). *Can we make education policy on the basis of evidence? What constitutes high quality education research and how can it be incorporated into policymaking?* Retrieved August 17, 2005, from http://www.brookings.edu/comm/transcripts/19991208.htm.

Carnegie Foundation for the Advancement of Teaching. (2005). *The gallery of teaching and learning.* Retrieved August 17, 2005, from http://www.carnegiefoundation.org.

Cazden, C. (2001). *Classroom discourse: The language of teaching and learning.* Portsmouth, NH: Heinemann.

Centers for Disease Control and Prevention. (1988). Guidelines for effective school health education to prevent the spread of AIDS. *Morbidity and Mortality Weekly Report,* 37(S-2). Atlanta, GA: CDC.

Centers for Disease Control and Prevention. (1992). *Developing and revising HIV policies. Handbook for evaluating HIV education* (Booklet 2). Atlanta, GA: CDC.

Chang, P. J., and Rosiek, J. (2003). Anti-colonialist antinomies in a biology lesson: A case study of cultural conflict in a science classroom. *Curriculum Inquiry* 33(3): 251–290.

Clandinin, D. J., and Connelly, M. F. (1996). Teachers' professional knowledge landscapes: Teacher stories. *Educational Researcher* 25(3): 24–31.

Clandinin, D. J., and Connelly, M. F., eds. (1999). *Shaping a professional identity: Stories of educational practice.* London, ON: Althouse Press.

Clandinin, D. J., and Connelly, M. F. (2000). *Narrative inquiry.* San Francisco: Jossey-Bass.

Cochran-Smith, M., and Lytle, S. (1993). *Inside/outside: Teacher research and knowledge.* New York: Teachers College Press.

Cochran-Smith, M., and Lytle, S. L. (1999). Relationships of knowledge and practice: Teacher learning in communities. *Review of Research in Education* 24: 249–305.

Darling-Hammond, L. (1996). The right to learn and the advancement of teaching: Research, policy, and practice for democratic education. *Educational Researcher* 25(6): 5–19.

Delpit, L. (1995). *Other people's children.* New York: The New Press.

DiClemente, R. J. (1998). Preventing sexually transmitted infections among adolescents: A clash of ideology and science. *Journal of the American Medical Association* 279: 1574–1575.

Dilworth, M. (1998). *Being responsive to cultural differences: How teachers learn.* Thousand Oaks, CA: Corwin Press.

Dufour, R., and Eaker, R. E. (1998). *Professional learning communities at work: Best practices for enhancing student achievement.* Bloomington, IN: National Educational Service.

Eng, T. R., and Butler, W. T. (1997). *The hidden epidemic: Confronting sexually transmitted diseases.* Washington, DC: National Academy Press.

Fisher, C. (1997). A relational perspective on ethics in science decision making for research with vulnerable populations. Contracted paper for the National Bioethics Advisory Commission. IRB: *A Review of Human Subjects Research* 19(5): 1–4.

Fullan, M. (2001). *Leading in a culture of change.* New York: John Wiley and Sons.

Gage, N. L. (1972). *Teacher effectiveness and teacher education: The search for a scientific basis.* Palo Alto, CA: Pacific Books.

Gage, N. L. (1978). *The scientific basis of the art of teaching.* New York: Teachers College Press.

Gay, G. (2000). *Culturally responsive teaching: Theory, research, and practice.* New York: Teachers College Press.

Gay, Lesbian, and Straight Education Network. (2002). *From denial to denigration: Understanding institutionalized heterosexism in our schools.* Retrieved August 17, 2005, from http://www.glsen.org/cgi-bin/iowa/all/library/record/1101.html.

Grossman, P. (1990). *The making of a teacher: Teacher knowledge and teacher education.* New York: Teachers College Press.

Grossman, P. L., and Stodolsky, S. (1995). Content as context: The role of school subjects in secondary school teaching. *Educational Researcher* 24(8): 5–11.

Hargreaves, A. (2000). *Learning from change.* New York: Jossey-Bass.

Hollingsworth, S., and Cody, A. (1994). *Teacher research and urban literacy education: Lessons and conversations in a feminist key.* New York: Teachers College Press.

Igoa, C. (1995). *The inner world of the immigrant child.* New York: Lawrence Erlbaum.

Ladson-Billings, G. (1995). Toward a theory of culturally relevant pedagogy. *American Educational Research Journal* 32(3): 465–493.

Macedo, D., and Bartolome, L. (2001). *Dancing with bigotry: Beyond the politics of tolerance.* New York: Palgrave Macmillan.

Madaus, G., and Clarke, M. (2001). The adverse impact of high-stakes testing on minority students: Evidence from one hundred years of test data. In G. Orfield and M. Kornhaber, eds., *Raising standards or raising barriers?*

Inequality and high-stakes testing in public education (pp. 85–106). New York: Century Foundation.

McEwan, E. K. (2002). *Ten traits of highly effective teachers: How to hire, coach, and mentor successful teachers.* Thousand Oaks, CA: Corwin Press.

McNeil, L. (2000). *Contradictions of school reform: Educational costs of standardized testing.* New York: Routledge Kegan Paul.

Meier, D. (2000). Educating a democracy. In J. Cohen and J. Rogers, eds., *Will standards save public education?* (pp. 3–31). Boston: Beacon.

Mohan, M., and Hull, R. E., eds. (1975). *Teaching effectiveness: Its meaning, assessment, and improvement.* Englewood Cliffs, NJ: Educational Technology Publications.

Muijs, D., and Reynolds, D. (2001). *Effective teaching: Evidence and practice.* London: Paul Chapman Publishing.

National School Boards Association. (1990). *Reducing the risk: A school leader's guide to AIDS education.* Alexandria, VA: NSBA.

Noddings, N. (1992). *The challenge to care in schools: An alternative approach to education.* New York: Teachers College Press.

Noddings, N. (2002). *Educating moral people: A caring alternative to character education.* New York: Teachers College Press.

Noddings, N. (2004). *Happiness and education: A caring alternative to character education.* New York: Teachers College Press.

Noffke, S. (1997). Professional, personal, and political dimensions of action research. *Review of Research and Education* 22: 305–343.

Office of National AIDS Policy. (2000). *Youth and HIV/AIDS policy 2000: A new American agenda.* Washington, DC: Author.

Orfield, G., and Wald, J. (2000). Testing, testing. *Nation* 270(22): 38–40.

Sarason, S. B. (1999). *Teaching as a performing art.* New York: Teachers College Press.

Scheurich, J. (2002). *Anti-racist scholarship: An advocacy.* New York: State University of New York Press.

Sconiers, Z., and Rosiek, J. (2000). Historical perspective as an important element of teacher knowledge: A sonata-form case study of equity issues in a chemistry classroom. *Harvard Educational Review* 70(3): 370–404.

Shulman, L. (1987). Knowledge and teaching: Foundations of the new reform. *Harvard Educational Review* 57: 1–22.

Shulman, L. (1992). Research on teaching: A historical and personal perspective. In F. K. Oser, D. Andreas, and J. L. Patry, eds., *Effective and responsible teaching: The new synthesis* (pp. 14–29). San Francisco: Jossey-Bass.

Shulman, L. (2000). Teacher development: Roles of domain expertise and pedagogical knowledge. *Journal of Applied Developmental Psychology* 25(1): 129–135.

Sleeter, C., and Grant, C. (1999). *Making choices for multicultural education: Five approaches to race, class, and gender.* New York: John Wiley and Sons.

Tell, C. (2001). Appreciating good teaching: A conversation with Lee Shulman. *Educational Leadership* 58(5): 6–11.

Willis, P. (1971). *Learning to labor.* New York: Columbia University Press.

Wilson, S., and Wineburg, S. (1993). Wrinkles in time and place: Using performance assessments to understand the knowledge of history teachers. *American Educational Research Journal* 30(4): 729–769.

Zeichner, K. M., and Liston, D. (1996). *Reflective teaching and the social conditions of schooling.* New York: Lawrence Erlbaum.

2

ON THE INDISPENSABLE QUALITIES OF PROGRESSIVE TEACHERS FOR THEIR BETTER PERFORMANCE

Paulo Freire

⊕

I would like to make it clear that the attributes I am going to speak about, which seem to me to be indispensable to the progressive teacher, are qualities acquired gradually through practice. Furthermore, they are developed through practice in concurrence with a political decision that the educator's role is crucial. Thus the attributes I am going to speak about are not attributes that we can be born with or that can be bestowed upon us by decree or as a gift. In addition, the order in which I list them here is not intended to rank their value. They are all necessary for a progressive educational practice.

I shall start with *humility*, which here by no means carries the connotation of a lack of self-respect, of resignation, or of cowardice. On the contrary, humility requires courage, self-confidence, self-respect, and respect for others.

Humility helps us to understand this obvious truth: No one knows it all; no one is ignorant of everything. We all know something; we are all ignorant of something. Without humility, one can hardly listen with respect to those one judges to be too far below one's own level of competence. But the humility that enables one to listen even to those considered less competent should not be an act of condescension or resemble the behavior of those fulfilling a vow: "I promise the Virgin Mary that, if the problem with my eyes turns out not to be serious, I will listen to the rude and ignorant parents of my students with attention." No. None of that. Listening to all that come to us, regardless of their intellectual level, is a human duty and reveals an identification with democracy and not with elitism.

In fact, I cannot see how one could reconcile adherence to an ideal of democracy and of overcoming prejudice with a proud or arrogant posture in which one feels full of oneself. How can I listen to the other, how can I hold a dialogue, if I can only listen to myself, if I can only see myself, if nothing or no one other than myself can touch me or move me? If while humble, one does undermine oneself or accepts humiliation, one is also always ready to teach and to learn. Humility helps me avoid being entrenched in the circuit of my own truth. One of the fundamental auxiliaries of humility is *common sense,* which serves to remind us that certain attitudes may lead us too close to becoming lost.

The arrogance of "You don't know who you are dealing with ... ," the *conceit* of the know-it-all with an unrestrained desire to make his or her knowledge known and recognized—none of this has anything to do with the *tameness* (which is not apathy) of the humble. Humility does not flourish in people's insecurities but in the insecure security of the more aware, and thus this insecure security is one of the expressions of humility, as is uncertain certainty, unlike certainty, which is excessively sure of itself. The authoritarians' stance, in contrast, is sectarian. Theirs is the only truth, and it must be imposed on others. It is in their truth that others' salvation resides. Their knowledge "illuminates" the obscurity or the ignorance of others, who then must be subjected to the knowledge and arrogance of the authoritarian.

I will return to my analysis of authoritarianism, whether that of parents or teachers. As one might expect, authoritarianism will at times cause children and students to adopt *rebellious* positions, defiant of any limit, discipline, or authority. But it will also lead to apathy, excessive obedience, uncritical conformity, lack of resistance against authoritarian discourse, self-abnegation, and fear of freedom.

In saying that authoritarianism may generate various types of reactions, I understand that on a human level things do not happen so *mechanically* and happily. Thus it is possible that certain children will go through the rigors of arbitrariness unscathed, which does not give us the license to gamble on that possibility and fail to make an effort to become less authoritarian. And if we can't make that effort for our dream for democracy, we should make it out of respect for beings in development, our children and our students.

But to the humility with which teachers perform and relate to their students, another quality needs to be added: *lovingness,* without which their work would lose its meaning. And here I mean lovingness not only toward the students but also toward the very process of teaching. I must confess, not meaning to cavil, that I do not believe educators can survive the negativities of their trade without some sort of "armed love," as the poet Tiago de Melo would say. Without it they could not survive all the injustice or the government's contempt, which is expressed in the shameful wages and the arbitrary treatment of teachers, not coddling mothers, who take a stand, who participate in protest activities through their union, who are punished, and who yet remain devoted to their work with students.

It is indeed necessary, however, that this love be an "armed love," the fighting love of those convinced of the right and the duty to fight, to denounce, and to announce. It is this form of love that is indispensable to the progressive educator and that we must all learn.

It so happens, however, that this lovingness I speak about, the dream for which I fight and for whose realization I constantly prepare myself, demands that I invent in myself, in my social experience, another quality: *courage,* to fight and to love.

Courage, as a virtue, is not something I can find outside myself. Because it comprises the conquering of my fears, it implies fear.

First of all, in speaking about fear we must make sure that we are speaking of something very concrete. In other words, fear is not an abstraction. Second, we must make sure that we understand that we are speaking of something very normal. And, when we speak about fear, we are faced with the need to be very clear of our choices, and that requires certain concrete procedures and practices, which are the very experiences that cause fear.

To the extent that I become clearer about my choices and my dreams, which are substantively political and attributively pedagogical, and to the extent that I recognize that though as an educator I am also a political agent, I can better understand why I fear and realize how far we still have to go to improve our democracy. I also understand that as we put into practice an education that critically provokes the learner's consciousness, we are necessarily working against myths that deform us. As we confront such myths, we also face the dominant power because those myths are nothing but the expression of this power, of its ideology.

When we are faced with concrete fears, such as that of losing our jobs or of not being promoted, we feel the need to set certain limits to our fear. Before anything else, we begin to recognize that fear is a manifestation of our being alive. I do not need to hide my fears. But I must not allow my fears to immobilize me. If I am secure in my political dream, having tactics that may lessen my risk, I must go on with the fight. Hence the need to be in control of my fear, to *educate* my fear, from which is finally born my courage.[1] Thus I must neither, on the one hand, deny my fears nor, on the other, surrender myself to them. Instead, I must control them, for it is in the very exercise of this control that my necessary courage is shared.

That is why though there may be fear without courage, the fear that devastates and paralyzes us, there may never be courage without fear, that which "speaks" of our humanness as we manage to limit, subject, and control it.

Tolerance is another virtue. Without it no serious pedagogical work is possible; without it no authentic democratic experience is viable; without it all progressive educational practice denies itself. Tolerance is not, however, the irresponsible position of those who play the game of make-believe.

Being tolerant does not mean acquiescing to the intolerable; it does not mean covering up disrespect; it does not mean coddling the aggressor or disguising aggression. Tolerance is the virtue that teaches us to live with the different. It teaches us to learn from and respect the different.

On an initial level, tolerance may almost seem to be a favor, as if being tolerant were a courteous, thoughtful way of accepting, of *tolerating*, the not-quite-desired presence of one's opposite, a civilized way of permitting a coexistence that might seem repugnant. That, however, is hypocrisy, not tolerance. Hypocrisy is a defect; it is degradation. Tolerance is a virtue. Thus if I live tolerance, I should embrace it. I must experience it as something that makes me coherent first with my historical being, inconclusive as that may sound, and second with my democratic political choice. I cannot see how one might be democratic without experiencing tolerance, coexistence with the different, as a fundamental principle.

No one can learn tolerance in a climate of irresponsibility, which does not produce democracy. The act of tolerating requires a climate in which limits may be established, in which there are principles to be respected. That is why tolerance is not coexistence with the intolerable. Under an authoritarian regime, in which authority is abused, or a permissive one, in which freedom is not limited, one can hardly learn tolerance. Tolerance requires respect, discipline, and ethics. The authoritarian, filled with sexual, racial, and class prejudices, can never become tolerant without first overcoming his or her prejudices. That is why a bigot's *progressive* discourse, which contrasts with his or her practice, is a false discourse. That is also why those who embrace scientism are equally intolerant, because they take science for the *ultimate truth*, outside of which nothing counts, believing that only science can provide certainty Those immersed in scientism cannot be tolerant, though that fact should not discredit science.

I would also like to add *decisiveness, security,* the tension between *patience and impatience,* and *joy of living* to the group of qualities to be nourished in ourselves if we are to be progressive educators.

An educator's ability to make decisions is absolutely necessary to his or her educational work. It is by demonstrating an ability to make decisions that an educator teaches the difficult virtue of decisiveness. Making decisions is difficult to the extent that it signifies breaking free to choose. No one ever decides anything without making a trade-off, weighing one thing against another, one point against another, one person against another. Thus every choice that follows a particular decision calls for careful evaluation in comparing and opting for one of the possible sides, persons, or positions. It is evaluation, with all its implications, that helps us to finally make choices.

Decision making is rupture and is not always an easy experience. But it is not possible to exist without rupturing, no matter how hard it may be.

One of the deficiencies that an educator may possess is an inability to make decisions. Such *indecision* is perceived by learners as either moral weakness or professional incompetence. Democratic educators must not nullify themselves in the name of being democratic. On the contrary, although they cannot take sole responsibility for the lives of their students, they must not, in the name of democracy, evade the responsibility of making decisions. At the same time, they must not be arbitrary in their decisions. Setting an example, as an authority figure, of not taking responsibility for one's duties, of allowing oneself to fall into permissiveness, is even more somber a fate for a teacher than abusing authority.

There are plenty of occasions when a good democracy-oriented pedagogical example is to make the decision in question with the students, after analyzing the problem. Other times, when the decision to be made is within the scope of the educator's expertise, there is no reason not to take action, to be negligent.

Indecision reveals a lack of confidence; but confidence is indispensable for anyone with responsibilities in government, whether of a class, a family, an institution, a company, or the state.

Security, confidence, on the other hand, requires scientific competence, political clarity, and ethical integrity.

One cannot be secure in one's actions without knowing how to support those actions scientifically, without at least some idea of what one does, why, and to what end. The same is true of allegiance: One must know whom or what one is for or against. Nor can one be secure in one's actions without being moved by them, or if one hurts the dignity of others, exposing them to embarrassing situations. Such ethical irresponsibility and cynicism show an inability to live up to the educator's task, which demands critically disciplined performance with which to challenge learners. On the one hand, such discipline reflects the educator's competence, as it is gradually revealed to the learners, discreetly and humbly, without arrogant outbursts; on the other, it affects the balance with which the educator exercises authority—secure, lucid, and determined.

None of this, however, can be realized if an educator lacks a taste for permanently seeking justice. No one can prevent a teacher from liking one student more than another, for any number of reasons. That is a teacher's right. What a teacher must not do is disregard the rights of the other students in favoring one student.

There is another fundamental quality that the progressive educator must not lack: He or she must exercise wisdom in experiencing the tension between *patience* and *impatience*. Neither *patience* nor *impatience* alone is what is called for. Patience alone may bring the educator to a position of resignation, of permissiveness, that denies the educator's democratic dream. Unaccompanied patience may lead to immobility, to inactivity. Conversely, impatience alone may lead the educator to blind activism, to action for its own sake, to a practice that does not respect the necessary relationship between tactics and strategy. Isolated patience tends to hinder the attainment of objectives central to the educator's practice, making it soft and ineffectual. Untempered impatience threatens the success of one's practice, which becomes lost in the arrogance of judging oneself the owner of history. Patience alone consumes itself in mere prattle; impatience alone consumes itself in irresponsible activism.

Virtue, then, does not lie in experiencing either without the other but, rather, in living the permanent tension between the two. The educator must live and work impatiently patiently, never surrendering entirely to either.

Alongside this harmonious, balanced way of being and working there must figure another quality, which I have been calling *verbal parsimony*. Verbal parsimony is implied in the assumption of patience-impatience. Those who live impatient patience will rarely lose control over their words; they will rarely exceed the limits of considered yet energetic discourse. Those who predominantly live patience alone stifle their legitimate anger, which then is expressed through weak and resigned discourse. Those, on the other hand, who are all uncontrolled impatience tend toward lack of restraint in discourse. The patient person's discourse is always *well-behaved*, whereas that of the impatient person generally goes beyond what reality itself could withstand.

Both of these kinds of discourse, the overly controlled as well as the undisciplined, contribute to the preservation of the status quo. The first falls short of the demands of the status quo; the second surpasses its limits.

The benevolent classroom discourse and practice of those who are only patient suggest to learners that anything, or almost anything, goes. There is in the air a sense of a nearly infinite patience. Nervous, arrogant, uncontrolled, unrealistic, unrestrained discourse will find itself immersed in inconsequence and irresponsibility.

In no way do these discourses contribute to the learners' education. There are also those who are excessively restrained in their discourse but who once in a while lose control. From absolute patience, they leap unexpectedly into uncontainable impatience, creating a climate of insecurity for everyone around them, always with terrible effects.

Countless mothers and fathers behave so. Today their words and their actions are permissive, but they transform tomorrow into the opposite, a universe of authoritarian discourse and orders, which not only leaves their sons and daughters appalled but, above all, makes them insecure. Such immoderate parental behavior limits children's emotional balance, which they need to grow up. Loving is not enough; one must know how to love.

Though I recognize that these reflections on qualities are incomplete, I would also like to briefly discuss *joy of living* as a fundamental virtue for democratic educational practice.

By completely giving myself to life rather than to death—without meaning either to deny death or to mythicize life—I can free myself to surrender to the joy of living, without having to hide the reasons for sadness in life, which prepares me to stimulate and champion joy in the school.

Whether or not we are willing to overcome slips or inconsistencies, by living humility, lovingness, courage, tolerance, competence, decisiveness, patience-impatience, and verbal parsimony, we contribute to creating a happy, joyful school. We forge a school-adventure, a school that marches on, that is not afraid of the risks, and that rejects immobility. It is a school that thinks, that participates, that creates, that speaks, that loves, that guesses, that passionately embraces and says yes to life. It is not a school that quiets down and quits.

Indeed the easy way out in dealing with the obstacles posed by governmental contempt and the arbitrariness of antidemocratic authorities is the fatalist resignation in which many of us find ourselves.

"What can I do? Whether they call me *teacher* or coddling mother, I am still underpaid, disregarded, and uncared for. Well, so be it." In reality, this is the most convenient position, but it is also the position of someone who quits the struggle, who quits history. It is the position of those who renounce conflict, the lack of which undermines the dignity of life. There may not be life or human existence without struggle and conflict. Conflict[2] shares in our conscience. Denying conflict, we ignore even the most mundane aspects of our vital and social experience. Trying to escape conflict, we preserve the status quo.

Thus I can see no alternative for educators to unity within the diversity of their interests in defending their rights. Such rights include the right to freedom in teaching, the right to speak, the right to better conditions for pedagogical work, the right to paid sabbaticals for continuing education, the right to be coherent, the right to criticize the authorities without fear of retaliation (which entails the duty to criticize truthfully), the right to the duty to be serious and coherent and to not have to lie to survive.

We must fight so that these rights are not just recognized but respected and implemented. At times we may need to fight side by side with the unions; at other times we may need to fight against them, if their leadership is sectarian, whether right or left. At other times we also need to fight as a progressive administration against the devilish anger of the obsolete; of the traditionalists, some of whom judge themselves progressive; and of the neoliberals, who see themselves as the culmination of history.

NOTES

1. See Paulo Freire and Ira Shor, *Medo e Ousadia, o Cotidiano do Professor* (Rio de Janeiro: Paz e Terra, 1987).

2. See Moacir Gadotti, Paulo Freire, and Sergio Guimaraes, *Pedagogy: Dialogue and Conflict* (Rio de Janeiro: Cortez, 1989).

3

DISABILITY STUDIES AS INSIGHT: DEPLOYING ENABLING PEDAGOGIES IN HIV/AIDS EDUCATION

Nirmala Erevelles

✒

> The point here, I think, is not to feel bad about the injustice or the suffering in the world.... . The point is to pull up short before the possibility that what you thought was true might not be, that what you thought was normal or natural might be the product of political struggle, and to start—from just that place—to *think,* which means to question, to critique, to experiment, to wonder, to imagine, to try.
> —*McWhorter, 2005, p. xvii*

> We condemn attempts to label us as "victims," which implies defeat, and we are only occasionally 'patients,' which implies passivity, helplessness, and dependence on the care of others. We are "people with AIDS."
> —*PWA Coalition, quoted in McRuer, 2002b, p. 222*

To conceptualize enabling pedagogies associated with HIV/AIDS education programs, educators must first critically question their assumptions regarding difference and disability in educational contexts. Notwithstanding progressive or radical critiques of education policy and praxis, most educators continue to uphold ideological assumptions of disability as commonsense, even if these assumptions have been used to justify some of the most oppressive hierarchies of difference in educational contexts (Slee, 1997; Erevelles, 2000). Mayo (2003) insightfully reveals the contradictions that are embedded in such assumptions. For example, in multicultural education we exhort our students to stop labeling difference associated with race, class, gender, and sexuality as "deviant" in order to explore the social, political, and economic conditions that produce these differences as deviant in the first place. At the same time, colleges of education across the country require their special education teacher candidates to pay close attention to the "facts" associated with different (disability) labels, without even asking why we have these labels in the first place, what implications such labeling has on the educational futures of students, and how labels serve to organize the education community into oppressive hierarchies based on the nebulous construct of "ability."

The reason I invoke the social construct of disability in this discussion on enabling pedagogies is because the makers of social policy associate HIV/AIDS with disability. In fact, the rights of students with HIV/AIDS are protected by the Individuals with Disabilities Education Act (IDEA) in K–12 settings and by the Americans with Disabilities Act (ADA) in postsecondary contexts. Notwithstanding the legal protection gained by the association of HIV/AIDS with disability, this association is also fraught with dangerous contradictions, especially as it relates to pedagogy. The impetus to talk about HIV/AIDS in educational contexts is to enable students to protect themselves from contracting the virus through the practices of safe sex and/or sexual abstinence. To bring to the attention of adolescents and young adults the deadly seriousness of this issue, the tone evoked in such pedagogical contexts is "a cross between awe and horror" (Nye, 2001, p. 230), especially when describing the real embodied experiences and material implications of contracting HIV/AIDS. Such pedagogical discussions of prevention are also mired in discourses of sexual morality based on ideological assumptions of who can and cannot be sexually active, how one is expected to express his/her sexuality, and what normative sexual practices are acceptable in educational settings.

In a pedagogical context that conjures up the "terror" of HIV/AIDS in order to exhort students to protect themselves from its "deadliness," in what ways do such discussions also shape how we relate to persons/students who have already contracted HIV/AIDS? Will such discussions produce a moral hierarchy in the context of disability—those who morally deserve to suffer their disability and those who as unwitting "victims" are worthy of our help and pity? Further, how do discourses of morality also implicitly set up normative codes that are then used to produce the oppressive binaries that separate those who are morally good (i.e., able-bodied) from those who are deviant (disabled)? What institutional practices in education and other contexts are specifically invoked to administer and propagate these segregationist practices that involve not only disability but also race, class, gender, and sexuality? What implications do such discussions of prevention have on a disability rights movement fighting the eugenic impulses of contemporary practices such as genetic counseling and physician-assisted suicide? Can objective, pedagogical discourses of prevention associated with a medical condition be easily disassociated from reactionary discourses that require the social annihilation of specific identity communities?

In this chapter, I argue that any discussion of enabling pedagogies associated with HIV/AIDS educational programs will be limited, despite their self-described social justice imperative, unless such pedagogies also urge students to critically engage with the political construct of disability situated within the hegemonic cult of normality. Disability studies scholars have demonstrated the limitations of the medical model of disability that focuses on the natural or biological aspect of disability and that describes disabled people as belonging to the "unfortunate few" who suffer these conditions (Michalko, 2002). These scholars have argued for a critical examination of the social, political, and economic conditions within which the cult of normality can flourish and of the violent implications of supporting without question certain normative directives. Echoing this position, I argue that pedagogical discussions of HIV/AIDS should not be limited to a dissemination of the facts associated with the virus but should also engage in a broader critique of the social politics of interpretation and the subsequent treatment of people marked as different/disabled. Resisting the construction of yet another oppressive "special" education program under the guise of empowering inclusivity, I will discuss in this chapter the implications and possibilities for an enabling pedagogy regarding HIV/AIDS that draws on the critical insight of a disability studies perspective.

Educators must reflect on their own ideological assumptions regarding both HIV/AIDS and disability as manifested in the teacher education knowledge base and in their own pedagogical interactions with their disabled students. Rather than providing a laundry list of what an enabling pedagogy for HIV/AIDS education could be, I will illuminate the oppressive implications embedded in particular ideological understandings of HIV/AIDS and disability and offer alternative readings of these ideologies. Therefore, discussions in different sections of this chapter focus on (a) the contested and contradictory relationship between HIV/AIDS and disability; (b) how educational policy and praxis produces disempowering discourses of HIV/AIDS and disability; and (c) how a disability studies perspective will serve as counter discourse to the prevailing ideologies of HIV/AIDS and disability.

HIV/AIDS AND DISABILITY: THINKING IN TANDEM?

Although members of the disability rights movement and AIDS activist groups might be wary of the framing of disability and HIV/AIDS as related conditions, this linkage may be explained by examining the contexts in which it has been forged. Official discourses that shape social and education policy draw on a medical model that describes HIV/AIDS as a health condition that results in a person's becoming disabled. Such a position is taken up by the World Health Organization (WHO), which has constructed the International Classification of Impairments, Disabilities, and Handicaps (ICIDH) to serve as a classification of the consequences of disease (Hwang and Nochajski, 2003). In 1992, in a presumably empowering move, the ICIDH was renamed the International Classification of Function, Disability, and Health (ICF) in an attempt to support a broader conceptual framework that emphasized "the dynamic and reciprocal nature of person–environment interactions within the health paradigm" so as to "provide a sound basis for understanding and studying the different dimensions of disablement as the consequences of health conditions and/or environmental interaction" (p. 4).

This move to classify disability as a product of the social environment drew its impetus from the struggles of the disability rights movement, both in the United States and in the United Kingdom (Oliver, 1990; Linton, 1998; Longmore, 2003). Here, disability studies activists and scholars, in an attempt to move away from the "personal tragedy theory" of disability as exemplified by the medical model of disability, argued for a social model of disability that made a critical distinction between *impairment,* which refers to physiological difference (limitations) and *disability,* which refers to the social and political response to this difference. Thus, according to the social model of disability, "it is not individual limitations of whatever kind, which are the causes of the problem [of disability], but society's failure to provide appropriate services and adequately ensure the needs of disabled people are fully

34

taken into account in its social organization" (Oliver, 1990, p. 32). By making this argument, these activists and scholars conceptualize disability as a political construct and disabled people as a minority group engaged in a civil rights struggle for social and political recognition. Based on this conceptualization,

> disability is never simply limitation in social and vocational functioning, never an objectively determinable, pathological clinical entity originating in the bodies of individuals. Rather, defying simple definition, it is an elastic social category shaped and reshaped by cultural values, societal arrangements, public policies, and professional practices. It is always an array of culturally constructed identities and highly mutable social roles. (Longmore, 2003, pp. 57–58)

The social model of disability has particular relevance to persons living with HIV/AIDS, even though this relation is fraught with both possibilities and tensions. Since the 1980s, improved medical care and pharmaceutical treatment has delayed the onset of AIDS and lengthened the survival time of people living with HIV/AIDS (Nye, 2001; Hwang and Nochajski, 2003). This change has resulted in a shift in the perception of HIV/AIDS from an "acute condition" to a "chronic disease model" (Hwang and Nochajski, 2003, p. 8) and a corresponding shift in how medical, educational, and rehabilitation institutions have treated what was formerly perceived as a terminal illness. The focus now is to provide appropriate resources and services to enhance the social, educational, occupational, and quality-of-life experiences of persons living with HIV/AIDS (Conyers, 2005; Ciasullo and Escovitz, 2005). As a result, the ICF qualifiers defined by the WHO that are used primarily to determine the kinds of services provided to persons with disabilities are also viewed as applicable to persons living with HIV/AIDS. These qualifiers include a description of the extent or magnitude of impairments (body functions), the nature of the change in body structure as a result of the impairment (body structures), the level of performance expected or anticipated in the person's current environment (activities and participation), and the extent of barriers and facilitators in the environment that prevent activity and participation (environmental factors).

Even though the ICF transformations claim to take a "whole-person" approach in the provision of services to persons with disabilities as well as persons living with HIV/AIDS, the overreliance on medical metaphors to describe factors associated with functioning, disability, and context continue to promote the individualistic or "personal tragedy" model of disability and HIV/AIDS—an approach that has been criticized by disability rights activists and scholars (Oliver, 1990; Russell, 1998; Thomas, 1999; Longmore, 2003). Further, even though the ICF claims to recognize the social dimension of disability, decisions relating to social context (e.g., occupation, recreation, housing) are nevertheless left in the hands of professionals who use scientific assessments to determine what course of action will be pursued by persons with disabilities and persons living with HIV/AIDS (Conyers, 2005; Thomas, 1999; Ciasullo and Escovitz, 2005). Locating even personal decisions within the purview of medical discourse serves to effectively deny personal choice and autonomy for both persons with disabilities and persons living with HIV/AIDS. For individuals with disabilities, many of whom do not have a persistent medical condition (e.g., persons with cognitive impairments), this conflation of disability with medical conditions such as HIV/AIDS forces them to live their lives within the dominating control of the so-called helping professions (e.g., special education and vocational rehabilitation).

At the same time, even though many persons living with HIV/AIDS will require critical medical interventions at times, medical discourses should not control all aspects of their lives. In fact, just like the disabled community, persons living with HIV/AIDS—notwithstanding social, cultural, economic, and even age differences—are often bound together by the collective experience of physical and emotional stigma associated with their impairment (Nye, 2001). In this context, just as disability rights activists have defined individuals with disabilities as an oppressed minority group, persons living with HIV/AIDS have followed suit by forming organizations such as the National Association of People with AIDS and the AIDS Coalition To Unleash Power (ACT-UP) (McRuer, 2002a). It is in their collective effort to challenge the overmedicalization of their lives and in their angry protest of the discrimination and isolation they face from mainstream society that activists for individuals with disabilities and with HIV/AIDS are intimately connected.

Persons living with HIV/AIDS and persons with disabilities are also collectively impacted by moralistic discourses of sexuality, albeit in different ways. Dominant discourses assume a causal relationship between infection by the HIV/AIDS virus and allegedly immoral, mostly sexual behavior such as homosexuality, sex outside marriage, and intravenous drug use. For persons with disabilities, on the other hand, merely having sex is considered deviant and therefore immoral (Erevelles and Mutua, 2005). Another relationship between HIV/AIDS and disability is evident in discussions that posit persons with disabilities as being at greater risk than the general population for contracting HIV/AIDS (Blanchett, 2000; Groce, 2003). Much of this risk has been attributed to the oppressive social conditions in which persons with disabilities live. A large number of them live in institution-like settings, where their physical vulnerability, poor and often abusive personal assistance services, and assumptions that they are not considered reliable witnesses in legal situations make them easy targets of sexual abuse (Groce, 2003; DiGiulio, 2003). Additionally, because of the erroneous assumption that persons with disabilities are mostly sexually inactive, there are few sex education programs that help them develop a well-rounded sense of sexuality, nor are there institutional or social structures that support their sexual activity, contributing to the problem that some disability scholars have dubbed "lack of sex access" (Shuttleworth and Mona, 2002). Further, social sanctions against marriage for persons with disabilities contribute to even less stable sexual relations (DiGiulio, 2003). Thus, both persons with disabilities and persons living with HIV/AIDS are seen to enact a "deviant" sexuality based on particular ideologies of morality that are limited, limiting, and discriminatory.

I have described here three key issues that are disruptive of the dominant, taken-for-granted knowledge base in teacher education. First, I have argued against the overreliance on the medical model that invokes an individualistic discourse of personal tragedy when applied to persons with disabilities and persons living with HIV/AIDS and that has resulted in the failure to respect their autonomy in making personal and social decisions. Second, I have argued that recognizing both persons with disabilities and persons living with HIV/AIDS as belonging to a minority group fighting for their civil rights requires that we also conceive of both disability and HIV/AIDS not just as physiological aberrations but as social/political constructs. Third, I have shown that our restrictive ideologies regarding disability and HIV/AIDS translate into restrictive social roles for persons with disabilities and persons living with HIV/AIDS, especially in the context of sexuality. Using these three key issues as an epistemological backdrop, in the next section I discuss the implications that oppressive understandings of HIV/AIDS and disability have on pedagogical praxis.

PEDAGOGY AS (IM)MORAL PRAXIS

As a teacher educator, I am confronted every year by a new batch of students who have all successfully passed their one mandatory course in special education. In this course, usually taught by a graduate assistant, students learn a laundry list of different disabilities and their key characteristics, laws that require that educational institutions provide these students with an education in the least restrictive environment, and a very cursory understanding about clinical interventions that are problematically considered pedagogy. More often than not, there is little if any information on the disability rights movement or HIV/AIDS activism and very little attention paid to the issue raised by both of these movements. Thus, in my Foundations of Education courses that focus on issues of social justice and difference, I draw on disability studies scholarship to offer a radical critique of how social difference is organized in educational institutions. This section of the course is sometimes met with resistance by both general education and special education teacher candidates. General education students resent the fact that they have limited instruction regarding how to teach "these" students and that "including" these students tends to take away from their broader pedagogical project of educating "regular" students. Special education students also resist the disability studies critiques of special education because such critiques render their specialized knowledge base as both limited and suspect.

When we broach the issue of sexuality and sex education in both general and special education, the silences are even more marked. In class discussions, it becomes painfully apparent that sex education is rarely part of the teacher education program or even an important part of the school curriculum. In public high schools, in particular, sex education is often relegated to a few sessions in a health course taught in sex-segregated settings by a biology teacher or coaching staff. In the conservative and religious southern United States where I teach, the vast majority of my preservice teachers report that they lack even this minimal education because their parents opted for them to receive instruction from their pastor at the church they attend. It is in this dismal context, ripe with the power of dangerous silences, that a discussion of pedagogy relating to HIV/AIDS, disability, and sexuality is situated.

Lupton and Tulloch (1996) argue that sex education is a contested discipline in which debates around moral values, sexual knowledge, the nature of childhood and adolescence, and the politics of pedagogy all collide. In contemporary discourses of sex education, there is the dominant assumption that the adolescent sexual body is an "unfinished" body in need of careful nurturing and protection before it can become fully sexual. Such a position also signals an urgency to monitor, control, and discipline the adolescent at a time when he or she might be also subject to "undesirable" influences (Lupton and Tulloch, 1996, p. 253). It is in this context, then, that sex education becomes more than just giving biomedical information to students about the sexual act, but, in fact, is also heavily embroiled in the political struggle over attitudes, emotions, feelings, and power relations.

The struggle, Lupton and Tulloch (1996) argue, is fought from two contentious positions—sexual romanticism (a conservative position that sees sexual activity as creating and reinforcing intimacy) and the libertarian position (which views sexual activity as having multiple purposes, including erotic pleasure for its own sake). Although both perspectives advocate the relationship of sexuality to the maintenance of a healthy body, the conservative perspective stresses abstinence or monogamous marriage, and the libertarian position advocates providing detailed information regarding safe sexual practices.

Certain segments in U.S. society prefer the conservative over the libertarian position, and schools become critical sites to disseminate this information. Because public schools are designated to be sites "for identifying, civilizing, and controlling that which is considered uncontrollable" (Fine, 1993, p. 76), the task of educating adolescents into normative sexual compliance requires that schools deploy particular discourses of sexuality that are both limited and limiting. Fine (1993) identifies four discourses that characterize the national debate over sex education curriculum. The first, *sexuality as violence,* argues that sex education courses terrorize students with discussions on sex, abuse, incest, and AIDS; proponents of this discourse call for an elimination of sex education programs in schools, preferring to rely instead on the family unit for this instruction. A dominant assumption in this perspective is that not learning about sexuality will cause adolescents to decrease or even cease sexual behavior. The second discourse, *sexuality as victimization,* exhorts adolescents (especially girls) to defend themselves against disease, pregnancy, and "being used"; most of the instruction, then, is geared toward practicing abstinence, understanding the social and emotional risks of sexual intimacy, and listing possible diseases (particularly HIV/AIDS) associated with sexual intimacy. The third discourse, *sexuality as individual morality,* teaches students "moral literacy" by deploying a language of self-control and self-respect although reminding students that sexual immorality breeds both individual and social problems. The fourth discourse, the *discourse of desire,* invites adolescents to discuss sexuality in terms of their experiences, needs, and limits—but this discourse is very rarely found in public schools.

The first three discourses of sexuality as articulated by Fine represent the intersection between normalizing discourses of sexuality and moralistic discourses of difference. According to Waldschmidt (2005), "normal" people are legally defined as those who are able to fit in, obey the law, and fulfill social expectations without active resistance. The first three discourses of sexuality are clearly *normalizing discourses,* setting up codes of sexual behavior that determine who can have sex (e.g., only heterosexual, able-bodied adults) and what forms of sexual expression are acceptable in education contexts (e.g., participation in the heterosexual school prom). *Moralistic discourses of difference* deployed in sex education programs manifest themselves in the silence on issues of homosexuality or in the characterization of teenage girls who engage in premarital sex as "bad" girls/sluts/whores (Tolman, 2000).

Adding disability to this discussion makes the terrain of sexuality discourse even more volatile. Disability activists constantly struggle against eugenic ideologies that discourage the recognition of adolescents and adults with disabilities as sexual beings. Characterized as asexual children (Milligan and Neufeldt, 2001), individuals with disabilities who express sexual desire risk being categorized as deviant, extremely vulnerable, and therefore a danger both to themselves and to others. The well-publicized sexual assault of an adolescent girl with mental retardation in Glen Ridge, New Jersey, by several of her male peers was situated in this sort of discourse that equated disabled sexual desire with deviant sexuality (Block, 2000).

Another reason why disabled girls in particular are perceived as deviant sexual subjects is because sex and disability are addressed in clinical contexts that draw on a biomedical viewpoint focused on regulating the fertility of the "dangerous" disabled female (Fiduccia, 2000). Girls with cognitive impairments have been especially restricted from expressing their sexuality on the grounds that they lack the capacity to engage in responsible sexual relationships—an ideology that has contributed in the past to eugenic practices of mass involuntary sterilization (Milligan and Neufeldt, 2001). In contemporary contexts, well-meaning parents and professionals justify their control of sexual decision making for girls and women with cognitive impairments through claims that they are seeking to protect their disabled daughters from future rejection, vulnerability to sexual abuse, and unwanted pregnancies (Milligan and Neufeldt, 2001). It is for all these reasons that disability studies author and activist Anne Finger writes "sexuality is often the source of our deepest oppression; it is also often the source of our deepest pain. It's easier for us to talk about and formulate strategies for changing discrimination in employment, education, and housing than to talk about our exclusion from sexuality and reproduction" (quoted in Shakespeare, 2000, p. 160).

It is in this context that pedagogies regarding HIV/AIDS and disability are expected to be disseminated. Schellenberg, Keil, and Bem (1995) point out that HIV/AIDS is mired in stigma because of its association in this country with male homosexuals and intravenous drug users, who are also disproportionately African American and Hispanic. In addition, those whose infection has resulted from "deviant" behaviors are contrasted with those whose infection has resulted from circumstances beyond their control (e.g., infants, hemophiliacs, and those who have received blood transfusions), thereby setting up a moral hierarchy of "deserving" and "nondeserving" victims of this condition.

According to Nye (2001), people who construct and disseminate information about HIV/AIDS use language that is burdened by moral overtones, tainting the disease as one of otherness and immorality. Military metaphors dominate popular discourse about HIV/AIDS, describing the virus as mysterious and deadly—a description that "overmobilizes, overdescribes, and powerfully contributes to the excommunicating and the stigmatizing of the ill" (Sontag, quoted in Nye, 2001, p. 231). McRuer (2002a) quotes Paula Treichler when he argues that people living with HIV/AIDS face not only "an epidemic of transmissible disease" but also an "epidemic of signification" (p. 221) that, in turn, is exacerbated by the racist, homophobic, sexist, and ableist attitudes that are reinvigorated through the AIDS crises, especially by those who imagine themselves as "immune" from the epidemic.

The manifestation of this epidemic of signification in educational praxis creates a kind of "pedagogy of terror" in which neither teachers nor students seem comfortable. In a qualitative study that examined how students experience HIV/AIDS and sexuality education in Australian schools, the researchers found that students wanted access to a more experiential and explicit understanding of HIV/AIDS and sexuality than what was provided to them (Lupton and Tulloch, 1996). Conscious that their teachers seemed ill at ease in addressing these subjects, students reported that discussions were often tense rather than relaxed. They were also critical about how teachers sounded both moralistic and judgmental because they clearly did not have personal experience in the area. As a result of the moral tensions, students did not believe they could trust teachers to maintain confidentiality, and they said they would have preferred qualified counselors and health workers sharing this information with them. Blanchett's (2000) study of young adults with learning disabilities in the United States supported similar findings. For the same reasons, Lemelle and Smith (2001) echo Lupton and Tulloch (1996) in arguing for an expansion of HIV/AIDS pedagogy from merely imparting biological and factual data to include discussions of personal relationships, feelings, and values; the acquisition of relevant negotiation skills that consider wider social pressures and cultural expectations; and personal accounts of people living with AIDS.

However, it is not just pragmatic changes in the curriculum and teaching style that will ensure a transformation in HIV/AIDS education programs. As stated earlier, an enabling pedagogy for HIV/AIDS education will be possible if and only if teacher educators and teachers are willing to critically examine the ideological bases of teachers' practical knowledge as it relates to disability, HIV/AIDS, and sexuality. More important, the knowledge base in teacher education has to also allow for a critique of prevailing discourses deployed in sex education that propagate hegemonic notions of "normal" sexuality and that regulate and normalize youth into taking up forms of sexuality that are approved by social institutions such as schools. If sex education programs, rather than being generative of critical discussion, are reduced to nothing but an administrative organ for the policing of sexuality, would we then identify such pedagogies as exemplars of moral praxis?

ADVANCING A CRITIQUE OF NORMATIVITY: A VIEW FROM DISABILITY STUDIES

In the previous section, I explained the normalizing imperative embedded in sex education programs. I also advanced the recommendation that educators engage in a "pedagogy of critique" rather than a "pedagogy of terror" when educating students on this subject. In this section, I explore the possibilities of a critique of normative sexuality and its relationship to disability and HIV/AIDS from the critical standpoint of disability studies.

Critiques of normativity do not fall under the unique purview of disability studies. Race theorists, feminists, and queer theorists have predated disability studies scholars in their critiques of the hegemonic norm. However, a disability studies perspective offers the most radical critique of the normal, because unlike other categories of difference (i.e., race, class, and gender) that can claim that their differences closely mirror the norm, albeit in diverse ways, the extraordinary body of the disabled subject, sometimes aided by an array of prosthetic devices, remains radically inassimilable. Disability is excluded even in discussions of transgressive body politics by radical cultural theorists: "Disabled bodies are not permitted to participate in the erotics of power, in the power of the erotic, in economies of transgression. There has been virtually no liberatory rhetoric—outside of the disability rights movement—tied to prostheses, wheelchairs, colostomy bags, canes, or leg braces" (Davis, 1995, p. 159).

Both dominant and radical representations categorize disability as the "abject" (Kristeva, 1982), the embodiment of inassimilable alterity whose marginal location marks the boundaries of normativity. Disability as *abject other* is, therefore, essential to the development of the cult of normality because "without the monstrous body to demarcate the borders of the generic, without the female body to distinguish the shape of the male, and without the pathological to give form to the normal, the taxonomies of bodily value that underlie political, social, and economic arrangements would collapse" (Thomson, 1997, p. 20).

Thomson's argument offers some insight into why dominant ideologies struggle to maintain distance between normality and disability—for example, when teachers of sex education programs go to great lengths to warn students about the terribleness embodied in "deviant" sexuality. Interjecting discourses of morality into these discussions contributes to the organization of sexual subjects into a hierarchy of identity that separates "us" (the moral, normative majority) from "them" (the deviant, disabled minority). McRuer (2002a) points out that these divisions are institutionalized by allowing individuals to claim the dominant identity (i.e., choose normalization) in order to immunize themselves against the loss of privilege experienced by those stigmatized as queer, deviant, or pathological (i.e., disabled). Claiming a normal identity while maintaining a distance from the "real" aberrancy of disability is amply rewarded in education contexts. The normative majority develops educational programs that will recruit more of "us" to shun "them." In the context of sex education and HIV/AIDS education programs, the discourses of morality are instrumental in assigning the following populations to the "them" category: pregnant teens, gay/lesbian/bisexual youth, transgendered youth, disabled youth, and youth living with HIV/AIDS.

Disability studies scholars, on other hand, aim to build bridges rather than maintaining distance from difference. McRuer (2002b) foregrounds possibilities for solidarity between disabled and queer interests on the grounds of shared experience by pointing out that people with disabilities are perceived as somewhat queer (i.e., oversexual or asexual) although queers are often understood as somewhat disabled (i.e., expressing deviant sexuality). In both instances the categorization of queer/disabled as deviant is used to maintain the fictional normative state of able-bodied heterosexuality.

This normative identity would be in crisis if teachers and students rejected the designation of queer/disabled as deviant and instead sought to mobilize and subvert the moral hierarchy of identity by "working the weakness in the norm" (McRuer, 2002b, p. 95). This subversion can occur, according to McRuer, by mounting what he calls a "severe critique": "[A] severe critique is a fierce critique ... [that] would reverse the able-bodied understanding of severely disabled bodies as the most marginalized, the most excluded from a privileged and always elusive normalcy, and it would suggest that it is precisely these bodies that are best positioned to refuse 'mere toleration' and to call out the inadequacies of compulsory able-bodiedness" (p. 96).

In practical terms, then, what would constitute a severe critique? In preceding sections of this chapter, I criticized so-called helping professions such as special education and vocational rehabilitation for deploying a language of inclusion and empowerment although denying both personal autonomy and choice to those communities they purport to help. Thus, one severe critique could be to expose such education contexts as antidemocratic because they support normalizing practices that organize hierarchies of identity along the oppressive continuum from normal to deviant students (Slee, 1997). In particular, Slee cautions against the unquestioning acceptance of pedagogical discourses that claim to support inclusion because such discourses can serve as "the Trojan horse for assimilation" (p. 411), welcoming and tolerating difference only if it will at some point be assimilable.

But what happens if disabled and HIV/AIDS communities resist assimilation? Would we then attempt to get rid of them via segregation and prevent the reproduction of more of their kind, because in the normative hierarchy of social value, they represent "useless difference" (Michalko, 2002, p. 93)? And would we then defend our annihilation of these identity communities by claiming that our practices serve to alleviate suffering?

In a thought-provoking book that blends personal narrative and phenomenological analysis of living with a disability, Michalko raises the critical question: Whose suffering? He offers a provocative definition of *suffering* that defies conventional wisdom by arguing that the only suffering faced by persons with disabilities (and, in turn, persons living with HIV/AIDS) is not located within the individual but is instead grounded in the social. According to Michalko, this distress includes "the suffering of the multitude of interpretations of disability, the political acts that culturally organize and define disability—the suffering of our society's choices made in regard to the meaning of disability" (p. 15). Thus, using a disability studies perspective to deconstruct the cult of normality and reinterpret the HIV/AIDS crisis will illuminate the context of social suffering that is caused by limited and limiting discourses that are deployed to describe, explain, rebuke, judge, and ultimately exterminate persons labeled deviant (in this case, those living with disabilities or HIV/AIDS).

IN SOLIDARITY: THE STRUGGLE FOR ENABLING PEDAGOGIES

In this chapter, I have argued that HIV/AIDS education programs are almost always situated in the complex politics of social difference—particularly the politics of disability. Educators working in these programs therefore have to be critically aware of the oppressive ideologies associated with sexuality, disability, and HIV/AIDS that are embedded in the teacher education knowledge base and that may influence their own pedagogical praxis. In an effort to deconstruct these ideologies that often masquerade as commonsense (e.g., disabled youth are ill-equipped to handle sexuality responsibly), an enabling pedagogy would have to foreground for teachers and students alike the social context of the unequal relations of power and access to privilege that frames all discussions about sexuality, disability, and HIV/AIDS. Deconstructing such ideologies would raise the following questions: Whose voices are privileged in discussions of sexuality, disability, and HIV/AIDS? What are the implications of including a diversity of voices in these discussions? Why is it that certain perspectives are privileged over others, and what are the consequences of silencing other perspectives?

I have also argued in this chapter that both disability and HIV/AIDS are more than an etiology of medical facts. I have shown that both disability and HIV/AIDS become critical identity positions associated with vibrant and passionate political communities that reject their designated status of "deviant" and instead struggle for political recognition as valued citizens. If educators are to become cognizant and supportive of this reconceptualization of disability and HIV/AIDS, they also need to find an alternative language and subscribe to discourses that are empowering rather than stigmatizing. This means that the teacher education knowledge base and pedagogical praxis should be designed in collaboration with persons with disabilities and persons living with AIDS—rather than depending on medical journals, rehabilitation manuals, and moral epigrams. Inclusion of these perspectives, especially those that document the political struggles of these communities for social equality, will support a more humanizing pedagogical praxis.

Perhaps most challenging is the question of how to talk about preventing the spread of HIV/AIDS without implying that those who are now living with HIV/AIDS are somehow inferior. Based on the disability studies perspective—that the "suffering" associated with living with a disability is grounded in the social—I propose that an enabling pedagogy for HIV/AIDS education should also address the social context in which sexuality, disability, and the disease are situated.

In concrete terms, rather than focusing predominantly on pedagogies that emphasize the dangers of individual sexual "deviancy," I suggest that sex education programs take a more social approach in exhorting students to practice safe sex. In other words, safe-sex programs should have less to do with condom use and more to do with how young adults can build trusting intimate relations that permit them the space to negotiate for both their partners' and their own sexual well-being. Safe-sex programs should address diverse ways to express sexual desire in contexts that are nurturing of the life goals of both partners involved. The programs should also permit open discussions that explore the possibilities of finding sexual partners with social identities that are not limited by the prevailing hegemony of able-bodied heterosexuality. Such discussions of safe sex would move away from the traditional emphasis on violence, danger, and terror to a more generative approach that situates sexuality as the search for intimacy in humanizing contexts where all bodies, not just some, are valued.

Brueggemann (2001) defines *enabling pedagogy* as a theory and practice of teaching that posits disability as insight. She writes, "Disability can create knowledge, open doors wider, build ramps to awareness that we all essentially have within us anyway. This happens when any body [teaches] anybody" (p. 800). I believe that in the context of humanizing sex education programs, disability does provide this insight.

REFERENCES

Blanchett, W. J. (2000). Sexual risk behaviors of young adults with LD and the need for HIV/AIDS education. *Remedial and Special Education* 21(6): 336–345.

Block, P. (2000). Sexuality, fertility, and danger: Twentieth-century images of women with cognitive disabilities. *Sexuality and Disability* 18(4): 239–254.

Brueggemann, B. J. (2001). An enabling pedagogy: Meditations on writing and disability. *Journal of Composition Theory* 21(4): 791–820.

Ciasullo, E. C., and Escovitz, K. (2005). Positive futures: The need for a paradigm shift in HIV/AIDS services. *Journal of Vocational Rehabilitation* 22: 125–128.

Conyers, L. M. (2005). HIV/AIDS as an emergent disability: The response of vocational rehabilitation. *Journal of Vocational Rehabilitation* 22: 67–73.

Davis, L. J. (1995). *Enforcing normalcy: Disability, deafness, and the body.* New York: Verso.

DiGiulio, G. (2003). Sexuality and people living with physical or developmental disabilities: A review of key issues. *Canadian Journal of Human Sexuality* 12(1): 53–68.

Erevelles, N. (2000). Educating unruly bodies: Critical pedagogy, disability studies and the politics of schooling. *Educational Theory* 50(1): 25–47.

Erevelles, N., and Mutua, K. (2005). "I am a woman, now!" Rewriting cartographies of girlhood from the critical standpoint of disability. In P. Bettis and N. Adams, eds., *Geographies of girlhood: Identities in-between* (pp. 253–270). New York: Erlbaum.

Fiduccia, B. W. (2000). Current issues in sexuality and the disability movement. *Sexuality and Disability* 18(3): 167–174.

Fine, M. (1993). Sexuality, schooling, and adolescent females: The missing discourse of desire. In L. Weis and M. Fine, eds., *Beyond silenced voices: Class, race, and gender in United States schools* (pp. 75–89). New York: State University of New York Press.

Groce, N. (2003). HIV/AIDS and people with disability. *Lancet* 361: 1401–1402.

Hwang, J., and Nochajski, S. M. (2003). The International Classification of Function, Disability, and Health (ICF) and its application with AIDS. *Journal of Rehabilitation* 69(4): 4–12.

Kristeva, J. (1982). *Powers of horror: An essay on abjection.* New York: Columbia University Press.

Lemelle, S. J., and Smith, V. G. (2001). HIV/AIDS knowledge sources and risk behavior among adolescent African American males: Towards developing HIV/AIDS pedagogy. *Journal of African American Men* 6(2): 3–17.

Linton, S. (1998). *Claiming disability: Knowledge and identity.* New York: New York University Press.

Longmore, P. K. (2003). *Why I burned my book and other essays on disability.* Philadelphia: Temple University Press.

Lupton, D., and Tulloch, J. (1996). "All red in the face": Students' views on school-based HIV/AIDS and sexuality education. *Sociological Review* 44(2): 252–271.

Mayo, C. (2003). Framing AIDS: Policy, politics, and the uncertainty of facts. *GLQ: A Journal of Lesbian and Gay Studies* 9(1–2): 321–327.

McRuer, R. (2002a). Critical investments: AIDS, Christopher Reeve, and queer/disability studies. *Journal of Medical Humanities* 23(3/4): 221–237.

McRuer, R. (2002b). Compulsory able-bodiedness and queer/disabled existence. In S. L. Snyder, B. J. Brueggemann, and R. Garland-Thomson, eds., *Disability studies: Enabling the humanities* (pp. 88–99). New York: Modern Language Association of America.

McWhorter, L. (2005). Foreword. In S. Tremain, ed., *Foucault and the government of disability* (pp. xiii–xvii). Ann Arbor: University of Michigan Press.

Michalko, R. (2002). *The difference that disability makes.* Philadelphia: Temple University Press.

Milligan, M. S., and Neufeldt, A. H. (2001). The myth of asexuality: A survey of social and empirical evidence. *Sexuality and Disability* 19(2): 91–109.

Nye, E. F. (2001). The rhetoric of AIDS: A new taxonomy. In J. C. Wilson and C. Lewiecki-Wilson, eds., *Embodied rhetorics: Disability in language and culture* (pp. 229–243). Carbondale: Southern Illinois University Press.

Oliver, M. (1990). *The politics of disablement.* New York: St. Martin's Press.

Russell, M. (1998). *Beyond ramps: Disability at the end of the racial contract.* Munroe, ME: Common Courage Press.

Schellenberg, E. G., Keil, J. M., and Bem, S. L. (1995). "Innocent victims" of AIDS: Identifying the subtext. *Journal of Applied Social Psychology* 25(20): 1790–1800.

Shuttleworth, R. P., and Mona, L. (2002). Introduction to the symposium. *Disability Studies Quarterly* 22(4): 2–9.

Slee, R. (1997). Imported or important theory? Sociological interrogations of disablement and special education. *British Journal of Sociology of Education* 18(3): 407–419.

Thomas, C. (1999). *Female forms: Experiencing and understanding disability.* New York: Taylor and Francis.

Thomson, R. G. (1997). *Extraordinary bodies: Figuring physical disability in American culture and literature.* New York: Columbia University Press.

Tolman, D. L. (2000). Object lessons: Romance, violation, and female adolescent sexual desire. *Journal of Sex Education and Therapy* 25(1): 70–80.

Waldschmidt, A. (2005). Who is normal? Who is deviant? In S. Tremain, ed., *Foucault and the government of disability* (pp. 191–207). Ann Arbor: University of Michigan Press.

4

BUILDING TRUST THROUGH COOPERATION IN THE AIDS EDUCATION CLASSROOM

James M. Mitchell

֍

This chapter demonstrates how cooperative learning and conflict resolution strategies help to build common bonds of trust and understanding in the AIDS education classroom. Readers will learn how to begin to build trust in AIDS education with simple yet effective strategies.

WHAT IS TRUST?

It can be difficult for us to trust people whom we don't know very well. Even people we see daily can become untrustworthy if they do something drastic such as violating a confidence, speaking an insult, or breaking a promise. "It is interesting to note that when we find ourselves not being comfortable with another person, regardless of the circumstances, we are not always able to articulate what this discomfort is about. What we experience is a strong gut feeling or hunch, which we are not able to explain. Not trusting someone means that we do not have full confidence in them" (Sieler, 1998).

Many people also believe that they know what trust is. Deutsch defined trust in behavioral terms and determined through his studies that "trust is strongly linked to confidence in, and overall optimism about, desirable events taking place" (1949, p. 136). Further research by McKnight and Chervany (1996) determined that "trust is the extent to which one party is willing to depend on something or somebody in a given situation with a feeling of security, even though negative consequences are possible" (p. 28).

Many teacher preparation programs promote the establishment of trust from the first day of kindergarten. The following selected strategies are emphasized for teachers to use from the very first day of school and are carried forth throughout the K–adult experience in some manner (Rockwell, 1995):

- Be as good as your word. If a treat, punishment, special activity, or assignment under the teacher's control is promised, follow through.
- Do not use intimidating actions or statements as a form of behavior control. While young children may respond out of fear, the price of such intimidation is high. The message teachers send by using intimidation tactics is that it's OK to frighten smaller, less physically capable people into submission. Older students are more apt to become physically aggressive toward a threatening adult.
- Deal with noncompliant behavior consistently.
- Make sure rewards and punishments relate logically to the student's actions.
- Use punishment as a tool of instruction rather than revenge.
- Be honest with students.
- Prepare students in advance for any changes. Substitute teachers, visitors, new classmates, schedule changes, fire drills, and even holiday vacations can catch students by surprise and cause an escalation of negative behavior. Talking about such events ahead of time and having a plan for dealing with them increases students' sense of self-control and trust. Even adults like to know "what lies ahead" without being surprised.
- As the students are ready, enlist them in some of the decision making in the classroom. If a weekly art or cooking activity is part of the schedule, allow the students to choose which activity they want to do. Giving them increasing opportunities to make appropriate choices increases their sense of trust, control, and positive regard for the rights of others.
- Use language that conveys acceptance and trust. Have students describe what they can do. De-emphasize what they cannot do. (Rockwell, 1995, p. 77)

TRUST AND AIDS EDUCATION

AIDS is a topic of conversation that is grounded in fear and mistrust (Joint United Nations Programme on HIV/AIDS [UNAIDS], 1997).

To many, it is the "elephant in the room" that few choose to talk about. Even the most educated people can be afraid to ask about it, share what they know, or engage in constructive discourse about the risk behaviors that can lead to HIV infection, at home or within their community. They fear the stigma of raised eyebrows, whispers, and pointed fingers (UNAIDS, 1997) because AIDS and AIDS education are still very controversial topics in some sectors of society. How can we reasonably expect our children to want to ask questions, share their knowledge, and engage in constructive discourse so that they may learn and apply as much constructive information about AIDS education as possible?

It is reasonable to assume that the teaching of AIDS education in K–12 classrooms is heavily dependent on trust, because the topic of AIDS education is both serious and sensitive. Herek and Capitanio determined that "AIDS educational programs can be effective only to the extent that their target audiences perceive them as credible" (1994, p. 368). Students are less inclined to share what they know and don't know with their peers and their teachers if they fear that "put-downs" or violations of psychological safety and well-being could occur. Such violations could be manifested in the form of "leaks" outside the classroom, such as "You wouldn't believe what Jerry said during our AIDS education class today!" Statements of this sort undermine efforts to create a viable community of learners based on trust among members. In order to learn effectively, students must recognize that confidences must be kept, criticisms should be impersonal and objective, and their thoughts may be shared freely in a safe atmosphere.

Likewise, teachers in AIDS education must believe that they can speak to their students with credibility, offering current information that is relevant to their students' lives both in and away from the classroom. Teachers must have their students thinking about the learning inside and outside of school, and not about gaffes the teacher may have made in the lesson's delivery. If teachers betray generation-based or cultural ignorance, for example, it is critical that the students be able to look past the error for the good of the group. Otherwise, the meaning of the lesson becomes skewed and the teacher's credibility is called into question. Therefore, in the AIDS education classroom, teachers must have trusting relationships with their students, and students must be able to trust each other.

THE ROLE OF COOPERATIVE LEARNING

The role of trust in education has been explored extensively through classroom research on the strategy of cooperative learning. Cooperative learning, used properly, can be a valuable strategy to ensure that a trusting climate is established. The essential components of trust-based cooperation are

(1) *positive interdependence,* a situation in which group members perceive that they are linked with each other in a way that one cannot succeed unless everyone succeeds; (2) *face-to-face promotive interaction,* where students see the need to do real work together in which they promote each other's success by sharing resources and helping, supporting, encouraging, and applauding each other's efforts to achieve; (3) *individual and group accountability,* where the group realizes that it must be accountable for achieving its goals and each member knows that he or she must be accountable for contributing his or her share of the work; (4) *interpersonal and small group skills;* and (5) *group processing.* (D. W. Johnson and R. Johnson, 1978b, p. 11)

These are the most crucial elements of cooperative learning. Teaching participants the required interpersonal and small-group skills and how to process overall group effectiveness is vitally important to establishing trust within the group community (D. W. Johnson and R. Johnson, 1989). Because cooperation and conflict are inherently related, the procedures and skills for managing conflicts constructively are especially important for the long-term trust-based success of learning groups. Members must believe that they can count on one another.

The development of this trust does not just benefit the group as a social unit; it also helps group members enhance their individual confidence and interpersonal skills. D. W. Johnson and R. Johnson found that "individual accountability is the key to ensuring that all group members are, in fact, strengthened by learning cooperatively. By each member ensuring his or her own success, the other group members see him/her as trustworthy, and being someone who is dependable" (1978a, p. 71).

Such positive interdependence results in *promotive interaction,* defined as "individuals encouraging and facilitating each other's efforts to achieve, complete tasks, and produce in order to reach the group's goals" (D. W. Johnson and R. Johnson, 1978b, p. 11). More specifically,

promotive interaction is characterized by individuals providing each other with efficient and effective help and assistance; exchanging needed resources, such as information and materials, and processing information more efficiently and effectively; providing each other with feedback in order to improve their subsequent performance; challenging each other's conclusions and reasoning in order to promote higher quality decision making and greater insight into the problems being considered; advocating the exertion of effort to achieve mutual goals; influencing each other's efforts to achieve the group's goals; acting in trusting and trustworthy ways; being motivated to strive for mutual benefit; and maintaining a moderate level of arousal characterized by low anxiety and stress. (D. W. Johnson and R. Johnson, 1989, ch. 2, p. 4)

A promotive atmosphere need not be one in which members cheer each other on with outward displays of support. Rather, a strong promotive environment is often found fostering an atmosphere of quiet respect and encouragement. Body language of students and teachers such as head-nodding, smiles, leaning forward, and friendly eye contact are all elements found in a promotive classroom environment.

In their book *Joining Together: Group Theory and Group Skills,* D. and F. Johnson write, "Students must be taught the social skills required for high-quality collaboration and be motivated to use them if cooperative groups are to be productive. The whole field of group dynamics is based on the premise that social skills are the key to group productivity" (1991, p. 237). For AIDS education in particular, the ability of all learners to work cooperatively with others is an important precursor to building and maintaining stable classrooms in which students feel safe to learn. The behaviors they learn should lead to stronger, more socially competent individuals and a better, more productive society.

ACADEMIC CONTROVERSY

A strategy associated with cooperative learning and building trust in classroom settings is *academic controversy,*

the instructional use of intellectual conflict to promote higher achievement and increase the quality of problem solving, decision making, critical thinking, reasoning, interpersonal relationships, and psychological health and well-being. To engage in an academic controversy students must *research and prepare* a position, *present and advocate* their position, *refute opposing positions* and rebut attacks on their own position, *reverse perspectives,* and *create a synthesis* that everyone can agree to. (D. W. Johnson and R. Johnson, 1989, ch. 3, p. 7)

In academic controversy, participants are assigned positions with which they might or might not agree. By having their roles assigned, participants do not feel personally vulnerable to any consequences of their debates. The sensitive nature of AIDS education discussions can be managed effectively with this method.

Further lowering the vulnerability of any individual participants, academic controversy assigns two or three students to collaboratively argue each position (D. W. Johnson and R. Johnson, 1989). These subgroups ensure that each other's arguments are given fair treatment by following a five-step procedure:

1. Research and prepare a position: Each advocacy subgroup re-searches its assigned position and organizes the evidence found into a persuasive argument for why the position should be adopted.
2. Present the best case possible for alternative positions: Each advocacy subgroup presents [its] position to all groups with the intent of persuading all others of the position's validity....
3. Open discussion to refute and rebut: Advocacy subgroups criticize the other positions and defend their own position from attack, by criticizing ideas and not personalities. This enables group members to learn the advantages and disadvantages of each alternative course of action while continuing to advocate their positions.
4. Perspective reversal: ... Members of each subgroup reverse perspectives by presenting the best case for one of the other alternative courses of action as if it were their own, adding new arguments, facts, and reasons when possible. This ensures that each subgroup listens carefully to the other presentations and comprehends their rationales completely.
5. Synthesize and decide: Advocacy subgroup members drop all advocacy, step back, strive for objectivity, attempt to see the issue from a variety of perspectives, summarize the best evidence from all sides, create a synthesis of the various positions, and decide what action to take to solve the problem.... Striving for synthe-sis helps the group make a decision as to what course of action would be most effective in solving the problem and achieving the group's goals. (D. W. Johnson and R. Johnson, 1989, ch. 6, p. 2)

Compared to other strategies for group decision making, such as *concurrence-seeking* (group members reach a decision quickly to avoid conflict), *debate* (individuals or groups argue a position before a judge, who decides which position is best), or *individualistic decision making* (an individual solves a problem alone), academic controversy "results in higher productivity, greater mastery and retention of ideas, more frequent use of complex reasoning, greater exchange of information, more creativity in problem solving, and higher quality decision making" (D. W. Johnson and R. Johnson, 1989, ch. 2, p. 5). Trust among group members is a positive outgrowth of the experience. The more academic controversy is practiced, the deeper the controversies may be structured, and stronger bonds of trust are created as a result.

The strategy of academic controversy cannot be easily taught, nor can it be learned quickly. Teachers need training in how to implement the procedure, and students must be given time to learn the mechanics, establish relationships with other class members in the controversy format, and reflect on the procedure as well as on the content of the lessons. Unfortunately, the increased emphasis in recent years on standards and assessment has caused teachers throughout the Western Hemisphere to find little time for pull-out programs and new curricular additions.

CONTROVERSY, TRUST, AND AIDS EDUCATION RESULTS

Academic controversies can be used in any subject area with students of almost any age. Scenarios related to HIV/AIDS prevention can be developed, for example, for high school mathematics using statistics related to the prevention of AIDS versus the prevention of pregnancy for a structured controversy (Mitchell, Johnson, and Johnson, 2002). Anecdotal summaries from people with AIDS may be used in English literature classroom controversies. Music classrooms might use controversies that involve songs about AIDS victims (Braithwaite and Taylor, 1998).

For example, Mitchell, Johnson, and Johnson (2002) investigated the relative impact of two types of cooperative learning—concurrence-seeking and academic controversy—on outcomes of a health education program focusing on tobacco use, alcohol use, and AIDS. Participants were 37 students from Grades 9–12 in a career-education track in a Midwestern, suburban high school. The students were classified as academically low performing and at risk for destructive health habits.

Students in the controversy condition, compared with those in the con-currence-seeking condition, significantly improved in knowledge about AIDS, developed healthier attitudes related to safe sex and cigarette use, developed higher academic self-esteem, generated greater social influence, and improved in constructive conflict skills.

Similarly, Braithwaite and Taylor (1998) sought to fill a void in the development of HIV/AIDS prevention efforts for African American adolescents and young adults by conducting discussions around hip-hop music, a form of music popularized by young African Americans. Braithwaite and Taylor found the music to be a highly effective vehicle for health promotion, including for teaching HIV/AIDS prevention:

> First, this method makes use of culturally relevant materials to address the educational and health needs of the target community. Second, it is grounded in an approach that serves to stimulate cooperative learning based on peer-developed content.... Such an approach holds heuristic value in dealing with HIV/AIDS prevention among [African American] young adults. Accordingly, part of the model was based on structured discussion around hip-hop music and AIDS education. (1998, p. 130)

SUMMARY REFLECTIONS

Teachers feel pressured to produce quality instruction based on content standards and oriented toward educating citizens who make valuable contributions to the workforce, but today we also see an overwhelming planetwide need for HIV/AIDS prevention. The use of an academic controversy approach in AIDS education promotes the development of skills necessary to fulfill this need.

Trust is itself a laudable goal, but it can be difficult to establish and maintain. Cooperative learning is a demonstrated strategy that pro-motes trust among participants, and academic controversy, a form of cooperative learning, is highly effective at teaching trust-based skills in an interdisciplinary manner. AIDS education can be taught through academic controversy, thereby promoting both trust and achievement in AIDS education classrooms.

REFERENCES

Braithwaite, R. L., and Taylor, S. E. (1998). Model for using hip-hop music for small group HIV/AIDS prevention counseling with African American adolescents and young adults. *Patient Education Counseling* 35(2): 127–137.

Deutsch, M. (1949). A theory of cooperation and competition. *Human Relations* 2: 129–152.

Herek, G. M., and Capitanio, J. P. (1994). Conspiracies, contagion, and compassion: Trust and public reactions to AIDS. *AIDS Prevention Education* 6(4): 365–375.

Johnson, D. W., and Johnson, F. (1991). *Joining together: Group theory and group skills.* 4th ed. Englewood Cliffs, NJ: Prentice-Hall.

Johnson, D. W., and Johnson, R. (1978a). An overview of cooperative learning. In J. Thousand, A. Nevin, and A. Villa, eds., *Creativity and collaborative learning* (pp. 68–79). Baltimore: Brookes Press.

Johnson, D. W., and Johnson, R. (1978b). Cooperative, competitive, and individualistic learning. *Journal of Research and Development in Education* 12: 8–15.

Johnson, D. W., and Johnson, R. (1989). *Cooperation and competition: Theory and research.* Edina, MN: Interaction.

Joint United Nations Programme on HIV/AIDS. (1997). *Learning and teaching about AIDS at school.* Geneva: Author.

McKnight, D. H., and Chervany, N. (1996). *The meanings of trust.* University of Minnesota, Carlson School of Management.

Mitchell, J., Johnson, D. W., and Johnson, R. (2002). Are all types of cooperation equal? Impact of academic controversy versus concurrence-seeking on health education. *Social Psychology of Education* 5(4): 329–344.

Rockwell, S. (1995). *Back off, cool down, try again: Teaching students how to control aggressive behavior.* Arlington, VA: Council for Exceptional Children.

Sieler, A. (1998). *Trust and relationships.* Retrieved September 29, 2005, from http://www.newfieldaus.com.au/articles/Trust_and_Relationships.htm.

PART II
THE SCIENCE AND SKILL OF
HIV AND AIDS PREVENTION

Overview, *Yolanda S. George*

ᴥ

The science and skill of HIV and AIDS prevention are two dynamic bodies of information that effective prevention agents inevitably encounter. This section provides one chapter that discusses HIV and AIDS science and two chapters intended to advance how the classroom practice might be supported by policy and specific practices and teaching formats.

Yolanda and Matthew George open the section with a scientific description of HIV and AIDS. "The Science, Treatment, and Prevention of HIV/AIDS" is organized into three sections that cover a myriad of topics including the structure of HIV, its infection cycle, the process by which HIV develops into AIDS, and AIDS treatment and prevention strategies. This primer is intended to fortify prevention agents with an understanding of the science of a disease that compels societal response.

Sattler and Armmer's "Inquiry-Based Approaches to HIV/AIDS Prevention Education: Standards, Practices, and Outcomes" is a reminder of how important education and educators are to an effective societal response to HIV and AIDS. They assert the value of national standards and policies, in both the private and public sectors, for advancing HIV/AIDS prevention, and they promote the use of inquiry-based teaching and learning. This strategy, designed to guide students to their own logical and meaningful answers, could be particularly effective in teaching ways to avoid risky behaviors associated with becoming infected with HIV.

The Mitchell, Ramirez-Marrero, and Hooks chapter, "Preparing Teachers as Prevention Agents: An On-Line Learning Course" explores the utility of distance learning for teaching HIV/AIDS prevention to teacher candidates. The chapter outlines the process of organizing best practices from the work of three schools of education that infused HIV/AIDS prevention into a distance course. The collaborative nature of this undertaking and its outcome are discussed, as are the technical and pragmatic considerations for developing on-line HIV/AIDS prevention instruction that offers easy access to learners.

5

THE SCIENCE, TREATMENT, AND PREVENTION OF HIV/AIDS

Yolanda S. George and Matthew George, Jr.

✧

This chapter includes 3 sections that explore primarily the science, treatment, and prevention of the Human Immunodeficiency Virus (HIV). The first section includes information on the science of HIV/AIDS including the genetic makeup of organisms, the structure of HIV, the HIV infection cycle, and the progression of HIV infection to the development of Acquired Immunodeficiency Syndrome (AIDS). The second section focuses on HIV testing and AIDS treatments, principally drugs. The final section provides information on prevention strategies to combat HIV infection, including awareness and education campaigns, as well as misconceptions and impediments associated with HIV/AIDS education campaigns.

THE SCIENCE OF HIV

The Genetic Makeup of Organisms

The genetic makeup or genome of most organisms, including HIV, is composed of DNA (deoxyribonucleic acid) or RNA (ribonucleic acid). DNA and RNA are responsible for the storage, replication, recombination, and transmission of genetic information. In a process known as genetic flow or gene flow, the genetic information found in DNA or RNA is converted into proteins, which are used by the cells of different organisms to provide cellular structure and do work within the cell. The conversion typically "flows" beginning with the DNA, whose genetic information is converted to RNA and then the RNA is translated into proteins (DNA→RNA→Protein). However, protein conversion in organisms such as HIV, which has a genome composed of RNA, differs in the way that genetic information flows: the RNA is first converted into DNA and then the typical process described above takes place (DNA↔RNA→Protein).

The Structure and Infection Cycle of the Human Immunodeficiency Virus (HIV)

HIV is a virus whose genome is composed of two identical single threads (or strands) of RNA surrounded by a protein coat or shell (core proteins), a lipid (fat) membrane, and proteins that specifically bind to certain types of immune cells (see Figure 5.1). HIV belongs to the family of viruses known as *retroviruses.*

HIV infects humans by binding to and invading the cells of the body's immune system, particularly immune cells known as CD+4 or T4 lymphocytes. These cells normally protect the body from different types of infections and foreign substances. During cell invasion, the DNA form of HIV becomes integrated primarily into the DNA of immune cells, making more HIV proteins and HIV RNA.[1]

Unlike most retroviruses, HIV kills its host cells (i.e., cells of the immune system). As more and more immune cells become infected and more HIV is made, the new viruses burst out of the infected cells by a "budding" process. During this process, part of the host cell's lipid membrane becomes wrapped around the newly made HIV. The large production and burst of newly made HIV leads to the death of the host cells. This process significantly reduces the number of immune cells capable of protecting the body from other infections or foreign substances. The gradual depletion of immune cells needed to protect the body from infections leads to an increase in the number of diseases that an infected individual contracts, including neurological diseases and rare forms of cancer.

Within the protein coat or shell of HIV are several specialized proteins: reverse transcriptase, for making new HIV RNA; integrase, for the integration process; and protease, for the production of properly sized HIV proteins. The genetic makeup of HIV also contains instructions for making envelope proteins that can bind to immune cells and HIV proteins needed for the overall production of new HIV. Drugs used to limit or disrupt the process of HIV binding and new HIV production

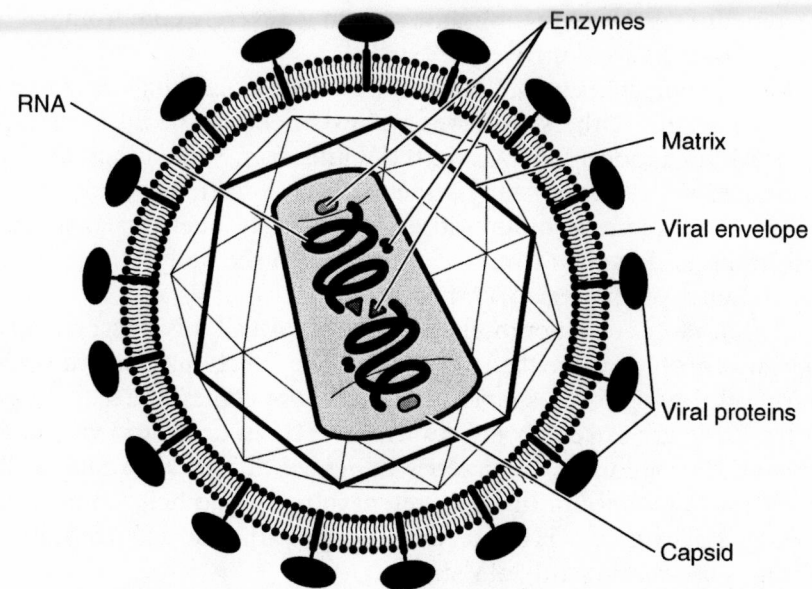

RNA

Enzymes

Matrix

Viral envelope

Viral proteins

Capsid

Figure 5.1. HIV Structure

Source: National Human Genome Research Institute of the National Institutes of Health (n.d.). Reprinted with permission.

This diagram shows the structure of HIV and its component parts. The HIV single-stranded RNA molecules are wrapped with proteins and along with the enzymes reverse transcriptase, protease, and integrase are located in a protein shell called a core or nucleocapsid. More proteins surround the nucleocapsid, and the structure is wrapped with a lipid bilayer (membrane) derived from the host cell. Within the lipid bilayer are envelope proteins that specifically bind to proteins called receptors on the surface of immune cells.

target the reverse transcriptase, integrase (in development), protease, and the envelope proteins.

The Progression of HIV to AIDS and AIDS Symptoms

The gradual loss of CD+4 immune cells leads to a weakening of the body's ability to fight off various infections, including HIV itself. When an individual initially becomes infected with HIV, the virus generally enters a type of immune cell known as a macrophage, although some central nervous system cells are also susceptible to HIV infection. While HIV is replicating in the macrophages, generally the macrophages are not killed by the budding process. Over time, however, the CD+4 cells become infected and the immune system is severely compromised as the CD+4 cells are destroyed.

Most people initially infected with HIV will usually have no or very mild symptoms. Others, however, will experience some flu-like symptoms within a month or two after HIV infection. Some other illnesses associated with the very early stages of HIV infection include fevers, headaches, tiredness, mouth sores, diarrhea, frequent vaginal yeast infections, and swollen lymph glands (areas of the body where cells of the immune system reside, such as in the neck).

Within a week to a month, these symptoms usually disappear and may appear as nothing more than a typical flu-like infection. Unfortunately, during this time, HIV is rapidly making more copies of itself. People at this stage are extremely infectious, and HIV is present in very large quantities or amounts, particularly in genital fluids. Determining the "viral load" or amount of HIV present in the blood helps in defining specific stages of the HIV-to-AIDS progression and in determining when to use certain anti-HIV drugs.

Although the time varies, generally it takes about 10 years for an individual's infection to progress from HIV to AIDS. With the use of drugs to combat HIV infection, however, the time for the progression to AIDS has been extended.

A key guideline used to determine when HIV infection has advanced to the AIDS state is a measure of the CD+4 cell count. Healthy people normally have a CD+4 cell count of 600 to 1,500 per microliter (cubic millimeter, mm^3) of blood serum. During the progression of HIV to AIDS, the number of CD+4 cells gradually drops. A person is defined as having AIDS when there is evidence of HIV infection and the CD+4 cell count is less than 200 (see Figure 5.2). As the immune system becomes more depleted of CD+4 cells, the resulting illnesses become more severe.

Among the more severe symptoms found in people with AIDS are weight loss, a loss of energy, AIDS dementia, persistent skin rashes, and frequent sweats and fevers. Opportunistic infections become more frequent and include a rare form of pneumonia caused by *Pneumocystis jiroveci* (formerly known as *carinii*). A rare form of cancer (Kaposi's sarcoma) has also been associated with AIDS patients.

HIV/AIDS Origin and Spread

Study of the HIV disease began in earnest in 1981.[2] This activity was sparked by an article in the Centers for Disease Control and Prevention's

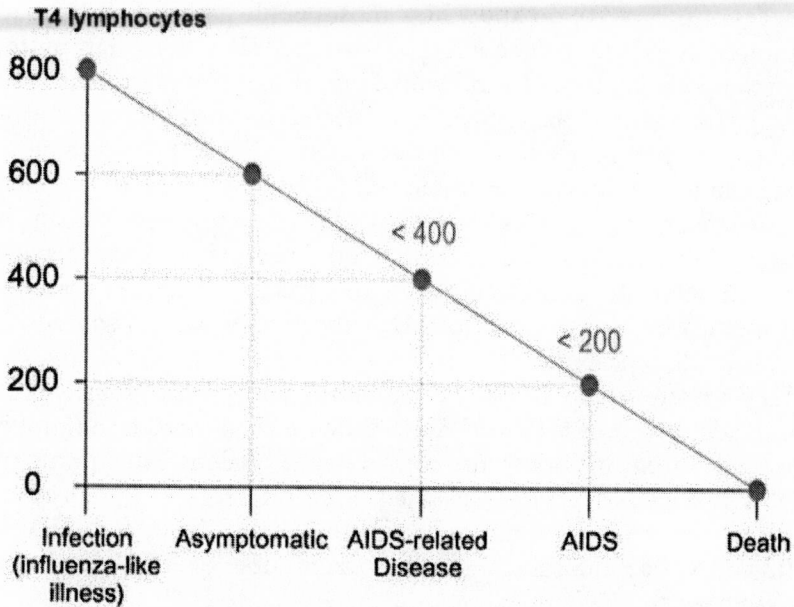

Figure 5.2. T4–Cell Counts and AIDS

Source: International Centre for Eye Health (2001).

A hallmark used in defining the AIDS condition is the depletion of CD+4 or T4 lymphocyte cells. A person is defined as having AIDS when he or she is diagnosed as being HIV positive and the T4–cell count drops below 200 per microliter of blood serum. The graph above shows the correlations between different illnesses and drops in the T4–cell count.

(CDC's) publication *Morbidity and Mortality Weekly Report* (*MMWR;* CDC, 1981a). The report described five young homosexual men in Los Angeles who had a rare form of pneumonia caused by *Pneumocystis jiroveci* and other unusual infections. Other early studies found in *MMWR* revealed that these same conditions were being found in other cities and states across America and elsewhere among homosexual men and, subsequently, intravenous drug users, hemophiliacs, female sexual partners of infected men, infants, prisoners, recipients of blood transfusions and blood products, Haitians, and Africans (CDC, 1981b, 1982). This led to a hunt for the causative agent, and in 1983 a human virus was discovered and later named HIV. We now know that HIV is the virus that leads to AIDS.

There is still some debate as to where and how HIV entered the human population, as there is a very similar virus found in the chimpanzees of Africa. We do know how most people get HIV: (a) by having unprotected sex with an infected partner (HIV can be transmitted from the body fluids of one individual into those of another individual through the lining of the vagina, vulva, penis, rectum, or mouth during sex); (b) by sharing needles or syringes among intravenous drug users who include an infected individual; and (c) by being born to a woman who is infected or drinking the breast milk of an infected woman. In the early 1980s, HIV could be contracted through blood transfusions, but since 1985 the nation's blood supply has been carefully screened and monitored, and the risk of HIV infection from this source has practically disappeared.

HIV infection and AIDS are pandemic and found globally. The worldwide spread of HIV and AIDS is being monitored by a number of organizations, including the Joint United Nations Programme on HIV/AIDS (UNAIDS) office and the World Health Organization. Table 5.1 presents the number of people globally living with HIV in 2003 and 2004, and Table 5.2 shows the number of AIDS deaths for the same years.

Of the approximately 40 million people living with HIV/AIDS, almost half are women (UNAIDS, 2005c; Quinn and Overbaugh, 2005). Women are particularly susceptible to HIV/AIDS for a variety

Table 5.1. People Living With HIV

Where	2003	2004	Percent change
Global total	37.8 million	39.4 million	4.2
Latin America	1.6 million	1.7 million	6.3
North America	1 million	1 million	0.0
Oceania	32,000	35,000	9.4
Sub-Saharan Africa	25 million	25.4 million	1.6
North Africa and Middle East	480,000	540,000	12.5
Western Europe	580,000	610,000	5.2
Eastern Europe and Central Asia	1.3 million	1.4 million	7.7
South and Southeast Asia	6.5 million	7.1 million	9.2
East Asia	900,000	1.1 million	22.2

Source: UNAIDS, 2005a.

Latin America includes Central America, the Caribbean, and South America; North America includes the United States and Canada; Oceania includes Australia and New Zealand; and Western Europe includes Spain, France, Italy, and England.

Table 5.2. AIDS Deaths

Region	2003	2004	Percent change
Latin America	84,000	95,000	13.0
North America	16,000	16,000	0.0
Oceania	700	700	0.0
Sub-Saharan Africa	2.2 million	2.3 million	4.5
North Africa and Middle East	24,000	28,000	16.7
Western Europe	6,000	6,500	8.3
Eastern Europe and Central Asia	49,000	60,000	22.4
South and SE Asia	460,000	490,000	6.5
East Asia	44,000	51,000	15.9

Source: UNAIDS, 2005a.

Latin America includes Central America, the Caribbean, and South America; North America includes the United States and Canada; Oceania includes Australia and New Zealand; and Western Europe includes Spain, France, Italy, and England.

of reasons that include social and cultural differences as well as their physiological makeup (Quinn and Overbaugh, 2005).

UNAIDS (2005a) predicts that AIDS could kill 80 million Africans by 2025, using a worst-case scenario. In addition, HIV infections could soar to 90 million by 2025 if more is not done to fight the disease (UNAIDS, 2005b; 2005c). Also, India's situation is particularly troubling:

India's epidemics are even more diverse than China's. Latest estimates show that about 5.1 million (2.5–8.5 million) people were living with HIV in India in 2003. Serious epidemics are underway in several states. In Tamil Nadu, HIV prevalence of 50 percent has been found among sex workers, while in each of Andhra Pradesh, Karnataka, Maharashtra and Nagaland, HIV prevalence has crossed the 1 percent mark among pregnant women. In Manipur, meanwhile, an epidemic driven by injecting drug use has been in full swing for more than a decade and has acquired a firm presence in the wider population .... HIV prevalence measured at antenatal clinics in the Manipur cities of Imphal and Churach has risen from below 1 percent to over 5 percent, with many of the women testing positive appearing to be the sex partners of male drug injectors. Several factors look set to sustain Manipur's epidemic, including the large proportion (about 20 percent) of female sex workers who inject drugs and the young ages of many injectors (40 percent of male injectors surveyed in 2002 were under 25 years of age). (UNAIDS, 2005c)

Yolanda S. George and Matthew George, Jr.

HIV TESTING AND TREATMENT

HIV Testing

HIV testing reveals whether a person is infected with the virus that causes AIDS. There are a number of tests used to determine the presence or absence of HIV infection, and there are other tests used to monitor the progression of HIV to the AIDS state. Also, HIV testing serves to help with diagnosis and management of HIV/AIDS.[3]

When an individual becomes infected with HIV, it takes the body's immune system between 3 weeks and 2 months to produce antibodies. Antibodies are proteins that attack and destroy specific foreign substances (such as viral proteins), known as antigens, in the body.

The initial tests for the presence or absence of HIV in blood samples are based on the use of antibodies generated against HIV proteins. The nation's blood supply is protected by the use of these tests. One such test is referred to as the HIV ELISA (Enzyme-Linked Immunosorbent Assay) test or HIV enzyme immunoassay (EIA). In the ELISA or EIA tests, HIV antibodies are added to the blood serum being examined. If HIV proteins are present, the antibodies will bind to them. Then an enzyme is added that binds to the antibody. When the enzyme binds to the antibody–HIV protein complex, a color change occurs, indicating the presence of HIV in the blood.

The other type of antibody-based test is known as a Western blot and is used to confirm the results of an ELISA test. Western blot analysis involves the separation of blood serum proteins based on size differences in a gel-like medium. The separated proteins are then transferred to special paper where antibodies that specifically bind to the different types of HIV proteins are added. The antibodies produce a color change on the paper when they are bound to the HIV proteins.

Since it takes from 3 weeks to 2 months for antibodies to be produced to fight HIV, the first tests may show no color changes. Therefore, it is recommended that people be tested again at 3- and 6-month intervals to confirm whether or not they are HIV positive. A positive HIV test means that the tested person has HIV antibodies and is infected with HIV, but it does not mean that the tested person has AIDS. An HIV-positive individual should be continuously monitored and tested to determine whether his or her HIV has progressed to the AIDS state.

In the initial stages of infection, an HIV-positive person is making large quantities of HIV. The viral load test, which helps to determine the stage of progression, is done by two methods: the Polymerase Chain Reaction (PCR) test and the branched DNA (bDNA) test. These tests are much more rapid and sensitive than the antibody-based tests and can detect up to approximately 2 million copies of HIV in blood samples. Both tests are used for diagnostic purposes.

The PCR test can detect the presence of HIV in blood a few days after HIV infection. PCR works by making copies of HIV found in blood samples. If there is no HIV in the sample, then no copies will be made. The bDNA test combines a material that gives off light or fluorescence when bound to HIV during a viral load test. This test can detect as few as 5 copies of HIV in a one-milliliter sample of blood.

In addition to viral load tests, HIV-positive individuals should take CD+4 or T4-cell tests to measure depletion of their lymphocytes (see Figure 5.2). Even with blood tests that are sensitive and rapid, though, one must keep in mind that only 2 percent of HIV is found in blood; it is also known to reside in lymph glands, the spleen, and the brain. Therefore, despite having an undetectable viral load, a person could still be infected and pass HIV to another individual.

AIDS Treatments

Much can be done to increase the lifespan and quality of life for individuals with HIV or AIDS. They need to receive continuing education about the disease and possible treatments so that they can be active partners in the decision-making process with their health care providers. HIV infection and AIDS cause a severe weakening of the immune system, preventing the body from effectively fighting off mild infections and other illnesses. Having AIDS creates a very stressful state for the individual and can lead to depression. Thus, affected individuals should try to keep themselves as physically fit as possible and join a support group in which others share the same problems and experiences.

Drug Regimens

Drugs developed to interfere with or suppress the life cycle of HIV first mainly targeted the enzyme (protein) reverse transcriptase, which makes DNA copies of the HIV RNA genome. Currently, other drugs inhibit or block the action of the HIV protease, which is used to make properly sized HIV proteins needed for HIV structure, copying, and

Table 5.3. Antiretroviral Drugs Approved by
the Food and Drug Administration*

Drug*	Site of action (inhibition)
Agenerase (amprenavir)	Protease inhibitor
Aptivus (tipranavir)	Protease inhibitor
Combivir (AZT, zidovudine)	Reverse transcriptase
Crixivan (indinavir, IDV, MKþ639)	Protease inhibitor
Emtriva (FTC, emtricitabine)	Reverse transcriptase
Epivir (lamivudine, 3TC)	Reverse transcriptase
Epzicom (abacavir/lamivudine)	Reverse transcriptase
Fortovase (saquinavir)	Protease inhibitor
Fuzeon (enfuvirtide, Tþ20)	HIV fusion inhibitor
Hivid (zalcitabine, ddC, dideoxycytidine)	Reverse transcriptase
Invirase (saquinavir mesylate, SQV)	Protease inhibitor
Kaletra (lopinavir, ritonavir)	Protease inhibitor
Norvir (ritonavir, ABTþ538)	Protease inhibitor
Rescriptor (delaviridine, DLV)	Reverse transcriptase
Retrovir (zidovudine, AZT)	Reverse transcriptase
Reyataz (atazanavir sulfate)	Protease inhibitor
Sustiva (efavirenz)	Reverse transcriptase
Trizivir (AZT+ 3TC + abacavir)	Reverse transcriptase
Truvada (tenofovir disoproxil/emtricitabine)	Reverse transcriptase
Videx (didanosine, ddI)	Reverse transcriptase
Viracept (nelfinavir mesylate, NFV)	Protease inhibitor
Viramune (nevirapine, BIþRGþ587)	Reverse transcriptase
Viread (tenofovir)	Reverse transcriptase
Zerit (stavudine, d4T)	Reverse transcriptase
Ziagen (abacavir)	Reverse transcriptase

Source: Food and Drug Administration (2005).

*Drugs listed by brand name; corresponding generic names are in parentheses.

integration. Additionally, the Food and Drug Administration (FDA) has approved at least one HIV fusion-inhibitor drug that prevents entry of HIV into susceptible cells. See Table 5.3 for a list of antiretroviral drugs currently in use.

When the CD+4 cell count falls below 500 (indicative of a weakened immune system) or a large quantity of HIV is found in the bloodstream, drug therapy is recommended. The major regimen of drug treatment is referred to as *highly active antiretroviral therapy* (HAART), in which multiple drugs are taken by the patient in a combination or "cocktail." This approach is used because HIV mutates rapidly, as the influenza virus does every year, only much faster. Thus, drugs that work effectively early on fail to work during the extended period of HIV-to-AIDS progression. In addition, different types of HIV are found throughout the world, with HIV-1 and HIV-2 the most prevalent. The medications used to effectively treat one form of the virus may work poorly or not at all on another.

Patients are advised to take all doses of their medications so that the immune system has sufficient time to repair itself. Taking medications at prescribed times and dosages also helps to prevent the virus from becoming resistant to the drugs.

Women who are pregnant and infected with HIV or have AIDS can transmit the virus to the baby. Generally, the child might be born with HIV antibodies that were generated by the mother. A HIV-positive mother can also transmit the virus by breast-feeding the child.

It is recommended that children of HIV-infected mothers be given the drug AZT for about 28 days after birth to limit the chances of contracting HIV. Recent studies from the 12th Annual Retrovirus Conference (UNAIDS, 2005c) suggest that pregnant women can significantly reduce the chances of transmitting HIV to their newborn children if they are on a combination therapy regimen (at least two antiretroviral drugs). It was also suggested at the conference that routine HIV testing be urged for nearly all Americans; the CDC is taking this recommendation under advisement.

PREVENTION OF HIV/AIDS

As previously noted, the most common modes of HIV transmission are unprotected sex with an infected partner and sharing needles and/ or syringes with an infected person. The risks of contracting HIV from infected blood products and infected mother to fetus have been significantly reduced or almost eliminated. According to the Institute of Human Virology (2005), HIV prevention strategies include the following:

- Do not have sexual contact with persons known or suspected of being infected with HIV.
- Do not have sex with numerous people or with people who have multiple partners. Do not have sex with prostitutes.
- Do not use intravenous (IV) drugs. If IV drugs are used, do not share needles or syringes. (Boiling or cleaning them with alcohol does not guarantee sterility.)

- Do not have sex with people who use IV drugs.
- People with AIDS or who have had positive HIV antibody tests may pass the disease on to others. They should not donate blood, plasma, body organs, or sperm. They should not exchange body fluids during sexual activity.
- Avoid oral, vaginal, or anal contact with semen.
- Avoid anal intercourse, since it causes small abrasions in the rectal tissues, through which HIV in an infected partner's semen may be injected directly into the recipient's blood.
- Avoid oral contact with the anus, and do not engage in the insertion of fingers or fists into the anus, as either an active or receptive partner.
- Do not allow a partner's urine to enter your mouth, anus, eyes, or open cuts or sores.
- Safer sex behaviors may reduce the risk of acquiring the infection. There is a risk of acquiring the infection even if "safe sex" is practiced with the use of condoms. Abstinence is the only sure way to prevent sexual transmission of the virus.

HIV prevention is also enhanced by education and behavior modification programs. However, there are many misconceptions concerning HIV/AIDS among different groups. As reported in the publication *HIV and AIDS: The Science Inside* (American Association for the Advancement of Science, 2005), a person cannot get HIV or AIDS:

- By being in daily contact (at home, at work, or in school) with an infected person
- By shaking hands with an infected person
- By hugging or casually kissing an infected person
- By using a toilet seat that an infected person has touched
- By using a drinking fountain that an infected person used
- From a pet that lives with an infected person
- From doorknobs, dishes, drinking glasses, or food

A recent study by Bogart and Thorburn (2005) about the attitudes of African Americans about HIV/AIDS and the use of condoms revealed some interesting beliefs. For example, 53.4 percent of African Americans surveyed agreed that an AIDS cure is kept from the poor; 48 percent believed that HIV was created by people; and 27 percent believed that a government lab created AIDS. Other erroneous beliefs included that those who take new HIV drugs are guinea pigs for the government (43.6 percent). Only 38 percent believed that HIV drugs save lives in the Black community or that the government tells the truth about AIDS.

Other untrue beliefs involving HIV/AIDS include the following:

- A new form of HIV is being transmitted through the air
- Infected syringes are being intentionally left on playgrounds in the United States
- If a man has sex with a virgin, he will be cured of AIDS (a belief held in some parts of Africa)
- AIDS is a "gay disease" occurring only among homosexual men (U.S.)
- The elderly don't get AIDS or visit prostitutes

These and other misconceptions concerning HIV/AIDS serve as impediments to the efforts aimed at educating the population about the devastating effects of this disease syndrome. Subsequent chapters in this section present ideas for enhancing education about HIV and AIDS.

NOTES

1. For more information about the life cycle of HIV, visit http://bioweb.wku.edu/courses/BIOL115/Wyatt/HIV/HIV.htm or http://www.hopkins-aids.edu/hiv_lifecycle/hivcycle_flsh.html

2. An excellent overview of HIV disease is found at http://hivinsite.ucsf.edu/InSite?page=kb-authorsanddoc=kb-03-01-01. This is a somewhat complex but comprehensive examination of HIV/AIDS written by C. Bradley Hare, M.D., of the University of California–San Francisco.

3. See also New Mexico AIDS InfoNet fact sheets 102, 124, and 125 at http://www.aidsinfonet.org and the Institute of Human Virology at the University of Maryland Biotechnology Institute, http://www.ihv.org/guides/hiv_symptoms.html.

REFERENCES

American Association for the Advancement of Science. (2005). *HIV and AIDS: The science inside.* Washington, DC: Author. Retrieved September 2, 2005, from http://www.healthlit.org/scienceInside/eb_hivandaids.htm.

Bogart, L. M., and Thorburn, S. (2005). Are HIV/AIDS conspiracy beliefs a barrier to HIV prevention among African Americans? *Journal of Acquired Immune Deficiency Syndromes* 38(2): 213–218.

Centers for Disease Control and Prevention. (1981a). Pneumocystis pneumonia—Los Angeles. *Morbidity and Mortality Weekly Report* 30(21): 250–252.

Centers for Disease Control and Prevention. (1981b). Kaposi's sarcoma and pneumocystis pneumonia among homosexual men—New York City and California. *Morbidity and Mortality Weekly Report* 30(25): 305–308.

Centers for Disease Control and Prevention. (1982). A cluster of Kaposi's sarcoma and pneumocystis carinii pneumonia among homosexual male residents of Los Angeles and Orange Counties, California. *Morbidity and Mortality Weekly Report* 31(23): 305–307.

Food and Drug Administration. (2005). *Drugs used in the treatment of HIV infection.* Retrieved September 1, 2005, from http://www.fda.gov/oashi/aids/virals.html.

Institute of Human Virology. (2005). *HIV information guide.* Retrieved September 2, 2005, from http://www.ihv.org/guides/hiv_prevention.html.

International Centre for Eye Health. (2001). Human immunodeficiency virus (HIV) and AIDS. *Teaching series: HIV/AIDS and the eye.* London: Author. Retrieved September 1, 2005, from http://www.iceh.org.uk/files/tsno8/text/02.htm.

Joint United Nations Programme on HIV/AIDS. (2005a). *AIDS epidemic update, December 2004.* Geneva, Switzerland: Author. Retrieved September 1, 2005, from http://www.unaids.org/wad2004/report.html.

Joint United Nations Programme on HIV/AIDS. (2005b). *AIDS in Africa: Three scenarios to 2025.* Geneva, Switzerland: Author. Retrieved September 1, 2005, from http://www.unaids.org/en/AIDS+in+Africa_Three+scenarios+to+2025.asp.

Joint United Nations Programme on HIV/AIDS. (2005c). *2004 Report on the global AIDS epidemic.* Geneva, Switzerland: Author. Retrieved September 1, 2005, from http://www.unaids.org/bangkok2004/report.html.

National Human Genome Research Institute of the National Institutes of Health. (n.d.). *HIV structure.* Retrieved September 1, 2005, from http://www.genome.gov/Pages/Hyperion//DIR/VIP/Glossary/Illustration/Pdf/hiv.pdf.

Quinn, T. C., and Overbaugh, J. (2005). HIV/AIDS in women: An expanding epidemic. *Science* 308: 1582–1583.

6

INQUIRY-BASED APPROACHES TO HIV/AIDS PREVENTION EDUCATION: STANDARDS, PRACTICES, AND OUTCOMES

Joan L. Sattler and Francesca Armmer

⊷

Education is the primary tool we have today to combat the world's HIV/AIDS pandemic. With half of all new infections in the United States affecting people under age 25 (U.S. Department of Health and Human Services, 2000), educators are on the front lines to provide a comprehensive, systematic approach to HIV/AIDS prevention education. This chapter addresses standards, policies, and evidence-based practices for health education and HIV/AIDS prevention education; methods, curriculum, and inquiry-based approaches to instructional practices; and contextual components such as community and culture and other quality-assurance factors in teaching about HIV/AIDS prevention. Finally, this chapter presents an inquiry-based decision making model for teaching HIV/AIDS prevention to serve as a conceptual framework for educators to use in planning instruction for preprimary through adult students.

THE PERVASIVE NATURE OF HIV/AIDS

The spread of the Human Immunodeficiency Virus (HIV) and Acquired Immune Deficiency Syndrome (AIDS) has reached pandemic proportions. The Joint United Nations Programme on HIV/AIDS (UNAIDS) estimated that in 2004, nearly 40 million people were living with HIV, including 25.4 million in the sub-Sahara region, 7.1 million in South and Southeast Asia, 1.7 million in Latin America, and 1 million in North

75

America (UNAIDS, 2004). Globally, new AIDS infections in 2004 included an estimated 640,000 children, infected primarily through mother-to-child transmissions, and women and girls were being infected with HIV in greater numbers than men (UNAIDS, 2004).

Over the last 5 years, the incidence of HIV infection and AIDS in the United States has continued to rise (McKay et al., 2004). This increase has affected primarily low-income, minority neighborhoods and others with poor access to health care. In response to the expansive impact of HIV/AIDS in the world, educators are challenged to prepare educational experiences that take into consideration student attentiveness, measures to strengthen student self-esteem, the extent of students' control of their sexual activities and of their cultural context for empowerment, and evolving views of the future.

THE IMPORTANCE OF A COMPREHENSIVE, SYSTEMATIC APPROACH TO HIV/AIDS PREVENTION EDUCATION

Health risks and unhealthy behaviors that contribute to illnesses, HIV infections, and other serious health problems often begin early in life. Prekindergarten through twelfth-grade (PK–12) students and college students are vulnerable groups.

A comprehensive approach to health literacy is an essential foundational component of the education of all children (U.S. Department of Health and Human Services, 2000). HIV/AIDS prevention education must be a major component of any health education strategy.

Educators can play a vital role in controlling the spread of HIV by teaching about health and behaviors that place young people at risk of serious health problems and by helping students develop skills for avoiding these risks. In U.S. elementary schools, classroom teachers are the primary providers of health education, which is required in every state. Yet only a few states require prospective elementary teachers to study health education. In secondary schools, the majority of teachers assigned to teach health and HIV/AIDS education are also not professionally prepared to teach health education (Council of Chief State School Officers, 2000).

HIV/AIDS affects not only the health of young people but also the economic, social, and cultural systems in which they live. Consequently, it is important to address HIV/AIDS prevention from multiple contexts, and colleges and universities should prepare teachers to do so.

STANDARDS-BASED HIV/AIDS PREVENTION EDUCATION

Educators should understand and use national standards, policies, and recommendations about HIV/AIDS prevention education. Preparation programs for teachers, counselors, and school administrators across the nation must ensure that their candidates understand various curriculum, instruction, and assessment programs that can be used for effective HIV/AIDS prevention education in PK–12 settings. A number of professional associations and governmental organizations have developed standards, guidelines, and recommendations about such programs.

The U.S. government does not prescribe health education nationally, as such policy falls in the jurisdiction of state and local governments (National Association of State Boards of Education, 2005). Most states do have policies about comprehensive school health education, and many states now have policies on HIV/AIDS prevention education in PK–12 schools (American Association of Colleges for Teacher Education, 2003). Educators should investigate these policies in their state and make certain that instructional programs used are aligned with state mandates.

National Health Education Standards for Prekindergarten–12 Students

The premiere set of professional standards on this topic is the National Health Education Standards (Joint Committee on National Health Education Standards, 1995), developed to help guide curriculum development, instruction, and the assessment of student performance in PK–12 settings. These standards were developed by members of the American Cancer Society, the Association for the Advancement of Health Education, the American Public Health Association, the American School Health Association, and the Society of State Directors of Health, Physical Education, and Recreation. The standards, listed in Table 6.1, promote student health literacy by encouraging characteristics such as critical thinking and problem solving; responsible, productive citizenship; self-directed learning; and effective communication. Each standard is accompanied by a rationale and performance indicators of knowledge, skills, and attitudes students should demonstrate by the end of kindergarten through Grade 4, Grades 5–8, and Grades 9–12.

Table 6.1. The National Health Education Standards

1. Students will comprehend concepts related to health promotion and disease prevention.
2. Students will demonstrate the ability to access valid health information and health-promoting products and services.
3. Students will demonstrate the ability to practice health-enhancing behaviors and reduce health risks.
4. Students will analyze the influence of culture, media, technology, and other factors on health.
5. Students will demonstrate the ability to use interpersonal communication skills to enhance health.
6. Students will demonstrate the ability to use goal-setting and decision-making skills to enhance health.
7. Students will demonstrate the ability to advocate for personal, family, and community health.

Source: Joint Committee on National Health Education Standards (1995)

A Grade-Level Framework for HIV/AIDS Prevention Education

Pateman (2003) constructed a framework that employs the National Health Education Standards in the context of HIV prevention education for prekindergarten through Grade 4, Grades 5–8, and Grades 9–12. The focus of this framework (see Table 6.2) is specifically on HIV education content, not on health education in general.

Standards and best practices are important elements that educators should identify in HIV/AIDS prevention education programs. Most adolescents are knowledgeable about HIV (Henry J. Kaiser Family Foundation, 2000). Consequently, HIV/AIDS prevention education programs must go beyond knowledge development and emphasize risk-reduction behaviors to prevent the spread of HIV (Kirby, 2002; Mueller, Bidwell, Okamoto, and Mann, 1998). Inquiry-based approaches to teaching and learning about HIV/AIDS prevention education are strategies that can be used to effect risk-reduction behaviors.

Standards for Health Education Teachers

National professional standards have been developed through an extensive credentialing process for the preparation of health educators. These standards are the basis for certification of individuals as well as for accreditation of teacher preparation programs in health education.

Table 6.2. HIV Prevention Education: Application of the National Health Education Standards by Grade Level

Standard	Grades PK–4	Grades 5–8	Grades 9–12
1. Core concepts	• Describe HIV as an infectious disease. • Explain that HIV is not transmitted through casual contact. • Describe correct procedures for handling blood or other body fluids. • Explain why it is safe to go to school with classmates who have HIV.	• Describe behaviors that do and do not transmit HIV. • Explain why behaviors, rather than who people are, transmit HIV. • Debunk myths and misperceptions about HIV transmission and people living with HIV. • Describe abstinence from sex and needle use as the only sure ways to prevent HIV infection.	• Explain why people can live with HIV without showing signs of illness. • Explain why a person's appearance does not reveal HIV status. • Explain that HIV compromises the immune system, making people susceptible to diseases associated with AIDS. • Describe treatments that show promise for helping people with HIV live longer and healthier.
2. Accessing information, products, and services	• List parents, teachers, and other trusted adults as information sources about HIV. • Explain that media may contain misinformation about HIV.	• Name agencies and organizations that provide accurate information about HIV over the Internet. • List Internet sites and toll-free phone numbers that provide accurate information about HIV.	• List organizations that provide reliable HIV testing. • Describe the correct and consistent use of latex condoms to help prevent HIV infection.
3. Self-management	• Practice universal precautions to help protect against HIV and other diseases. • Demonstrate self-care for nosebleeds and scrapes.	• Practice abstinence from sexual behaviors and needle use to protect against HIV. • Abstain from alcohol and other drug use, which influence HIV-related risk behaviors.	• Describe personal commitment to protect self and others from HIV infection. • Role-play ways to avoid, leave, or negotiate to protect oneself in HIV risk situations.

(continued)

Table 6.2. *(continued)*

Standard	Grades PK–4	Grades 5–8	Grades 9–12
4. Analysis of influences	• Discuss family influences on health beliefs and behaviors. • Describe media messages related to health behaviors.	• Analyze the influence of friends, as well as family, on health behaviors. • Examine personal beliefs, likes/dislikes, attitudes, and experiences as influences on health behaviors.	• List pressure lines others may use to promote risky behaviors. • Evaluate the strength of various influences on HIV protective or risk behaviors.
5. Interpersonal communication	• Tell others how to protect themselves against blood and body fluid spills. • Communicate care and support for people living with HIV.	• Practice effective responses to avoid or leave HIV risk situations. • Communicate to help others avoid or leave HIV risk situations.	• Demonstrate negotiation skills to protect oneself in an HIV risk situation. • Communicate to help others avoid or leave HIV risk situations.
6. Decision making and goal setting	• Describe important decisions for staying healthy. • Set personal goals for staying healthy.	• List important steps in decision making to protect oneself against HIV infection. • Set personal goals that provide reasons to stay healthy.	• List important steps in decision making to protect oneself against HIV infection. • Set personal goals that provide reasons to stay healthy.
7. Advocacy	• Discuss healthy lifestyles with family members. • Create a classroom book about how to treat a friend who has special health needs.	• Design an advocacy campaign to help eliminate misperceptions about HIV. • Support others who make positive health choices.	• Serve as peer educators to inform others about HIV and important health practices. • Advocate for effective HIV education for all grade levels.

Source: Pateman (2003, pp. 27–28). Copyright American Association of Colleges for Teacher Education. Reprinted with permission.

These standards can be found on the Web sites of the American Association for Health Education (2005) and the National Council for Accreditation of Teacher Education (NCATE, 2005). Also, teachers may seek master-teacher certification from the National Board for Professional Teaching Standards (NBPTS, 2002). NBPTS has established 11 standards of accomplished practice for health education teachers, defining the comprehensive background and knowledge, skills, and dispositions such educators need to teach about health, including HIV/AIDS education. However, most teachers who teach health are not credentialed as health educators and did not major in health education.

HIV/AIDS Education Taught Across the Curriculum

All PK–12 students should have instruction on HIV/AIDS prevention through comprehensive school health education programs. In addition, the overall PK–12 curriculum provides supplementary opportunities to reinforce HIV/AIDS prevention education across the curriculum. Consequently, all teachers should have some ability and preparation to teach about HIV/AIDS prevention education. Schools of education must prepare teachers to address this critical public health issue in their classrooms as a deliberate part of the overall curriculum.

Elementary, middle school, secondary, and special education teachers who are not health education specialists need to possess the knowledge, skills, and attitudes to prepare students to make positive choices to promote a healthy lifestyle. NCATE has established program standards for elementary teacher preparation on what prospective teachers should know and be able to do to help students learn. Elementary standard 2g addresses health education: "Candidates know, understand, and use the major concepts in the subject matter of health education to create opportunities for student development and practice of skills that contribute to good health" (NCATE, 2000).

Teaching and learning about HIV/AIDS prevention education can occur across the PK–12 curriculum in such subject areas as science, mathematics, English/language arts, civics, the arts, social studies, and technology. Integration of this topic in the various disciplines is limited only by the educator's imagination; Pateman (2003) provides examples of ways to incorporate HIV information across the PK–12 curriculum (see Table 6.3).

Table 6.3. Learning About HIV Prevention Across the PK–12 Curriculum

Subject area	Links to HIV prevention education
English/language arts	• Read fiction and nonfiction related to HIV infection, living with HIV, effects on families, death and dying, and issues of discrimination. • Write a story about a young person infected with HIV. • Dramatize situations related to HIV issues, such as discrimination, decision making, and going for testing.
Mathematics	• Design a mathematical model to show the potential spread of HIV infection resulting from unprotected intercourse with multiple partners. • Calculate potential years of life lost to HIV infection among U.S. adolescents and young adults.
Science	• Identify the period during which HIV antibody testing reflects infection and explain why. • Describe the challenges scientists face in developing an HIV vaccine.
Foreign language study	• Compare culturally sensitive methods of teaching about HIV prevention education in various cultures. • Describe differences in languages used to discuss HIV risks.
Civics and government	• Explain U.S. efforts to research and prevent HIV infection. • Compare government intervention for HIV prevention education among different countries.
Economics	• Estimate the impact and potential impact of HIV on the U.S. economy. • Calculate the costs of prevention versus treatment for HIV infection.
Fine arts	• Study the works of artists who have lost their lives to HIV. • Review photography, cinema, theater, and music related to HIV and AIDS.
History and social studies	• Compare the spread of HIV with the spread of other epidemics in history. • Examine the social stigma associated with HIV and AIDS in various societies.
Geography	• Track the spread of HIV around the world. • Examine differences in access to treatment and care around the world.

Table 6.3. *(Continued)*

Subject area	Links to HIV prevention education
Physical education	• Describe the role of physical activity in overall health. • Debunk myths about HIV infection and athletic participation.
Technology	• Locate the most current and accurate information about HIV on the Internet. • Design persuasive HIV prevention education materials for peers.

Source: Pateman (2003, p. 29). Copyright American Association of Colleges for Teacher Education. Reprinted with permission.

METHODS, CURRICULUM, AND INQUIRY-BASED APPROACHES TO TEACHING AND LEARNING ABOUT HIV/AIDS PREVENTION

Inquiry-Based Teaching and Learning

Inquiry learning implies involvement that leads to understanding. For educators, inquiry-based approaches to teaching and learning involve the development of student inquiry skills and the nurturing of inquiring attitudes or habits of mind that will enable individuals to continue the quest for knowledge throughout life (Educational Broadcasting Corporation, 2004). The use of the scientific method is inquiry-based learning. However, inquiry learning can be applied to all disciplines by using that discipline's unique perspective, values, and disciplinary ground rules. For example, the study of literature often uses opinions and subjective interpretations as a source of information rather than relying on scientific facts.

Inquiry-based teaching and learning is a process in which students and teachers formulate investigative questions, obtain factual and interpretative information, and build knowledge that ultimately reflects their answers to the original questions. In this approach, teachers pose questions and problems, then guide students to help them find their own answers. The approach helps students learn how to learn, transforming them from passive learners to active participants in the learning process. Some examples of inquiry-based teaching strategies are the case study approach, project-based learning, role playing, conducting experiments, and real-world problem solving such as investigating topics through strategic use of the World Wide Web. Students become engaged by applying their existing knowledge and experience and by learning to hypothesize, test theories, and draw conclusions from their findings.

"Effective learning is predicated on students' active participation in the learning process, interactive communication with peers and instructors, and the application of new knowledge to their current experiences" (Sileo, Prater, Luckner, Rhine, and Rude, 1998, p. 187). Some of these inquiry-based approaches suggested by Sileo et al. in health-related curricula are technology-based simulations, service-learning, journaling, videotapes with peer-assisted reflection, storyboarding, concept maps, and cooperative learning activities. These strategies can be used to teach HIV/AIDS education across the curriculum and not merely in health education classes.

Methods Consistent With Research on Changing HIV-Related Risk Behaviors

Educators must be prepared to teach about HIV/AIDS prevention based on research on changing HIV-related risk behaviors among youth. Much of the research notes that inquiry-based teaching and learning approaches are most effective. Kirby (1997) identified some characteristics of effective HIV/AIDS prevention education programs that involve active, inquiry-based approaches, such as using teaching methods to involve students and to help them personalize information, providing modeling and practice in communication and refusal skills regarding risky behaviors, and addressing social pressures on sexual behavior.

Kirby (2002) reviewed 73 studies of programs on sexuality education and found that many of the programs have some positive effects on some outcomes, such as greater knowledge, but only some of the programs delay the initiation of sex, increase condom or contraceptive use, and reduce unprotected sex among youth. The most effective programs were within four groups: comprehensive sex- and HIV-education programs; programs involving clinical protocols; service-learning programs; and long-term, intensive programs. These programs for adolescents showed strong evidence for effectiveness in reducing behaviors that place students at risk for contracting HIV and other sexually transmitted diseases.

Behavior mapping is another effective way for teachers to develop curriculum and teaching methods to address the risk behaviors associated with HIV/AIDS. Wooley (1995) proposes using behavior maps to identify factors that influence individual decisions about behaviors.

Components of a behavior map include behavioral goals, predisposers to the behavior, enablers, and reinforcers. Once completed, the behavior map can be used by the teacher as a tool for questioning and developing goals, instruction, and priorities for use of classroom time. It is helpful to focus instruction on objectives and outcomes to ultimately alter behaviors (Wooley, 1995).

The Curriculum at Various Age and Grade Levels

To increase students' knowledge and tolerance and influence subsequent behavior, HIV/AIDS prevention education programs should have a concentrated focus; give accurate information; use active learning methods; include small-group discussions; examine media and social influences; and, most important, emphasize skill modeling and practice, including decision-making and refusal skills and attention to the issue of self-esteem (Kirby, Short, and Collins, 1994). The programs should be developmentally appropriate to the age and grade level of students (Pateman, 2003; see Table 6.2) and be ethnically and culturally sensitive.

The elementary school curriculum for HIV/AIDS education should emphasize general concepts of health and disease, cleanliness, the role of microorganisms in disease, and the prevention of infection. The content should define HIV and AIDS and differentiate between myth and fact, explain the effects on the immune system, and identify appropriate resource people to clarify unresolved issues (Centers for Disease Control and Prevention, 1988).

Middle and high school students must have extensive exposure to health education because of their significant potential for engaging in high-risk behaviors. The curriculum should include the scope and history of HIV/AIDS as an infectious disease, the effect on the immune system, methods of transmission, testing issues, prevention and treatments, the relationship of substance abuse and HIV transmission, social and psychological aspects of the disease, and legal and discrimination issues (Committee on Pediatric AIDS, 1998).

CONTEXTUAL COMPONENTS OF COMMUNITY AND CULTURE AND OTHER QUALITY-ASSURANCE FACTORS

The development of an inquiry-based approach to HIV/AIDS prevention education will need to address contextual components of community and culture as well as the curricular and pedagogical components necessary to assure quality of instruction. The student learner, the teaching topic, and the community all become integral to the inquiry-based approach.

Consider the student learner. Teachers must be aware of the technological infrastructure, as a contextual referent, that many children and youth experience daily. The impact of this infrastructure compels educators to give specific focus to the notion of *attentional economy* (Castell and Jenson, 2004). *Economy* refers to the use of scarce resources; *attentional economy* refers to the scarcity of student attention or student attentiveness. Previous unimodal approaches to the teaching of selected topics might need to be replaced with multimodal activities, many of which are being derived from advances in technology.

The Joint United Nations Programme on HIV/AIDS (UNAIDS) Best Practice Collection (UNAIDS, 1997) identifies two contextual factors that must be considered in a comprehensive, systematic HIV/AIDS prevention program. Those factors are the impact of peer pressure on the young person and the nondiscriminatory attitudes often reflected in young people. To be sure, peer pressure might be negative, such as encouragement to engage in risky health behaviors, or might be very positive, such as sharing the messages of HIV/AIDS education. Young people's tendency to learn to adopt nondiscriminatory attitudes and behaviors toward persons with HIV/AIDS more readily than adults allows for a more open approach to the discussion of HIV/AIDS information. The UNAIDS document also cites evidence that a sound, comprehensive HIV/AIDS education program delays the age of sexual intercourse, refuting the popular presumption that such a program would lead to increased sexual activity.

Maintenance of quality is another factor to be considered in the contextual planning of an inquiry-based approach to HIV/AIDS prevention education. Two hallmarks of quality for this topic are cultural sensitivity and ethical soundness. When working with culturally diverse populations, professionals must demonstrate respect for the values, beliefs, traditions, expectations, experiences, and priorities of families. These diverse beliefs and values confront teachers from students of all age groups. In the context of HIV/AIDS prevention education, teachers must be careful to avoid stereotyping and illusions of racial homogeneity that might be implied in the case studies, writing activities, and even guest speakers that could become a part of the planning.

This idea of cultural sensitivity, reinforced in the writing of Pinzon-Perez (2003), who identified lessons learned from working in international settings, may readily assist the HIV/AIDS prevention educator. One lesson reported by Pinzon-Perez is that the development of a healthy lifestyle is a universal priority. Yet when the demands of day-to-day survival exist, due to poverty, destitution, or illness, clearly survival takes precedence over all else. The question for the educator becomes "How can HIV/AIDS prevention education assist the individual who is facing these day-to-day survival issues?" By answering this question, the educator strengthens the quality of the program that will be presented.

Another lesson described by Pinzon-Perez (2003) is that poverty is a key concern, even to industrialized nations. In the midst of an industrialized environment, educators are challenged not only to develop multimodal learning activities but to serve as a resource for students who cannot economically afford to access technological tools.

Pinzon-Perez (2003) also learned the importance and value of cultural sensitivity in health education. The complexity embedded in multicultural issues becomes more easily addressed when the educator makes deliberate efforts to cultivate a program that is culturally sensitive.

The second hallmark of quality for inquiry-based HIV/AIDS prevention education programs, ethical soundness, is difficult to attain because of the emergence of *ethical dilemmas*—moral situations in which people must decide between two or more mutually exclusive, morally correct actions (Brown and Simpson, 2000). One example of such a dilemma could be whether to promote abstinence or safer sex. Educators might be faced with this dilemma when deciding on the breadth and depth of HIV/AIDS prevention education that will be allowed within their particular district, state, or province. If the answer to a dilemma is not found in district or state policy, educators should consider the following questions when focusing the lesson or program:

- What is the problem or ethical dilemma?
- Whose problem is it?
- Who should make the decision? Who are the key participants?
- Who is affected by the decision? (Brown and Simpson, 2000)

When developing the curricular component of a high-quality, comprehensive, systematic approach, educators might need to modify their teaching in order to challenge their students and to incorporate the culture and community. This shift may be characterized by multiple modes of communication, "virtual" and in real time, as well as a diverse set of teaching strategies (Goodwin, 2003). Activities should challenge students to think critically and to share the conclusions derived from those activities. Technology can be used to facilitate a constructivist foundation that allows for an ongoing discussion of questions related to HIV/AIDS prevention.

AN INQUIRY-BASED DECISION-MAKING MODEL FOR TEACHING HIV/AIDS PREVENTION

Educators are confronted with a myriad of curricular programs, standards, and policies regarding the content and process of teaching about HIV/AIDS prevention. This information might prompt teachers to ask questions such as these:

- What ideas should I consider in planning and developing instruction for my classroom of children or youth?
- What types of standards, rationale, curricular content, and pedagogical skills should I consider using?
- What types of contextual components, such as community and culture, are important to consider in developing instruction for my students?
- What research and resources are available to me in deciding on a curricular program or in designing my own instruction?
- Should I use a packaged curricular program designed for HIV/AIDS instruction, or should I design the instructional program, lesson, or unit myself?
- What instructional outcomes do I expect?
- How will I assess and evaluate the program and then use that outcome information to modify and redesign future instruction?

Planning and Decision Making

Educators are involved in planning and decision making continually. Arends (1998) refers to these phases as the *preinstructional planning phase,* the *interactive planning phase,* and the *postinstructional planning phase.* In the preinstructional planning phase, educators question, investigate, and choose content and an instructional approach, and they determine time, space, structures, and motivation. In the interactive planning phase, educators are implementing the curriculum through teaching and learning activities, some of which are questioning, guiding learners, using inquiry-based approaches, providing opportunities for skills practice, and using informal and formal assessments and evaluations. In the postinstructional planning phase, educators continue to use informal and formal methods of assessment and evaluation by checking for understanding, providing feedback, and testing and then analyzing data and feedback to modify and redesign instruction. This continual planning and decision-making process is used as a foundational component of the inquiry-based model.

The actions of the educator throughout these three phases include questioning, investigating, selecting or designing instruction, teaching and learning, assessing and evaluating, and modifying and redesigning instruction (see Figure 6.1).

A Model to Assist Educators

Figure 6.2 suggests a model to help educators conduct this continual planning and resource exploration and to serve as a catalyst for educators' own creative process. This model is also appropriate for other human service professionals who have educational responsibilities, such as school nurses, counselors, and administrators in schools and in other settings.

Questioning. Educators begin with their own questions about HIV/AIDS prevention education: What do students already know about the topic? Are other educators teaching these students about the topic? How much time is available? Questions such as these form the basis for educators' decision about what curricular program to use or create. Teachers must determine what the students need to know, should be able to do, and which attitudes they should form regarding the topic of HIV/AIDS prevention. This program could be in the context of a comprehensive school health education program; through a school discipline other than health education, such as mathematics, science, literature, or technology; or through a supplemental educational experience.

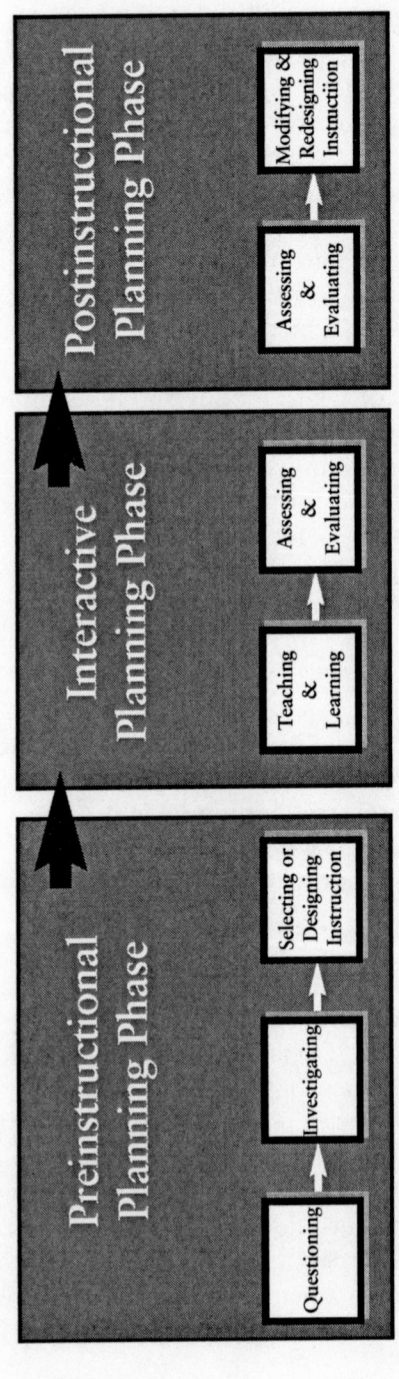

Figure 6.1. Continual Planning and Decision-Making by Educators

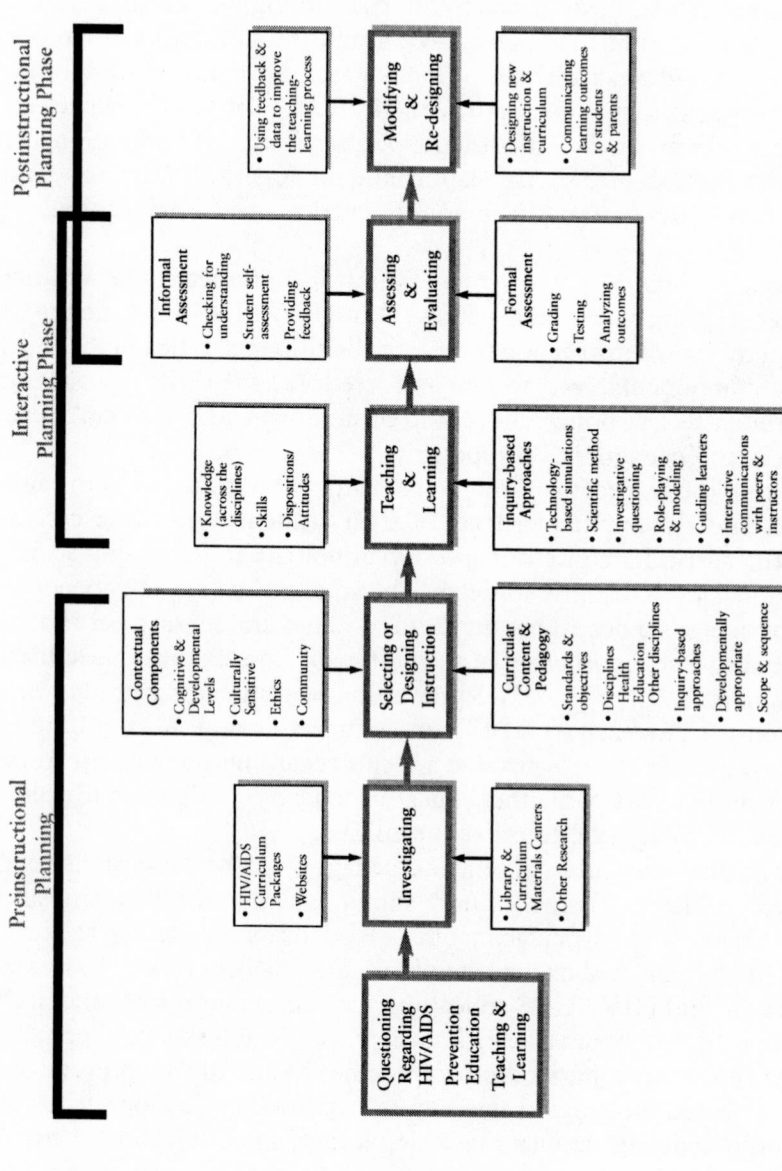

Figure 6.2. An Inquiry-Based Decision-Making Model for Teaching HIV/AIDS Prevention

91

Investigating. Educators then begin to research those questions by reviewing HIV/AIDS curricular packages that are currently available. Some of these materials can be found through the school district's curricular specialists, through state-endorsed programs, and through the Internet. Excellent materials are also available from government sources, such as the Centers for Disease Control and Prevention; from professional organizations, such as the American Association of Colleges for Teacher Education, the American Association for Health Education, the American School Health Association, and the American Red Cross; and from school or community libraries or curricular materials centers.

Selecting or Designing Instruction. Educators must determine whether to select existing curricular materials about HIV/AIDS prevention or to design their own instruction to best fit the students to be taught. Two major components need to be considered: (a) the context involving the students, classroom, culture, and community and (b) the curricular content and pedagogical components.

Within the category of context, educators need to consider the age, grade, and developmental level of their students and make certain that the curricular content is appropriate for the cognitive and social-emotional levels of those students. The students' community needs to be considered to determine the cultural values and sensitivities related to racial, ethnic, or other social and cultural factors. Some of the ethical dilemmas raised in HIV/AIDS prevention education can provide a rich environment to teach students to use critical thinking. Also, educators need to explore their own value systems regarding the content to be taught and to work with other educators to gain confidence in teaching content that might be considered sensitive.

Regarding curricular content and pedagogy, many dimensions need to be considered. First, educators should examine the standards and objectives of the curricular materials to determine whether they are aligned with national or state standards and practices related to health education and HIV/AIDS education. Instruction for middle and high school students should also include exposure to and skill development in risk reduction behaviors to promote health and disease prevention. Inquiry-based pedagogical approaches help students develop such skills through modeling, simulations, role-playing, and other various investigative procedures. Educators also need to consider how best to teach the content within health education or in any other subject taught in school. Finally, the scope and sequence of the lesson or program must be determined along with the timeline in which it will be implemented.

Teaching and Learning. During the interactive planning phase, educators are implementing instruction and guiding students through the curricular materials. Here is where teachers' creativity comes into play in developing students' knowledge, skills, and attitudes about HIV/AIDS prevention, using various inquiry-based approaches to involve students actively in their own learning. These approaches might use technology-based simulations, experiments using the scientific method, role playing and modeling, investigative questioning, and various interactive communications with peers and instructors.

Assessing and Evaluating. In the interactive planning phase, educators use various forms of informal and formal assessments to determine whether students are learning the material and analyze the outcomes to evaluate the lesson or program. Informal assessments might have the students use self-assessments, check for understanding, and provide feedback. Formal assessments might involve testing, grading rubrics, and outcomes analysis.

Modifying and Redesigning Instruction. In the postinstructional planning phase, educators continue to assess and evaluate and then modify their instruction based on what is learned from the outcome data. Educators also need to communicate the learning outcomes to the students and, depending upon the age of the students, to the parents. This continual planning and decision-making helps keep the material fresh, up-to-date, and adapted to the specific students and community. Because knowledge about HIV/AIDS is evolving and new educational materials frequently become available, it is especially important that teachers continually update their lessons.

CONCLUSIONS

Educators are confronted with an enormous task of providing students with the knowledge, skills, and attitudes about HIV/AIDS to keep them healthy, alive, and free from infection. It takes time and energy to cull through the wealth of information on this topic, to review curricular programs available, and to learn about the standards and practices and how to plan instruction related to this topic. This chapter assists educators in this process by providing educational standards, evidence-based practices, and resources regarding HIV/AIDS prevention education as well as a decision-making model for educators to use in planning instruction.

Besides educators, other human service professionals such as nurses and counselors may use this versatile decision-making model. It can be used in elementary or secondary settings as well as in higher education and other adult settings. This model could serve as a planning guide for teacher preparation programs to use in HIV/AIDS prevention education with preservice and in-service teachers. Also, multidisciplinary teams of health and education professionals could use the model to develop a comprehensive, integrated-services approach for designing curriculum to best fit the culture of specific schools and communities.

Ultimately, success with HIV/AIDS prevention education will be evident if educators can change HIV-related risk behaviors of young people. Indeed, if educators can keep young people from becoming HIV infected and promote healthy lifestyles, then they will have an impact on this generation and generations to come and help to ensure a healthy country and world population.

REFERENCES

American Association for Health Education. (2005). *AAHE/NCATE health education standards and key elements*. Retrieved September 14, 2005, from http://www.aahperd.org/aahe/template.cfm?Template=ncate_elements.html.

American Association of Colleges for Teacher Education. (2003). *Matching expectations: What states say that young people need to know about health and HIV and how well teachers are prepared to provide it*. Washington, DC: Author.

Arends, R. I. (1998). *Learning to teach*. 4th ed. New York: McGraw-Hill.

Brown, E., and Simpson, E. (2000). Comprehensive STD/HIV prevention education targeting U.S. adolescents: Review of an ethical dilemma and proposed ethical framework. *Nursing Ethics* 7(4): 339–349.

Castell, S., and Jenson, J. (2004). Paying attention to attention: New economies for learning. *Educational Theory* 54(4): 381–397.

Centers for Disease Control and Prevention. (1988). Guidelines for effective school health education to prevent the spread of AIDS. *Morbidity and Mortality Weekly Report* 37(S-2): 1–14.

Committee on Pediatric AIDS. (1998). American Academy of Pediatrics: Virus/Acquired Immunodeficiency Syndrome education in schools. *Pediatrics* 101(5): 933–935.

Council of Chief State School Officers. (2000). *Key state education policies on K–12 education 2000: Time and attendance, graduation requirements, content standards, teacher licensure, school leader licensure, student assessment.* Washington, DC: Author.

Educational Broadcasting Corporation. (2004). *Workshop: Inquiry-based learning.* Thirteen ed. online. Retrieved September 14, 2005, from http://www.thirteen.org/edonline/concept2class/inquiry/index.html.

Goodwin, S. (2003). Health conundrums. *American Journal of Health Education* 34(1): 56–59.

Henry J. Kaiser Family Foundation. (2000). *Sex education in America: Summary of findings (2000).* Menlo Park, CA: Author.

Joint Committee on National Health Education Standards. (1995). *National health education standards: Achieving health literacy.* Atlanta, GA: American Cancer Society.

Joint United Nations Programme on HIV/AIDS. (1997). *Learning and teaching about AIDS at school.* Retrieved September 8, 2005, from http://www.unaids.org/html/pub/publications/irc-pub04/schooltu_en_pdf.pdf.

Joint United Nations Programme on HIV/AIDS. (2004). *Epidemiology.* Retrieved September 8, 2005, from http://www.unaids.org/en/resources/epidemiology.asp.

Kirby, D. (1997). *No easy answers: Research findings on programs to reduce teen pregnancy.* Washington, DC: National Campaign to Prevent Teen Pregnancy.

Kirby, D. (2002). Effective approaches to reducing adolescent unprotected sex, pregnancy, and childbearing. *Journal of Sex Research* 39(1): 51–57.

Kirby, D., Short, L., and Collins, J. (1994). School-based programs to reduce sexual risk behaviors: A review of effectiveness. *Public Health Reports* 109(3): 339–360.

McKay, M., Chasse, K., McKinney, L., Baptiste, D., Coleman, D., Madison, S., et al. (2004). Family-level impact of the CHAMP family program: A community collaborative effort to support urban families and reduce youth HIV risk exposure. *Family Process* 43(1): 79–92.

Mueller, D., Bidwell, R., Okamoto, S., and Mann, E. (1998). Preventing HIV disease in adolescents. In J. Wordarski and B. Thyer, eds., *Handbook of empirical social work: Social problems and practice issues* (pp. 1–20). New York: Wiley.

National Association of State Boards of Education. (2005). *Healthy schools.* Retrieved September 8, 2005, from http://www.nasbe.org/Healthy-Schools/States/Federal_Laws.html.

National Board for Professional Teaching Standards. (2002). *Health education standards for teachers of students ages 11–18+.* Arlington, VA: Author.

National Council for Accreditation of Teacher Education. (2000). *Program standards for elementary teacher preparation: Standard 2g.* Retrieved September 14, 2005, from http://www.acei.org/rubrics2g.htm.

National Council for Accreditation of Teacher Education. (2005). *Program standards and report forms: Health education.* Retrieved September 14, 2005, from http://www.ncate.org/public/programStandards. asp?ch=4#AAHE.

Pateman, B. (2003). *Linking national subject standards with priority health-risk issues in PK–12 curricula and teacher education programs.* Washington, DC: American Association of Colleges for Teacher Education.

Pinzon-Perez, H. (2003). Lessons from developing countries: Health education in the global village. *American Journal of Health Education* 34(2): 101–103.

Sileo, T. W., Prater, M. A., Luckner, J. L., Rhine, B., and Rude, H. A. (1998). Strategies to facilitate preservice teachers' active involvement in learning. *Teacher Education and Special Education* 21(3): 187–204.

U.S. Department of Health and Human Services. (2000, November). *Healthy people 2010: Understanding and improving health.* 2nd ed. Washington, DC: U.S. Government Printing Office.

Wooley, S. F. (1995). Behavioral mapping: A tool for identifying priorities for health education curricula and instruction. *Journal of Health Education* 26(4): 200–206.

7

PREPARING TEACHERS AS PREVENTION AGENTS: AN ON-LINE LEARNING COURSE

James M. Mitchell, Farah A. Ramirez-Marrero,
and Mose Yvonne Brooks Hooks

⊕

> Authentic on-line learning is a multidimensional pursuit. Lifelong learning environments that promote student-centered, self-directed study foster a way of engaging on-line learners in a voyage of personal discovery. Such an educational journey can lead to a transformative learning encounter where on-line learners can better understand themselves and the changing world in which they live.... This type of participatory environment represents the pathway to genuine engagement.
>
> —*Ryan, 2005, p. vii*

This "voyage of personal discovery" transpires in a nonthreatening atmosphere in which the learner has the freedom to choose to be inspired, motivated, and empowered (Ryan, 2005). This environment is well suited to goal-oriented adult learners who already possess a rich reservoir of experience. An ambiance of mutual respect, appreciation for previous experience, collegial rapport, equity, shared authority, and participation creates a climate that is both safe and stimulating. Such an environment can be particularly effective for teaching and learning about HIV/AIDS prevention using problem-solving orientations that consistently offer a message of hope and inclusion.

Some learning environments are optimal for on-line education. To enter such an atmosphere one must first approach the affective domain. Brain research indicates that on-line learners think through their feelings (Knowles, 1980, 1984; Ryan, 2005); how the student feels about what is to be taught can virtually open or close the door to cognitive learning. The affective domain, which includes inspiration, motivation, and empowerment (Ryan, 2005), is primal to learning. One's affective disposition overlays one's cognitive ability. This chapter aims to give educators a coherent approach to the on-line learner through one example of an HIV/AIDS education course designed by three academic professionals.

PROFILE OF ON-LINE LEARNERS

Developers of on-line courses for adult students might begin by considering Malcolm Knowles's (1984) research on teaching adults; the adult learning model, or *andragogy*, posits that adults learn differently than children or adolescents. Adult learners tend to be self-directed, experienced, goal-oriented, and motivated (Knowles, 1984).

To match the first trait, educators might employ a model of self-directed education, an inherently empowering notion that puts the responsibility for one's education squarely on the learner (Knowles, 1980, 1984). In an on-line course, for example, adult learners could be given a variety of assignments from which to choose (Ryan, 2005). The second characteristic of adult learners, life experience, provides a unique basis for the associative processes that learning entails. Adults who are given opportunities to tell their life stories, within the context of what is being studied, combine practice with theory—a strong learning paradigm. In addition, the use of analogies related to common experiences among adult learners is an effective way to introduce new ideas (Ryan, 2005).

Knowles (1984) identified the third characteristic of adult learners as goal orientation, based on adults' inclination to complete a specific task or goal, in contrast to the subject matter orientation typical of younger learners. Hence, education or training that leads to the accomplishment of a specific goal is critical for the adult learner, particularly in an on-line environment where there is usually no face-to-face interaction. Students need to see evidence of their progress through regular feedback on assignments, discussions, and electronic questioning. Goal orientation is especially prevalent among mature learners who are working toward a diploma or other credential—and ultimately a job. Correspondingly, the personal intrinsic drive of motivation, the fourth characteristic identified by Knowles (1984), becomes the engine that inspires and ultimately empowers the adult learner to succeed (Ryan, 2005). Because adult learners are generally motivated to learn (intrinsic factors) instead of needing external motivation (extrinsic factors), such as incentives, on-line educators of adults need to know how to create an environment that nurtures their inspiration.

In sum, the enlightened on-line educator of adults should provide a learner-centered instructional setting that provides opportunities for self-directed, task-oriented experiences from learners who bring experience and motivation to the learning venue. When the learner's goal-oriented aspirations are valued (an affective occurrence), the cognitive and psychomotor domains can follow with step-by-step strategies to think, plan, and act. This synergistic interaction among the three domains produces practical learning.

Robert Boyd (1991), expanding on Carl Jung's notion of individuation, delved into the affective nature of adult learning by examining psychosocial aspects and the critical role that the dynamic unconscious mind plays in sculpting feelings and thoughts. The feelings that emerge during the learning process stem from unconscious concerns. These concerns, independent from the conscious ego, emanate from compulsions, impulses, complexes, and even obsessions. Transformation occurs when students begin to understand themselves and the world through mythopoetic images rather than through concepts or words (Brookfield, 1999). To interconnect the cognitive and the affective, adult educators might use ancient myths and contemporary narratives to present archetypes that traverse students' imagination, dialogue, and writing.

The course described here, which focuses on the biological, psychosocial, and curriculum perspective of HIV/AIDS education, holds true to these principles.

A WORLDWIDE PLATFORM FOR HIV/AIDS EDUCATION

HIV/AIDS directly or indirectly affects us all. The physical and emotional burden of this epidemic makes us all vulnerable and in need of finding ways to effectively prevent its spread and improve the quality of life of those already infected or otherwise affected by it. While we wait for a cure, education and prevention are our best defense against HIV/AIDS. Teachers must be prepared to become prevention agents. On-line learning provides a unique opportunity for all teachers—both in-service and preservice—to expand their professional training by participating in a learning community that has no geographical boundaries.

HIV/AIDS EDUCATION IN TEACHER PREPARATION PROGRAMS

The infusion of HIV/AIDS education into teacher preparation programs is a challenge to many institutions of higher education because of their limited capacity to expand an already overloaded curriculum. Creative ways must be found to provide teachers with tools to help them integrate HIV/AIDS education into activities for their students inside and outside the classroom. Here, we present a model developed by three institutions—California State University, East Bay; Langston University; and University of Puerto Rico–Rio Piedras—to help infuse HIV/AIDS education experience into teacher preparation programs. The institutions were demonstration sites funded by the American Association of Colleges for Teacher Education (AACTE) through its initiative with the Centers for Disease Control and Prevention (CDC) called Build a Future Without AIDS. The model is an on-line course for teacher education students at all three universities to communicate with each other.

ABOUT THE COLLABORATING INSTITUTIONS

California State University, East Bay is one of the 23 California State Universities and has campuses in Hayward, Concord, and Oakland. For the Build a Future Without AIDS project, students in two teacher education courses, TED 5351—Psychological Foundations of Education and TED 6901—Graduate Synthesis, were taught a conflict resolution and an AIDS education curriculum. TED 5351 students participated by traveling in pairs to two high school sites and teaching the AIDS education curriculum using the conflict-resolution framework known as *academic controversy* (see chapter 4 or http://www.co-operation.org). TED 6901 students traveled in three- and four-member groups to visit two separate sites with the Alameda County Office of Education (ACOE).

The high school students who received the curriculum were part of the continuation day school population for ACOE, which

provides educational services for students ages 12 to 17 who are "at risk" of dropping out of school. The program is an alternative "regular" education program designed primarily to serve youth who are wards or dependents of the court or status offenders (incorrigible) and who are under the supervision of the Juvenile Court, Probation Department, or Social Services Agency. The program provides small classrooms staffed with credentialed teachers and instructional aides. Each student's academic educational needs are assessed and addressed through a self-paced, highly structured, individualized instructional program. The students in the program receive supervision and counseling services from Probation, Social Services, or community-based organizations.... Referral to the program is through the Hayward [CA] District interagency discipline hearing committee which is chaired by the school district of residence. (Alameda County Office of Education, 2005)

These ACOE students had been expelled from previous traditional assignments, and many had served time in juvenile hall.

The second participating institution, Langston University, is one of the 117 historically Black colleges and universities (HBCUs) in the nation and the only one in the state of Oklahoma. The university's student body is approximately 47 percent African American, 46 percent Caucasian, and 7 percent other. As of 1978, the university adopted an urban mission and established upper-division urban centers in Tulsa and Oklahoma City. The university's School of Education and Behavioral Sciences took leadership for the Build a Future Without AIDS program as part of its effort to identify and address vital issues of concern for the community.

The Build a Future Without AIDS project's goals were (a) to provide opportunities for teacher education majors and public school personnel to develop and evaluate curriculum to be used with junior high and high school students; (b) to enhance the students' knowledge related to HIV/AIDS and other infectious diseases; and (c) to provide a forum for preservice and in-service teachers to discuss the HIV/AIDS problems that relate to education in public schools.

The program objectives included researching curriculum on HIV/AIDS prevention; developing curriculum related to the topic with personnel from partner public schools; compiling curriculum guides; offering workshops and seminars to share HIV/AIDS curriculum; and participating in an international HIV/AIDS conference at the university. In addition, the project incorporated Build a Future Without AIDS curricula in the following courses in the teacher education program: educational sociology, classroom management, instructional strategies, clinical teaching seminar, and clinical teaching. In the latter three courses, candidates developed and studied lesson plans that could be implemented across the curriculum in all content areas. Opportunities for developing the HIV/AIDS and health-related curricula are available during each course at the present time.

The third participating institution, the University of Puerto Rico (UPR), Rio Piedras, has the oldest accredited teacher preparation program in Puerto Rico. About 3,500 undergraduate and more than 500 graduate students enroll in more than 11 different areas of specialty in teacher education instructed by over 200 faculty members. With the grant from AACTE, a project was set in motion to infuse HIV/AIDS education into the program. The project started with a 2-day conference and focus group discussions in which faculty, students, supervising teachers, cooperating teachers, and community members shared knowledge, experiences, and ideas about HIV/AIDS education and prevention. The conference covered topics such as social, cultural, and historical aspects of HIV/AIDS; legal aspects and human rights; risk behaviors among adolescents; the biological aspects of the infection and the disease; and educational strategies for HIV/AIDS integration into the school curriculum. Focus groups discussions concentrated on designing educational activities into which HIV/AIDS education could be integrated.

From the information provided in the conference and focus group activities, a manual titled *HIV/AIDS Education and Prevention: A Guide for Teachers* was developed. The manual, written in Spanish, contains information on HIV/AIDS from biological, social, cultural, and emotional perspectives; curricular issues; and practical activities for the classroom categorized by subject matter and grade level. A graduate student wrote a short animated story for the manual. Over 2 years, the project also sponsored 1-day seminars for student teachers each semester. All participants received a variety of handouts with HIV/AIDS prevention information. A copy of the manual was also developed in digital format.

The UPR College of Education has integrated the seminar on HIV/AIDS education and prevention into each semester's official calendar of events for student teachers. Approximately 70 to 100 student teachers have participated per semester in the lectures and discussions offered during the seminars. They continue to receive HIV/AIDS prevention materials and the manual in digital format free of charge.

DEVELOPING AN ON-LINE LEARNING COURSE ON HIV/AIDS EDUCATION: A MULTIDISCIPLINARY AND INTERINSTITUTIONAL MODEL

Humanizing pedagogy through on-line learning about HIV/AIDS might sound incongruent to those who think of computers and electronic communications as cold and impersonal. However, the unlimited opportunities for interaction between students and teachers from different geographical locations can make it a very humanizing experience. To achieve this goal, effective on-line class activities must be constructed that facilitate interaction and account for different levels of experience among participants and different areas of expertise of instructors. Because on-line learning activities are heavily dependent on students' participation, instructors must assume a facilitating/moderating role, leaving aside the authoritative behavior that teachers sometimes exhibit in a regular classroom. Participants must be able to easily navigate through the on-line platform, find the information needed, perform the tasks assigned, and submit their work without unnecessary frustrations. Assignments must provoke the participants' curiosity and challenge them to read, reflect, and ultimately engage in effective and provocatively profound discussions and arguments in writing.

As a continuation of their involvement in the Build a Future Without AIDS project, the authors developed a preliminary on-line learning experience focusing on the basic biological, psychosocial and emotional, and curriculum aspects of HIV/AIDS education and prevention. The instructors' differing expertise facilitated the course's multidisciplinary perspective. The course was offered bilingually, as Spanish is the primary language of one of the author/instructors. The bilingual conceptual map for this initial course is presented in Figure 7.1.

ELECTRONIC PLATFORM

Blackboard (Bb®) is the electronic platform selected for the development of the HIV/AIDS on-line learning course. When students enter the course after accessing Bb® through the Internet, they first see an announcement screen with the following message:

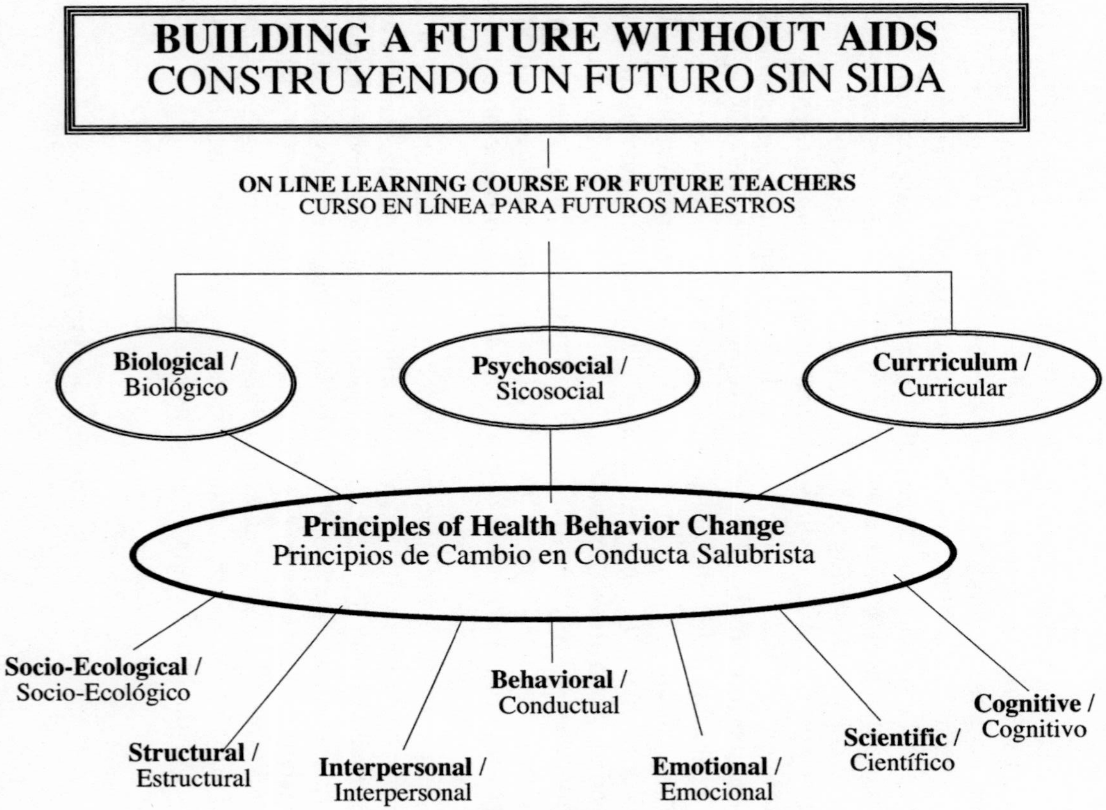

BUILDING A FUTURE WITHOUT AIDS
CONSTRUYENDO UN FUTURO SIN SIDA

ON LINE LEARNING COURSE FOR FUTURE TEACHERS
CURSO EN LÍNEA PARA FUTUROS MAESTROS

Biological / Biológico

Psychosocial / Sicosocial

Curriculum / Curricular

Principles of Health Behavior Change
Principios de Cambio en Conducta Salubrista

Socio-Ecological / Socio-Ecológico

Structural / Estructural

Interpersonal / Interpersonal

Behavioral / Conductual

Emotional / Emocional

Scientific / Científico

Cognitive / Cognitivo

Figure 7.1

104

Welcome to this HIV/AIDS online learning course. By participating in this course you will have the unique opportunity to share with three professors and students from three different academic institutions: the University of Puerto Rico, California State University at East Bay, and Langston University in Oklahoma. The course has been divided in four sections: Introduction, Biological Perspective, Psychosocial and Emotional Perspective, and Curriculum Issues. For more details of each section, objectives, and course policies (participation and grading), please read the course syllabus located under Course Information. Most of the reading materials are located under Course Documents. Browse through the buttons at the left side of the screen to get familiarized with all that is offered in this online learning environment.

We will be using this announcement page to keep you updated about class activities, deadlines for assignments, and any changes that might occur as we move along. Also, under Tools, you will find the course calendar.

After you read the course syllabus, please introduce yourself in the "Coffee break" discussion board. We hope that this experience contributes to your personal and professional growth as an educator. (*AACTE HIV Distance Learning Course Web Site,* 2005)

The announcement screen also offers the navigation buttons that allow the student to see and download documents, submit documents, participate in discussions, prepare a home page, organize in groups, send collective or individual e-mails, complete evaluation instruments (exams, surveys, quizzes), check their grades, and link to other Web sites related to the course.

COORDINATING THE COLLABORATION: ON-LINE TEAM TEACHING

The course's three instructors used a "division of labor" teaching model in which each takes charge of one perspective corresponding to his or her area of expertise (Ko and Rossen, 2004). Instructors post assignments and evaluate students' work accordingly. While each instructor is expected to keep track of discussions in all sections, active participation from all instructors occurs only in the introductory section. The on-line course syllabus details the timeframe for each course section, the name of the instructor, deadlines to submit assignments, and expected date of evaluation.

An on-line course syllabus needs to be more explicit than a traditional syllabus, presenting a complete course outline. Because this document represents a contractual agreement between the instructors and the course participants, it should present a clear "geography" of the course. Instructors must agree on every aspect of the syllabus. Some elements to consider include:

- course description
- goals and objectives
- schedule of topics, readings, activities, and assignments
- expected outcomes
- terms of class interaction, including ethical and confidentiality issues
- grading policies and procedures
- ethics, discipline, and confidentiality
- policy on late assignments / time zone considerations
- opportunities for synchronous activities (virtual office, chat)

ON-LINE INTERACTIONS AMONG PARTICIPANTS

Interaction opportunities among instructors and participants in on-line learning environments must be organized and scheduled. The HIV/AIDS on-line learning course provides electronic discussion boards for the course introduction and for the separate biological, psychosocial and emotional, and curriculum areas. Electronic discussion boards are structured and focused on a particular subject, and the guidelines for participation are provided in advance. However, students also have the opportunity to introduce at least one topic and lead the discussion of that topic for extra credit. A list of readings and Web sites is provided for students to be prepared before the initiation of the electronic discussions. To receive full credit, each student is required to provide at least two postings that contribute to the overall discussion.

The "coffee break" discussion board provides an informal communication opportunity for participants to introduce themselves and share non–class-related topics, although the course's ethics and discipline guidelines also apply in this informal setting. In order for classmates and instructors to put a human face to a name, each student is required to create a home page, including a photo, information about himself or herself (interests, hobbies, and goals), links to favorite Web sites, and expectations about the course. Each participant's home page must be completed by the end of the first week of the course. The Bb® electronic platform also allows participants to send individual and collective electronic mail. Mail is sent to the electronic address indicated by participants when they open the account in the electronic platform.

CONSIDERING LOGISTICAL AND CROSS-CULTURAL ISSUES

Before launching a course sponsored by multiple institutions, logistical administrative issues such as credits, fees, and instructors' time must be determined. In this case, the University of Puerto Rico provides access to the electronic platform. No institutional credit hours are offered, but students do receive a certificate of completion from AACTE. The instructors' time is individually negotiated with their academic institutions. These arrangements and agreements could change as the course develops further.

Cross-cultural exchange is also offered in this HIV/AIDS on-line learning course. Most reading documents and Web sites are provided in both English and Spanish. This provides the opportunity for students to read the materials and search the information in their native language. However, English is the common language used for the discussion boards. Students with difficulty communicating in English are assisted by one instructor and/or course assistant. Students know in advance which instructor will be providing that assistance. Also, at least one discussion board is completely in Spanish.

Time zones are another issue to consider when students from different geographical regions participate in an on-line course. Confusion is avoided when deadlines include the day, month, year, and time zone (e.g., Eastern, Pacific, Atlantic, Central).

ON-LINE DOCUMENTS, SOFTWARE, AND INTERNET COMMUNICATION

For this course, students are required to use Microsoft Office software such as Word and PowerPoint. Documents can be uploaded to the electronic platform or downloaded from the platform using this software. In addition, documents in Office applications can be converted easily to Adobe Portable Document Format (PDF) files, a format that allows users to view and print the documents even if they do not have the originating application. Acrobat Reader, required for viewing PDF files, can be downloaded from the Internet at no cost.

Participants must be aware that long documents with diagrams, figures, and photos can take a long time to download over slower connections. Dividing large documents into a number of smaller pieces is recommended to give students easier access. Also, documents that will not be discussed during the course should not be included on the platform; they take unnecessary space and can cause confusion among participants. Copyright issues also must be considered when posting documents on the electronic platform.

EVALUATION

A grading rubric is useful for showing students exactly what is expected from each assignment. This document is included in the "Course Information" section of Bb® where grading policies are presented. The course syllabus also provides information on the total points needed to receive the certificate of course completion from AACTE. Students can check their progress periodically by searching "My Gradebook" in the "Tools" section of the Bb® electronic platform. With this feature, students are able to see only their own grades.

A VIEW TO FUTURE ON-LINE LEARNING COURSES ON HIV/ AIDS PREVENTION: NEW HEIGHTS OF INNOVATION

Others who plan to undertake a project such as this one should consider the following:

1. Leaders of multi-institution on-line projects should submit detailed plans regarding how they will coordinate the collaboration.
2. Overall logistics should be as clear as possible and understood before the project begins.
3. Some travel may be necessary for face to face communication by the project's leaders in order to build relationships.
4. Meetings, whether face to face or virtual, must be planned in advance because of differing academic calendars.
5. Cultural and regional differences may arise during the collaboration, and policies among institutions may conflict.
6. Students on different campuses may use different software.

7. Keeping communication going among on-line course participants must be planned in detail for the course to be successful.
8. Degrees of trust must be developed among participants to share some thoughts. More opportunities to communicate on line may bring about more levels of trust.

HIV/AIDS on-line learning opportunities are needed to continue expanding education and prevention efforts against this pandemic. Teachers as HIV/AIDS prevention agents can take advantage of on-line environments to keep updated with current knowledge and teaching strategies. The course described here is an introductory one with three different perspectives: biological, psychosocial, and emotional. However, each perspective could become an independent on-line course and more perspectives could be explored. For example, the economical, political, epidemiological, and sociocultural aspects of HIV/AIDS could be developed as independent courses.

REFERENCES

AACTE HIV Distance Learning Course Web Site. (2005). Available to subscribers at http://virtual.uprrp.edu.

Alameda County Office of Education. (2005). *Juvenile court schools and community day schools.* Retrieved September 30, 2005, from http://www.alameda-coe.k12.ca.us/apps/page.asp?Q=291andT=Pages.

Boyd, R. D., ed. (1991). *Personal transformations in small groups: A Jungian perspective.* London: Routledge.

Brookfield, S. D. (1999). What is college really like for adult students? *About Campus* 3(6): 10–15.

Knowles, M. S. (1980). *The modern practice of adult education.* Rev. ed. Chicago: Association Press/Follett.

Knowles, M. S. (1984). Introduction: The art and science of helping adults learn. In *Andragogy in action: Applying modern principles of adult learning.* San Francisco: Jossey-Bass.

Ko, S., and Rossen, S. (2004). *Teaching online: A practical guide.* 2nd ed. Boston: Houghton Mifflin.

Ryan, M. (2005). *Ask the professor: A practitioner's guide to setting an environment for professional development.* Boston: Pearson Education.

PART III
DIVERSITY IN TEACHING AND LEARNING

Overview, *Thomas W. Sileo*

⊕

Educators in the United States and across the world face many challenges related to social, economic, and political contexts that are difficult to address in school settings. HIV/AIDS prevention may be one of the greatest contemporary challenges in the field of education, as the disease can affect all individuals. Teaching and learning about its prevention requires honest discussions of issues associated with the epidemic. Such conversations in educator preparation programs enhance teachers' awareness and understanding of ways the disease affects a variety of populations. Furthermore, the discussions help to increase educators' tolerance to address the topic and facilitate acceptance of differences.

Teacher preparation programs, because of their ability to reach the majority of future educators, might be the most critical factor in ensuring comprehensive and effective HIV/AIDS prevention education for all children, youth, and young adults. Teachers must understand the social, political, economic, and human rights repercussions that surround the disease as bases for designing, implementing, and evaluating HIV/AIDS prevention programs. This section of the book, about diversity in teaching and learning, explores the inherent value of diversity to all mankind as well as its power to democratize teaching and learning processes. In a democratic environment, differences may become agents that amplify people's perspectives.

This section includes four chapters, each of which considers issues of diversity and their implications for designing HIV/AIDS prevention education. The chapters present a rich portrait regarding the extent of HIV/AIDS across the nation and around the world by focusing on human rights issues as well as on topics related to ethnicity, gender, socialization, sexual orientation, and people's HIV-positive or HIV-negative status.

First, Sileo and Sileo examine human rights implications of the disease and the impact of concomitant vulnerabilities on the spread of the disease. In addition, they consider improvements to teachers' knowledge, skills, and dispositions that are necessary to develop and implement HIV/AIDS prevention programs.

Hooks, Sileo, and Mazzotti address influences of people's origins, sociohistorical experiences, and ecological adaptations on decisions to engage in risk behaviors that heighten their susceptibility to HIV/AIDS. They offer suggestions for developing HIV/AIDS prevention programs that address the cultural, linguistic, and religious construction of family values.

Blanchett and Prater focus on the intersection of sexuality, disability, and HIV/AIDS. They address the importance of educational equity to ensure access to contextualized HIV/AIDS curricula and instructional strategies that complement students' cognitive, behavioral, and learning styles; home and community experiences; and active participation in learning. In addition, they provide insight into the preparation of general, special, and health education teachers to accommodate the learning needs of students with disabilities regarding HIV/AIDS.

The chapter by Fennell, with contributions from Parker, concerns the effects of male socialization, gender role theories, and issues of sexuality, race, and ethnicity on men's sexual behaviors and HIV/AIDS. These authors offer examples to illustrate the impact of socialization on men's behaviors and to heighten teachers' understanding about men's decisions and behavioral choices. Finally, they suggest methods and approaches to build effective HIV/AIDS prevention messages that influence positive behavioral change.

Rather than including separate chapters on the impact of injection drug use and male and female prostitution on the spread of HIV/AIDS, this section addresses these issues throughout its chapters. Injection drug users and commercial sex workers contribute significantly to the magnitude of HIV infections worldwide and in the United States. Educators should understand these linkages as a foundation for developing and implementing comprehensive and effective prevention curriculum and instructional practices.

8
HIV/AIDS: A GLOBAL HUMAN RIGHTS ISSUE

Nancy M. Sileo and Thomas W. Sileo

⊷

> What does it say about the world that we can tolerate the slow and
> unnecessary death of millions [from AIDS] whose lives would be
> rescued with treatment? The tsunami must be seen to be the turning
> point. The publics of the world have shown their desperate concern
> for the human condition. How long will it take for governments to
> do the same?
>
> —*Stephen Lewis, United Nations Special Envoy for HIV/AIDS in Africa,*
> *Joint United Nations Programme on HIV/AIDS (UNAIDS), 2005*

The United Nations (1992) defines human rights as "those rights which
are inherent in our nature and without which we cannot live as human
beings. Human rights and fundamental freedoms allow us to fully develop and use our human qualities, our intelligence, our talents, and our
conscience to satisfy our spiritual and other needs. They are basic for
mankind's increasing demand for a life in which the inherent dignity and
worth of each human being will receive respect and protection" (p. 5).

Denial of human rights results in tragedy and triggers political unrest,
violence, and conflict among individuals, groups, and nations. Human
rights violations occur daily as AIDS assaults people in the prime of their
lives and each day causes an estimated 8,500 slow, painful, and costly
deaths (UNAIDS, 2004a). The disease does not discriminate according to race, religion, age, gender, sexual orientation, national origin,
or economic and social status. For the first time in the 20-year history
of the disease, as many women as men are identified with HIV/AIDS.
The shift toward women exacerbates the spread of disease through
unprotected sexual activity, childbirth, and breast-feeding.

Current trends indicate that AIDS will be the leading infectious killer during the next 20 years and cause the deaths of tens of millions of people (Piot, as cited in Clifton, 2003). The pandemic is spreading at alarming rates in Eastern Europe, Central Asia, and China, where it was almost nonexistent a few years ago. In addition, it continues to spread in sub-Saharan Africa as well as the Caribbean Islands, where Haiti is the epicenter of the disease. HIV/AIDS in Haiti is transferred primarily through heterosexual contact; it affects more than 235,000 adults and 11,000 children, of whom 80 percent live in abject poverty (Winfield, 2003).

AIDS threatens to destabilize countries, including strategically important nations such as China, Russia, and India, and disrupt their social, political, and economic growth. Moreover, the disease decimates entire generations of families and diminishes ethnic and cultural heritage. According to Clifton (2004), "While weapons of mass destruction and terrorism have the capacity to kill in a moment of violence, AIDS has proven that it can and does destroy the social and economic structure of communities and countries—slowly and silently" (p. 17).

Investment in HIV/AIDS prevention is critical if we are to save people's lives, preserve families and communities, and maintain the current balance of power. Many governments and other groups and individuals are making such an investment through the Global Fund to Fight AIDS, Tuberculosis, and Malaria, established at the prompting of United Nations Secretary General Kofi Annan to direct resources to regions affected most by these diseases (Piot, as cited in Clifton, 2003). This chapter addresses (a) the extent of HIV/AIDS on international and national bases; (b) human rights issues that contribute to the spread of disease and that confront people with HIV/AIDS; and (c) practices that help deter spread of the epidemic.

HIV/AIDS: A WORLDWIDE PERSPECTIVE

The spread of HIV infection results from behavioral risks, including sexual transmission patterns, injection drug use with contaminated needles, and mother-to-child transmission. Furthermore, ecological risks such as widespread malnutrition and preexisting infectious diseases deter the body's ability to fight sickness. According to UNAIDS (2004c), in 2003, there were an estimated 5 million new HIV infections, more than any other year since the beginning of the pandemic. From

2002 to 2004 alone, there were 5.6 million AIDS-related deaths, which added to the existing 24.8 million deaths, worldwide, since beginning of the epidemic. Approximately 610,000 of the deaths in that 2-year period were among children (UNAIDS, 2004b, 2004c).

Most people with HIV/AIDS live in nations other than the United States. At the end of 2003, an estimated 42 million people worldwide, including 38.6 million adults and 3.2 million children younger than 15 years of age, were infected with HIV/AIDS. This number had increased fourfold in the preceding 12 years. Currently, there are about 14,000 new HIV infections daily with more than 40 percent among young people who are 15 to 24 years of age (UNAIDS, 2004b, 2004c).

Approximately 29.4 million people with HIV/AIDS (70 percent of cases worldwide) live in sub-Saharan Africa and another 7.2 million people (17 percent) in Eurasia. About 30 percent of all adults ages 15 to 49 in four African countries are identified with HIV infection. Adult infections in Botswana have reached an unimaginable 40 percent of the population.

Africa's AIDS catastrophe is a humanitarian disaster of historic proportions with concomitant economic and political reverberations within the African continent. Fewer repercussions occur outside Africa due to the area's marginal status in global economics and politics. Circumstances differ, however, in other regions of the world with rapid spread of HIV infection. Eurasia, which is home to a majority of the global population, has great economic, political, and military power. Estimates indicate that the crisis could shift from Africa to Eurasia within the next generation. The unfolding HIV/AIDS epidemic in Russia, India, and China will have major ramifications that affect the balance of economic and political power throughout the world (Eberstadt, 2002).

The infection rate in Russia is soaring, with an estimated 1.5 million reported HIV/AIDS cases. The spread of the disease is due to societal transitions and rapid changes in economic status over the past 10 years, which have led to social dislocation and poverty. In addition, new freedoms associated with the collapse of the Soviet Union, such as extramarital sexual intercourse, prostitution, release of prison populations with HIV infection, and rise in the availability of illegal drugs and subsequent injection drug use, contribute to the spread of HIV. Projections indicate that the HIV/AIDS cases in Russia will increase to 5 to 8 million people and have a 6 to 10 percent prevalence rate by the end of the decade (Eberstadt, 2002).

An estimated 4 to 8 million people are infected with HIV in India, where the virus occurs in major urban areas as a result of injection drug use and unprotected sexual activity among men who engage in extramarital affairs, sex with other men, and commercial sex workers and who, in turn, infect their spouses and female partners. Contributing factors to the spread of the epidemic include strong taboos about discussing sex, power imbalances between men and women, widespread discrimination against people with the disease, and poverty. Projections indicate that by 2010, HIV/AIDS cases in India will increase to 20 to 25 million people and have a 3 to 4 percent prevalence rate (Eberstadt, 2002; Piot, as cited in Clifton, 2003).

India now accounts for at least 10 percent of global HIV infections, a rate second only to South Africa's. Many of the people understand little about the disease, suffer from stigma and discrimination, and lack access to quality health care. The impact of the country's epidemic is obscured by India's huge population of over a billion people who live in its vast regions and speak different languages. A seemingly current low national prevalence rate of less than 1 percent can equate to a large number of infected people.

Between 850,000 and 6 million people in China are infected with HIV; according to Eberstadt (2002), an overwhelming majority of current and new infections in China are undocumented and untreated, so estimates rely heavily on guesswork. The spread of disease occurs primarily among rural poor people and transient migrant workers, who typically have little knowledge about the disease and condom use. The migrant workers most often are young, male laborers who travel extensively between rural and urban areas and engage in unprotected sex with commercial sex workers. Other causes of infection include heterosexual marital intercourse, injection drug use, and commercial sex employed by "unmarriageable males"—the surplus of men, resulting from China's policy of one child per family, who often have no alternative sexual outlet over the course of their lives (Cook, Flynn, Merchant, and Pietrandoni, 2003). Gay men are also an emergent high-risk group.

The sale of contaminated blood in the 1990s contributed greatly to unprecedented increases in HIV infections in China. An estimated 250,000 poor people were infected after selling blood to commercial companies that used unhygienic procedures. The blood centers pooled and centrifuged blood from paid donors, separated the plasma, and then reinfused the red blood cells to the donors so they could sell blood more frequently without incurring anemia. The practice, unfortunately, turned out to be a very efficient way to transmit HIV infection. Forecasts project that HIV/AIDS cases in China will increase to 10 to 20 million people by the end of the decade and have a 1.3 to 2.5 percent prevalence rate (Cohen, 2004b; Eberstadt, 2002; Piot, as cited in Clifton, 2003).

AIDS is the leading cause of death among men 15 to 44 years old in the English-speaking Caribbean and among women of the same age in the Dominican Republic. The rate of infection is increasing among expectant mothers in the Dominican Republic, where many male spouses desert their sick mates and children.

Children abandoned by the disease are filling orphanages and children's homes worldwide. They are stigmatized by and marginalized from society through their association with HIV/AIDS and plunged into economic crises and insecurity by their parents' deaths (Bok and Morales, 2002). Furthermore, these children are malnourished, uneducated, and damaged psychologically, and they have a higher risk of becoming infected with the disease (Vazquez, 2003). Children who are orphaned by AIDS are subject to more exploitation and abuse than other orphans. They also struggle without services and extended support systems in impoverished communities burdened by violence.

Estimates regarding the extent of the epidemic are only the tip of the iceberg when one considers the long incubation period for AIDS. The prognosis for the pandemic depends on governmental recognition of and response to the disease, which should include monitoring the spread of infection, engaging in campaigns for public awareness and prevention education, tending to curable sexually transmitted diseases that fuel spread of HIV infection, and intervening with HIV-risk groups to encourage behavior change and lifestyles that court fewer dangers (Eberstadt, 2002).

HIV/AIDS: A UNITED STATES PERSPECTIVE

In the United States, an estimated 42,000 people are identified with AIDS each year. The disease is increasing most notably among women, through heterosexual contact, as well as among young men from diverse racial, ethnic, and cultural communities who engage in sex with men. Recent success in treating HIV/AIDS raises concerns that the United States public may be growing complacent about prevention. Many people who engage in sex with multiple partners, both men and women, often do not use condoms (Allan and Leonard, 2005; Sanchez, 2005;

Vazquez, 2004). Vazquez notes that people are more likely to engage in unprotected sex if they feel optimistic about sexual risk-taking.

AIDS is the fifth leading cause of death among all Americans 25 to 44 years of age. It is the leading cause of death among African American women ages 25 to 34 and the third leading cause of death among African American men of the same age. The Centers for Disease Control and Prevention (2003) estimates that as of the end of 2002, 161,976 Americans were living with HIV infection and 362,827 people had AIDS. Approximately 37 percent were Caucasian, 42 percent were African American, 20 percent were Hispanic, and 1 percent were Asian/Pacific Islander Americans, American Indians, or Alaska Natives.

Fortunately, AIDS is on the verge of elimination among babies in the United States as a result of safer sex practices, better drugs such as AZT, and more rigorous testing among pregnant women to identify their HIV status prior to giving birth. AZT, when taken during the second trimester of pregnancy and administered during labor, reduces presence of the virus in the mother's bloodstream and significantly reduces chances of mother-to-child transmission (Santora, 2005).

HIV/AIDS AND HUMAN RIGHTS ISSUES

The battle against HIV/AIDS affects human rights and has social, political, and economic implications. The disease reduces life expectancy and derails economic progress in developing countries. Discrimination against women, children, and other exploited groups plays a major role in the spread of HIV. Moreover, adolescent sexuality receives little or no attention in many countries, thereby contributing to increases of HIV/AIDS among this population. Human rights issues related to HIV/AIDS include (a) gender inequity and lack of women's rights; (b) discrimination against HIV-positive persons and others at risk of infection; (c) lack of adequate HIV/AIDS prevention education for children, youth, and young adults; and (d) global inequities regarding the availability and distribution of health care resources (Bok and Morales, 2002; Eberstadt, 2002).

Gender Inequity and Lack of Women's Rights

Cultural norms and taboos often thwart HIV/AIDS prevention efforts. In many instances, there are vast cultural differences in attitudes toward sexuality among men and women. In many cultures, promiscuity is more acceptable in men, which exposes them to heightened risk of infection and increases the possibility that they will transmit HIV to their female partners.

Worldwide, women with HIV suffer stigma, discrimination, and isolation. They often are shunned by family members and neighbors or even stoned to death, and their children may be ostracized in school (Clifton, 2004). Women comprise half of all adults with HIV/AIDS. Their HIV risk status is heightened due to efficient transmission of infection through vaginal intercourse (Faryna and Morales, 2000); vulnerability to silence and denial about HIV/AIDS because sex is not discussed in many cultures; expectations of submissiveness in sexual relations; and traditions of polygamy and multiple partners among men.

Moreover, women are increasingly more susceptible to infection due to poverty and powerlessness. They lack power to negotiate sexual relationships because of gender inequities as well as lower social and economic status (Bok and Morales, 2002; Cervero, 2005). In some instances, women are forced to exchange sex for survival and sustenance (Clifton, 2004); an estimated 20 percent of prostitutes in Vietnam are HIV-positive. In sub-Saharan Africa, two times as many women as men have HIV/AIDS, and in South Africa alone, 25 percent of women experience forced initial sexual experiences. Many South Africans perceive sexual violence against women in marital and nonmarital relationships as a legitimate expression of masculinity.

In China, men's extramarital affairs and the commercial sex trade are devastating to women who believe they are protected from disease because they remain monogamous to their husbands. Women with HIV/AIDS are more likely to experience family rejection and be denied treatment, care, and basic human rights. Yet they bear the burden of caring for spouses, brothers, and fathers with HIV/AIDS. Widows and children in rural China who are forced to work often turn to commercial sex or other harsh labor conditions for survival (Cook et al., 2003).

Women in South Asia have the lowest status in the world (Bok and Morales, 2002; Cohen, 2004a; Eberstadt, 2002). In India, high illiteracy levels among women and taboos concerning sexually transmitted diseases preclude availability of information about HIV risks. In addition, abstinence is not preached or practiced, and public discussion of sexual conduct is limited. Women are uninformed about sex when they wed, often to older men, in marriages arranged by families. Condom use is forbidden, and women who become infected with HIV, even as a result of their husbands' sexual indiscretions, may experience rejection and life-threatening abuse. Often, their husbands' parents and other family members blame them for bringing the disease into their homes.

Women account for approximately 25 percent of HIV infections in India, and nearly 90 percent of those who are sero-positive have monogamous relationships. According to Bok and Morales (2002), women with HIV/AIDS resist disclosure because of the sexual stigma associated with the disease; this secrecy inadvertently erects a barrier to prevention.

In the United States, HIV/AIDS among women from diverse ethnic communities results primarily from injection drug use and heterosexual relationships. Approximately 45 percent of American Indian and Alaska Native women with HIV indicate exposure through contaminated needles. African American, Asian/Pacific Islander, and Hispanic women, on the other hand, report exposure occurrences primarily through heterosexual contact with older men who are HIV-positive and high health-risk partners (Centers for Disease Control and Prevention, 2003). Many of these men engage in injection drug use as well as extramarital sexual relationships. Reports substantiate the practice of some Southeast Asian men who live in the United States and engage in unprotected sex behaviors with commercial sex workers during visits to their native countries. Upon returning to the United States, the men neglect to wear condoms or inform their wives and sex partners of their sexual exploits, thereby contributing to the increased incidence of HIV/AIDS among American women (Jemmott, Maula, and Bush, 1999). In addition, female commercial sex workers of Asian descent, employed in massage parlors, may participate in unsafe sex practices that place them at risk of sexually transmitted diseases. Their survival needs often take priority over the risk of HIV/AIDS and access to health care (Passar and Johnson, 1996).

Power imbalances between men and women also create problems in sexual communication. Women are not expected to negotiate condom use or ask about their partners' sexual activities. Moreover, they may be expected to share injection drug needles with male sexual partners, a behavior that is related to gender role socialization (Flaskerud, 1995). Drug use prior to and during sexual activity diminishes judgment and inhibitions and decreases condom use. Furthermore, some women act in a helpless and servile manner in the presence of potential male sexual partners and therefore do not insist on condom use (Amorampah, 1989; Fullilove, Fullilove, Haynes, and Gross, 1990). Finally, women may be unaware of their partners' unprotected sexual behaviors with multiple partners, which could include male-to-male sexual contact. Many men across all racial, ethnic, and cultural groups often identify as heterosexual but engage in clandestine same-sex behaviors even while they are in heterosexual relationships (Bryant, 2004; Clay, 2002; Egan, 2005).

HIV/AIDS prevention campaigns in the United States traditionally have targeted men and overlooked women, especially women of color and those with low economic status. Many of these women experience sexual intercourse at a very early age and report multiple sex partners, unintended pregnancies, sexually transmitted diseases, and concerns about a waning pool of partners. They are less likely to report rape, sexual abuse, or abuse of any type (Wyatt et al., 1997).

African American women tend to be less knowledgeable about transmission of HIV through heterosexual exposure than their male counterparts. An estimated 27 percent of African American women live at or below the poverty level. In addition, many women are unemployed and, consequently, have limited access to health education, medical insurance, and medications. The relationship of poverty and ill health helps to explain the unbalanced prevalence of HIV/AIDS among indigent African American women (Duh, 1991). In addition, preexisting poor health, pregnancy, sexually transmitted diseases, and injection drug use may undermine the immune system and facilitate conveyance of HIV infection (Flaskerud, 1995).

As mentioned earlier, Hispanic women are most likely to be infected with HIV through heterosexual contact or injection drug use. One in five Hispanic women in the United States lives in poverty. Poverty, lack of health services and insurance, and limited education increase the risk of exposure to HIV among Hispanic women. Culture and social status may also lead Hispanic women to be reluctant to discuss condom use with their male partners out of fear of emotional or physical abuse or discontinuation of financial support (Centers for Disease Control and Prevention, 2005).

Discrimination Against HIV-Positive Persons and Others At Risk of Disease

Human rights protections for people with HIV/AIDS are a low priority worldwide. Few countries shield people with HIV/AIDS from social discrimination, and some countries require forced quarantine for people with the disease. China, for example, uses a quarantine method and limits access to villages with high incidence rates of HIV/AIDS. Cuba, too, has a modified quarantine approach. The lack of confidential policies and discrimination in workplace, educational, and medical settings are powerful incentives to conceal and misrepresent one's HIV status. People worldwide fear disclosure of their illness and loss of employment, housing, and families (Bok and Morales, 2002).

Discrimination against people with HIV/AIDS, women, children, and other exploited groups is also a major contributor to the spread of the disease. The stigma attached to contracting HIV through extramarital, illicit, or male-to-male sex or through injection drug use has crippled efforts to prevent transmission of the disease in many countries. People would rather not know their HIV status, resist testing and, therefore, unwittingly transmit the disease.

In the United States, the extent of HIV/AIDS among diverse racial, ethnic, and cultural populations must be considered in light of the effects of prejudice and discrimination and their influences on socioeconomic, political, and environmental contexts as well as on equitable access to quality health care (Cervero, 2005). For example, an estimated 84 percent of African Americans live in urban communities with elevated rates of poverty, unemployment, welfare dependency, alcohol and drug use, and sexually transmitted diseases. Infections such as syphilis, gonorrhea, chlamydia, and herpes cause open genital sores, which fuel the sexual spread of HIV (Maldanado, 1999a).

Similarly, two in every five Hispanics 25 years of age and older have not completed high school and are likely to be underemployed or unemployed. Moreover, income levels among Hispanics are comparatively low, with 21.5 percent of all Hispanics in the United States living below the poverty level in 2002 (Human Resources and Services Administration, 2005). Poverty and cultural and language barriers complicate Hispanics' ability to access HIV prevention information, adequate and appropriate health care facilities, and HIV/AIDS treatment programs.

A similar situation exists among Cambodian, Laotian, and Vietnamese Americans, many of whom struggle to survive in urban ghettos. They often have limited access to health care, fall below national poverty levels in income and education, and live amidst violence and drugs. Many Americans of Southeast Asian descent engage in HIV-risk behaviors;

they have the highest rate of pneumocystis carinii pneumonia as their AIDS-defining illness among all racial and ethnic groups (Chen and Hawks, 1995; Eckholdt and Chin, 1997).

Poverty is also endemic among the nation's indigenous populations and advances their poor health and general lack of well-being. Many American Indians and Alaska Natives do not have health insurance or an adequate health care system, which contributes to their lack of awareness about HIV/AIDS; delayed HIV testing, counseling, and diagnosis; and limited access to physicians experienced in HIV/AIDS treatment regimens. Adolescents and young adults in reservation settings also experience high incidences of alcohol and substance abuse, which elevates the number of indigenous people with HIV/AIDS. Their injection drug use advances the disease through both shared needles and related sexual contact.

Confidentiality issues also arise among American Indians and Alaska Natives who reside in reservation settings or small villages and receive medical care in public health clinics (Maldanado, 1999b). A perceived lack of confidentiality contributes to their unwillingness to seek testing for HIV infection and thereby leads to elevated rates of HIV/AIDS and other sexually transmitted diseases. Furthermore, many Asian/Pacific Islander Americans who are at risk of HIV/AIDS avoid testing and treatment based on fear that public knowledge about the illness would bring shame to their families. Public disclosure often threatens family rejection, stigmatization, and loss of support within their ethnic communities, which normally provide a sense of belonging (Wong, Chng, Ross, and Mayer, 1998).

These factors add to the HIV/AIDS epidemic when coupled with misunderstandings about the validity of information, distrust of health professionals, and reluctance to seek health care. Some Asian/Pacific Islander Americans are also less than comfortable with and distrust the quality of health services (Chng, 1999; Wong et al., 1998). Furthermore, many African Americans believe that AIDS is a form of genocide introduced and allowed to spread within the African American community because of racist motivations to control population size; emphasis on condom use to prevent HIV infection is also suspected to be an attempt to reduce births (Bogart and Thorburn, 2005; Quinn, 1997). African Americans are often skeptical about medical research and their roles as guinea pigs for medical experimentation and are reluctant to access new drugs and treatments for HIV/AIDS (Bogart and Thorburn,

2005; Hagen, 2005). These beliefs harm efforts to prevent the spread of the disease among African Americans.

Lack of Adequate HIV/AIDS Prevention Education for Youth

Many political, community, and religious leaders across the world view adolescent sexuality as a politically volatile subject and believe sexuality education promotes promiscuity. Furthermore, educators and parents often know little about sexuality and are not prepared to discuss HIV/AIDS and its transmission, prevention, and treatment (Bok and Morales, 2002).

People in developing countries, therefore, may resist discussion of HIV/AIDS prevention education and use of condoms. Schools in South Africa, for example, do not offer HIV/AIDS education programs or opportunities for testing. Teenagers' access to condoms is nonexistent, and adults refuse their purchase. As a result, approximately 25 percent of women younger than 20 years old may be infected with the disease, and more than half of South African 15-year-olds may die of AIDS-related illnesses (Bok and Morales, 2002).

Global Inequities and Health Care Resources

Poverty is often related to race and rooted in colonization and oppression of people in developing countries. Many African and Caribbean nations have struggled to overcome racial and class inequities created during periods of colonization. Yet many people continue to experience stereotyping, prejudice, and racism that amount to physical, cultural, and psychological genocide. They are marginalized and devalued members of society and often live in impoverished geographic regions.

Poverty is a dominant issue linked with HIV/AIDS. Many poor countries receive funds to fight malnutrition and infectious diseases, such as malaria, tuberculosis, measles, and hepatitis B, all of which affect millions of people annually; these countries must decide whether to allocate these much-needed funds to HIV prevention education, testing, and treatment or to use funds for the treatment of other, less controversial, curable or manageable infectious diseases (Bok and Morales, 2002).

It is imperative that patients who receive HIV/AIDS medications understand how the drugs work, the importance of adherence to drug regimens, and culturally appropriate education and medical regimes that are effective in improving medical compliance. However, achieving such understanding in the United States can be difficult among American Indian, Alaska Native, and Asian populations who might prefer health care that combines traditional, natural, and herbal medications and healing approaches with religious practices.

Poor adherence to antiretroviral drug regimens lowers resistance to opportunistic infections. Education is needed, therefore, to heighten people's awareness of long-term antiretroviral therapy (Cook et al., 2003). Treatment helps prevent the spread of infection because people with low viral levels are less likely to transmit the disease to others. Availability of treatment also gives people a reason to get tested and draws them into health clinics where they learn safe-sex practices.

Although high drug prices are one obstacle to treating HIV/AIDS in poor countries, many African and Asian nations also lack resolve, medical facilities, and personnel to treat people with the disease (Bok and Morales, 2002). The politics and ethics of AIDS and related research affect funding and access to care. Health care must become a priority in developing regions; people who receive regular health care are more likely to practice lower HIV-risk behaviors. In addition, participation in a health care system leads to the treatment of other deadly communicable diseases.

The cost, availability, and distribution of life-saving antiretroviral drugs have received considerable attention worldwide. Fortunately, recent changes have increased access and availability, as major drug companies commit funds to fight AIDS and others revise copyright laws to allow production of less expensive generic drugs for distribution. Still, many people with HIV/AIDS in developing countries lack access to the drugs.

The South African government resists distribution of antiretroviral AIDS drugs and opts instead to treat opportunistic infections. Antiretroviral drugs are available to less than 1 percent of the 28.5 million Africans with the disease. Similarly, the Indian government resists distribution of antiretroviral drugs, even at reduced prices, preferring to treat more curable diseases (Bok and Morales, 2002; Eberstadt, 2002). In China, only government employees are covered by national health insurance, thereby leaving most rural populations without health coverage. Only 10 to 20 percent of the one million or more Chinese with HIV/AIDS can access available treatments (Cook et al., 2003).

According to UNAIDS Executive Director Peter Piot, "of the six million people in the developing world in need of antiretroviral drug therapy ... less than 4 percent were receiving antiretroviral drugs at the end of 2001" (Clifton, 2003, p. 18).

Piot has declared the battle against HIV/AIDS to be a global human rights issue and moral imperative (Clifton, 2003). The fight is connected with environmental, contextual, and social vulnerabilities that influence HIV-risk behaviors. Vulnerabilities include extreme poverty, sexual and economic exploitation, and discrimination and marginalization due to race and ethnicity, gender, sexual orientation, and disability (Cervero, 2005). The reduction of these vulnerabilities is allied closely with HIV/AIDS prevention and requires expanding access to education, elimination of discrimination, promotion of gender equity, collaboration across sectors, and partnerships between schools and their communities (UNAIDS Inter Agency Task Team on Education, 2002, p. 29). Countries must set aside cultural traditions, customs, and ways of life and protect the rights of their citizens, especially women and children and other vulnerable groups, such as homosexuals and prostitutes.

SUMMARY AND CONCLUSIONS

HIV/AIDS affects global human rights and has social, political, and economic implications. The disease continues to spread in the United States and internationally; it has reduced life expectancy and derailed economic progress in developing countries. Discrimination against women and children and other exploited groups plays a major role in the spread of the disease.

HIV/AIDS prevention and treatment programs must focus on gender inequities, reduction in mother-to-infant transmission, access to antiretroviral drugs and other medical resources, availability of health care workers, and elimination of prejudice and discrimination against people with HIV/AIDS. Prevention goals must be applied equitably across all populations and countries. These programs should consider the differing needs of various populations and should concentrate on strategies that have proven successful in the past. National education and health organizations must strive to understand peoples' attitudes, beliefs, and perceptions regarding susceptibility to HIV/AIDS and must take into account the sociocultural views and values of differing populations as a foundation for developing culturally competent prevention programs (Allan and Leonard, 2005; Sileo, 2005; Wilson and Miller, 2003).

IMPLICATIONS FOR TEACHER EDUCATION PROGRAMS

The majority of individuals with HIV/AIDS are young adults who were infected during adolescence. Consequently, HIV/AIDS prevention education must target youth, particularly when they start to engage in HIV-risk behaviors, although it can begin as early as kindergarten with basic directions such as "do not touch someone else's blood" and "wash your hands thoroughly if you touch someone else's blood." HIV prevention strategies that result in behavior change and risk reduction ultimately could save millions of lives, and they are more cost effective than antiretroviral drugs.

All educators must be knowledgeable of the HIV/AIDS pandemic and translate their understandings into culturally competent curriculum and instructional practices. However, a dearth of knowledgeable teachers who care about these issues is a major concern. The preparation of educators may be the most important factor in ensuring effective HIV/AIDS prevention (Byrom and Katz, 1991). Colleges of education are ideally suited to integrate prevention education initiatives into their curricula. Preparation programs must provide teachers with an understanding about the human rights, social, political, and economic repercussions that surround the disease. In addition, teachers must know about (a) HIV/AIDS infection, transmission, and prevention; (b) universal precautions related to infection control in school settings; (c) educational, psychosocial, and medical effects of HIV/AIDS; (d) ethical and legal requirements for confidentiality; (e) religious and medical issues regarding sexuality, death, and dying; and (f) cultural attitudes, values, and beliefs that influence young people's HIV-risk behaviors (Evans, Melville, and Cass, 1992; Skripak and Summerfield, 1996; Thomas, 1998). Finally, teachers must be comfortable with their own sexuality and the language of sex as a prerequisite to conducting open and honest interactions with others.

Teacher education activities might include reading and discussing sexuality issues with peers, increasing exposure to a wide range of sexual expressions and values, becoming knowledgeable about sexual and relationship problems, increasing familiarity with curriculum guides and published curricula, and demonstrating how sexuality topics and HIV/

AIDS prevention education can be integrated across the curriculum (Brantlinger, 1992). Some teachers, regardless of the quantity or quality of preparation, may face emotional barriers concerning HIV/AIDS prevention education, which requires knowledge of and willingness to discuss topics such as sexuality, transmission of sexually transmitted diseases, and injection drug use. In addition, the disease is fatal, and few people are comfortable discussing death and dying. Moreover, HIV/AIDS is commonly associated with disenfranchised groups, such as homosexuals, prostitutes, and injection drug users. These barriers may be diminished by becoming informed about HIV/AIDS as a means to discriminate myth from fact and to examine personal stereotypes, attitudes, and values necessary to developing tolerance for diversity (Sileo, 1998).

REFERENCES

Allan, B., and Leonard, W. (2005). Asserting a positive role: HIV-positive people in prevention. In J. P. Egan, ed., *HIV/AIDS Education for Adults* (pp. 43–54). San Francisco: Jossey-Bass.

Amorampah, O. (1989). Black male-female relationships: Some observations. *Journal of Black Studies* 19: 320–342.

Bogart, L. M., and Thorburn, S. (2005). Are HIV/AIDS conspiracy beliefs a barrier to HIV prevention among African Americans? *Journal of Acquired Immune Deficiency Syndromes* 38(2): 213–218.

Bok, M., and Morales, J. (2002). AIDS at 20: A global human rights concern. *Journal of HIV/AIDS Prevention and Education for Adolescents and Children* 5(1/2): 139–151.

Brantlinger, E. (1992). Sexuality education in the secondary school curriculum: Teachers' perceptions and concerns. *Teacher Education and Special Education* 15: 32–40.

Bryant, L. (2004). *Demystifying the "down low": Black masculinity, sexuality, and HIV among black men who have sex with men.* Paper presented at the U.S. Conference on AIDS, Philadelphia, PA.

Byrom, E., and Katz, G., eds. (1991). *HIV prevention and AIDS education: Resources for special educators.* Reston, VA: Council for Exceptional Children.

Centers for Disease Control and Prevention. (2003). Table 11: Estimated numbers of persons living with AIDS at the end of 2002, by race/ethnicity, sex, and exposure category—United States. In *HIV/AIDS surveillance report: Cases of HIV infection and AIDS in the United States, 2002, 14.* Retrieved September 19, 2005, from http://www.cdc.gov/hiv/stats/hasr1402/table11.htm.

Centers for Disease Control and Prevention. (2005). *HIV/AIDS among Hispanics.* Retrieved September 19, 2005, from http://www.cdc.gov/hiv/PUBS/Facts/hispanic.htm.

Cervero, R. M. (2005). The struggle for meaning and power in HIV/AIDS education. In J. P. Egan, ed., *HIV/AIDS Education for Adults* (pp. 5–10). San Francisco: Jossey-Bass.

Chen, M. S., and Hawks, B. L. (1995). A debunking of the myth of healthy Asian Americans and Pacific Islanders. *American Journal of Health Promotion* 9: 261–268.

Chng, C. L. (1999). Asians and Pacific Islander Americans. In *Cultural competence for providing technical assistance, evaluation, and training for HIV prevention programs: A research synthesis* (pp. 12–23). Washington, DC: CRP, Inc. Contract No. 200–97–0644(P), funded by the Centers for Disease Control and Prevention.

Clay, S. B. (2002). Villains or victims? *HIV Plus* 5(7): 28–31.

Clifton, C. E. (2003). One-on-one with Dr. Pete Piot. *Positively Aware* 14(2): 17–19.

Clifton, C. E. (2004). The politics of leadership. *Positively Aware* 15(5): 12–17.

Cohen, J. (2004a). Till death do us part. *Science* 304: 513.

Cohen, J. (2004b). Poised for takeoff? *Science* 304: 1430–1432.

Cook, S., Flynn, J., Merchant, S., and Pietrandoni, G. (2003). At the crossroads: HIV and the People's Republic of China. *Positively Aware* 14(2): 20–24.

Duh, S. M. (1991). *Blacks and AIDS: Causes and origins.* Newberry Park, CA: Sage.

Eberstadt, N. (2002). The future of AIDS. *Foreign Affairs* 81(6). Retrieved September 16, 2005, from http://www.foreignaffairs.org/20021101faessay9990/nicholas-eberstadt/the-future-of-aids.html.

Eckholdt, H., and Chin, J. (1997). Pneumocystis carinii in Asians and Pacific Islanders. *Clinical Infectious Diseases* 24: 1265–1267.

Egan, J. P. (2005). Marginalized, not marginal: Adult education's unique contribution to the fight against HIV/AIDS. In J. P. Egan, ed., *HIV/AIDS Education for Adults* (pp. 85–94). San Francisco: Jossey-Bass.

Evans, E. D., Melville, G. A., and Cass, M. A. (1992). AIDS: Special educators' knowledge and attitudes. *Teacher Education and Special Education* 15(4): 300–306.

Faryna, E. L., and Morales, E. (2000). Self-efficacy and HIV-related risk behaviors among multiethnic adolescents. *Cultural Diversity and Ethnic Minority Psychology* 6(1): 42–56.

Flaskerud, J. H. (1995). Culture and ethnicity. In J. H. Flaskerud and P. J. Ungvarski, eds., *HIV/AIDS: A guide to nursing care.* 3rd ed. (pp. 405–432). Philadelphia: W. B. Saunders.

Fullilove, M., Fullilove, R., Haynes, K., and Gross, S. (1990). Black women and AIDS prevention: A view towards understanding the gender rules. *Journal of Sex Research* 27: 47–63.

Hagen, K. S. (2005). Bad blood: The Tuskegee syphilis study and legacy recruitment for experimental AIDS vaccines. In J. P. Egan, ed., *HIV/AIDS Education for Adults* (pp. 11–20). San Francisco: Jossey-Bass.

Human Resources and Services Administration. (2005). *Hispanics and HIV/AIDS* (HRSA Fact Sheet, January 2005). Retrieved September 16, 2005, from http://hab.hrsa.gov/history/fact2005/hispanics_and_hivaids.htm.

Jemmott, L. S., Maula, E. C., and Bush, E. (1999). Hearing our voices: Assessing HIV prevention needs among Asian and Pacific Islander women. *Journal of Transcultural Nursing* 10: 102–111.

Joint United Nations Programme on HIV/AIDS. (2004a). *2004 report on the global AIDS epidemic.* Retrieved September 16, 2005, from http://www.unaids.org/bangkok2004/GAR2004_html/GAR2004_00_en.htm.

Joint United Nations Programme on HIV/AIDS. (2004b). *Around the world: 2004 facts and figures.* Retrieved February 9, 2005, from http://www.unaids.org/html/pub/media/pressreleases02/PR_Globalreport2004_06Jul04_en_pdf/PR.

Joint United Nations Programme on HIV/AIDS. (2004c). *Understanding the latest estimates of the global AIDS epidemic—July 2004.* Retrieved September 16, 2005, from http://www.unaids.org/html/pub/una-docs/q-a_epi_en_pdf.htm.

Joint United Nations Programme on HIV/AIDS. (2005, January 18). *Press briefing by Stephen Lewis, UN Secretary-General's special envoy for HIV/AIDS in Africa, on his recent trips to Malawi and Tanzania.* Retrieved September 28, 2005, from http://www.aegis.com/news/unaids/2005/UN050103.html.

Joint United Nations Programme on HIV/AIDS (UNAIDS) Inter Agency Task Team on Education. (2002, May). *HIV/AIDS and education: A strategic approach.* New York: Author.

Maldanado, M. (1999a). *HIV/AIDS and African Americans.* Washington, DC: National Minority AIDS Council.

Maldanado. M. (1999b). *HIV/AIDS and Native Americans.* Washington, DC: National Minority AIDS Council.

Passar, D., and Johnson, R. (1996). *Working in the massage parlors: Reaching Asian women at high risk for infection.* Abstract Pub. C 1262. Presentation at the 11th International Conference on AIDS, Vancouver, BC.

Quinn, S. C. (1997). Belief in AIDS as a form of genocide: Implications for HIV prevention programs for African Americans. *Journal of Health Education* 28(6): S-6–11.

Sanchez, M. (2005, January 15). Americans with AIDS survive longer, but lives remain a struggle. *Anchorage Daily News,* pp. A1, A7.

Santora, M. (2005). U.S. is close to eliminating AIDS in infants, officials say. *New York Times.* Retrieved September 16, 2005, from http://www.nytimes.com/2005/01/30/nyregion/30aids.html.

Sileo, N. M. (1998). Pediatric HIV/AIDS: Knowledge, attitudes, and perceptions of early childhood professionals. (Abstract.) Retrieved September 26, 2005, from Digital Dissertations database.

Sileo, N. M. (2005). HIV/AIDS prevention education: What are classroom teachers' roles and responsibilities? *Intervention in School and Clinic* 40(3): 177–181.

Skripak, D., and Summerfield, L. (1996). *HIV/AIDS education in teacher preparation programs* (ERIC Digest). Washington, DC: ERIC Clearinghouse on Teaching and Teacher Education. (ERIC Document Reproduction Service No. ED403264).

Thomas, S. B. (1998, August). *Cultural issues and HIV prevention: Implications for historically black colleges and universities.* Paper presented at the National Collaborative Preservice Forum, Landsdowne, VA.

United Nations. (1992). *Teaching and learning about human rights: A manual for schools of social work and the social work profession.* Geneva, Switzerland: Centre for Human Rights.

Vazquez, E. (2003). The most vulnerable of the epidemic: Orphans. *Positively Aware* 14(2): 26.

Vazquez, E. (2004). Update on the U.S. *Positively Aware* 15(5): 29–31.

Wilson, B. D. M., and Miller, R. L. (2003). Examining strategies for culturally grounded HIV prevention: A review. *AIDS Education and Prevention* 15(2): 184–202.

Winfield, C. (2003). Haiti: A battle against poverty and HIV. *Positively Aware* 14(2): 30.

Wong, F. Y., Chng, C. L., Ross, M. W., and Mayer, K. H. (1998). Sexualities as roles among Asian and Pacific Islander American gay, lesbian, bisexual, and transgender individuals: Implications for community-based health education and prevention. *Journal of the Gay and Lesbian Medical Association* 2(4): 157–165.

Wyatt, G. E., Tucker, M. B., Romero, G. J., Carmona, J. V., Newcomb, N. D., Wayment, H. A., et al. (1997). Adapting a comprehensive approach to African American women's sexual risk-taking. *Journal of Health Education* 28(6): S-52–60.

9

INFLUENCES OF FAMILY AND CULTURAL VALUES, LANGUAGE, AND RELIGION ON HIV/AIDS BEHAVIOR CHANGE

Mose Yvonne Brooks Hooks, Thomas W. Sileo, and Valerie L. Mazzotti

↩

Numerous challenges confront educators as they create HIV/AIDS prevention education programs that meet the diverse needs of children, youth, and young adults. Individuals' decisions to engage in HIV-risk behaviors must be considered in light of family and cultural values, language, and religious considerations. Educators must acknowledge these perspectives and design programs and strategies that reduce the spread of disease. This chapter addresses (a) the current status of HIV/AIDS globally and in the United States; (b) variables that contribute to growth of the epidemic, especially among the nation's various racial, ethnic, and cultural communities; and (c) principles of health behavior change that facilitate educators' understanding of the beliefs and attitudes that underlie HIV-risk behaviors.

THE SPREAD OF AIDS: INTERNATIONAL AND UNITED STATES PERSPECTIVES

An International Perspective

The global AIDS crisis is one of the world's greatest health catastrophes. The disease has infected 65 million people in the past 25 years and continues to spread at a vigorous pace. Approximately 42 million adults and children worldwide are living with HIV/AIDS (Joint United Nations Programme on HIV/AIDS, 2004). The U.S. National Intelligence Council (2002) forecast sustained growth in new cases through the end of this decade, with total projections in China, India, Russia, Ethiopia, and Nigeria that range from 50 to 75 million people by 2010. Some of the fastest growing HIV/AIDS epidemics occur in Asia, where an estimated 1.1 million new infections were diagnosed in 2003. Without significant prevention efforts, Asia will have appreciably more HIV infections than sub-Saharan Africa by the end of the decade. The National Intelligence Council predicts an excess of 15 million people in China and 25 million people in India with HIV infections. Projections also point to 25 million children and youth younger than 18 years old who will lose one or both parents as a result of AIDS; 80 percent of them reside in sub-Saharan Africa (U.S. National Intelligence Council, 2002).

The AIDS pandemic exemplifies stories of politics, bureaucracy, disease, warfare, and negligence. Its spread, if unchecked, will result in negative economic growth and government instability in sub-Saharan Africa, Eastern Europe, and Asia. Eurasia is home to a majority of the world's population, and it possesses substantial global economic, political, and military strength. The aftershock of the unfolding epidemic in these countries will affect the balance of trade, industry, political power, and security interests in the rest of the world (Behrman, 2004).

A United States Perspective

HIV/AIDS also continues to gain strength in the United States despite availability of effective drug therapies that enable people to live longer and defy the virus' early image as a death sentence. At least 405,000 Americans currently live with the disease (Centers for Disease Control and Prevention [CDC], 2004). Prior to the accessibility of powerful drugs, the average time from infection to developing AIDS was about 9 years, and people usually lived an additional year and a half before dying from AIDS-related complications. People now live with the virus at least 11 years, on average, before an AIDS diagnosis and another 6 years after identification of the disease (Sanchez, 2005).

Although drugs have decreased AIDS-related deaths, spread of the disease remains relatively constant at about 42,000 new HIV infections annually (CDC, 2004). HIV/AIDS extends across urban and suburban neighborhoods as well as rural and remote areas among men and women of all racial, ethnic, and cultural groups. A contributing factor to the spread of infection is the denial of some communities to join the fight against AIDS. This negative response is due, in part, to cultural values such as a sense of *machismo,* in which communities are reluctant to acknowledge men's risky sexual behaviors (Diaz, 2000). Many men who engage in sex with other men identify as heterosexual and do not relate to HIV/AIDS prevention messages crafted for gay men (CDC, 2000; Diaz, 2000; Egan, 2005). Their identification as heterosexual is due to homophobia and social stigma associated with gay lifestyles. Quite often, these men who secretly have sex with men also engage in unprotected sexual activity with women (Bryant, 2004; Clay, 2002; Egan, 2005; Rowell, 1997).

HIV/AIDS is increasing among African Americans and Hispanics, who constitute 66 percent of the estimated 850,000 to 950,000 HIV/AIDS cases reported to the CDC since the beginning of the epidemic (CDC, 2004). The CDC reports that African Americans make up 41 percent of all AIDS cases in the United States, yet they comprise only 12 percent of the population. Hispanics represent 19 percent of all AIDS cases and constitute approximately 13 percent of the U.S. population (CDC, 2004).

The disease is also swelling among Asian Pacific Islander and indigenous populations. Growth in HIV/AIDS cases in these groups, however, is not always acknowledged as a significant threat due to their small population sizes. Asian Pacific Islanders and Native Americans collectively comprise about 5 percent of the U.S. population. Spread of the disease among these groups constitutes less than 2 percent of reported HIV/AIDS infections nationwide (CDC, 2004), but underreporting and lack of detailed surveillance data masks a realistic picture regarding the extent of the epidemic. Underreporting occurs due to racial misclassifications (Maldanado, 1999) and lack of national standards for race and ethnicity; data are aggregated within federal definitions of Asian/Pacific Islander and American Indian/Alaska Native to adjust for smaller populations. Underreporting also results from cultural prohibitions, social taboos, language barriers, and lower education levels among people who may be less knowledgeable about HIV/AIDS (Faryna and Morales, 2000; Yep, 1993).

Finally, the rate of new infections is rising among a generation of young, gay men within all racial and ethnic groups whose HIV-risk behaviors include unprotected male-to-male sex, sex in combination with drugs and alcohol, and injection drug use. Their behaviors may be attributed to misperceptions about severity of the disease in light of life-prolonging drugs as well as to beliefs that sex with barriers is unnatural—leading them to resist condom use (Allan and Leonard, 2005; Rowell, 1996).

VARIABLES THAT CONTRIBUTE TO HIV/AIDS IN DIVERSE RACIAL AND ETHNIC COMMUNITIES

HIV/AIDS, to be understood in context, must be viewed from the perspectives of oppression, prejudice, and racism and their impact on socioeconomic and environmental resources as well as on access to prevention education and quality health care (Cervero, 2005; Egan, 2005). At times, members of various racial and ethnic communities are viewed by mainstream society as culturally, economically, and socially disadvantaged. This perception may result in low behavioral expectations and negative self-perceptions among children, youth, and young adults who internalize adverse messages and acquiesce to dominant-group standards. The internalization creates notions of inferiority, constricts individuals' overall development, and negates the unique experiences within their cultural settings. Their academic and social performance mirrors perceived beliefs of others' low expectations and results in failure (Ladson-Billings, 2000).

Oppression, prejudice, and racism align with political, social, and environmental circumstances that contribute to the health-risk behaviors of many adolescents and young adults and heighten their chances of HIV infection. They often reside in poverty-ridden situations and lack health insurance and an adequate health care system, which in turn advances poor health and a general lack of well-being. These factors also contribute to higher instances of alcohol and drug use; circumscribed awareness about HIV/AIDS and other sexually transmitted diseases; delayed testing, counseling, and diagnosis; and limited access to physicians experienced in HIV/AIDS treatment options (Cervero, 2005; Egan, 2005). Additional variables that contribute to elevated rates of HIV/AIDS and sexually transmitted diseases are a perceived lack of confidentiality and a dearth of culturally appropriate health care.

A number of factors challenge professionals as they design HIV/AIDS prevention programs. In the past, HIV/AIDS education was addressed in a simplistic manner that involved disseminating knowledge about transmission of the disease due to high-risk sexual practices, sharing injection drug needles, and contact with body fluids. The intention was that various audiences would listen to the messages, adhere to prevention methods, and curtail the disease. Unfortunately, these methods have not been successful, and the virus continues to spread. Raising awareness about HIV and its transmission does not equate to changing people's attitudes and risk behaviors.

Why do people continue life-threatening behaviors despite having knowledge about the disease, its transmission, and prevention practices? Clearly, the concept of one-size-fits-all HIV/AIDS prevention programs is not effective. Standardized generic programs are even more questionable in light of the disparate characteristics of the nation's overall population—a multitude of languages; varying levels of education; and continuing beliefs in sensitive, value-laden, and culturally based notions about sexuality and sexual behaviors. The following discussion identifies environmental circumstances and cultural perspectives that must be considered as cornerstones when designing HIV/AIDS education programs. These variables are viewed in light of health behavior principles that influence people's behaviors and attitudes regarding HIV/AIDS.

PRINCIPLES OF HEALTH BEHAVIOR CHANGE

The principles of health behavior change provide insight into peoples' perceptions and attitudes regarding their well-being as well as the variables that influence their actions. The principles also illuminate individuals' health-risk behaviors. Therefore, educators should be aware of these principles as they design HIV/AIDS prevention programs and strategies. In addition, educators should recognize that the principles are not mutually exclusive and are interrelated regarding their application to effective HIV/AIDS prevention education.

The Cognitive Principle

The cognitive principle concerns individuals' knowledge about the disease, its transmission and prevention, and related high-risk behaviors. Linley and Joseph (2004) indicate that knowledge about the disease and positive self-affirmation enable people to recognize and accept negative perspectives associated with an illness. In addition, positive beliefs promote preventive behaviors and decrease progression of the disease in persons diagnosed with HIV/AIDS (Linley and Joseph, 2004).

Knowledge about HIV/AIDS often is inadequate or lacking among residents of underdeveloped countries; young people of diverse racial, ethnic, and cultural heritage; youth who live in low socioeconomic and poverty-ridden areas; and individuals with disabilities. HIV/AIDS prevention programs must fit their intended audience. As such, they should be developmentally appropriate, culturally sensitive, and rooted in community values and beliefs (Wilson and Miller, 2003).

HIV/AIDS education may begin as early as preschool where teachers use juvenile nonfiction books, role-play, guest speakers, and videos to teach concepts (Sileo, 2005). It is also important to design district-wide HIV/AIDS education programs that intersect curricular areas and are appropriate for all age and grade levels. Sileo, Prater, Pateman, and Sileo (2002) discuss mnemonic strategies such as rhyme to teach universal precautions to elementary-age students of diverse racial and ethnic heritages. These and similar strategies enhance students' knowledge about HIV/AIDS and allow them to generalize information and use preventive measures outside classroom environments. The chapter by Blanchett and Prater provides detailed discussion about developmentally appropriate prevention programs; the importance of specific, contextualized HIV/AIDS prevention messages for people with disabilities; and generalization strategies across settings.

Cultural Sensitivity and Responsiveness

Culturally competent HIV/AIDS prevention education programs are designed and delivered in collaboration with community leaders and role models who, as stakeholders, equip learners with practical knowledge, skills, and competencies about the disease as well as motivation to apply newly acquired skills. For example, Barnhardt and Kawagley (2005) believe that cross-generational learning and natural environments, such as those in which American Indian and Alaska Native elders share knowledge with students, have positive implications for curriculum, pedagogical strategies, and enhancing students' learning. Similarly, programs for Asian/Pacific Islanders should be developed and implemented by people of similar racial and ethnic background who speak the languages of the community and share cultural values and practices (Sileo et al., 2002). It is especially beneficial when participants recognize program personnel for their understanding and sensitivity to the community's cultural dynamics and health education needs (Flaskerud, 1995; Jemmott, Maula, and Bush, 1999).

According to Jester (2002), culturally relevant, place-based curricula and pedagogy facilitate learners' acquisition of content knowledge, promote respect for and connection to their cultural identity, and enhance their understanding of educational and social inequities. Linking education to learners' physical, linguistic, and cultural environments and contexts enriches their educational experiences and enhances their comprehension. Educators, therefore, must make certain that HIV/AIDS program goals, objectives, and activities are presented with clarity across age and grade levels (Fan, Conner, and Villarreal, 2004) and that prevention messages are appropriate and purposeful in language, style, and venue.

Culture and language may be barriers that interfere with individuals' learning about HIV/AIDS and seeking health care. It is extremely important, therefore, to ensure that linguistically appropriate and culturally responsive programs and strategies target the concerns of specific populations. For example, Hostos Community College at the City University of New York has developed an HIV/AIDS prevention curriculum for learners who speak English as a second language. The curriculum, which is based on the assumption that non-English speakers may have limited access to school and community-based AIDS education, provides program objectives, lessons, and strategies that integrate best practices for teaching English as a second language as well as HIV/AIDS prevention (Lesnick, 2001).

It also may be appropriate to present HIV/AIDS prevention content in multiple languages to meet the linguistic needs of racial and ethnic groups such as Asian/Pacific Islanders, American Indians, and Alaska Natives. In addition, when discussing HIV/AIDS prevention with some Native American populations, it may be necessary to use a combination of English and indigenous language words because some terms, including HIV/AIDS itself, do not hold meaning in native languages. Moreover, many traditional American Indians and Alaska Natives generally do not discuss sex—heterosexuality, homosexuality, or bisexuality (Sileo and Gooden, 2003).

The Emotional Principle

Emotions play a significant role in facilitating people's ability to integrate new knowledge, skills, and dispositions about HIV/AIDS transmission and prevention with previous understandings and experiences. Scholarship about the interplay of emotions and learning acknowledges that fear as an emotion can be useful in health behavior change communications. Yet excessive use of fear may alienate people and result in continued HIV-risk behaviors (Allan and Leonard, 2005; Dejong, 2000; Fan et al., 2004).

Information about HIV/AIDS should be presented in a straightforward, optimistic, and accessible manner that exemplifies concern for intended audiences. It is important to capitalize on people's positive emotions to facilitate their learning (Allan and Leonard, 2005). The chapter in this section by Fennell includes a discussion about imagery and role-play activities that connect to people's emotions in an attempt to develop their compassion for persons with HIV/AIDS.

A current approach to sensitizing the general public about HIV/AIDS and the importance of knowing one's HIV status is the multimedia, multithemed, multinational public service campaign called Know HIV/AIDS. The campaign, which was developed by the Viacom media giant and the nonprofit Kaiser Family Foundation, uses billboards, radio, television public service announcements, and a Web site to promote the significance of its message. The campaign's theme for 2005, *Knowing Is Beautiful,* is designed to motivate young people to test regularly for HIV infection (Kahn, 2005). The campaign targets groups hardest hit by HIV/AIDS including women, people of diverse heritage, and men who have sex with men. It eschews frightening, statistic-driven messages and visual images that address the advanced stages of the disease; these forms of dissuasion may have a negative impact on people's emotions and cause them to turn away from HIV/AIDS prevention education (Allan and Leonard, 2005). Instead, the advertisements employ positive imagery: a flower-shaped HIV-test bandage as a trademark along with Grammy Award–winning hip-hop artist Common, whose voice and face are behind the theme.

Many people view the campaign as controversial and as airbrushing the harsh realities of the disease. They believe the advertisements negate safe-sex messages and undermine the difficult task of getting young people to practice safe sex. Furthermore, some people believe the comeliness of the advertisements may alienate young people who do not perceive themselves as attractive. As Kahn (2005) notes, however, people's early knowledge of HIV sero-positivity can lead to early treatment and a longer life.

The Behavioral Principle

HIV/AIDS prevention messages, to be effective, should be specific, clear, and purposeful. People do not respond to vague information with unclear connections to HIV/AIDS. For instance, a picture of a person placing a mitten on a hand has little connection to a verbal message about using condoms to prevent the spread of disease. It may be more appropriate to explain the association and to use a banana and a condom for a more specific demonstration.

HIV/AIDS prevention educators also must be aware of students' education levels, their cognitive and comprehension levels, and their ability to codify, interpret, and use the information for preventive purposes. For example, individuals with disabilities who participate in HIV/AIDS prevention programs might not use strategies if the program lacks developmental appropriateness. In addition, educators must be knowledgeable about HIV/AIDS and understand the extent to which individuals perceive their susceptibility to the disease.

Individuals who believe they are not susceptible to HIV infection often do not use prevention methods. For example, youth and young adults of Asian/Pacific Islander, American Indian, Alaska Native, and Hispanic descent might not generalize precaution behaviors to their lifestyles if they perceive the face of AIDS as a Western epidemic among gay and bisexual men and indigent drug users. Consequently, they engage in risk behaviors such as unprotected vaginal and anal intercourse, multiple sex partners, same-sex behaviors, and use of drugs and alcohol in connection with sex (Flaskerud and Nyamathi, 1998; Jemmott et al., 1999). Therefore, it is imperative to present information that is appropriate to individuals' environmental and cultural contexts (Wilson and Miller, 2003).

Furthermore, many individuals view the threat of disease as inconsequential and do not use condoms or worry about results of their actions. This attitude results from *optimistic bias,* a consistent tendency to underestimate personal risk and susceptibility to HIV/AIDS that minimizes peoples' perceptions about the reality of infection, likelihood of harm resulting from unprotected sex, and potential concomitant negative life events (Yep, 1993). Another important issue concerns personal beliefs about the effectiveness of the prevention method; individuals do not feel pressured to use a prevention method if they underrate its results (Fan et al., 2004). Others distrust the intention behind certain preventive measures; for example, many African Americans perceive efforts to increase condom use as an attempt to reduce pregnancies and births and thereby control population size (Bogart and Thorburn, 2005; Hagen, 2005; Quinn, 1997).

According to Hayman, Mahon, and Turner (2002), people's behavior beliefs focus on (a) their attitudes toward a specific behavior, (b) whether significant others approve of the behavior, and (c) personal confidence in performing a specific behavior. Jemmott, Jemmott, Spears, Hewitt, and Cruz-Collins (2002) identify three behavioral beliefs in relation to condom use: The *prevention belief* addresses a condom's effectiveness in preventing HIV transmission; the *hedonistic belief* concerns the effect of using a condom on sexual pleasure; and the *partner reaction belief* considers the partner's reaction to the decision to use a condom.

Condom use is also affected by four behavior-control beliefs. The *availability belief* concerns the ready availability of condoms; the *negotiation belief* focuses on the potential difficulty in negotiating condom use; *impulse control belief* addresses people's ability to control their sexual excitement long enough to use a condom; and the *technical skills belief* considers whether condom use will "ruin the mood." Other factors such as socioeconomics, ethnicity, personal feelings, family, and peers must be considered regarding condom use. All of these beliefs together create the theory of planned behavior, which signifies a person's intentions and behaviors toward taking precautions against HIV/AIDS (Hayman et al., 2002).

The Interpersonal Principle

The interpersonal principle recognizes the significance of people's social environments and acknowledges that their lives interconnect as members of various groups that often assume social responsibility for others' well-being. As such, the principle considers people's immediate social networks and spheres of influence, which encompass family, gender roles, and communication styles.

Family Considerations

African Americans' social identity may be characterized by the concept of *fictive kinship,* in which people reach out to traditional and nontraditional family members and subscribe to group-specific values and communication styles. African American families typically stress parent-child and sibling ties, fosterage of children, and social networks that underscore a sense of community and survival of its members (Cartledge and Middleton, 1996). Extended families and social interactions among African Americans are humanistic and focus on informality, expressiveness, and a strong sense of connectedness to historical roots.

Many traditional Asian/Pacific Islander families are patriarchal and guided by a concept of *filial piety*, which centers on respecting the father figure, fulfilling parental wishes, valuing elders, continuing obligations to past generations, conforming to group standards, and establishing harmonious interpersonal relationships (Cartledge and Feng, 1996). Family members gauge their behaviors in terms of this concept as the cornerstone for resolving conflicts in a compromising and peaceful manner.

American Indian and Alaska Native families are distinguished by shared values that stress spirituality and living in harmony with the creator, nature, and humanity. They demonstrate ongoing appreciation for life and interactions among physical, mental, emotional, and spiritual well-being (Hunt, Gooden, and Barkdull, 2001). Indigenous people strive to bring honor and respect to their families, accord respect to elders, and embrace family and tribal solidarity. Families customarily have strong cooperative and supportive structures and networks. Grandparents traditionally participate in childcare and teach children about autonomy and responsibility for behaviors, loyalty, self-discipline, and generosity; youth are socialized to make and abide by their decisions. Adults assume minimal authoritative posture and seldom reprimand children verbally or punish them physically; rather, they respond to inappropriate behaviors with disapproving looks, ridicule, and shaming (Lee and Cartledge, 1996). Children and youth identify with and engage in cooperative endeavors and are inspired to develop unique talents, knowledge, and skills that benefit themselves and society. Personal mastery motivates their cognitive, physical, social, and spiritual development; self-improvement is valued over comparison to and competition with others (Hunt et al., 2001).

Many Hispanic families are characterized by the concept of *familisimo*, which connotes family-centeredness, integrity, and relationships as well as cooperation and defined roles (Cochran and Cartledge, 1996). Families typically are intergenerational and patriarchal; fathers discipline children and mothers nurture and oversee their overall development and education. Family members exhibit patterns of social interaction and behavioral styles that resonate with unique cultural traditions and expressions of deference for individuals based on social relations. Children customarily bestow respect on parents, and there is an abiding sense of devotion for elders (Cochran and Cartledge, 1996).

In summary, children and youth in African American, American Indian/Alaska Native, Asian/Pacific Islander, and Hispanic communities are socialized to a family orientation; extended family members assist with child rearing and influence youths' understandings, attitudes, and behaviors. Some family structures do not condone homosexuality and emphasize instead the importance of marrying, procreation, and continuing the family lineage. For example, behaviors outside these perceived norms in many Asian American families are considered nonconforming and shameful. Therefore, youth and young adults often conceal their same-sex orientation in order to avoid bringing shame to the family. Their lack of disclosure, in turn, may lead to risky sexual activities that expose them to HIV infection as well as to avoidance of HIV testing and treatment (Sileo, Prater, Pateman, and Sileo, 2001). In addition, Asian American families often show an aversion to speaking about sex and sex-related issues. As a result, children and youth may have little understanding about HIV/AIDS, which precludes their avoidance of HIV-risk behaviors.

HIV/AIDS prevention educators must understand family and social norms that govern behaviors of individuals within and among racial, ethnic, and cultural groups. Effective HIV/AIDS prevention education honors traditional cultural beliefs and attitudes that reflect interdependence among individuals (Cervero, 2005). Programs should be grounded in the reality of people's lives, stress the social unacceptability of health-risk behaviors, and emphasize the importance of communal responsibility toward reducing sexual behaviors that may lead to HIV/AIDS (Chng, 1999; Mueller et al., 1997).

Gender Role Differences

Prevention educators also must be knowledgeable of male and female roles within the family constellation and of differences in sexual roles and purposes among men and women from various racial, ethnic, and cultural groups. In the African American community, for example, men often portray the attitude that procreation contributes to their adult image, and therefore they avoid use of condoms. Women may be submissive to male sexual partners and believe it is unacceptable to discuss men's multiple sexual encounters, sex partners, and condom use. This behavior, which also appears in Asian American communities, contributes to the spread of HIV in women. Finally, cultural factors within Hispanic communities tend to reinforce traditional gender roles, contribute to women's difficulties communicating about sex, and add to their increased risk of HIV infection. Some women, including those who suspect their partners are at risk of HIV infection, are reluctant to discuss condom use for fear of emotional or physical reprisals and withdrawal of financial support (Diaz, 2000; Raffaelli and Suarez-Al-Adam, 1998; Suarez-Al-Adam, Raffaelli, and O'Leary, 2000).

An estimated 64 percent of African American women, 75 percent of Asian/Pacific Islander women, and 65 percent of Hispanic women with AIDS attribute their exposure to heterosexual contact (CDC, 2003). Not only do power imbalances between men and women create problems in sexual communication, but women may be unaware of their partners' HIV-risk behaviors. They may also be expected to share injection drug needles with male sexual partners, a behavior that is related to gender role socialization (Flaskerud, 1995). Women must understand the fatal consequences of HIV-risk behaviors, overcome power struggles, and establish parameters that ensure safe sex. The final chapter in this book addresses strategies to improve women's health behaviors.

Communication Styles

Cultures vary in the extent to which they view and interact with their environments, social surroundings, and organizational structures. African Americans, Asian/Pacific Islanders, Hispanics, and various indigenous populations rely on strong social networks to develop their identities. They value interdependence and intragroup interactions as well as cohesive, person-oriented relationships that benefit group members.

HIV/AIDS prevention educators also should be aware of communication styles that influence learning and changing behaviors. For example, people of African American and Asian/Pacific Islander heritage often communicate behavioral standards through implicit nonverbal cues in which "a look, a word, or a gesture may convey the equivalent of paragraphs of spoken words" (Chng, 1999, p. 17). Sometimes, however, communication may be harsh and abrupt if an individual is passionate about a topic. Educators should acknowledge and harness the energy to educate youth and young adults about the disease.

In American Indian and Alaska Native settings, silence is often the norm, and people tend toward long pauses in conversation. They speak in low-keyed, monotone voices with a slow pace of discourse, and they communicate with select words and gestures. They seldom exert dominance over or provide excessive directions to others, nor do they address acquaintances in an overly familiar way. Finally, their conversational language may be allegorical, because content of the message is more important than emotional reactions (Lee and Cartledge, 1996). Educators of students from these backgrounds should use proverbs, small-group discussions, story telling, and role-play strategies to respect learners' communication style.

The interpersonal principle strengthens educators' awareness about the need for HIV/AIDS prevention messages that are developed and implemented in collaboration with community members and that align with cultural, interpersonal, and communication characteristics (Fan et al., 2004; Wilson and Miller, 2003). Community groups may not sanction school-based instructional programs about HIV/AIDS and other sexually transmitted diseases. Program planners, therefore, should conduct ethnographic interviews, observations, and pilot studies to determine community and cultural attitudes and concerns toward sex, sexuality, and risk-taking behaviors. They should design and implement programs that ensure an accurate and clear presentation of HIV/AIDS content accompanied by positive interactions based on participants' developmental maturity, cultural norms, belief systems, language backgrounds, and family characteristics. Ultimately, the programs should promote behavior change that deters HIV infection.

The Social Ecological Principle

Individuals' behavior changes are influenced by their current circles of friends and relatives, prior experiences with important people in their lives, and knowledge of others' beliefs and perceptions about their behaviors. The social ecological principle acknowledges the influence of social and cultural standards on people's behaviors that extend beyond family and friends. It considers the significance of religion as well as role models and respected community leaders who help to set behavioral standards.

Religious Perspectives

Religion often occupies an important place in peoples' lives and influences their behaviors, including sexual ones. Some people may abstain from sexual activities due to religious influences, while others may engage in unprotected sex because some forms of birth control have negative religious connotations (Liskin, Church, Piotrow, and Harris, 1989). This behavior is especially prevalent among Hispanics who have strong familial values related to Catholicism and who believe that religion offers significant guidance in their lives. Most Hispanics are highly conservative regarding moral and ethical issues; Catholicism does not condone the use of condoms for contraceptive purposes (Espinosa, Elizondo, and Miranda, 2003). Religious beliefs and family values, therefore, may prevent Hispanics from using condoms, even to prevent the spread of HIV infection and other sexually transmitted diseases.

Many African Americans, too, maintain a strong commitment to religious values and church participation. Churches are the foundation of family support and guidance for some African Americans as well as venues for communicating community values and desires (Frazier, 1963). At the same time, churches may avoid discussions about HIV/AIDS prevention, which hinders congregational members from seeking assistance or information about the disease and thereby fosters continued participation in health-risk behaviors. Some denominations believe that community health organizations and associations should address the issue of HIV/AIDS and its prevention. According to Lemelle (2004), many African American churches are homophobic and recognize only heterosexual relationships in marriage as an acceptable lifestyle. They argue against homosexuality, refuse to acknowledge HIV/AIDS as a heterosexual disease, and do not respond to preventive measures. Yet heightened numbers of young African Americans are becoming infected with the disease and dying from AIDS-related illnesses. Thomas (1998) believes that many churches are missing opportunities to educate their members when they do not create acceptable environments and capitalize on situations where it is suitable to discuss HIV/AIDS and its impact on the African American community. Many faith-based organizations perceive their support for HIV/AIDS prevention as an endorsement of homosexuality.

Studies indicate that the incidence of HIV/AIDS among Muslims and the Islamic Nation is less than that of other religions. According to

Gray (2004), the Muslim religion prohibits alcohol and substance use as well as premarital and extramarital sex. Islamic views require people to exhibit modesty in their discussions about sex and sexual matters; talking about sex and sexuality is considered taboo within some family constellations. Hendrick et al. (2002) found that Muslim youth have little knowledge about contraceptives and sexually transmitted diseases. A girl's virginity contributes to determining the honor and status of a family in society. Therefore, prohibitions regarding sexual encounters are more stringent for young women than for men. Family and social consequences regarding sexual activity before marriage instill fear among women, and sexual contacts usually occur under extremely secretive circumstances.

The importance of preserving virginity also is emphasized for adolescent Muslim boys. However, exceptions may be made because young men's sexual drives often are perceived as overwhelming; some people believe it is important for young men to fulfill sexual desires to be "real men." Most often, young men do not turn to women they know for sexual pleasures but rather secretly engage in sex with prostitutes, which can lead to the spread of HIV (Hendrick et al., 2002). Islamic marital codes also allow men to divorce easily and to marry as many as four wives. The increase in sexual partners may heighten the risk of HIV/AIDS and other sexually transmitted diseases (Gray, 2004), so men should know how to protect themselves and their sexual partners from infection. Once again, culturally responsive HIV/AIDS prevention programs must be implemented to deter spread of the disease.

Traditional American Indian/Alaska Native religious practices value environmental customs and enduring beliefs about spirituality, humanity, and living in harmony with nature. Religious beliefs are based on origin, place of creation, and emergence from the earth (Hendry, 2003). In many communities, illness and misfortune are attributed to supernatural causes such as witchcraft, spells, and spirit loss, as well as to natural causes that may include breaching cultural taboos, accidents, and acculturation (Joe and Malach, 1998).

People of American Indian and Alaska Native heritage often engage in traditional healing rituals and ceremonies to cure disease. Individuals with HIV/AIDS may turn to healing rites and spiritual leaders to guide and redirect their lives toward good health and healing. In addition, many Native Americans view death as a continuation of life, making discussions about health issues, disability, and death unacceptable because they may interfere with an individual's destiny (Sileo and Gooden, 2003). HIV/AIDS prevention education for Native Americans, therefore, should consider good health and respect for life in order to have a positive impact on the culture. Prevention programs must integrate cultural beliefs and healing ceremonies with Western medical practices in an attempt to meet the needs of Native American tribal communities.

Some Native American tribes accept traditional beliefs about *two-spirit* people, which emphasize sacred status for such individuals that results from a special calling or prophesy. Currently, many people equate the two-spirit status with homosexuality. Other tribes disregard these traditional beliefs and align themselves with Christianity and mainstream cultural values, which may not accept homosexuality (Sileo and Gooden, 2003). In such cases, gay American Indian men may be ostracized by their tribal communities and forced to lead secretive lives in which they practice unsafe sex. These individuals may engage in male-to-male sex in urban settings, return to tribal lands, and infect others with HIV/AIDS (Rowell, 1997). In addition, they often lack easy access to relevant HIV/AIDS prevention information.

HIV/AIDS Ministries

Various faith initiatives globally and in the United States participate in HIV/AIDS prevention and treatment activities. For example, The Balm in Gilead is a nonprofit, nongovernmental organization whose primary mission is HIV/AIDS prevention throughout the African Diaspora. Its focus is to build the capacity of faith communities to provide AIDS education and support networks for all people living with and affected by HIV/AIDS. The Balm in Gilead encourages faith institutions to respond to the HIV/AIDS crisis among African people across the world through the development and implementation of comprehensive programs that help Black churches become centers for AIDS ministry, education, and compassion.

Major church denominations, caucuses and coalitions, and independent churches endorse the goals of The Balm in Gilead, which are to (a) develop and disseminate culturally sensitive and responsive educational materials to the Christian community; (b) provide training, organization, and technical assistance to faith-based institutions as well as to HIV/AIDS service agencies and health departments; (c) heighten the understanding of HIV/AIDS community agencies and health departments about the African and African American communities as a means to engage the church in culturally competent HIV/AIDS prevention and treatment; and (d) disseminate information to the media regarding the church's response to the HIV/AIDS education needs of congregations and communities (*Week of Prayer Magazine*, 2003).

The National Black Leadership Commission on AIDS is another faith-based organization that participates in the fight against HIV/AIDS. The organization, which was formed in 1987, believes it is important for the clergy to be knowledgeable about HIV/AIDS transmission and prevention. It also mobilizes the media, medical profession, businessmen and women, politicians, and people involved in social policy issues to fight against spread of the disease within African American communities (Lemelle, 2004).

The AIDS National Interfaith Network was formed in 1987 with representatives from across Christian, Jewish, Unitarian, and other denominations to provide a religious voice in federal AIDS public policy and to improve the overall functioning of the AIDS ministries in the United States. These ministries attend to people's spiritual needs and provide a range of social services and treatment to people living with AIDS as well as HIV/AIDS prevention education.

In 1991, the United Synagogue of Conservative Judaism passed a resolution at its biennial convention for its congregations to (a) institute comprehensive, age-appropriate HIV/AIDS prevention education programs; (b) reach out in an empathic manner to people with AIDS and their families; (c) protect individuals with AIDS from legal discrimination in housing, employment, health care, and synagogue settings; and (d) prepare rabbis, cantors, and other Jewish professionals to accept and counsel people with AIDS and their families (M. Waldman, personal communication, September 27, 2005). The organization provides resources about HIV/AIDS and its interface with Judaism as well as suggestions for congregations to design and implement HIV/AIDS prevention education programs and to provide support for individuals and their families who are affected by the disease.

The Islamic community acknowledges that many Muslims are affected by AIDS and that people with the disease should not be judged or condemned but rather afforded compassion and allowed to live with dignity. In addition, the Muslim community believes that HIV/AIDS prevention education programs should emphasize Islamic moral values and inform people about methods of protection such as abstinence until marriage, monogamy, and condom use.

Many members of the Catholic Church believe the face of AIDS does not inhabit a particular individual but rather is a global face that demands a worldwide, bold, creative, moral, and humane response to its prevention and treatment. Catholic hospitals and faith organizations are playing an important role in the fight against HIV/AIDS by providing health and social services as well as spiritual support to people diagnosed with HIV/AIDS and their families. Currently, the Catholic Church provides 25 percent of all medical care for persons living with HIV/AIDS worldwide, and in the United States, an estimated 45 percent of 600 Catholic hospitals provide HIV/AIDS care as compared to 32 percent of hospitals overall (Fuller and Keenan, 2004). Many Catholic ministries have adopted the "ABC" approach to preventing the sexual transmission of HIV infection: Abstinence from sexual activity until marriage; Being faithful to a partner and practicing monogamy if already in a sexual relationship; and Condom use if sexual relations are with multiple partners.

Some Catholic theologians consider the use of condoms to be a necessary component of HIV/AIDS prevention (Fuller and Keenan, 2001). They believe that Catholic traditions, based on various seventeenth-century theological principles of morality, support and justify condom use for HIV/AIDS prevention when people engage in sexual intercourse despite a known risk of HIV infection. However, these theologians are very careful to state that any form of contraception, including condoms, is wrong regardless of the circumstances (Fuller and Keenan, 2001, 2004). Consequently, condom use may be justified medically between spouses when one person has HIV/AIDS as long as the intent is to protect the healthy partner from infection and not to prevent pregnancy.

Catholic doctrine maintains that sexual activity outside of marriage is wrong because it violates the principle of chastity. For someone who does engage in sexual relations outside of matrimony, however, condom use may be justified, as unprotected sexual activity could cause HIV infection and ultimately lead to someone's death. The use of condoms becomes a matter of justice and is deemed to be a lesser evil, valuing the protection of human life (Fuller and Keenan, 2001).

The Catholic Church also believes that illicit sexual actions are morally wrong, people who are sero-positive for HIV should practice abstinence, and transmission of HIV infection endangers the common good. Keenan (1989) states, however, that the Catholic principle of toleration allows education programs to include information about prophylactics, and counselors may advise HIV-positive people who continue to engage in sexual activity to use condoms.

It appears that some of the leadership in the Catholic Church is beginning to change its position regarding the prophylactic function of condoms to stem the spread of HIV/AIDS. The change in thinking is based on the enormity of the AIDS pandemic, extensive suffering of people worldwide, and a belief that "in the overall context of HIV prevention, condoms continue to remain a critical and effective strategy when abstinence is not pursued and these populations remain at risk" (Fuller and Keenan, 2001, p. 461).

Role Models

In addition to possessing their own credibility with community and program recipients, practitioners who design and deliver HIV/AIDS education programs may wish to connect with individuals who are role models for the community's young people. For example, Earvin "Magic" Johnson is a basketball icon to many male urban youth as well as a reputable leader within the African American community. In 1991, he acknowledged his HIV sero-positivity and founded the Magic Johnson Foundation for AIDS Research. The foundation, which focuses on the health, education, and social needs of inner-city youth, enhances young people's knowledge about HIV/AIDS prevention (Eldridge, 2004).

Magic Johnson helps to establish social standards within the African American community, and his message about HIV/AIDS prevention is effective among African American males. However, it might not have as positive an effect on African American females 18 to 45 years of age, who are contracting the disease at an alarming rate. A variety of role models, therefore, may be necessary to stem the growing number of HIV/AIDS infections among different populations, and role models should fit their target audiences (Fan et al., 2004).

Other athletic role models participate in HIV/AIDS prevention efforts. They include Olympic diving champion Greg Louganis and Olympic ice skating champion Rudy Galindo, both of whom have AIDS. Louganis, who is of Samoan heritage, lectures at colleges and universities across the country about the importance of HIV/AIDS testing, leading a closeted life as a gay man, unsafe sex, low self-esteem, and contracting HIV

(Greiner, 1995; Louganis and Marcus, 1995). Galindo is an important figure in the Hispanic community who promotes health education about HIV-related anemia. In 2003, he and songstress Patti LaBelle served as honorary cochairs of the National Minority AIDS Council (Galindo and Marcus, 1997; Official Rudy Galindo Web Site, 2004).

Allan and Leonard (2005) believe that HIV-positive individuals should be at the center of HIV/AIDS program design, implementation, and evaluation because they bring their experiences and insights of living with the disease into the development of prevention strategies. The involvement of people with AIDS in prevention activities helps to put a human face on AIDS and to incorporate the lived experiences of people into prevention activities. In addition, it has proven to be one of the most effective and accessible forms of community education. HIV-positive people can shed light on the trials and tribulations of living with the disease as well as on treatment regimens and their side effects (Allan and Leonard, 2005). The voices of people with the disease can have a positive impact on the prevention of HIV infection.

Finally, in addition to persons with AIDS, role models may include other sports and media personalities to help maximize the scope of prevention messages. The National Basketball Association (NBA), in partnership with the International Basketball Federation (FIBA), runs the Basketball Without Borders program, an international basketball and community relations outreach initiative since 2001 (T. Jacobson, personal communication, June 6, 2005). Basketball Without Borders is a cornerstone of the NBA's global outreach efforts and incorporates a basketball instructional camp for top young players on each continent while at the same time promoting education, leadership, life skills, healthy living, and HIV/AIDS awareness and prevention.

In response to the overwhelming AIDS epidemic in Africa, the NBA and FIBA brought the program to that continent in 2003 to promote education, HIV/AIDS awareness and prevention, and basketball instruction. The camp included NBA players as well as the 100 top young basketball players from 21 African countries. Partners on the program included the U.S. Embassy in South Africa, South Africa's "Lovelife" national HIV prevention program for youth, and the Ithuteng Trust, a program in Soweto that assists at-risk youth with life skills and education (Babcock, 2005; T. Jacobson, personal communication, June 6, 2005). In 2005, Basketball Without Borders is expanding to four continents: Africa, Europe, South America, and Asia.

Similar programs are in place in other regions around the world where HIV/AIDS is spreading rapidly. For example, U.S. actor, humanitarian, and AIDS activist Richard Gere has created a public charity, Healing the Divide. The charity is dedicated to helping communities in Asia, India, and the United States to tackle pressing social and cultural challenges. The charity's early efforts in India include an HIV/AIDS awareness project and development of culturally sensitive secondary school curricula designed to stop the spread of AIDS. Gere's most ambitious program is The Heroes Project, which also involves India's government and industry in the fight against HIV/AIDS (*Healing the Divide Newsletter,* 2004). The project attempts to reduce the stigma and discrimination associated with the disease by reaching out to the people of India through television and radio public service announcements, on-line and print resources, and events that educate and raise people's awareness about the severity of HIV/AIDS. The safe-sex television advertisements feature Indian cricket star Rahul Dravid, who is a role model to youth and young adults in India.

The Structural Principle

HIV/AIDS prevention programs, because of our heterogeneous world, must respond to a variety of physical and contextual environments as well as legal considerations. These environments are the structural elements that complement or conflict with social and cultural norms.

Environmental Variables

According to Levenson (2004), the HIV/AIDS epidemic links to urban decay and concomitant contributing forces that may include, but are not limited to, public housing policy and related housing destruction; crack cocaine and heroin scourges; ill-conceived architecture of the war on drugs; media failure to grasp the interrelated dimensions of the HIV/AIDS epidemic, drugs, and violence; contours and cultures of the African American church; aftermath of the great southern migration of African Americans to northern urban areas; and gaps in national prevention and surveillance plans.

Levenson (2004) argues that if race is largely about segregation, and segregation is about place, then the story of urban decay helps to illuminate the social disintegration that underlies the intersecting epidemics of AIDS, drugs, and violence. Although African American parents endeavor to be positive role models for their children, intersecting environmental influences of poverty, low-income housing, domestic violence, and gang activity often cripple their efforts.

Numerous Southeast Asian immigrants also live in a world of poverty, violence, and drugs (Yin, 2000). They have low education levels and poor access to health care as well as a tendency to engage in risk behaviors associated with HIV/AIDS. As a result, this group incurs high rates of tuberculosis, hepatitis-B, and pneumocystis carinii pneumonia (Chen and Hawks, 1995; Eckholdt and Chin, 1997).

Hispanics, too, in both urban and rural areas, may not have adequate skill levels for employment, live below federal poverty levels, and lack access to health information and high-quality health care. Cultural and linguistic barriers mitigate their ability to communicate with health care providers. Hispanics tend to seek HIV testing late in their illness and are more likely to have AIDS-defining illnesses at the time of testing and diagnosis of infection (CDC, 2003). Socioeconomic circumstances are especially dire for Hispanic migrant farm workers who have low education levels and do not speak English (Human Resources and Services Administration, 2005).

Finally, many residents of American Indian reservations and Alaska Native villages are very poor—a condition which, as with other groups, is linked to low levels of education and poor health. Many indigenous people have little awareness about HIV/AIDS and other sexually transmitted diseases, and they experience higher incidences of alcohol and drug abuse than other populations. Injection drug use further exacerbates their risk of contracting HIV through shared needles and drug-related sexual encounters.

In summary, psychological, social, and economic variables as well as myriad situational factors influence individuals' health-risk behaviors. Youth and young adults from diverse racial and ethnic communities often attribute their high-risk behaviors to a sense of fatalism derived from their impoverished environment.

Legal Perspectives

Legislation often determines social and cultural standards, yet neither legal nor social structures always protect individuals at risk of HIV infection. For example, there are few truly confidential HIV testing sites and well-trained counselors. A decision to seek HIV testing is complex because individuals must weigh the benefits against the costs of testing: HIV sero-positivity, breaches of confidentiality, and financial expenses (Auerbach, Wypijewska, and Brodie, 1994). An increase in availability of testing sites and a concomitant decrease in the cost of testing could create a significant difference in people's decisions to seek HIV testing.

In addition, people may be more willing to seek testing if they are ensured confidentiality. When positive test results are disclosed, individuals may suffer discrimination as well as multiple repercussions related to loss of interpersonal relationships, housing, employment, and child custody. Health information contains personal details that deserve protection and, if violated, can take emotional and physical tolls on individuals and their families. Medical and legal fields acknowledge the importance of confidentiality, yet violations often occur at testing sites (Canadian HIV/AIDS Legal Network, 2002–2004). Confidentiality is a major concern among American Indians and Alaska Natives who seek HIV testing at Indian Health Service hospitals in reservation and village settings. Even when people do submit to testing, there is a high level of initial nonacceptance among persons who test positively for the disease.

Teachers, administrators, and other school personnel also need to be knowledgeable about legal considerations, especially as they concern students' rights to a free, appropriate public education; due process safeguards; and issues of confidentiality. Quite often, children and youth with HIV/AIDS, depending on the stage of their illness, may have concomitant physical and cognitive difficulties and, therefore, be eligible for special education and related services. According to the Office of Civil Rights, they qualify for services under "Section 504 due to the substantial limitation imposed on a major life activity caused either by a physical impairment or the reaction of others to the perceived contagiousness of the disease" (cited in Katsiyannis, 1992, p. 220).

A primary consideration regarding the education of students with HIV/AIDS relates to the setting. The concept of inclusive education suggests that all students attend schools nearest their homes and participate in least restrictive educational settings with age and grade peers. Accordingly, children and youth with HIV/AIDS should attend general classroom settings, to the extent possible, where they receive appropriate educational, medical, and habilitative services, based on progression of the disease. Therefore, educators must create caring school climates that foster compassion and tolerance for individual differences; support students' academic, social, and emotional well-being;

and maintain confidentiality for youth and other family members who may be affected by the disease.

The U.S. Constitution upholds the principle that professionals have a duty to preserve an individual's privacy rights. Students and their families have a right to privacy about health issues, disclosure of their HIV status, and the persons eligible to receive the information. In addition, the information should be excluded from educational and health records that are accessible to persons beyond those identified by the students, parents, or guardian. Unauthorized disclosure of HIV-related information could have a negative impact on a student's privacy and provoke potential harassment and discrimination. Furthermore, school personnel could experience individual liability as well as criminal or civil suits when they violate confidentiality issues.

Finally, many members of society perceive HIV/AIDS as a social stigma associated with same-sex orientation, unprotected sexual activity, and injection drug use. Consequently, students and family members may experience feelings of shame, guilt, and confusion, as well as a sense of isolation and abandonment. Educators must ensure a sense of belonging and perhaps even serve as advocates and care coordinators for students and their families (Prater and Sileo, 1994; Prater, Serna, Sileo, and Katz, 1995).

The Scientific Principle

Considerable financial and individual resources have been expended nationally and internationally to identify the biological and immunological causes of HIV/AIDS, medical treatments and cure for the disease, and effective means to change people's HIV-risk behaviors. The enormous nature of the pandemic limits the ability to make deep inroads into diminishing its prevalence. Research is needed to assess people's general knowledge about HIV/AIDS as well as perceptions about their susceptibility to the disease. In addition, research should determine the effectiveness of HIV/AIDS prevention and intervention campaigns, programs, and materials on target communities to inform decision-making about the need for program change.

The studies might include scientific, objective assessments that yield quantitative data to detect changes that occur in experimental and control groups as a result of HIV/AIDS prevention programs and treatments. In addition, ethnographic studies should be conducted among people living with HIV/AIDS—as well as family and other care providers, community agency personnel, and education professionals, among others—to identify their experiences as individuals affected by the disease (Fan et al., 2004).

SUMMARY AND CONCLUSIONS

The AIDS pandemic continues to spread nationally and globally. It is the fourth leading cause of death worldwide, after heart disease, strokes, and acute lower respiratory infections. The lack of a medical cure necessitates significant change in people's sexual behaviors to decrease spread of the disease. The application of health behavior principles discussed in this chapter will assist those developing HIV/AIDS prevention education programs.

Successful HIV/AIDS prevention education requires careful attention to the influences of environmental constructs on people's behaviors. Health behavior change principles are linked closely with family and cultural values, language, and religious viewpoints regarding HIV/AIDS. Although this chapter serves as a general foundation to facilitate readers' understanding about the disease among the nation's diverse racial, ethnic, and cultural populations, the authors acknowledge the heterogeneity within every group and caution readers against generalizing these traits to all group members. Traditional values and folkways are modified by proximity to and interaction with mainstream society's values and practices, and cultural scripts change as people adapt to new customs and lessen ties with their home country and language. In addition, patterns among immigrants and refugees may differ depending on assimilation rates; immigrants often are eager to embrace the language and culture of their new country, whereas refugees may be slower in adopting language and cultural mores (Cochran and Cartledge, 1996). As they design and implement HIV/AIDS prevention programs, educators should consider typical patterns as well as the broad range of acculturation and adaptation that occurs among all populations.

REFERENCES

Allan, B., and Leonard, W. (2005). Asserting a positive role: HIV-positive people in prevention. In J. P. Egan, ed., *HIV/AIDS Education for Adults* (pp. 43–54). San Francisco: Jossey-Bass.

Auerbach, J. D., Wypijewska, C., and Brodie, H. K. H., eds. (1994). *AIDS and behavior: An integrated approach*. Washington, DC: National Academy Press.

Babcock, R. (2005). *Timberwolves: Africa 100 camp*. NBA Media Ventures. Retrieved September 19, 2005, from http://aol.nba.com/timberwolves/news/africa100_03.html.

Barnhardt, R., and Kawagley, A. O. (2005). Indigenous knowledge systems and Alaska Native ways of knowing. *Anthropology and Education Quarterly* 35(1): 8–23.

Behrman, G. (2004). *The invisible people*. New York: Free Press.

Bogart, L. M., and Thorburn, S. (2005). Are HIV/AIDS conspiracy beliefs a barrier to HIV prevention among African Americans? *Journal of Acquired Immune Deficiency Syndromes* 38(2): 213–218.

Bryant, L. (2004, October). *Demystifying the "down low": Black masculinity, sexuality, and HIV among Black men who have sex with men*. Paper presented at the U.S. Conference on AIDS, Philadelphia, PA.

Canadian HIV/AIDS Legal Network. (2002–2004). Privacy: Human rights, public policy, and law. In *Privacy protection and the disclosure of health information: Legal issues for people living with HIV/AIDS in Canada* (pp. 1–3). Canada: Canadian HIV/AIDS Legal Network.

Cartledge, G., and Feng, H. (1996). Asian Americans. In G. Cartledge and J. F. Milburn, eds., *Cultural diversity and social skills instruction: Understanding ethnic and gender differences* (pp. 87–132). Champaign, IL: Research Press.

Cartledge, G., and Middleton, M. B. (1996). African Americans. In G. Cartledge and J. F. Milburn, eds., *Cultural diversity and social skills instruction: Understanding ethnic and gender differences* (pp. 133–204). Champaign, IL: Research Press.

Centers for Disease Control and Prevention. (2000). HIV/AIDS among racial/ethnic minority men who have sex with men: United States, 1989–1998. *Morbidity and Mortality Weekly Report* 49: 4–11.

Centers for Disease Control and Prevention. (2003). Late versus early testing of HIV: 16 sites, United States, 2002–2003. *Morbidity and Mortality Weekly Report* 52(25): 581–586.

Centers for Disease Control and Prevention. (2004). *HIV/AIDS surveillance report: Cases of HIV infection and AIDS in the United States, 2003*. Retrieved September 19, 2005, from http://www.cdc.gov/hiv/stats/2003SurveillanceReport.htm.

Cervero, R. M. (2005). The struggle for meaning and power in HIV/AIDS education. In J. P. Egan, ed., *HIV/AIDS Education for Adults* (pp. 5–10). San Francisco: Jossey-Bass.

Chen, M. S., and Hawks, B. L. (1995). A debunking of the myth of healthy Asian Americans and Pacific Islanders. *American Journal of Health Promotion* 9: 261–268.

Chng, C. L. (1999). Asians and Pacific Islander Americans. In *Cultural competence for providing technical assistance, evaluation, and training for HIV prevention programs: A research synthesis* (pp. 12–23). Washington, DC: CRP.

Clay, S. B. (2002). Life on the down low: Villains or victims? *HIV Plus* 5(7): 28–31.

Cochran, L. L., and Cartledge, G. (1996). Hispanic Americans. In G. Cartledge and J. F. Milburn, eds., *Cultural diversity and social skills instruction: Understanding ethnic and gender differences* (pp. 245–296). Champaign, IL: Research Press.

Dejong, W. (2000, January). Language matters. *Prevention Pipeline Newsletter* 3.

Diaz, R. M. (2000). Latino gay men and psycho-cultural barriers to AIDS prevention. In M. P. Levine, P. M. Nardi, and J. H. Gagnon, eds., *Changing times: Gay men and lesbians encounter HIV/AIDS* (pp. 221–244). Chicago: University of Chicago Press.

Eckholdt, H., and Chin, J. (1997). Pneumocystis carinii pneumonia in Asians and Pacific Islanders. *Clinical Infectious Diseases* 24: 1265–1267.

Egan, J. P. (2005). Marginalized, not marginal: Adult education's unique contribution to the fight against HIV/AIDS. In J. P. Egan, ed., *HIV/AIDS education for adults* (pp. 85–94). San Francisco: Jossey-Bass.

Eldridge, E. (2004). Rebounding from basketball court to boardroom. *USA Today* [on-line]. Retrieved September 28, 2005, from http://www.usatoday.com/money/companies/management/2004–11–07–magic_x.htm.

Espinosa, G., Elizondo, V., and Miranda, J. (2003). Hispanic churches in American public life: Summary of findings. *Interim Reports* 2003 (2): 7–28.

Fan, H., Conner, R. F., and Villarreal, L. P. (2004). *AIDS, science, and society.* Sudsbury, MA: Jones and Bartlett.

Faryna, E. L., and Morales, E. (2000). Self-efficacy and HIV-related risk behaviors among multiethnic adolescents. *Cultural Diversity and Ethnic Minority Psychology* 6(1): 42–56.

Flaskerud, J. H. (1995). Culture and ethnicity. In J. H. Flaskerud and J. P. Ungvarski, eds., *HIV/AIDS: A guide to nursing care*. 3rd ed. (pp. 405–432). Philadelphia: W. B. Saunders.

Flaskerud, J. H., and Nyamathi, A. (1998). An AIDS education program for Vietnamese women. *New York State Journal of Medicine* 88: 632–637.

Frazier, E. (1963). *The Negro church in America*. New York: Schocken.

Fuller, J. D., and Keenan, J. F. (2001). Condoms, Catholics, and HIV/AIDS prevention. *Furrow* 52: 459–467.

Fuller, J. D., and Keenan, J. F. (2004). Church politics and HIV prevention: Why is the condom question so significant and so neuralgic? In L. Hogan and B. FitzGerald, eds., *Between poetry and politics: Essays in honor of Edna McDonagh* (pp. 158–181). Dublin: The Columba Press.

Galindo, R., and Marcus, E. (1997). *Icebreaker: The autobiography of Rudy Galindo*. New York: Pocket Books.

Gray, P. B. (2004). HIV and Islam: Is HIV prevalence lower among Muslims? *Social Science and Medicine* 58(9): 1751–1756.

Greiner, K. (1995, November 6). Greg Louganis breaks the surface: Former Olympian tells his story. *Monroe Street Journal*. Retrieved September 19, 2005, from http://www.umich.edu/~msjrnl/backmsj/110695/loug.html.

Hagen, K. S. (2005). Bad blood: The Tuskegee syphilis study and legacy recruitment for experimental AIDS vaccines. In J. P. Egan, ed., *HIV/AIDS Education for Adults* (pp. 11–20). San Francisco: Jossey-Bass.

Hayman, L. L., Mahon, M. M., and Turner, J. R., eds. (2002). *Health and behavior in childhood and adolescence*. New York: Springer.

Healing the Divide Newsletter. (2004). 1–7. Retrieved September 19, 2005, from http://www.healingthedivide.org/newsletter/index.html.

Hendrick, K., Lodewijck, E., Van Royen, P., and Denekens, J. (2002). Sexual behavior of second generation Moroccan immigrants balancing between traditional attitudes and safe sex. *Patient Education and Counseling* 47(2): 89–94.

Hendry, J. (2003). Mining the sacred mountain: The clash between the Western dualistic framework and Native American religions. *Multicultural Perspectives* 5(1): 3–10.

Human Resources and Services Administration. (2005). *Hispanics and HIV/AIDS* (HRSA Fact Sheet). Retrieved September 16, 2005, from http://hab.hrsa.gov/history/fact2005/hispanics_and_hivaids.htm.

Hunt, D. E., Gooden, M., and Barkdull, C. (2001). Walking in moccasins: Indian child welfare in the 21st century. In A. L. Sallee, H. A. Lawson, and K. Briar-Lawson, eds., *Innovative practices with vulnerable children and families* (pp. 165–187). Dubuque, IA: Eddie Bowers.

Jemmott, J. B., Jemmott, L. W., Spears, H., Hewitt, N., and Cruz-Collins, M. (2002). Self-efficacy, hedonistic expectancies, and condom-use intentions among inner-city black adolescent women: A social cognitive approach to AIDS risk behavior. *Journal on Adolescent Health* 13(6): 512–519.

Jemmott, L. S., Maula, E. C., and Bush, E. (1999). Hearing our voices: Assessing HIV prevention needs among Asian and Pacific Islander women. *Journal of Transcultural Nursing* 10: 102–111.

Jester, T. E. (2002). Healing the "unhealthy native": Encounters with standards-based education in rural Alaska. *Journal of American Indian Education* 41(3): 1–21.

Joe, J. R., and Malach, R. S. (1998). Families with Native American roots. In E. W. Lynch and M. J. Hanson, eds., *Developing cross-cultural competence*. 2nd ed. (pp. 127–164). Baltimore: Paul H. Brookes.

Joint United Nations Programme on HIV/AIDS. (2004). *2004 report on the global AIDS epidemic.* Retrieved September 16, 2005, from http://www.unaids.org/bangkok2004/GAR2004_html/GAR2004_00_en.htm.

Kahn, R. (2005, March 20). Knowing is beautiful—or is it? *Boston Globe*, p. C-1.

Katsiyannis, A. (1992). Policy issues of school attendance of children with AIDS: A national survey. *Journal of Special Education* 26: 219–226.

Keenan, J. F. (1989). Prophylactics, toleration, and cooperation: Contemporary problems and traditional problems. *International Philosophical Quarterly* 29(2): 205–220.

Ladson-Billings, G. (2000). Fighting for our lives: Preparing teachers to teach African American students. *Journal of Teacher Education* 51: 206–214.

Lee, J. W., and Cartledge, G. (1996). Native Americans. In G. Cartledge and J. F. Milburn, eds., *Cultural diversity and social skills instruction: Understanding ethnic and gender differences* (pp. 205–244). Champaign, IL: Research Press.

Lemelle, A. J., Jr. (2004). African American attitudes toward gay males: Faith-based initiatives and implications for HIV/AIDS services. *Journal of African American Studies* 7(4): 59–74.

Lesnick, H. (2001). *It's up to us: An AIDS education curriculum for ESL students and other English language learners.* Bronx: City University of New York, Hostos Community College, Department of Language and Cognition. Retrieved September 19, 2005, from http://www.hostos.cuny.edu/homepages/lesnick/aids.

Levenson, J. (2004). *The secret epidemic: The story of AIDS and Black America.* New York: Pantheon Books.

Linley, P. A., and Joseph, S., eds. (2004). *Positive psychology in practice.* Hoboken, NJ: John Wiley and Sons.

Liskin, L., Church, C. A., Piotrow, P. T., and Harris, J. A. (1989). *AIDS education: A beginning. Population Reports* (Series L 8: 25–27). New York: Printed Matter/Irvington Publisher.

Louganis, G., and Marcus, E. (1995). *Breaking the surface.* New York: Random House.

Maldanado, M. (1999). *HIV/AIDS and Native Americans.* Washington, DC: National Minority AIDS Council.

Mueller, C. W., Bidwell, R., Manning, E., Mew, S., Goo, C., Dunbar, H., and Lovely, R. H. (1997). Adolescent construction of HIV and HIV prevention. *Journal of HIV/AIDS Prevention and Education for Adolescents and Children* 1(2): 13–27.

Official Rudy Galindo Web Site. (2004). *More about Rudy.* Retrieved September 19, 2005, from http://www.rudy-galindo.com/more1.htm.

Prater, M. A., and Sileo, T. W. (1994). HIV/AIDS and abuse issues: Preparing future school personnel. In P. C. Long, ed., *Quality outcomes: A showcase for education proceedings* (pp. 150–158). Melbourne: Australian Association for Special Education.

Prater, M. A., Serna, L. A., Sileo, T. W., and Katz, A. R. (1995). HIV Disease: Implications for special educators. *Remedial and Special Education* 16: 68–78.

Quinn, S. C. (1997). Belief in AIDS as a form of genocide: Implications of HIV prevention programs for African Americans. *Journal of Health Education* 28(6): S-6–11.

Raffaelli, M., and Suarez-Al-Adam, M. (1998). Reconsidering the HIV prevention needs of Latino women in the United States. In N. L. Roth and L. K. Fuller, eds., *Women and AIDS: Negotiating safer practices, care, and representation* (pp. 7–43). Binghamton, NY: Harrington Park/Haworth.

Rowell, R. (1996). *HIV prevention for gay/bisexual/two-spirit Native American men.* Oakland, CA: National Native American AIDS Prevention Center.

Rowell, R. (1997). Developing AIDS services for Native Americans: Rural and urban contrasts. In L. B. Brown, ed., *Two spirit people: American Indian lesbian women and gay men* (pp. 85–95). New York: Haworth.

Sanchez, M. (2005, January 15). Americans with AIDS survive longer, but lives remain a struggle. *Anchorage Daily News,* pp. A-1, A-7.

Sileo, N. M. (2005). Design HIV/AIDS prevention education: What are the roles and responsibilities of classroom teachers? *Intervention in School and Clinic* 40(3): 177–181.

Sileo, T. W., and Gooden, M. A. (2003). HIV/AIDS prevention in American Indian and Alaska Native communities. *Tribal College Journal* 14(4): 44–48.

Sileo, T. W., Prater, M. A., Pateman, B., and Sileo, N. M. (2001). Multicultural considerations for HIV/AIDS prevention education: An Asian Pacific Islander American perspective. *Journal of HIV/AIDS Prevention and Education for Adolescents and Children* 4(4): 23–41.

Sileo, T. W., Prater, M. A., Pateman, B., and Sileo, N. M. (2002). HIV/AIDS prevention education: Culturally sensitive and responsive strategies for Asian Pacific Islander American adolescents and young adults. *Journal of HIV/AIDS Prevention and Education for Adolescents and Children* 5(1/2): 61–85.

Suarez-Al-Adam, M., Raffaelli, M., and O'Leary, A. (2000). Influence of abuse and partner hypermasculinity on the sexual behavior of Latinas. *AIDS Education and Prevention* 12: 263–274.

Thomas, S. B. (1998, August). *Cultural implications and HIV prevention: Implications for historically Black colleges and universities.* Paper presented at the National Collaborative Preservice Forum, Landsdowne, VA.

U.S. National Intelligence Council. (2002). *The next wave of HIV/AIDS: Nigeria, Ethiopia, Russia, India, and China* (Intelligence Community Assessment, ICA 2002–04D). Retrieved September 19, 2005, from http://www.cia.gov/nic/special_nextwaveHIV.html.

Week of Prayer Magazine. (2003). The Balm in Gilead, pp. 20–21.

Wilson, B. D. M., and Miller, R. L. (2003). Examining strategies for culturally grounded HIV prevention: A review. *AIDS Education and Prevention* 15(2): 184–202.

Yep, G. A. (1993). HIV/AIDS prevention among Asian-American college students: Does the health belief model work? *Journal of American College Health* 41: 199–205.

Yin, X. (2000, May 14). Economic, educational influences divide Asian Americans. *Honolulu Advertiser,* p. B-1.

10

HIV/AIDS: SEXUALITY AND DISABILITY

Wanda J. Blanchett and Mary Anne Prater

⊸⊝

Persons with disabilities at all severity levels are in public school settings across the country and rightfully so, yet many do not receive equitable access to HIV/AIDS prevention education. Consequently, they may lack understanding regarding what behaviors could put them at risk for contracting HIV/AIDS and other sexually transmitted diseases.

Discussion in this chapter addresses the preparation of educators to teach HIV/AIDS prevention; the characteristics of individuals with disabilities and their relationship to HIV-risk behaviors; issues of sexuality; and the importance of pedagogical equity and instructional strategies that (a) mesh with students' cognitive, behavioral, and learning styles; (b) contextualize learning experiences; and (c) actively involve students in learning and help them personalize new knowledge.

Since the late 1980s, several articles (e.g., Colson and Carlson, 1993; Prater, Serna, Sileo, and Katz, 1995) have appeared in the special education professional literature that call attention to the need to provide HIV/AIDS prevention education to students with disabilities and others at risk of educational failure. Students with disabilities are more vulnerable to HIV infection and other sexually transmitted diseases, sexual abuse, and teen pregnancy than their peers without disabilities (Council for Exceptional Children, 1991). Particularly, students with disabilities may be at increased risk due to (a) lack of knowledge and information about their bodies and sexuality, (b) misinformation and inability to distinguish between reality and unreality, (c) limited social skills, (d) susceptibility to others' influences, and (e) poor judgment in social situations. In addition, research highlights the poor decision-making and problem-solving skills of some students with disabilities that may place them at heightened risk of HIV infection (Blanchett, 2000; Colson and Carlson, 1993).

Little has been done to educate students with disabilities about HIV prevention despite the profession's knowledge that personal learning and social characteristics may predispose these students to HIV infection. Calls to provide comprehensive health education, including HIV/AIDS prevention, to students with disabilities (e.g., Colson and Carlson, 1993; Prater et al., 1995) appear to have gone unnoticed; research suggests that such education is not offered consistently to this population (Blanchett, 2000). Students' access to HIV/AIDS prevention seems to be related to the setting in which they receive educational services. Students with learning disabilities who are in general education classrooms for at least 75 percent of the day are more likely to participate in HIV/AIDS education than their peers who spend a minimum of 25 percent of their time in special education classes (Blanchett, 2000). Moreover, HIV/AIDS prevention education is seldom tailored to students' unique learning characteristics, styles, or preferences.

This lack of developmentally appropriate instruction continues even as the number of students with disabilities is increasing, and they have greater access to general education settings than in the past. During the 2000–2001 school year, approximately 5.8 million students, ages 6 to 21 years, were served nationwide in 13 disability categories. The categories with the largest numbers included students identified with specific learning disabilities (50 percent), speech and language impairments (18.9 percent), mental retardation (10.6 percent), and emotional disturbance (8.2 percent). In these groups as a whole, students' racial and ethnic backgrounds were 62.0 percent White, 19.8 percent Black, 14.5 percent Hispanic, 1.9 percent Asian/Pacific Islander, and 1.5 percent American Indian/Alaska Native (U.S. Department of Education, 2002). The inclusive education movement has brought about significant changes in educational placement and in the quality of services that students with disabilities receive in schools. A significant percentage of students with disabilities spend a portion, if not all, of the school day in general education settings (U.S. Department of Education, 2002).

Despite this progress regarding access to general education environments and curricula, many students with disabilities do not receive HIV/AIDS prevention education in these settings, and programs often are delivered in an inaccessible manner. A number of issues impede students' access to HIV/AIDS education, including misperceptions regarding their sexuality, sexual expression, risk factors, and behaviors, as well as teachers' lack of preparation to address issues of sexuality and disabilities. Although it might seem that special education teachers would be better equipped than general education teachers to address these issues, research suggests that neither group receives appropriate preparation because curricula rarely address human sexuality and HIV/AIDS (Rodriguez, Young, Renfro, Asencio, and Haffner, 1997; May and Kundert, 1996).

Effective HIV/AIDS prevention education and subsequent risk reduction are the only available weapons to stem the rate of infection and spread of disease. According to the Centers for Disease Control and Prevention (CDC, 1988), HIV/AIDS prevention education is most effective when it is aligned with the developmental levels and risk behaviors of a targeted group, offered as a component of a comprehensive health education program, and taught by qualified teachers. Qualified teachers are knowledgeable about HIV/AIDS prevention, capable of selecting and implementing curricula tailored to students' developmental levels and sexual risk behaviors, and comfortable teaching the content.

SPECIAL EDUCATORS' PREPARATION RELATED TO HIV/AIDS AND STUDENTS WITH DISABILITIES

Although special educators' lack of preparation to provide health education is well documented, few attempts have been made to improve their training. Surveys of preservice preparation programs suggest that only 50 percent provide special education teacher candidates with coursework related to HIV/AIDS prevention, sex education, and drug abuse (May and Kundert, 1996; May, Kundert, and Akpan, 1994). More important, most preservice programs do not require such coursework as a curricular component. Some 41 percent of special education programs in the May and Kundert (1996) study did not include any sex education in their curricula. When health or sex education content is included in special education teacher preparation, it is not required consistently.

In this same study, about 66 percent of programs indicated that sex education was covered in a required course and 14 percent in an elective course; 20 percent did not answer the question. When asked where students receive sex education coursework, 11 percent of respondents indicated a separate special education course and 19 percent reported a separate course offered by another department. May and Kundert (1996) found that there was more coverage of sex education in required special education courses in the 1990s than the 1980s. However, the total time allotted to sex education in special education classes decreased, although the time increased in courses offered by other departments. The average amount of time per semester devoted to sex education content in special education courses and those offered by other departments was 3.6 hours and 7.7 hours, respectively.

Studies in the 1990s of special educators who state that preservice preparation did not prepare them to meet students' needs regarding sex education support the belief that special education programs provide limited health education training (Foley, 1995; Foley and Dudzinski, 1995; Rabak-Wagener, Ellery, and Stacy, 1997). Three later studies provide additional evidence that special education teachers do not receive adequate preparation in this area. First, Ubbes et al. (1999) reported that only 26 states required health education coursework as a prerequisite to elementary education certification with only nine of these requiring courses in methods and materials. Second, in a study that examined what and how risk-related content is addressed in special education teacher preparation programs, Prater, Sileo, and Black (2000) found that HIV/AIDS was one of the topics least likely to be covered. Third, an analysis of textbooks providing an introduction to exceptionalities, which are used in courses usually required of all general and special education majors, revealed that only 1 of 11 texts provided comprehensive coverage of HIV/AIDS and disabilities; 1 text did not address the topic at all (Foulk, Gessner, and Koorland, 2001).

GENERAL EDUCATORS' PREPARATION RELATED TO HIV/AIDS AND STUDENTS WITH DISABILITIES

General educators also play a critical role in teaching skills and concepts associated with comprehensive health education. In elementary schools, general education classroom teachers bear primary responsibility for providing health education to all students (Hausman and Ruzek, 1995), including those with disabilities. Many of the studies cited above did not include general educators in their surveys to ascertain special and health educators' perceptions regarding their preparation to teach health and HIV/AIDS education to students with disabilities. Little is known about elementary teachers' preparation or competency to teach health education to students with disabilities.

Research findings suggest that most teacher certification programs require few health education, human sexuality, or HIV/AIDS prevention courses. One study (Rodriguez et al., 1997) found that only 14 percent of teacher preparation programs require a health education course for all preservice teachers; none of the programs surveyed require courses that address HIV/AIDS or sexuality. Only 48 percent of elementary teacher preparation programs require a health course (Rodriguez et al., 1997). In secondary education settings, health education is often provided by specialized health and physical educators; however, few secondary teachers are prepared to reinforce health education skills and concepts. Only 1 in 6 teacher preparation programs require health education courses for preservice secondary teachers who do not specialize in health or physical education (Rodriguez et al., 1997). If teachers prepared in general education programs lack training in health or HIV/AIDS prevention education, it is unlikely that they will be able to teach the content to any students, let alone those with a wide range of learning characteristics and abilities.

Teachers' lack of preparation compounds the challenges already facing students with disabilities regarding sexuality and HIV/AIDS prevention. These students have an elevated risk for contracting HIV because they may be more vulnerable than their peers to sexual abuse and drug abuse. Their vulnerability is attributed partially to characteristics of increased impulsivity, lack of resistance to peer pressure, and deficient problem-solving strategies (Prater et al., 1995). Other risk factors for substance abuse include difficulty with abstractions, attention, memory, and goal persistence; low self-esteem; and deficits in social and academic skills (Weinberg, 2001), all of which are difficulty areas for many students with disabilities.

Cocco and Harper (2002) explain the relationship between personal characteristics and vulnerability to abuse among certain individuals with disabilities: "People with mental retardation tend to binge drink when they do engage in substance use .... For an individual who is already dealing with a disability that affects one's cognitive abilities, being in social environments while intoxicated could put him or her in serious danger by impairing his or her capacity to make decisions and exercise sound judgment" (p. 38).

Some data indicate that students with disabilities might actually contract HIV/AIDS at greater rates than their peers. For example, a study of more than 8,000 Medicaid beneficiaries with HIV infection identified a larger percentage of individuals diagnosed with mental retardation than are present in the general population (Walker, Sambamoorthi, and Crystal, 1999). Transmission of HIV to these individuals cannot be pinpointed, but drug abuse most likely played a role, as most subjects in the group were substance abusers with a "registry-based injection drug use ... classification" (Walker et al., p. 360).

Of course, individuals with disabilities may be more susceptible to HIV/AIDS due to their limited exposure to school-based prevention curricula. Professionals do not always agree about their responsibility for teaching HIV/AIDS prevention to students with and without disabilities. Most educators believe HIV prevention should be taught by a health instructor, school nurse, or other trained medical specialist (Lavin, Porter, Shaw, Weill, Crocker, and Palfrey, 1994). However, other school personnel, including physical education, science, and social studies teachers, have also been identified as appropriate instructors (Prater et al., 1995).

Segregated teacher preparation programs compound the confusion about what teachers are responsible for the content. Currently, many programs are dual systems in which general and special educators are prepared separately (Carroll, Forlin, and Jobling, 2003). A potential outgrowth of segregated systems is that general educators are not prepared to work with diverse populations. They often perceive that they are prepared inadequately to work with students with disabilities (Lombard, Miller, and Hazelkorn, 1998). If general educators are responsible for teaching HIV/AIDS prevention, they also must have the skills to select and adapt appropriate curriculum and instructional strategies for students with special needs.

Teacher educators need specific knowledge about the characteristics of students with disabilities as well as curricular and instructional modifications. They also need fundamental understanding of these issues to prepare future general educators. We propose that classroom teachers and teacher educators must be knowledgeable about six major areas in the context of teaching sexuality and HIV/AIDS prevention to students with disabilities:

1. Understand the importance of addressing the HIV/AIDS prevention education needs of students with disabilities.
2. Know the learning characteristics of students with disabilities and their particular HIV/AIDS risk factors and behaviors as

well as how disabilities can affect HIV/AIDS prevention instruction.

3. Be comfortable discussing and addressing issues related to HIV/AIDS prevention such as death and dying, sexuality, disability, and the intersection of sexuality with disability and culture.

4. Be familiar with developmentally appropriate HIV/AIDS curriculum and instruction for students with disabilities.

5. Gain expertise with adapting and modifying HIV/AIDS prevention education curricula and instructional materials and strategies for students with varying abilities.

6. Develop skill in forming and maintaining collaborative relationships with professionals essential to educating students with disabilities.

EFFORTS TO INCLUDE STUDENTS WITH DISABILITIES IN HIV/AIDS PREVENTION EDUCATION

In 1988, the CDC published Guidelines for Effective School Health Education to Prevent the Spread of AIDS. The publication was an attempt to ensure uniformity regarding the purposes of HIV/AIDS education; program planning, implementation, and evaluation; and curriculum content, instructional strategies, and assessments. Unfortunately, the document did not address students with disabilities. During the following year, the Council for Exceptional Children and the Association for the Advancement of Health Education, in conjunction with an HIV prevention project funded by the CDC, held a forum to assess the extent to which children with disabilities were at risk of HIV infection and to discuss their HIV/AIDS prevention needs. An outcome of this meeting was a resource guide (Association for the Advancement of Health Education/American Alliance for Health, Physical Education, Recreation, and Dance [AAHE/AAHPERD], 1995) that included basic information about transmission of HIV and recommendations, including curricular adaptations, to provide HIV/AIDS education to students with disabilities. The forum also outlined policy implications and directions for the preservice and in-service preparation of special and health educators to meet the needs of students with disabilities.

The efforts of these organizations, although laudable, did not result in addressing the HIV/AIDS education needs of students with disabilities or ensuring that their teachers receive appropriate preparation.

Furthermore, although suggestions were made to guide preparation of special and health educators and establish collaborative efforts between the fields of special and health education, the roles and contributions of general educators were not addressed. The forum outcomes were not disseminated widely, and few special or health educators and their teacher preparation program faculty are aware of these recommendations.

HIV/AIDS KNOWLEDGE AND RISKS FOR INDIVIDUALS WITH DISABILITIES

Although studies (Bowler, Sheon, D'Angelo, and Vermund, 1992; Ford and Norris, 1993) have examined the HIV/AIDS knowledge and risk behaviors of U.S. adolescents, even of incarcerated youth (Kanterbury, Calvet, McGarvey, and Koopman, 1999), researchers did not indicate inclusion of youth and young adults with disabilities in their samples. Research concerning such individuals' knowledge about HIV/AIDS and risk behaviors is limited to a few small studies of youth and young adults with learning and behavioral disabilities and mild mental retardation. Findings suggest that students with learning disabilities (Bell, Feraios, and Bryan, 1991) and emotional disorders (Singh, Zemitzsch, Ellis, Best, and Singh, 1994) have limited exposure to HIV/AIDS prevention education and, consequently, possess misconceptions about HIV transmission. Students with disabilities who do participate in HIV/AIDS education have fewer misconceptions about transmission of the disease (Blanchett, 2000).

The sexual risk behaviors of students with learning disabilities mirror those of their peers without disabilities: Approximately 51 percent report that they engaged in behaviors during high school that place them at risk for HIV infection (Blanchett, 2000). Blanchett found that young adults with learning disabilities seldom or never used condoms during oral sex (49 percent), vaginal intercourse (38 percent), and anal intercourse (11 percent). Forty-two percent of participants indicated that they had sex with two or more partners who were strangers, and 36 percent reported using alcohol or drugs before or during sexual activity. When questioned about their sexual risk behaviors, participants indicated that they engaged in sexual activity before they were ready to do so, or they did not use condoms because unprotected sex was the "thing to do" or "everyone was doing it." These findings are consistent with the special education literature that documents susceptibility of students with disabilities to succumb to peer pressure and substance use. In addition, many individuals with mental retardation and other developmental disabilities often are victims of sexual abuse and exploitation, although students with learning and behavioral disabilities are less likely to be victims of this type of abuse.

The extent of HIV/AIDS among individuals with disabilities is inadequately documented. As early as 1990, certain individuals with mental retardation who were served by the developmental disabilities service system were believed to have HIV. In 1990, a survey estimated that more than 500 individuals with mental retardation were infected (Marchetti, Nathanson, Kastner, and Owens, 1990). A recent study of New Jersey's Medicaid recipients documented the largest single group of HIV-infected persons with mental retardation (N=119; Walker et al., 1999). The researchers reported that individuals with mental retardation, in comparison to other HIV-infected Medicaid recipients, were more likely to be female, Black, and injection drug users.

Although Walker et al. (1999) make a significant contribution to our understanding of HIV infection and individuals with disabilities, the study tracked only people with mental retardation. This investigation did not examine HIV infection among individuals with learning disabilities and emotional or behavior disorders, who are more likely to receive services that are not tracked easily. In addition, the study did not consider individuals with low-incidence diseases such as deafness, blindness, or physical and other health impairments. The prevalence of HIV/AIDS among individuals with disabilities remains largely a mystery because the CDC does not include disability as a variable for HIV/AIDS reporting agencies. In addition, few disability service agencies actually track such data. If other states identified HIV infections among individuals with disabilities at rates similar to those in New Jersey, an estimated 3,000 to 6,000 individuals with disabilities could be infected with HIV.

LEARNING CHARACTERISTICS OF STUDENTS WITH DISABILITIES

To design and implement effective instruction in any area, educators must be familiar with students' learning characteristics and these traits' effect on learning. Students with disabilities, who receive special education and related services under the Individuals with Disabilities Education Act, increasingly participate in general education settings, where teachers sometimes have little expertise in accommodating the wide range of abilities. Teachers must understand the nature and manifestation of students' disabilities as a basis for ensuring that students receive accessible HIV/AIDS prevention education (Byrom and Katz, 1991).

Students may be identified with high-incidence and low-incidence disabilities. High-incidence categories include learning disabilities, behavioral or emotional behavioral disorders, and mild mental retardation. The majority of students who receive special education services are diagnosed in these categories. For students with high-incidence disabilities to reap maximum benefits of HIV/AIDS prevention education, teachers should

- Develop and improve students' social skills, including their relationship-building skills.
- Employ multisensory teaching strategies.
- Teach self-regulatory and self-management skills.
- Teach and model problem solving and decision-making associated with HIV-risk reduction.
- Promote development of positive self-concepts.
- Help students connect their behavior and HIV/AIDS risk factors, when appropriate.
- Use role-plays to increase likelihood of students' ability to generalize skills and concepts.
- Present content, concepts, and skills in a concrete manner.
- Repeat or restate students' questions and responses during class discussion.
- Teach lessons that are developmentally and age appropriate (AAHE/AAHPERD, 1995).

Low-incidence disability areas include blindness and visual impairments, physical and other health impairments such as multiple disabilities and orthopedic impairments, and deafness and hearing disorders. Low-incidence disability categories house a small percentage of individuals with disabilities. The instructional and curricular needs of students with low-incidence disabilities, particularly those with sensory impairments, usually involve adapting and modifying materials and the environment rather than employing specific instructional strategies or techniques. For students with low-incidence disabilities to reap maximum benefits of HIV/AIDS prevention education, teachers should

- Involve students actively in all aspects of lessons.
- Provide an interpreter, when applicable.
- Allow for partial participation, when appropriate.
- Watch for fatigue among students with physical or health impairments.
- Provide enlarged-print materials for students with visual impairments.
- Support use of hearing aides by students with hearing impairments.
- Ensure students' physical access to all curriculum materials.
- Provide audiotapes of reading materials, when applicable.
- Provide materials and readings in Braille, when applicable.
- Use appropriate amplification systems, when applicable (AAHE/ AAHPERD, 1995).

In addition to addressing students' diverse learning characteristics when providing HIV/AIDS prevention education, teachers must provide culturally responsive HIV/AIDS prevention curriculum, pedagogy, and instructional practices for students with disabilities who are members of diverse racial, ethnic, and cultural populations. According to Gay (2000), educators who provide culturally responsive instruction

- Teach to and through students' prior knowledge, experiences, learning styles, and preferences to ensure effective and relevant learning.
- Build meaningful bridges between students' home and school experiences.
- Incorporate multicultural information, resources, and materials into curricula and school experiences.
- Create a sense of community in the classroom where students work together rather than in competition with each other.
- Develop and employ curricula that empower and enable students' success.

COMFORT LEVEL AND COMPETENCE OF TEACHER EDUCATORS

Teacher educators must be competent and comfortable discussing issues of sexuality, disability, and the intersection of the two areas as a foundation for preparing the next generation of teachers to meet the needs of students with disabilities relative to HIV/AIDS prevention. Competence includes the ability to separate facts and myths related to sexuality and disability. Common myths assert that individuals with disabilities are perpetual children incapable of consenting to sexual expression; contributing to an intimate, long-term relationship or marriage; and caring for offspring. Other myths promote ideas that people with disabilities are sterile, asexual with little or no interest in sexuality or sexual expression, or sexual deviants who are more promiscuous and more likely to be sex offenders than their peers without disabilities.

Teacher educators must also be comfortable addressing issues of sexuality prior to designing and implementing preservice and in-service curricula aimed at increasing teachers' capacity to address the needs of students with disabilities related to sexuality and HIV/AIDS prevention. Hence, teacher educators must

- Examine and clarify their personal beliefs and values about sexuality, sexual expression, and personal rights related to choice.
- Engage in professional development to ensure that they possess current knowledge, skills, and dispositions associated with effective HIV/AIDS prevention, which may include addressing issues of sexuality, disability, and the intersection of the two areas.
- Acknowledge and address their limitations in knowledge, skills, and dispositions related to the topic.

DEVELOPMENTALLY APPROPRIATE HIV/AIDS CURRICULUM FOR STUDENTS WITH DISABILITIES

The Individuals with Disabilities Education Act requires that students with disabilities have access to the general curriculum. More than curriculum availability, this access refers to students' opportunities to interact with the curriculum as a basis for learning (Orkwis and McLane, 1998). Students' physical, sensory, or cognitive disabilities may create obvious barriers to accessing the curriculum. Students with less obvious learning disabilities or emotional and behavioral disorders also need to engage actively with instructional materials and concepts in order to achieve meaningful access. In effect, all barriers must be removed.

Universal design is a concept in the field of special education that addresses access to the general curriculum. Universally designed curricular materials are created to be fully accessible to the broadest range of student learners (Pisha and Coyne, 2001). The instructional materials "allow the learning goals to be achievable by individuals with wide differences in their abilities to see, hear, speak, move, read, write and understand English, attend, organize, engage, and remember" (Orkwis and McLane, 1998, p. 9). Flexibility and alternatives built into the curriculum design allow access without the need for teachers to plan adaptations for students with special needs. Unfortunately, we are unaware of any universally designed curriculum materials for HIV/AIDS prevention.

The lack of developmentally appropriate health curriculum materials has been identified as a significant problem in the field (Ellery, Rabak-Wagener, and Stacy, 1997). Existing curricula and materials regarding sexuality and HIV/AIDS prevention tend to be designed for two distinct populations: students without disabilities; and students with significant disabling conditions. Both sets of materials are inappropriate for students with a wide range of disabilities. General, special, and health educators need a broader selection of developmentally appropriate health education curricula that include HIV/AIDS prevention for students with a variety of disabilities and, perhaps, disability-specific curricula (Ellery et al., 1997).

MAKING INSTRUCTIONAL AND CURRICULUM ADAPTATIONS AND MODIFICATIONS

Although universal design is an ideal goal, no curriculum or materials can ever be completely universally designed (Orkwis and McLane, 1998). Some adaptations for specific students will always be necessary, and general educators need to know how to *accommodate* and *modify* existing curricula and instructional strategies to meet the needs of students with disabilities in their classrooms.

An accommodation is usually a service or support that allows students to fully access the content and instruction and to demonstrate validly what has been learned (Nolet and McLaughlin, 2000). Accommodations may be as simple as providing large-print books or as complex as allowing a student to answer a paper-and-pencil exam verbally. Teachers must understand the content to ensure that accommodations designed for individual students do not alter the major learning outcomes of overall instruction. Most instructional accommodations fall into five broad categories: input, level of support, time, participation, and output, defined as follows:

- Input—accommodations to the manner in which instruction is delivered, such as adding structure to the lesson or visual or auditory prompts.
- Level of support—accommodations to the amount of assistance a student receives, including a peer tutor, paraeducator, or additional materials such as audiotaped books.
- Time—accommodations to the time allotted to the learning process, such as decreasing the pace of instruction or increasing the amount of time allowed to complete assignments or exams.
- Participation—accommodations to the type of a student's involvement in a task, such as assigning different roles in cooperative learning groups.
- Output—accommodations to the manner in which a student demonstrates knowledge and skills, such as allowing oral presentation (Deschenes, Ebeling, and Sprague, 1994).

Modifications differ from accommodations. When modifications are made, either the content is altered or the student's performance expectation is changed (Nolet and McLaughlin, 2000). Three examples of modifications in HIV/AIDS prevention education are (a) rewording vocabulary and terminology to more simplified terms; (b) focusing on the critical elements of instruction necessary for prevention education; and (c) including a sufficient amount of modeling, role-play, and practice for skill acquisition.

Vocabulary

All written and spoken language in curricular materials or instruction should be at an appropriate developmental level for students with disabilities. Sensitivity to the type of disability and developmental levels is paramount. Students with reading disabilities might understand most of the spoken language in instruction but will incur difficulty reading similar language. Students with cognitive disabilities need instruction and materials on a simpler level. Teachers should use basic language and terms, as needed, to communicate prevention education. For example, rather than explaining that AIDS stands for Acquired Immune Deficiency Syndrome, students can be taught the acronym only.

Critical Elements of Prevention Education

All students should not necessarily be accountable for every element of HIV/AIDS prevention curriculum. For example, curricula often include foundational or historical information prior to addressing skills focused on prevention. Historical information may not be necessary or helpful for students with disabilities. They may only need the knowledge and, particularly, the skills to prevent contracting HIV.

Modeling, Role-Play, and Practicing

Most HIV/AIDS curricula focus on knowledge, attitudes, and behaviors. Students are taught facts about HIV "in the belief that they will then act on the basis of what they know" (Aggleton, 2002, p. 5). This form of instruction is insufficient for students with disabilities. They need to acquire skills. Some curricula focus on skills acquisition, particularly decision-making and sexual communication and negotiation skills (Aggleton, 2002). Generally speaking, students with disabilities need to learn explicit skill steps and practice them through role-play until they have mastered the skills. For example, teaching students how to say "no" when approached by peers to participate in unhealthy activities—and practicing their responses—is more powerful than the discussion method often used in many curricular materials (Ellery et al., 1997).

COLLABORATIVE RELATIONSHIPS

If special and general educators are not fully prepared to teach students with disabilities about sexuality and HIV/AIDS prevention, and if health educators are not prepared to teach students with disabilities, collaborative relationships among general, special, and health educators may be the most effective tool to meet students' needs in these areas (Blanchett, 2002). Teacher educators can help develop these relationships by doing the following:

1. Prepare general, special, and health educators in integrated programs that model collaboration.

2. Establish an HIV/AIDS Prevention Education Council that consists of faculty and staff from professional programs across the campus community, including representatives from nursing, health education, and other relevant programs as well as students and current practicing educators.

3. Convene monthly council meetings to examine curricula in teacher education programs as well as in health professions to ensure that issues of disability, sexuality, and HIV/AIDS prevention education are infused into the respective program curricula, while adhering to national professional and content standards.

4. Work collaboratively with the council to develop new courses and to modify or revise existing coursework and program structures so that students in professional programs across the university have an opportunity to take courses together to enrich class discussions and develop professional relationships that will be sustained beyond program completion.

5. Initiate collaborative skill-building and professional development activities on college and university campuses to raise awareness regarding HIV/AIDS education and to retool professionals who are charged with preparing future educators and health care providers.

CONCLUSIONS AND RECOMMENDATIONS

Despite having increased access to the general education curriculum and their peers without disabilities, most students with disabilities do not receive HIV/AIDS prevention education designed to address their learning characteristics and risk behaviors. This situation is dangerous, given these students' learning characteristics, limited knowledge regarding issues of sexuality and HIV/AIDS prevention, risk behaviors, and susceptibility to sexual abuse. Many students with disabilities experience difficulty in critical skill areas, such as problem solving and decision-making, associated with HIV/AIDS prevention. If all educators are prepared to address program content and skill development, it could save these students' lives. HIV/AIDS prevention education is important for all students, but it is especially critical for students with disabilities. Rather than simply watering down existing HIV/AIDS prevention curricula, the general education curriculum and instruction should be made fully accessible to students with disabilities.

General educators should be proficient in six skill areas in order to meet the HIV/AIDS prevention needs of students with disabilities. They must (a) recognize the importance of addressing students' HIV/AIDS prevention needs; (b) realize that students' learning characteristics, health risk factors, and behaviors have an impact on instruction; (c) discuss and address issues related to HIV/AIDS prevention such as sexuality, disability, and the interface of these areas with culture; (d) understand and implement developmentally appropriate HIV/AIDS curriculum and instruction; (e) value the importance of adapting and modifying curricular materials and instructional strategies to accommodate students' diverse abilities; and (f) develop and maintain collaborative relationships with other professionals.

Students with disabilities are a diverse group of learners with regard to learning characteristics, styles, and preferences. Therefore, educators should employ the features and components of universal design when developing and implementing HIV/AIDS prevention curricula. In addition, teacher educators should develop and sustain collaborative relationships with colleagues in the fields of special and health education as well as with professionals in nursing and other relevant health professions who can assist them in preparing candidates to provide effective HIV/AIDS education to students with disabilities. The following recommendations aim to improve the preparation of all educators in the area of HIV/AIDS prevention education.

- Preservice teacher education programs must acknowledge the importance of preparing teachers to address students' educational needs, including HIV/AIDS prevention. These programs should infuse, as required preservice curricular components, courses and course content about HIV/AIDS prevention education and accommodations for learners with diverse learning characteristics and ethnic backgrounds.
- The fields of special, general, and health education should work together to establish HIV/AIDS prevention education competencies for students with disabilities in their respective teacher education programs.
- Teacher educators must foster collaborative relationships across special, general, and health education to ensure that they prepare teachers who recognize and value the importance of collaboration in HIV/AIDS prevention.

- Special, general, and health educator preparation programs must prepare culturally competent teachers who use responsive pedagogy to meet the HIV/AIDS prevention needs of ethnically, culturally, and linguistically diverse students.
- Reward and evaluation structures in academe should be revised to reflect the legitimacy of cross-disciplinary collaboration in preparing preservice and in-service teachers.
- Faculty members should participate in professional development opportunities that enable them to acquire appropriate knowledge, skills, and dispositions to prepare teachers about the interface of HIV/AIDS prevention and students' diverse learning characteristics and backgrounds.
- Assessment and evaluation research should document ongoing efforts to prepare special, general, and health educators about HIV/AIDS prevention education as a means of informing decisions about preservice and in-service teacher education curricular modifications and program change (Blanchett, 2002).

REFERENCES

Aggleton, P. (2002). HIV/AIDS prevention and sexuality education must change to meet their promise. *SIECUS Report* 31(1): 5–7.

Association for the Advancement of Health Education/American Alliance for Health, Physical Education, Recreation, and Dance. (1995). *HIV/AIDS education for students with special needs: A guide for teachers.* Fairfax, VA: Authors.

Bell, D., Feraios, A. J., and Bryan, T. (1991). Learning disabled adolescents' knowledge and attitudes about AIDS. *Learning Disabilities Research and Practice* 6: 104–111.

Blanchett, W. J. (2000). Sexual risk behaviors of young adults with LD and the need for HIV/AIDS education. *Remedial and Special Education* 21(6): 336–345.

Blanchett, W. J. (2002). State of professional preparation of special educators in health education. In *Proceedings of the National Preservice Forum: Implications for professional preparation of special education teachers in health education* (pp. 10–12). Fairfax, VA: American Association for Health Education/American Alliance for Health, Physical Education, Recreation, and Dance.

Bowler, S., Sheon, A. R., D'Angelo, L. J., and Vermund, S. H. (1992). HIV and AIDS among adolescents in the United States: Increasing risk in the 1990s. *Journal of Adolescence* 15: 345–371.

Byrom, E., and Katz, G. (1991). *HIV prevention and AIDS education: Resources for special educators.* Reston, VA: Council for Exceptional Children.

Carroll, A., Forlin, C., and Jobling, A. (2003). The impact of teacher training in special education on the attitudes of Australian preservice general educators towards people with disabilities. *Teacher Education Quarterly* 30(3): 65–79.

Centers for Disease Control and Prevention. (1988). Guidelines for effective school health education to prevent the spread of AIDS. *Morbidity and Mortality Weekly Report* 37(S-2): 1–14.

Cocco, K. M., and Harper, D. C. (2002). Substance use in people with mental retardation: A missing link in understanding community outcomes? *Rehabilitation Counseling Bulletin* 46: 34–41.

Colson, S. E., and Carlson, J. K. (1993). HIV/AIDS education for students with special need. *Intervention in School and Clinic* 28(5): 262–274.

Council for Exceptional Children. (1991). *HIV prevention education for exceptional youth: Why HIV prevention education is important* (ERIC Digest No. E507). Reston, VA: ERIC Clearinghouse on Handicapped and Gifted Children. (ERIC Document Reproduction Service No. ED340151).

Deschenes, C., Ebeling, D. G., and Sprague, J. (1994). *Adapting curriculum and instruction in inclusive classrooms: A teacher's desk reference.* Bloomington, IN: The Center for School and Community Integration Institution for the Study of Developmental Disabilities.

Ellery, P. J., Rabak-Wagener, J., and Stacy, R. D. (1997). Special educators who teach health education: Their role and perceived ability. *Remedial and Special Education* 18: 105–112.

Foley, R. M. (1995). Special educators' competencies and preparation for the delivery of sex education. *Special Services in the Schools* 19(1): 95–112.

Foley, R. M., and Dudzinski, M. (1995). Human sexuality education: Are special educators prepared to meet the educational needs of disabled youth? *Journal of Sex Education and Therapy* 21(3): 182–191.

Ford, K., and Norris, A. E. (1993). Knowledge of AIDS transmission risk behavior, and perceptions of risk among urban, low income, African-American and Hispanic youth. *American Journal of Preventive Medicine* 9: 297–306.

Foulk, D., Gessner, L. J., and Koorland, M. A. (2001). Human Immunodeficiency Virus/Acquired Immune Deficiency Syndrome (HIV/AIDS) content in introduction to exceptionalities textbooks. *Action in Teacher Education* 23(1): 47–54.

Gay, G. (2000). *Culturally responsive teaching: Theory, research, and practice.* New York: Teachers College Press.

Hausman, A. J., and Ruzek, S. B. (1995). Implementation of comprehensive school health education in elementary schools: Focus on teacher concerns. *Journal of School Health* 65: 81–86.

Kanterbury, R. J., Calvet, G. J., McGarvey, E. L., and Koopman, C. (1999). HIV risk-related attitudes and behaviors of incarcerated adolescents: Implications for public school students. *High School Journal* 82(1): 1–10.

Lavin, A. T., Porter, S. M., Shaw, D. M., Weill, K. S., Crocker, A. C., and Palfrey, J. S. (1994). School health services in the age of AIDS. *Journal of School Health* 64: 27–31.

Lombard, R. C., Miller, R. J., and Hazelkorn, M. N. (1998). School-to-work and technical preparation: Teacher attitudes and practices regarding the inclusion of students with disabilities. *Career Development for Exceptional Individuals* 21: 161–172.

Marchetti, A., Nathanson, R., Kastner, T., and Owens, R. (1990). AIDS and state developmental disability agencies: A national survey. *American Journal of Public Health* 80: 54–56.

May, D. C., and Kundert, D. K. (1996). Are special educators prepared to meet the sex education needs of their students? A progress report. *Journal of Special Education* 29(4): 433–441.

May, D., Kundert, D., and Akpan, C. (1994). Are we preparing special educators for the issues facing schools in the 1990s? *Teacher Education and Special Education* 17(3): 192–199.

Nolet, V., and McLaughlin, M. J. (2000). *Accessing the general curriculum: Including students with disabilities in standards-based reform.* Thousands Oaks, CA: Corwin.

Orkwis, R., and McLane, K. (1998). *A curriculum every student can use: Design principles for student access.* Reston, VA: The ERIC Clearinghouse on Disabilities and Gifted Education.

Pisha, B., and Coyne, P. (2001). Smart from the start: The promise of universal design for learning. *Remedial and Special Education* 22: 197–203.

Prater, M. A., Serna, L. A., Sileo, T. W., and Katz, A. R. (1995). HIV disease: Implications for special educators. *Remedial and Special Education* 16: 68–78.

Prater, M. A., Sileo, T. W., and Black, R. S. (2000). Preparing educators and related school personnel to work with at-risk students. *Teacher Education and Special Education* 23: 51–64.

Rabak-Wagener, J., Ellery, P. J., and Stacy, R. D. (1997). An analysis of health education provided to students with disabilities in Nebraska. *Journal of Health Education* 28: 165–170.

Rodriguez, M., Young, R., Renfro, S., Asencio, M., and Haffner, D. W. (1997). Teaching our teachers to teach: A study on preparation for sexuality education and HIV/AIDS prevention. *Journal of Psychology and Human Sexuality* 9(3/4): 121–141.

Singh, A. N., Zemitzsch, A. A., Ellis, C. R., Best, A. M., and Singh, N. N. (1994). Seriously emotionally disturbed students' knowledge and attitudes about AIDS. *Journal of Emotional and Behavioral Disorders* 2: 156–163.

Ubbes, V. A., Cottrell, R. R., Ausherman, J. A., Black, J. M., Wilson, P., Gill, C., and Snider, J. (1999). Professional preparation of elementary teachers in Ohio: Status of K–6 health education. *Journal of School Health* 69(1): 17–21.

U.S. Department of Education. (2002). To assure the free appropriate public education of all children with disabilities. *Twenty-fourth annual report to Congress on the implementation of the Individuals with Disabilities Education Act.* Washington, DC: Author.

Walker, J., Sambamoorthi, U., and Crystal, S. (1999). Characteristics of persons with mental retardation and HIV/AIDS infection in a statewide Medicaid population. *American Journal on Mental Retardation* 104: 356–363.

Weinberg, N. Z. (2001). Risk factors for adolescent substance abuse. *Journal of Learning Disabilities* 34: 343–351.

11

HIV/AIDS: UNDERSTANDING MEN'S DECISIONS AND CHOICES

Reginald Fennell

᪰

Imagine two men embracing, kissing, and smiling as others delight in their unbridled joy. Most people accept such behavior as appropriate if it accompanies a sports victory, but if the embrace is celebrating a marriage or civil union between two men, many people find it socially unacceptable.

This phenomenon is just one example of the nuances of male socialization and gender roles in our society. This chapter discusses these topics, particularly as they relate to gay men, as well as issues of sexuality, race, and ethnicity, each of which affects men's choices and decisions regarding health and sexual behaviors. Knowledge of these variables helps educators to understand the intersection of men's behaviors and HIV/AIDS, including the transmission of HIV, HIV/AIDS prevention education, and harm reduction behaviors. Specific examples are provided to illustrate the impact of socialization on men's behaviors, and educational methods and approaches are suggested as guides to build effective HIV/AIDS prevention messages and influence positive change in men's behaviors regarding HIV/AIDS.

According to Keeling and Engstrom (1992), the

> spectrum of male–male sexual behavior is broad and diverse: it includes men whose sexual contact with other men is limited to a certain period of their lives (such as, for example, while in college), or to particular circumstances that recur now and then; men who have, or have had, sex with women as well as with men; men whose only historical or current sexual activity is

185

with other men; and men who have not yet had sexual contact with other men, but whose fantasy life is dominated by male-male intimacy and who may, at some time, experience sex with another man. In the same broad spectrum are men who have never been married, are separated or divorced from one or more women, or are currently married; men who are childless and men who have, or have adopted, children; and men who are committed to a long-term relationship with another man. Like men who never had (and do not generally fantasize about) sex with other men and whose primary affective attachments are to women, men who have (and do fantasize about) sex with other men and whose primary affective attachments are to men are variably caring and cold, interesting and dull, conventional and unusual, clever and predictable. (p. 55)

In short, the issues of men and male sexuality are complicated and cannot be addressed without understanding why and how men are socialized and their resulting behaviors. Keeling and Engstrom (1992) explain that the spectrum

incorporates men who define themselves as gay, or homosexual; men who label themselves bisexual; and men who call themselves heterosexual. A pattern of some type, frequency, and duration of homosexual behavior—having sexual contacts with others of the same [sex]—is part of the life experience of many men, most of whom would not label themselves homosexual. Regardless of the existence of homosexual behavior or fantasy, many men (and many cultures) are uncomfortable with naming the behavior, or fantasy, homosexual (or gay, for that matter), or with acknowledging that the behavior happens. Society does a disservice to all of these "homosexual and bisexual men," the whole spectrum of them—and just as critically, to men in general and to itself—when it insists on labels that limit and stereotype them, wholly defining them by naming a sexual behavior and overlooking the broad diversity that characterizes their lives, hearts, and minds. Thus the term *homosexual* describes certain behaviors, but it is inadequate to describe people. (pp. 55–56)

Sexual orientation concerns gay, lesbian, bisexual, and transgender identities of people from diverse racial, ethnic, and cultural heritages (Mobley, 2000). People of diverse backgrounds who are gay or lesbian experience minority perspectives based on both heritage and sexual orientation (Kumashiro, 2002). Consequently, they could be identified as *double identity* individuals who could experience *double marginalization* in mainstream society as well as in their own racial and ethnic communities. Double identity and marginalization also could be affected by other identities. Hoban and Ward (2003) elaborate on the "connection between HIV and culture," encouraging educators to recognize the "heterogeneity within cultural groups and the multiple identities of individuals" (p. 137) in their instruction. Fennell (2003) also emphasizes this concept, saying that "students are not a monolith ... a student could be a lesbian Hispanic female, a transgender White male, a bisexual Asian female, a gay Black male, a lesbian Native American female, or a GLBTQ student who uses a wheelchair" (p. 102).

MALE SOCIALIZATION AND GENDER ROLE THEORIES

Socialization influences people's reactions to almost everything, including men, sex, and sexual orientation. Common definitions of the terms *sex, gender, roles, gender roles, androgynous,* and *gender role strain* (see Table 11.1) can help educators better understand boys and men as well as the complexities involved in educating them.

David and Brannon (1976) describe four major themes in male socialization processes and traditional masculinity:

- *No Sissy Stuff:* The stigma of all stereotyped feminine characteristics and qualities, including openness and vulnerability.
- *Be a Big Wheel:* Success, status, and the need to be looked up to.

Table 11.1. Definition of Terms

Sex:	The biological state of being male or female.
Gender:	The psychosocial condition of being feminine or masculine; the collection of particular behaviors, traits, and interests that people agree to be masculine or feminine.
Roles:	Any pattern of behaviors that a given individual in a specified situation is expected, encouraged, and trained to perform.
Gender roles:	Behaviors, personality, characteristics, and lifestyles that a culture or society expects of an individual based on the individual's sex.
Androgynous:	Having both masculine and feminine characteristics.
Gender role strain:	Excessive mental or physical tension caused by gender role conflict and the effects of masculine, feminine, or androgynous roles.

Source: Adapted from David and Brannon (1976), McAnulty and Burnette (2003), and O'Neil (1981).

- *Be a Sturdy Oak:* A manly air of toughness, confidence, and self-reliance.
- *Give 'Em Hell!* The aura of aggression, violence, and daring. (p. 12)

Together with the terms defined in Table 11.1, these themes provide a context for understanding gender role strains, which result from tensions caused by conflicts and the effects of masculine, feminine, and androgynous roles. O'Neil's (1981) theory of gender role strains contains six categories that emanate from men's fear of femininity. He defines the classifications as follows:

- *Restrictive emotionality* implies that men will have difficulty expressing feelings openly, giving up emotional control, and being vulnerable to self and others. These deficits imply that some men will have difficulty in self-disclosure, recognizing feelings, and processing the complexities of interpersonal life.
- *Socialized control, power, and competition.* Control implies to regulate, restrain, and have others or situations under one's command. Power is [the ability] to obtain authority, influence, or ascendancy over others. Competition is an act of striving against others to gain something or the comparison of self with others to establish one's superiority in a given situation.
- *Homophobia* ... (a) a belief system that holds discrimination on the basis of sexual orientation as justifiable; (b) the use of language or slang (e.g., *fag* or *queer*) that is offensive to gay people; and (c) any belief system that does not value homosexual lifestyles. Homophobia does not exist in most cases as an isolated prejudice but is characteristic of an individual who is generally rigid and sexist.
- *Restrictive sexual and affectionate behavior* is having limited ways of expressing one's sexuality and affection toward others. For men, this is caused by their inability to express their feminine sides and also rigid adherence to their values of the masculine mystique.
- *Obsession with achievement and success* is men's persistent and disturbing preoccupation with work, accomplishments, and eminence as a means of substantiating their masculinity and personal value. Fear of femininity is a primary emotion that may produce in men obsessive work behavior, particularly in early adulthood.

Many men associate masculinity with competition, achievement, ambition, success, status, wealth, power, and influence.

- *Health care problems* [preclude] maintaining positive health care in terms of nutrition, exercise, relaxation, and stress management. Many men have been socialized to ignore the physical symptoms that lead to acute illness or chronic health problems. The male gender role and its stereotypic rigidities project men as tireless, invincible workers with superhuman limits. (pp. 206–209)

Understanding the effects of socialization and gender role strains can assist educators in comprehending how boys and men behave and the rationale behind their behaviors, thereby informing instruction related to men and HIV infection. Entertainment media are a powerful influence on the socialization of boys and men of all cultural backgrounds and can serve as catalysts for teachers and students to discuss gender, gender roles, and gender role strain, especially films with Vin Diesel, Bruce Lee, Richard Roundtree, Sylvester Stallone, Arnold Schwarzenegger, Will Smith, Wesley Snipes, Antonio Banderas, John Wayne, and many other "real men." Analysis of such films may help teachers and students understand the psychological pressures on men and illuminate some reasons why they engage in risky sexual behavior.

Gender role strains as described by O'Neil (1981) and David and Brannon (1976) have a powerful influence on the socialization of boys and often create particular strains for gay men. Malesky (Malesky and Fennell, 1992) describes how, from the moment his parents learned they were expecting a boy until his years as a college student, his family, friends, schools, college, fraternity, and others in his life socialized his behaviors toward masculinity:

> My dad would rub my mom's stomach and say, "You're going to be a big man some day." ... I was sent home in a nice pair of blue pajamas. When I got home, my mom took me upstairs to my new room.... The room was painted blue and a football helmet and a baseball bat were hanging from the wall. At that moment, I knew I was meant to be an athlete.... As I became older, more and more gender role strains were placed on me. The first things I learned were that only babies and girls cry (restrictive emotionality) and that men can tough it out if they get hurt or sick (healthcare problems). I was also taught to be all that I can be, because the only way to make it in this world is by hard work (obsession with achievement and success). Along with this, I was taught to be better than everyone else because only the best

can survive (socialized control, power, and competition). In time, I also learned that it was no longer masculine to hug my friends and other people. I also found out what it meant to be a real man— "Make out with as many girls as possible, but never let anyone know if you really like somebody, especially that person" (restrictive sexual and affectionate behavior). Finally, I learned to fear being perceived as feminine or homosexual (homophobia). (Malesky and Fennell, 1992, pp. 83–84)

Malesky's description illustrates the powerful force of socialization in a boy's early growth and development as well as in his maturation to young adulthood. Pleck's (1981, 1995) explanation of gender role (or sex role) strains indicates that

- Sex roles are defined operationally by sex role stereotypes.
- Sex roles are contradictory and inconsistent.
- A high proportion of individuals violate sex roles.
- Violation of sex roles leads to social condemnation.
- Violation of sex roles leads to negative psychological consequences.
- Violation of sex roles, whether actual or imagined, leads to over-conformity by individuals in their attempt to adhere to sex roles.
- Violation of sex roles has more severe consequences for males than for females.
- Certain characteristics prescribed by sex roles are psychologically dysfunctional.
- Men and women experience sex role strain in work and family roles.
- Historical change causes sex role strain.

The gender role strain related to health care is particularly problematic in HIV/AIDS prevention. How many men ignore physical symptoms that may be indicative of illness or a health problem? Davies et al. (2000) found that college men do not seek assistance from campus health services due to perceived hindrances that result from male socialization. "The primary barrier appeared to be men's socialization to be independent and to conceal their vulnerability from others. Men prefer to try to help themselves first, and they feel pressure from peers and society in general to avoid seeking help. Men's lack of knowledge and their misinformation about services and lack of trust in healthcare providers were seen as barriers to seeking services" (pp. 264–265).

Davies et al. (2000) also convey the powerful influence of socialization on boys and men and its implications for HIV/AIDS prevention education. Even gay and bisexual men who are largely unconcerned about traditional notions of masculinity indicate that they have difficulty admitting that they need help. This finding might reflect the strength of male socialization processes in discouraging help-seeking behavior, but it could also reflect the concerns of gay and bisexual men and transgender persons about being accepted and understood by health care providers and counselors. Their perceptions can have a profound impact on HIV prevention efforts if gay and bisexual men do not seek assistance for fear of discrimination in health care settings.

Educators have an important obligation to be inclusive of the diverse populations in their classrooms. Teachers' use of heterosexual examples, such as Mom and Dad or boyfriend and girlfriend, in school settings can send messages to gay, lesbian, bisexual, and transgender students that devalue their existence. These terms also can create problems for students because they could have a negative impact on students' health care–seeking behaviors as well as on their classroom experiences.

MEN'S DECISIONS AND CHOICES

It is important that educators engage in discourse that facilitates awareness and understanding about men's decisions and choices. One could generate many hypotheses regarding the reasons men continue to engage in risky sexual behaviors. For example, some men might continue to engage in high-risk sexual behaviors because of the pressures that gender role strains such as "be a sturdy oak" or "restrictive affectionate behavior" place on their lives. However, it could be that individuals with high internal and external self-esteem avoid risk better than individuals with low internal and external self-esteem. Hypothetically, a person could have high internal self-esteem but, externally, feel less than valued by family members, coworkers, and other members of society. Such a person—heterosexual, homosexual, or bisexual—might be more likely to engage in risky sexual behaviors, which can have an impact on seemingly monogamous relationships that place their partners at risk of HIV/AIDS and other sexually transmitted infections (STIs). Researchers have found that men often are not as likely as women to disclose their STI history to either heterosexual or homosexual partners (Burdon, 1996; Ciccarone et al., 2003; Marelich and Clark, 2004).

Research articles, editorials, television news reports, and talk shows often address issues related to men who engage in high-risk sexual behaviors. We must acknowledge, however, that not all men who have sex engage in risky sexual behaviors. It is important, therefore, to avoid generalizing research findings, particularly when the findings are about men who have sex with men, because the resulting news stories have the potential to reinforce homophobia in society.

News reports of men who have sex with men and who engage in high-risk sexual behaviors generally do not mention the context of a society where gay men are still victims of discrimination, often taunted, and sometimes killed. Reporters often seem to make value judgments of gay men but not on other groups such as teenagers whose sexual behaviors result in unintended pregnancies and STIs. Yet HIV and other STIs occur because men *and* women do not use risk reduction behaviors to decrease the transmission of infection, and heterosexuals do not always use contraception to reduce chances of unintended pregnancies. Nearly one million teenage pregnancies occur in the United States each year; nearly half of these pregnancies terminate in abortions (Alan Guttmacher Institute, 1999). While value judgments are made about gay men, some of whom are teenagers who engage in high-risk sexual behaviors, these same value judgments are not made about heterosexual teenagers who engage in unprotected sexual behaviors that result in unintended pregnancies or infection with HIV or other STIs.

These value judgments do not reduce infections, but they do perpetuate negative stereotypes. Educators need to do their part to help all people appreciate the worth and importance of *all* individuals, regardless of their diverse nature and lifestyles. According to the California Task Force (1990), designed to promote self-esteem as well as personal and social responsibility,

> Every human being deserves to be recognized and appreciated as a unique and valuable individual. To see and appreciate the contribution each of us makes to other people and the world, we need to acknowledge our unique strengths, positive qualities, and personality traits.... . The importance of accepting and appreciating people as they are cannot be exaggerated. This includes accepting each person's feelings, thoughts, body, mind, and spirit. It also includes appreciating people's individual and cultural differences.

We must make sure that we do not require others to deny or disown their real selves to earn our approval or love. (p. 29)

In short, we must value the worth of all people as a foundation for influencing positively their decisions and, subsequently, reducing barriers to seeking help. For men, these barriers include, but are not limited to, socialization, HIV sero-positivity, self-esteem, prejudice, homophobia, and other interconnected factors that affect men's self-esteem as well as their choices and decisions.

Aggleton (2002) writes that the greatest social ill associated with the HIV/AIDS epidemic is "the willingness of people to ostracize, vilify, and reject their brothers and sisters, sons and daughters, friends, and lovers.... [HIV/AIDS] education programs are among the relatively few educational programs to date where stigma, discrimination, and human rights are central to prevention work" (p. 6). Fennell (2004), in recognition of the stigma and discrimination associated with HIV/AIDS, provides a guided imagery activity that helps others develop compassion for people living with HIV/AIDS. The guided imagery activity allows an individual to imagine what it would be like to receive positive test results from an HIV antibody test. This activity can elicit empathy and compassion for people who are living with HIV/AIDS.

Similarly, Sechrist (1997) offers a role-play activity that helps adolescents personalize the possibility of contracting HIV infection and develop understanding and concern for people with HIV/AIDS. In the activity, participants role-play an appointment for HIV pretest counseling, imaginary drawing of a blood specimen, and receipt of fictitious test results in which they learn of their HIV sero-positivity. The participants then write a letter to a significant person in their lives about testing positive for HIV antibodies; they share the contents of the letters with peers. The role-play is intended to help youth and young adults confront the illusion of their invincibility to HIV/AIDS. Sechrist states that the value of the role-play lies "in the *process* of thinking about oneself as being [HIV] infected" (p. 107) and imagining the subsequent challenges to overall physical health, interpersonal relationships, emotional well-being, economic security, and career opportunities.

These two activities may deter high-risk sexual behaviors among adolescents and young adults and make them more sensitive to individuals with HIV/AIDS. This sensitivity is needed to combat people's tendency to judge others, especially men, for what society perceives to be irresponsible behaviors. By adopting a more compassionate outlook, people will come to realize that the "tragedy of [HIV/AIDS] is not that so many people live such desperate lives that they choose to die [from complications of AIDS]. It is that so many people are dying for no reason other than that they took the kinds of risks we all take in our efforts to lead meaningful lives. Taking risks and losing is not the same as choosing to die" (Bérubé, 1989, p. 2).

Compassion requires an understanding of human behavior. Public outcry often ensues when media headlines report that someone with HIV did not inform his or her partner(s) of his or her status. People wonder, *Why would someone behave in such a reckless and uncaring manner? How could anyone do this to another person?* But we should avoid placing complete blame on sero-positive people; except in cases of sexual assault, people are responsible for their own bodies. Sero-negative people have the choice to be informed, ask questions, and take measures to protect themselves from HIV infection—and from any other ills.

Indeed, we do not always make healthy behavioral choices. We make excuses, such as not having enough time to eat nutritious foods or to sleep as much as we should. Belloc and Breslow (1972) found that people who followed seven basic health practices—sleeping 7 to 8 hours each night, eating breakfast, avoiding junk food, exercising regularly, maintaining an ideal weight, limiting alcohol intake, and avoiding cigarettes—were in better health than those who failed to follow them independent of sex, age, and economic status. In fact, compliant people in their 60s and 70s had physical health that paralleled "those 30 years younger who followed few or none of these practices" (p. 419).

Acknowledging the fact that many people do not practice healthy behaviors should help people relate to men's decisions regarding sexual behaviors. Some people may argue that the seven health practices differ from sexual behaviors and that more than one person is involved in a sexual relationship. The daily health practices might seem to affect only the individual who does or does not practice them, but in fact we are impacted by the health choices of each individual in our lives. If an individual has a single-car accident, for example, and his or her injury or loss of life could have been prevented if a seat belt had been worn, the individual's decision not to use a seat belt still has an impact on others. Similarly, if someone does not follow a healthy diet and develops cardiovascular disease, the behavior has an impact on the individual as well as on those who love him or her.

MULTICULTURAL CONSIDERATIONS

Any discussion about men, HIV/AIDS, and the interface of men and HIV/AIDS must acknowledge that men of color are disproportionately infected with HIV (Centers for Disease Control and Prevention, 2005). Oppression, prejudice, and racism influence socioeconomic and environmental contexts as well as access to quality health care. Chapter 9 in this volume (Hooks, Sileo, and Mazzotti) explores this topic in greater depth.

According to the Institutes of Medicine (IOM) of the National Academies (2002), prejudice is "an unjustified negative attitude based on a person's group membership" (p. 4). Furthermore, "institutional racism in the United States has resulted in segregation, stigmatization, and alienation for minority peoples. All these maltreatments have profound impacts on people's behavior and senses of self" (Kilmartin, 2000, p. 122).

Many variables—race, ethnicity, class, sex, gender, and socialization, among others—have a negative impact on the behavioral choices of men of color as well as on how others see and treat them based on these factors. Consequently, educators must contextualize lessons about HIV/AIDS prevention around these variables to facilitate students' knowledge and appreciation of the behaviors of others. Even a simple explanation of these disparities would be a refreshing beginning, since typically statistics are given by race and ethnicity with few if any explanatory remarks. Contextual teaching increases awareness and understanding about men of color so that they are not reduced to mere statistical pathological entities.

The Kaiser Permanente National Diversity Council (2000) has developed a series of handbooks that address culturally competent health care for diverse populations including African Americans, Asian/Pacific Islander Americans, Native Americans, Latinos, and gay, lesbian, bisexual, and transgender persons. Each handbook also provides culturally relevant information for HIV/AIDS prevention and intervention. "The term 'culturally competent care' describes healthcare that is sensitive to the health beliefs and behaviors, epidemiology and treatment efficacy of different population groups. Increasingly, healthcare organizations are being evaluated by consumers for their ability to provide such care. Additionally, studies are now indicating that sexual orientation and gender identity are as important as age or race in understanding healthcare utilization patterns and cost of care" (Kaiser Permanente, 2000, p. 1). Teachers, like health care providers, must be able to provide culturally competent education to their students.

The National Board for Professional Teaching Standards (NBPTS) has identified national teaching standards in 22 certificate areas that address diversity, equality, and fairness as integral components of each standard. NBPTS sets standards for what accomplished teachers should know and be able to do; for example, "accomplished health education teachers demonstrate equity and fairness and promote respect and appreciation for diversity" (NBPTS, 2002a, p. 35).

> Accomplished health educators are aware of issues students may face related to human sexuality, including sexual orientation, and to the varying stages of adolescent growth and development. Teachers establish a climate in their classrooms that promotes an understanding and acceptance of these differences. They take measures to reduce incidents of teasing, bullying, and harassment. Health educators value diversity and promote respect for others by modeling appreciation for and a richness of culture and ethnicity. (NBPTS, 2002a, p. 36)

APPROACHES TO TEACHING FOR UNDERSTANDING GENDER, SEXUALITY, AND HIV/AIDS

The ability of accomplished teachers to reach all students in their classrooms is the hallmark of their success. They foster an environment that encompasses a spirit of inquiry and reflective conversation about individuals' backgrounds, cultures, and knowledge. According to NBPTS (2002b), reflective teaching and learning are driven by the diligent pursuit of teachers to understand the circumstances that surround teaching and learning. Furthermore, effective teachers strive to create the intellectual conditions that ensure significant learning for all students. This same environment supports teachers when discussing gender and sexuality issues as well as HIV/AIDS.

Teachers must have a clear perspective as they deliver factual, nonjudgmental, and culturally responsive messages. The American Red Cross (1999) characterizes *nonjudgmental instruction* as educators' ability to (a) accept others' rights to possess personal values, attitudes, and beliefs; (b) avoid sharing or imposing their personal values and beliefs on others; (c) acknowledge their personal lack of understanding about others' traditions or beliefs; (d) avoid reinforcing others' expressed prejudices; (e) maintain awareness of verbal and nonverbal messages; and (f) respond in ways that respect divergent perspectives and cultural values.

Similarly, the American Red Cross (1999) characterizes *cultural responsiveness* as educators' ability to (a) comprehend the important notion that culture is more than race or ethnicity; (b) understand that culture can also be defined by other group membership, including by gender, age, sexual orientation, and religion; (c) consider different communities' languages, customs, world views, religions, spirituality, health beliefs, gender roles, sexuality, and family relationships; (d) recognize that all groups and communities have their own sets of values, attitudes, beliefs, and traditions; and (e) use particular aspects of personal culture to construct and facilitate HIV/AIDS prevention messages.

These points are the fundamental principles that support positive discourse among teachers and learners. They also serve as rules or guidelines that provide a "safe space" for teachers and learners to explore discussions about HIV/AIDS prevention. These characteristics can be woven throughout instructional strategies to create effective educational approaches.

Teachers may ask, *How do I cover the content needed for HIV/AIDS prevention while at the same time concentrating on how it is presented in a classroom setting?* School systems continually identify specific content knowledge for HIV/AIDS curricula, but what are the parameters necessary to deliver a message to all learners regardless of their cultural backgrounds, gender, or sexuality? How do we weave those characteristics into well-constructed lessons? What are the facts about HIV/AIDS and how do they affect human differences in learners? Teacher educators and practicing teachers must strike this balance with careful attention to many details.

While developing *What Teachers Should Know and Be Able to Do* (1997), NBPTS focused on core propositions that speak directly to the "how and what" of teaching and learning. Particular action is placed on treating students equitably:

> As stewards for the interests of students, accomplished teachers are vigilant in ensuring that all pupils receive their fair share of attention and that biases on real or perceived ability differences, handicaps or disabilities, social or cultural background, language, race, religion, or gender, do not distort relationships between them and their students. Accomplished teachers do not treat all students alike, for similar treatment is not necessarily equiva-

lent or equitable education. In responding to differences among students, teachers are careful to counter potential inequities and avoid favoritism. This requires a well-tuned alertness to such matters and is difficult, as we have only modest knowledge of human differences and how best to respond to them. Hence, accomplished teachers employ what is known about effectual and effective practice with diverse groups of children, while striving to know more about how best to accommodate those differences. (NBPTS, 1997, p. 16)

As the need for more accurate, factual, and nonbiased messages becomes paramount, all teachers, regardless of their content knowledge, must develop a clear and concise HIV/AIDS prevention message. According to Daria and Campbell (2004), teachers must feel comfortable teaching about and answering students' questions related to sexuality. In addition, educators should possess several key characteristics, including (a) enthusiasm for and comfort with the subject matter, (b) thorough knowledge of human sexuality, (c) respect for adolescents, (d) clarity about their own personal values, (e) ability to accept others' values and beliefs, and (f) good group facilitation skills (Manley, 1986).

HIV/AIDS has a tremendous effect on people throughout the United States and the world. Socialization, gender, and cultural diversity are significant influences on men's decisions and behavioral choices. Teachers and teacher educators need to develop multifaceted methods to teaching and learning that respect sexuality and culture as they design HIV/AIDS education messages for youth and young adults. If teachers are true change agents, then they must send forth a clear message that frees learning environments of biases and ensures that HIV/AIDS prevention education meets the needs of the learning community and addresses every voice in the community.

CONCLUSION

NBPTS (1997) asserts that a teacher's mission extends beyond developing students' cognitive capacity; instruction must consider the *whole learner*. Good teachers are concerned with students' self-concept and motivation, the effects of learning on peer relationships, and students' development of character, aspirations, and civic virtues. Proficient teachers consider students' potential in the broadest sense when they make decisions about how and what to teach.

The cultural patterns that influence HIV/AIDS prevention strategies are rooted in people's attitudes, values, and cultures, as well as in their communities' socioeconomic factors (Airhihenbuwa and Pineiro, 1988). As teacher educators and teachers become more empowered with knowledge about HIV/AIDS, they must adapt prevention messages to ensure that they address students' diverse cultural, gender, and sexuality needs.

This chapter has shown that multiple variables, including male socialization and gender role strain, influence individuals' decisions. People's choices have an impact on their health as well as on the health of those they love and of those who love them. Societal forces often complicate men's decisions about sexual behavior, and some people make unhealthy choices. By infusing a perspective of unconditional acceptance of others into educational programs, educators can make a significant difference in the lives of young people.

NOTE

The author would like to thank Wilbur Parker, manager of minority recruitment at the National Board for Professional Teaching Standards in Arlington, VA, for his contributions to this chapter.

REFERENCES

Aggleton, P. (2002). HIV/AIDS prevention and sexuality education must change to meet their promise. *SIECUS Report* 31: 5–7.

Airhihenbuwa, C. O., and Pineiro, O. (1988). Cross-cultural health education: A pedagogical challenge. *Journal of School Health* 58(5): 240–242.

Alan Guttmacher Institute. (1999). *Facts in brief: Teen sex and pregnancy.* Retrieved October 3, 2005, from http://www.agi-usa.org/pubs/fb_teen_sex.html.

American Red Cross. (1999). *African American fundamentals: HIV/AIDS instructors' manual.* Falls Church, VA: Author.

Belloc, N. B., and Breslow, L. (1972). Relationship of physical health status and health practices. *Preventive Medicine* 1: 409–421.

Bérubé, A. (1989). The AIDS health project. *Focus: A Guide to AIDS Research and Counseling* 5: 1–2.

Burdon, W. M. (1996). Deception in intimate relationships: A comparison of heterosexuals and homosexuals/bisexuals. *Journal of Homosexuality* 32: 77–93.

California Task Force. (1990). *Toward a state of esteem: The final report of the California task force to promote self-esteem and personal and social responsibility.* Sacramento: California State Department of Education.

Centers for Disease Control and Prevention. (2005). *AIDS cases by race/ethnicity.* Retrieved October 3, 2005, from http://www.cdc.gov/hiv/stats.htm#aidsrace.

Ciccarone, D. H., Kanouse, D. E., Collins, R. L., et al. (2003). Sex without disclosure of positive HIV serostatus in a U.S. probability sample of persons receiving medical care for HIV infection. *American Journal of Public Health* 93: 949–954.

Daria, M. P., and Campbell, K. J. (2004, October 10). Schools need sexuality programs. *Electronic Journal of Human Sexuality* 7. Retrieved October 3, 2005, from http://www.ejhs.org/volume7/sexed.html.

David, D., and Brannon, R., eds. (1976). *The forty-nine percent majority: The male sex role.* Reading, MA: Addison-Wesley.

Davies, J., McCrae, B. P., Frank, J., Dochnahl, A., Pickering, T., Harrison, B., et al. (2000). Identifying male college students' perceived health needs, barriers to seeking help, and recommendations to help men. *Journal of American College Health* 48: 259–267.

Fennell, R. (2003). Multiculturalism, social justice, and campus health. *Journal of American College Health* 52: 101–103.

Fennell, R. (2004). Developing compassion for people living with HIV/AIDS. *American Journal of Health Education* 35: 245–247.

Hoban, M. T., and Ward, R. L. (2003). Building culturally competent health programs. *Journal of American College Health* 52: 137–141.

Institutes of Medicine of the National Academies. (2002). *Unequal treatment: What healthcare providers need to know about racial and ethnic disparities in health care.* Washington, DC: National Academy Press.

Kaiser Permanente National Diversity Council and Kaiser Permanente National Diversity Department. (2000). *A provider's handbook on culturally competent care: Lesbian, gay, bisexual and transgendered populations.* Oakland, CA: Kaiser Permanente.

Keeling, R. P., and Engstrom, E. L. (1992). Sexual health promotion for men who have sex with other men. In R. P. Keeling, ed., *Effective AIDS education on campus.* San Francisco: Jossey-Bass.

Kilmartin, C. T. (2000). *The masculine self.* Boston: McGraw-Hill.

Kumashiro, K. K. (2002). *Troubling education: Queer activism and antioppressive pedagogy.* New York: Routledge Falmer.

Malesky, D., and Fennell, R. (1992). Gender role strains: One man's awakening. *Journal of American College Health* 41: 83–84.

Manley, J. (1986). Teacher selection for sex education. *SIECUS Report* 15: 10–11.

Marelich, W. D., and Clark, T. (2004). Human Immunodeficiency Virus (HIV) testing and false disclosures in heterosexual college students. *Journal of American College Health* 53: 109–115.

McAnulty, R. D., and Burnette, M. M. (2003). *Exploring human sexuality: Making healthy decisions.* Needham Heights, MA: Allyn and Bacon.

Mobley, M. (2000). Cultural guardianship: A model for supporting gay African American boys/men. In M. C. Brown and E. D. Davis, eds., *Black sons to mother: Compliments, critiques, and challenges for cultural workers* (pp. 173–192). New York: Peter Lang.

National Board for Professional Teaching Standards. (1997). *What teachers should know and be able to do.* Arlington, VA: Author.

National Board for Professional Teaching Standards. (2002a). Standard VIII: Equity, fairness, and diversity. In *NBPTS: Health education standards* (pp. 35–36). Arlington, VA: Author.

National Board for Professional Teaching Standards. (2002b). Standard XIII: Self reflection. In *NBPTS: Adolescence and young adulthood English language arts standards* (pp. 73–78). Arlington, VA: Author.

O'Neil, J. M. (1981). Patterns of gender role conflict and strain: Sexism and fear of femininity in men's lives. *Personnel and Guidance Journal* 60: 203–210.

Pleck, J. H. (1981). *The myth of masculinity.* Cambridge, MA: MIT Press.

Pleck, J. H. (1995). The gender role strain paradigm: An update. In R. R. Levant and W. S. Pollack, eds., *A new psychology of men* (pp. 11–32). New York: Basic Books.

Sechrist, W. (1997). Personalizing HIV infection: Moving students closer to believing ... "this could actually happen to me!" *Journal of HIV/AIDS Prevention and Education for Adolescents and Children* 1(1): 105–107.

PART IV
INTERNATIONAL DIMENSIONS OF PREVENTION

Overview, *Beverly Lindsay*

✦

When I received the invitation from AACTE to spearhead the international component of the Build a Future Without AIDS project and of this volume, my plate was already full with "normal" university research. Yet the incredible and severe effects of the HIV/AIDS pandemic on the Southern Hemisphere demanded that I expand my agenda. After consultations with AACTE and communications with the World Bank, the U.S. Agency for International Development, the Council on Foreign Relations, and similar bodies, I assembled a team of professionals involved in domestic and international HIV/AIDS matters in postsecondary education. Each author wrote a chapter that contributes his or her individual expertise, collectively assisting the international university community in broadening its public engagement role to address the most acute educational, health, and social phenomenon of our generation.

The chapters assembled in this section explicate and analyze multiple dimensions of the HIV/AIDS pandemic in relationship to higher education. The initial chapter, "Multifaceted Policy Challenges and Motifs Concerning HIV/AIDS in International Higher Education Venues," by Beverly Lindsay, provides comprehensive sociocultural perspectives by using illustrations from Africa, Australia, the Caribbean, Great Britain, and the Netherlands. Subsequent chapters by Ladislaus Semali, "Postcolonial Perspectives in Constructing Teacher Knowledge About HIV/AIDS," and Barnabas Otaala, "African Tertiary Institutions' Response to the HIV/AIDS Epidemic: Current Practices and the Way Forward," focus on Anglophone (English-speaking), Francophone (French-speaking), and Lusophone (Portuguese-speaking) Africa. The chapter by Neena Khanna, "HIV and AIDS Affecting Postsecondary Education in South Asia," concentrates on India and Indonesia, the world's first and third largest democracies.

All chapters examine the critical interrelations between global and national phenomena of HIV/AIDS and higher education institutions. All further present critical statistics on the phenomenal impact of HIV/AIDS in various nations wherein about 40 million people worldwide are currently infected.

Our chapters specifically and collectively serve several purposes:

1. Explore the role of higher education institutions in addressing how select domestic groups are affected by the disease with special focus on students, faculty, and administrators in colleges and universities.
2. Examine the social constructs of various African and Indian cultural groups vis-à-vis HIV/AIDS.
3. Analyze the role of university professional education programs in the preparation of students and professionals for a range of teaching, education, and other career roles.
4. Present emerging program options for African, Indian, and Indonesian universities to incorporate HIV/AIDS awareness into the curriculum.
5. Portray current university policies and posit new policy options for alternative models to help ensure that viable socioeconomic and democratic societies continue in countries ravished by HIV/AIDS.

The content of our chapters explicates that the spread of the disease in national and international settings affects basic human rights issues. These issues include, inter alia, (a) global inequities regarding poverty, racism, and the availability and distribution of health care resources; (b) in-country effects on gender, age, and other demographic variables; and (c) the importance of pedagogical equity and instructional strategies that mesh with students' cognitive, behavioral, and learning styles regardless of the presence or absence of the disease. Finally, we posit the impact of HIV/AIDS on "intellectual migration" among transnational university settings, the creation of new knowledge, and subsequent dissemination in order to help alleviate the pandemic.

12

MULTIFACETED POLICY CHALLENGES AND MOTIFS CONCERNING HIV/AIDS IN INTERNATIONAL HIGHER EDUCATION VENUES

Beverly Lindsay

↶

There is a tsunami every month in Africa.
—*Commission for Africa, 2005, p. 18*

In the course of history, there comes a time when humanity is called to shift to a new level of consciousness, to reach a higher moral ground. A time when we have to shed our fear and give hope to each other. That time is now.
—*Maathai, 2004*

GLOBAL STAGES FOR CONTEMPORARY CHALLENGES

Throughout the spring and early summer of 2005, the media in the United States and Great Britain vigorously promoted plans for the global Live 8 Concerts and the G-8 Summit. The latter event, convened in Gleneagles, Scotland, included the world's wealthiest industrialized nations: the United States, Canada, France, Germany, Great Britain, Italy, Japan, and Russia. Both the concerts[1] and the G-8 Summit highlighted global poverty, especially poverty in sub-Saharan Africa. These events built on the work of the Commission for Africa, initiated in March 2004 by British Prime Minister Tony Blair to reexamine Africa's history and to ascertain the international community's roles therein. The Commission[2] quickly identified multifaceted dimensions of poverty on the continent, such as the lack of fiscal and material resources; inadequate basic and higher education; and the absence of and poor access to adequate health care. This combination of factors contributes to the most devastating health crisis of modern times: the HIV/AIDS pandemic, which has been compared in magnitude to the Black Plague of the thirteenth century (Commission for Africa, 2005; Garrett, 2005). The harsh effects of HIV/AIDS and other communicable diseases cause the death of 300,000 Africans every month—a toll equivalent to the number of December 2004 tsunami victims in several Asian countries.

In some quarters, this reality is acknowledged, and policies and programs are emerging and being enhanced to address this acute problem. On a Senior Fulbright grant in Zimbabwe, for example, I attended the convocation ceremony at Africa University, a United Methodist institution. This ceremony welcomed first-year students, in particular, and provided general orientation information. The university's vice chancellor (equivalent to an American university's president) delivered an impassioned address in which he informed students about the effects of HIV/AIDS, about testing and counseling services, and about prophylactic measures. His comments resonated with the students, who recognized that the information could save their lives. Compare this orientation to those typically given for American university students; although information on binge drinking is imparted to Americans students to save lives, the information often deals with curriculum and co-curricular activities. American students may be oblivious to HIV/AIDS, but even if they do contract HIV, they likely will have access to medical treatment that could prolong their lives. Such options rarely exist for Africans due to the multifaceted negative effects of HIV/AIDS.

The overarching, sad reality is that the HIV/AIDS crisis often is not fully acknowledged or accepted—by societies, governments, or even individuals. When acknowledged, it is not always a priority. Nor are viable policies and programs being implemented to halt the deadly pandemic. With such extensive media coverage on the ravages of poverty in African nations, why is there not adequate acknowledgement of the role of HIV/AIDS? What structural, economic, and sociopolitical phenomena in both developed and developing nations impede progress toward comprehensive solutions? What are the critical scholarly and public engagement roles of the university community in alleviating the problem?

This chapter seeks to analyze macro-level global socioeconomic, political, and cultural conditions that contribute to poverty and HIV/

AIDS; to examine the particular roles and responsibilities of universities; and to elucidate policies and programs that have worked and may present cross-national lessons. This chapter includes illustrations from the subsequent chapters, which explore HIV/AIDS and higher education in Southern and East Africa, India, and Indonesia. The authors of these chapters were engaged in field research in Asia and Africa and worked with organizations and universities with foci on HIV/AIDS policies and programs. This chapter also includes select examples from Australia and the Netherlands to reveal the presence of HIV/AIDS in industrialized non-G-8 nations and in the Caribbean. (In some regards, Caribbean nations are in fluid transition toward national development.) The final section of this chapter posits five macro- and micro-level tasks for HIV/AIDS intervention initiatives: awareness/acknowledgement, acceptance, analysis, action, and assessment.

MACRO-LEVEL DIMENSIONS AND PORTRAITS
OF POVERTY AFFECTING HIV/AIDS

In analyzing poverty in African nations, the 17-member Commission for Africa, appointed by Prime Minister Blair, articulated several critical points in its seminal report, *Our Common Interest*. The title highlights how African and industrialized nations are linked, although there are epic differences in stages of national development. Contemporary globalization is a multidimensional and multilevel phenomenon that has contributed to vastly different levels of economic development (Lindsay, 2005). Stromquist (2002) posits that the G-8 countries set in motion and sustain economic conditions (including international trade, labor, and intellectual property rights) that affect comprehensive sectors of individual societies and international relations. Many of these economic conditions, according to Stromquist and *Our Common Interest*, contribute to poverty because they are designed to favor industrialized nations.

The devastating realities of poverty are overwhelming in Africa and other regions. The executive summary of the Commission's report declares, "Africa must accelerate reform. The developed world must increase and improve its aid, and stop doing those things which hinder Africa's progress. *The developed world has a moral duty* [italics added]— as well as a powerful motive of self-interest—to assist Africa" (Commission for Africa, 2005, p. 11). *In essence, the ethical and humanistic treatment of people, regardless of their geographical location or material resources, should provide the bedrock for addressing poverty*—and we have a similar moral responsibility to address the HIV/AIDS pandemic, which disproportionately affects the poor. *To accomplish this aim, partnerships, rather than charity, should characterize relations among African nations and the developed world, particularly the G-8 nations.* The Commission further maintains that "leaving no one out" is mandatory (p. 13). Poverty reduction and elimination are part of fundamental human rights and social justice. In many African regions (and in other regions with acute poverty) about one half of the population lives on less than $2 per day in American dollars (Rice, 2005). Reducing poverty and disease, which too often go hand-in-hand, is a sound economic principle that will contribute to and sustain national development. Toward this end, development aid should be given to ratchet up the services to help address the catastrophe of HIV/AIDS, which kills more people in sub-Saharan Africa than in any other area of the world.

Grim statistics portray the deadly effects of HIV/AIDS. Over 40 million people currently live with HIV/AIDS, about 30 million have died, and over 12 million children have been orphaned (Garrett, 2005; Commission for Africa, 2005). On the African continent, over 25 million people are infected. Because most of these individuals have little if any access to HIV/AIDS medication and medical care, well over 2 million will die of AIDS each year. In Zambia, for example, 1 in every 3 children will become an orphan. The United Nations has estimated that 1 in every 12 people in sub-Saharan Africa is HIV positive (Saint, 2004).

Within the higher education community, the statistics are extremely grim. In discussions, one South African vice chancellor stated that university students were permitted to test voluntarily for HIV. Over one-quarter of those tested were HIV-positive. The vice chancellor speculated that within the undergraduate student body, the figures were as high if not higher. Using a modeling exercise undertaken with South African universities, similar statistics were evinced. The HIV infection rate was estimated at 22 percent and expected to increase to 33 percent by the end of 2005. For technikons (technical institutions that offer degrees and diploma certification), the percentage is 24 percent, with an expected increase to 36 percent before 2006. For university graduate students, the rate is 11 percent, with an anticipated increase to 21 percent as 2005 ends (Kinghorn, 2000; Saint, 2004). Furthermore, at the University of Natal, 33 percent of the graduating nurses died within 3 years of graduation (Saint, 2004). Who will care for the sick and dying when such health care professionals die?

We can compare these statistics and percentages to Caribbean nations and to Australia and the Netherlands. The Caribbean region has the highest rate of HIV/AIDS after sub-Saharan Africa. And the portrait appears to worsen among the 15 member nations of the Caribbean Community (Caricom). The Caribbean Commission on Health and Development estimates that over 500,000 Caribbeans are living with HIV/AIDS (Richards, 2005). By 2009, the figure is projected to increase to nearly 700,000. About 250,000 will die within 5 years if the pandemic is not halted. Measures designed to foster national and regional development among Caricom nations may, in effect, halt progress. The Caricom Single Market and Economy will permit the unfettered movement of labor, services, and products among the countries—and with them, infectious diseases such as HIV/AIDS (Richards, 2005). Hardest hit will be the 15–45 age cohort. As in Africa, deaths from HIV/AIDS will halt economic and social development and political stability through the loss of human resources.

Indonesia, the world's third largest democracy, with about 230 million citizens, is concerned about the rise of HIV/AIDS. The national government speculates about HIV transmission via tourists from neighboring Australia. Those fears are further elaborated in Neena Khanna's chapter, "HIV/AIDS Affecting Postsecondary Education in South Asia." The overall HIV/AIDS statistical portrait of Australia would appear to allay some of Indonesia's concern. Australian HIV/AIDS infection and disease peaked in the mid-1990s. Since then, there has been a decrease. In 2003, there were only 20,000 Australians living with HIV/AIDS in a population of over 20.2 million (HIV InSite, 2005a). In short, less than one-thousandth of the population is infected. Fewer than 200 Australians died from AIDS complications each year in the early 2000s. Even for those who are infected, medical care is accessible through one of the world's best health care systems. Nevertheless, there is concern within Australia about accessibility to medical care for the nation's poor and for recent immigrants with limited personal resources.

On the European continent, we can note the statistics regarding HIV/AIDS infection in the Netherlands, which has a population of 16.3 million people. Of those, about 19,000 are living with HIV/AIDS, and fewer than 100 deaths resulted from the disease in 2003 (HIV In-Site, 2005b). Well under 1 percent of the population is infected. As in Australia, those in the Netherlands who are infected with HIV/AIDS have access to comprehensive medical care. Moreover, various aspects of health education have been included in the Dutch secondary school curriculum. In addition to their level of overall socioeconomic and political development, the Dutch have established progressive national policies toward HIV/AIDS. In fact, Americans have criticized some Dutch wellness programs because condoms and needles have been provided to some sectors as a preventive measure. In contrast, sub-Saharan nations and the Caribbean are experiencing cruel effects of HIV/AIDS. Khanna in her chapter examines India, the world's largest democracy, and the rising rates of infections in that nation. Again, the prevalence and treatment of HIV/AIDS are linked to socioeconomic national development.

Although HIV/AIDS and other communicable deadly diseases exist and are linked to poverty, there is often unawareness or, more accurately, failure to acknowledge the effects of such devastation on the affected nations, on the G-8, and on other Western and Eastern nations. In a penetrating article, former Assistant Secretary of State for Africa Susan E. Rice (2005) portrays the intermediate and long-range effects of HIV/AIDS throughout the world, even in nations with low rates of infection. She contends that poverty in seemingly remote places undermines national security for all nations. The failure to address health problems is part of the transnational globalization equation. Over 90 percent of the globe's acute–diseases burden falls on low- and middle-income countries; such nations account for only 11 percent of worldwide spending on health. Nations affected by poverty use scarce fiscal resources when they attempt to be responsive to HIV/AIDS and other communicable diseases. Some positive results are being witnessed, however. For example, in Uganda, HIV prevalence was 30 percent in 1992, and in 2003 it was 8 percent (Saint, 2004).

Rice (2005) demonstrates how poverty undermines the world's security: Vulnerable states and individuals are susceptible to negative forces that sometimes employ horrific means to achieve their goals. In short, various forms of terrorism may be the result for states and individuals with little recourse. An American senior executive told me after his trip to an African nation, "The poverty is so extreme. Anyone or any group that offers some alternatives can influence the country whether for good or bad." As Rice further articulates, "poor countries are weak in other respects. Often unable to meet their citizens' needs for food, education, and health care, such states are easy prey for extremist religious groups and charities" (2005, p. A13).

The Commission for Africa (2005) clearly articulated the interrelations among poverty, health care for HIV/AIDS and other severe diseases, African development, and global well-being. Although the Commission acknowledged the responsibilities of African nations, it recognized the necessity for genuine economic and educational partnerships—rather than charity—between G-8 and poverty-stricken countries to promote socioeconomic development. Given the historical and contemporary dominance of G-8 nations, the Commission contends that such nations have a moral responsibility to engage in concrete and viable plans for African development and the elimination of poverty. Indeed, Ladi Semali's chapter, "Postcolonial Perspectives in Constructing Teacher Knowledge About HIV/AIDS," explicates historical colonial conditions and their continuing effects on African development.

The Commission discusses how African debts (incurred in the postcolonial period) are after-effects of colonization that stagger contemporary economic development. Industrialized nations have been reluctant to remove the oppressive debts that contribute to daily burdens. Such debts should be relieved, and aid should be designed to reduce poverty in developing countries rather than to support the political and industrial interests of rich nations through fiscal subsidies to select organizations and groups in the latter (Commission for Africa, 2005). Authentic aid should be directed to health care, education, and other parts of the basic infrastructure.

The Commission stressed that life expectancy in much of Africa has decreased because of HIV/AIDS. The life expectancy in many African countries is now 47 years, compared to 63 years in India. Yet at their respective times of independence, life expectancies on the African continent and Indian subcontinent were not vastly different. Through the 1980s, life expectancy increased in both regions. Now, the African gains are being obliterated. We must approach this illustration with caution, however. Khanna points out later in this book that HIV/AIDS is increasing in India, and measures must be undertaken to check the spread of the disease. Increases in HIV/AIDS infection also may occur due to extremely crowed urban conditions, as witnessed in India and parts of Africa. For example, in Nairobi, 60 percent of the populace (the poor and very poor) live on 5 percent of the land (Commission for Africa, 2005). Such crowded urban living provides fertile conditions for communicable disease proliferation in Nairobi, Calcutta, and New Delhi.

The extreme loss of lives during their productive years means development and peaceful solutions to problems can be thwarted. Development and peace cannot occur without people (Commission for Africa, 2005). Decades of progress are being lost absent viable policy development and solutions in countries already ravished by HIV/AIDS and in nations beginning to acknowledge and experience the effects. The following illustrations regarding two professional men who contracted HIV more than a decade ago highlight the interplay among a nation's national development (including the relative levels of poverty), its willingness to develop HIV/AIDS policies, and its ability to engage in peaceful solutions to problems without being sidetracked by civil strife.

In January 2005, former South African President Nelson Mandela announced that his son had died of AIDS complications. Buoyed by this announcement, British Member of Parliament (MP) Chris Smith revealed days later that he has been living with HIV since 1987 (Bright, 2005). In these contrasting situations, the former president's son died within a few years of contracting HIV, whereas a British MP has been living in relatively good health for nearly 20 years. Being the president's son did not prevent death. Living in a G-8 nation and being in a position to shape national policy extended the life expectancy for a gay MP who is HIV-positive.

THE ROLES AND RESPONSIBILITIES OF UNIVERSITIES

The preceding discussion has highlighted global and regional effects of HIV/AIDS. A salient issue is the role of universities in addressing the problem, especially since many African faculty members, administrators, and staff are affected by the disease. Lindsay (2004), Saint (2004), and Hayward and Ncayiyana (2003) point out that universities periodically develop and/or refine their mission statements and engage in academic and strategic planning. Until recently, many tertiary institutions did not include HIV/AIDS in their strategic planning. As Saint (2004) maintains, within institutional SWOT (strengths, weaknesses, opportunities, and threats) analyses, African universities were not atypical in the absence of HIV/AIDS in their strategic planning. Oblivion was the norm regarding the HIV/AIDS presence on campus and in the surrounding communities. When recognized, there was a "conspiracy of silence," according to Kelly (2001). Through the 1990s, there was a noticeable silence surrounding the disease at the institutional, academic, and personal levels.

This silence—as Barnabas Otaala's chapter, "African Tertiary Institutions' Response to the HIV/AIDS Epidemic: Current Practices and the Way Forward," explicates in this book—is due to a variety of factors that include cultural taboos, psychological discomfort, and absence of resources. Otaala discusses the critical importance of developing institution-wide policies to address various facets of the problem. Toward this end, the Association of African Universities (AAU), with its 113 members from 32 countries, has spearheaded projects at particular universities and regions (AAU, 2005).

We must note the extreme importance of (a) being aware of the multifaceted causes and dimensions of HIV/AIDS, (b) undertaking appropriate analysis to comprehend those dimensions, and (c) engaging in subsequent policy and program development to alleviate those dimensions. Saint (2004), Kelly (2001), and Lyman (2004) articulate that institutions—whether in Africa, the Caribbean, India, or Indonesia—should recognize HIV/AIDS as a central leadership matter, a development issue, an individual and university matter, and a human-resource development issue. In addition, the issue necessitates the creation of a body of knowledge. In various modes, Semali, Otaala, and Khanna examine such factors and present solutions.

Leadership by senior administrators can yield efforts to establish institutional policies and set the tone for how HIV/AIDS will be addressed on campuses by various sectors. Decision-making support structures and staff training in academic, student affairs, and health services units could be established by senior university executives. Universities also must allocate, or in some case reallocate, resources for HIV/AIDS.

University and teacher-training curricula and practice must incorporate the multiple facets of HIV/AIDS in African, Asian, European, and Caribbean regions *and* in relation to globalization where mutable borders enable instant interactions and transmissions. Salient illustrations regarding the nature of globalization, the absence of development, and the relationship between poverty and communicable diseases should be integral components of university-wide curriculum. Training on HIV/AIDS should not be limited to health and education courses.

Curriculum modules also should include cultural components on local ethnic groups and other practical approaches. For example, when I conducted research in East Africa, several female university students explained that they would have difficulty marrying their boyfriends if they were not pregnant because the ability to produce children is an absolute requirement for marriage. Having unprotected sexual relations flies in the face of HIV/AIDS prevention; yet cultural norms also mean that males can engage in nonmonogamous relations. The rate of HIV infection, however, is higher among female than among male university students due to the tendency of younger women to have relations with older men. The older men can provide financial resources for tuition, books, and living expenses. Male university students of comparable age to their female cohort do not have the financial resources of older men with multiple wives and/or girlfriends (Lyman, 2004; Saint, 2004). Key curricular and practicum endeavors may be altered so that new, healthy practices for female and male college students are established.

Despite the overwhelming presence of HIV/AIDS in Africa, the incorporation of AIDS education into the university curriculum differs among the Anglophone (English-speaking), Francophone (French-speaking), and Lusophone (Portuguese-speaking) countries; the Anglophone countries are farthest ahead. East and Southern Africa are farther ahead than are Central and West Africa. Many of the Francophone countries are just beginning to address the issue (Otaala, 2000, 2004). Successes in Anglophone and Southern African nations could be shared among African universities and with those in India and Indonesia.

Although much of the HIV/AIDS research and the development of medical solutions have occurred in G-8 and other Western nations, this fact does not preclude new possibilities and actual involvement of African universities in joint ventures. Viable partnerships among universities, not as junior partners, would be one way to conduct research. The central roles for universities would include advocating and altering the creation of intellectual and disciplinary paradigms in light of African, Asian, and Caribbean contexts. Otaala's and Semali's chapters discuss such possibilities. Equally important is the critical role that Otaala and other African scholars and policy makers play in presenting proposals to the G-8 for funding, as they did for the 2005 summit.

In India, which has the second highest number of HIV/AIDS cases after South Africa, scientists are administering an experimental HIV/AIDS vaccine. Indian university professors and researchers should be integrally involved in the development and monitoring of the vaccine as it is administered in trial runs. Their fundamental responsibility should be ensuring appropriate and ethical protocols in light of national and international standards. As part of their scholarly and public engagement roles, universities would be indispensable to assessments of the overall experimental project. Vaccine development becomes even more urgent in light of the discovery in the United States in early 2005 of a new strand of HIV that does not appear to respond to current retrovirus treatments; hence this new virulent strand progresses quickly to full-blown AIDS (Altman and Samura, 2005). The introduction of an experimental vaccine coupled with the presence of a quickly lethal form of HIV necessitates critical roles for universities in devising solutions.

With university involvement in vaccine trials, we could witness the positive impact of intellectual migration among transnational university settings in India, Africa, and the United States (Lindsay, 2004). Knowledge creation should not be limited to select universities in industrialized nations; the creation and dissemination of knowledge should occur among various global regions. In recent years, universities have developed alternative delivery modes via technology such as the youth radio station at the University of Namibia, which works in partnership with Johns Hopkins University to incorporate HIV/AIDS programs as part of their regular talk-show format. They have altered and enhanced human management structures and reallocated existing university funds to priority areas such as HIV/AIDS prevention and research (Lindsay, 2005; Lyman, 2004; Otaala, 2004). These developments illustrate intellectual migration. Through intellectual migration, permanent physical migration could be curtailed (Commission for Africa, 2005; Garrett, 2005) so that home universities in Africa, India, or the Caribbean could fully reap the benefits in the institutional and societal spheres.

TOWARD ALL "A'S" FOR TRANSFORMATIVE POLICIES AND PROGRAMS

In July 2005, British Prime Minister Blair, as chairman of the G-8 summit, planned to highlight and push for the goals articulated in *Our Common Interest*. Unfortunately, the London subway and bus systems were bombed July 7, diverting Blair's attention and that of the media away from the summit's major goals: Africa and climate change. Like other

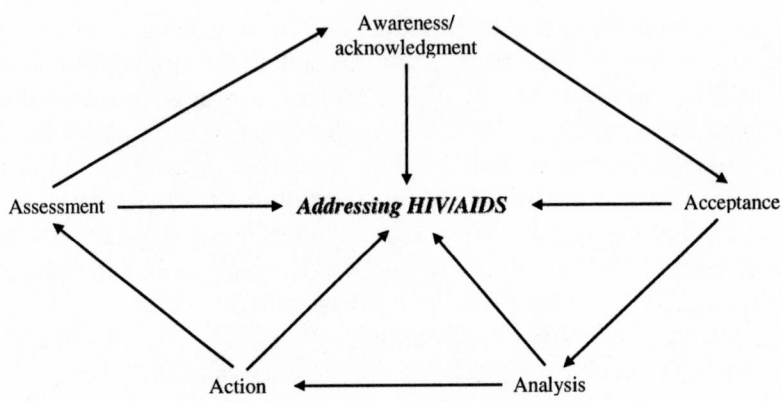

Figure 12.1. The Five "A's"

recent atrocities of terrorism—the August 1998 simultaneous bombings in Nairobi and Dar es Salaam, the attacks of September 2001 in the United States—the horrific events diverted fiscal and human resources from HIV/AIDS, which kills far more people every month in Africa. Multifaceted aspects of development in Africa, including extreme poverty and HIV/AIDS, were overshadowed by the London bombings.

The heads of state from Nigeria, South Africa, and India, for instance, participated in the G-8 summit in order to advocate for their nations and the continents via cooperative political, economic, and scientific partnerships.

Figure 12.1 portrays the centrality of addressing HIV/AIDS through the interactive effects of awareness/acknowledgement, acceptance, analysis, action, and assessment. The G-8 leaders and guest heads of state acknowledged and were apprised of global conditions that have negatively affected various regions. The leaders did not concur on the level of acceptance for the disparities or on various solutions. My discussion of the initial "A's" begins with that discrepancy.

Various global actors must couple awareness and acknowledgement of HIV/AIDS with acceptance of responsibility. Acceptance was partially demonstrated by the G-8 pledge to commit $25 billion a year to the African continent by 2010. In addition, approximately $55 billion in debt is to be relieved. Simultaneously, African nations are to accept responsibility for ensuring sound governments and fiscal policies by initiating and/or enhancing policies to ensure transparent, participative, democratic governments (AAU, 2004; Blair, 2005; New Partnership for Africa's Development [NEPAD], 2001, 2005). Indeed, NEPAD of the African Union has advocated transparent, democratic government for several years. There are success stories; however, until relatively recently, African states have been reluctant to become involved in the internal strife and the oppressive governments of fellow states.

In addition to the need for African countries to accept responsibility, Western universities and professional and scientific associations also must acknowledge and accept responsibility for global phenomena, rather than hiding behind the illusion of the quest for scientific truth (Bunche, 1940/in press; Lindsay, in press). African, Asian, and American universities, as part of their public engagement roles, should address concrete social problems such as the HIV/AIDS pandemic. While this priority might appear self-evident, often this is not the reality, as recently demonstrated in summer 2005 by one major American higher education association. When a proposal addressing its conference theme on the social responsibilities of universities, "University Program and Policy Research Regarding HIV/AIDS: Illustrations from Domestic and International Venues," was submitted, it was praised for its innovation, conceptual and methodological framework, and the knowledge of panelists. It was summarily rejected, however, because reviewers believed it was not of sufficient appeal to higher education scholars and policy makers. The absence of awareness and/or acknowledgement by the reviewers and the program committee was disconcerting given the magnitude of the HIV/AIDS pandemic. HIV/AIDS was marginalized.

The faculty and leaders of African, Indian, and Indonesian universities must analyze the dimensions of HIV/AIDS and the macro-level transnational matters affecting the disease. The AAU developed proposals and presented them to G-8 leaders, calling for sponsored research and the creation of scientific centers of excellence. The G-8 summit leaders did not endorse particular objectives or determine funds for such programs (Dickson, 2005); however, the proposals lucidly demonstrated the role of African scholars and researchers in helping to develop African solutions. Semali's and Otaala's chapters in this volume articulate the importance of indigenous answers. For several years, NEPAD (2005) and the AAU (2005) have emphasized policies to develop and enhance science, technology, and human development within NEPAD nations and in cooperation with industrialized nations.

Our next step after acceptance and analysis must be to take action. Otaala's chapter outlines several concrete actions that have been undertaken at select African universities. These actions include the introduction by the university vice chancellor of institutional policies on HIV/AIDS that make voluntary testing and counseling available; student peer tutoring and counseling; and curriculum integration so that students have multiple opportunities to learn about and address issues associated with HIV/AIDS. Semali's chapter extensively addresses curriculum actions that can be initiated. Given numerous fiscal constrains, university executives may initiate zero-based budget policies that have limited costs, and/or they may reallocate funds. Otaala's chapter also explicates the coordination of university policies with national HIV/AIDS policies. To the extent that such integration occurs, nations may experience a decline in HIV infection, as witnessed in Uganda. Modified cross-national lessons and policies can serve as models for other Asian and Caribbean nations, as Khanna's chapter explicates.

Some nations spent several years debating the existence of HIV/AIDS, the influence of Western lifestyles, and the deliberate or negligent attempts that spread infection among populations (Lyman, 2004). That debate now has abated. Some African leaders, however, have not fully distanced themselves from such animated discussions regarding the causes of HIV/AIDS; their connection to earlier debate has stifled their ability to fight the epidemic.

Simultaneously, Western nations such as the United States have pledged $15 billion for the HIV/AIDS pandemic in Africa and the Caribbean. Requests from the G-8 and from the African Union advocate an increase in the amount, rather than diverting funding already earmarked for African aid and assistance. When authentic new allocations occur, then the United States and other industrialized nations will be demonstrating their commitment through their actions.

Finally, nations must assess or evaluate and document successful policies and programs to ascertain areas for improvement. For example, the apparent HIV/AIDS declines in Uganda can be assessed to determine what factors contributed to the decline. Such information can be disseminated globally. Certainly, we must assess the effectiveness of experimental vaccines, but we also must assess curricular policies and peer tutoring for their roles in publicizing information. In short, assessments and evaluations inform us of what needs to be changed, altered, or initiated.

The Five "A's," depicted in Figure 12.1, can inform us regarding how to proceed. Recasting the future prospects of HIV/AIDS means altering the creation of intellectual and transnational paradigms that help professionals and policy makers actively address global issues, domestic issues, and the interconnectivity between the two. As awareness/acknowledgement, acceptance, analysis, action, and assessment are intertwined successfully, we may paraphrase Nobel Peace Laureate and University of Nairobi Professor Wangari Maathai (2004) by saying that now we have reached a higher moral ground and addressed one of the most significant contemporary challenges facing humanity.

NOTES

1. The 2005 Live 8 Concerts—like their counterpart from 20 years earlier, the worldwide LiveAid Concerts, which addressed the incredible Ethiopian famine—were spearheaded by popular entertainment mogul Sir Bob Geldof and aimed to raise global awareness and funds for the incredibly ravishing effects of poverty in Africa.

2. Besides Prime Minister Blair, members of the Commission for Africa included a female former American senator and a British Chancellor of the Exchequer, but the majority of members were prominent African civic, policy, and scholarly leaders.

REFERENCES

Altman, L. K., and Samura, M. (2005). Search for origin of new AIDS strain widens. *New York Times,* p. B1.

Association of African Universities. (2004). *Workshop on the implications of WTO/GATS for higher education in Africa.* Retrieved October 6, 2005, from http://www.aau.org/wto-gats.

Association of African Universities. (2005, July 3). *The Abertay conversation: Communique to G8 leaders.* Retrieved October 6, 2005, from http://www.aau.org/announce/abertay.htm.

Blair, T. (2005). *Prime Minister's statement. Gleneagles, Scotland: G-8 Summit.* Retrieved October 6, 2005, from http://www.g8.gov.uk/servlet/Front?pagename=OpenMarket/Xcelerate/ShowPageandc=Pageandcid=1078995903270anda=KArticleandaid=1119519013377.

Bright, M. (2005, January 30). I'm HIV positive says Chris Smith. *The Observer.* Retrieved October 6, 2005, from http://observer.guardian.co.uk/politics/story/0,6903,1401956,00.html.

Bunche, R. J. (In press). *The role of the university in the political orientation of Negro youth.* In B. Lindsay, ed., *Ralph Johnson Bunche: Public Intellectual and Nobel Peace Laureate.* Urbana: University of Illinois Press (original work published 1940).

Commission for Africa. (2005). *Our common interest: Report of the Commission for Africa.* New York: Penguin.

Dickson, D. (2005). *G-8 leaders give indirect boost for science in Africa.* Retrieved July 8, 2005, from http://allafrica.com/stories/200507110003. html.

Garrett, L. (2005). *HIV and national security: Where are the links?* New York: Council on Foreign Relations.

Hayward, F. M., and Ncayiyana, D. J. (2003). *Strategic planning: A guide for African higher education institutions.* Sunnyside, South Africa: Center for Higher Education Transformation.

HIV InSite. (2005a). *Australia.* San Francisco: University of California–San Francisco, Center for HIV Information. Retrieved October 6, 2005, from http://hivinsite.ucsf.edu/global?page=cr01–as-00.

HIV InSite. (2005b). *The Netherlands.* San Francisco: University of California–San Francisco, Center for HIV Information. Retrieved October 6, 2005, from http://hivinsite.ucsf.edu/global?page=cr10–nl-00.

Kelly, M. J. (2001). *Challenging the challenger: Understanding and expanding the response of universities in Africa to HIV/AIDS.* Washington, DC: World Bank, ADEA Working Group on Higher Education.

Kinghorn, A. (2000). *The impact of HIV/AIDS on tertiary education.* Presentation to South African Universities Vice Chancellors Association. Johannesburg, South Africa: Abt Associates.

Lindsay, B. (2004). Transforming African and African American sociopolitical and educational realities: Possibilities or pipe dreams? *African Studies Quarterly* 7(4): 41–47.

Lindsay, B. (2005). Initiating transformations of realities in African and African American universities. In J. King, ed., *Black education: A transformative research and action agenda for the new century* (pp. 183–194). Washington, DC: American Educational Research Association and Mahwah, NJ: Lawrence Erlbaum Associates.

Lindsay, B. et al. (In press). *Ralph Johnson Bunche: Public intellectual and Nobel Peace Laureate.* Urbana: University of Illinois Press.

Lyman, P. (2004). *Addressing the HIV/AIDS pandemic: A U.S. global AIDS strategy for the long term.* New York: Council on Foreign Relations.

Maathai, W. (2004, December). Nobel Peace Laureate lecture presented in Oslo, Norway. Retrieved October 6, 2005, from http://nobelprize.org/peace/laureates/2004/maathai-lecture.html.

New Partnership for Africa's Development. (2001). *The millennium partnership for the African recovery programme: A market access action plan for Africa.* Pretoria, South Africa: Department of Trade and Industry.

New Partnership for Africa's Development. (2005). *What is NEPAD?* Retrieved October 6, 2005, from http://www.nepad.org/2005/files/inbrief.php.

Otaala, B. (2000). *Impact of HIV/AIDS on the University of Namibia and the university's response.* Study commissioned by the ADEA Working Group on Higher Education. Windhoek, Namibia.

Otaala, B. (2004). Institutional policies for managing HIV/AIDS in Africa. In W. Saint, ed., *Crafting institutional responses to HIV/AIDS: Guidelines and resources for tertiary institutions in Sub-Saharan Africa.* Washington, DC: World Bank.

Rice, S. (2005). We must put more on the plate to fight poverty. *Washington Post,* p. A13.

Richards, P. (2005, July 20). *Health-Caribbean: AIDS could kill quarter million by 2010.* Retrieved July 21, 2005, from http://www.ipsnews. net/dominologin.asp?Db=ips\eng.nsfandwView=vwWebMainViewandD ocID=6295179AD1E4403DC1257044005C0A89.

Saint, W. (2004). The response begins at home: HIV/AIDS and tertiary education in sub-Saharan Africa. In W. Saint, ed., *Crafting institutional responses to HIV/AIDS: Guidelines and resources for tertiary institutions in sub-Saharan Africa* (pp. 4–14). Washington, DC: The World Bank.

Stromquist, N. P. (2002). *Education in a globalized world: The connectivity of economic power, technology, and knowledge.* Lanham, MD: Rowman and Littlefield.

13

POSTCOLONIAL PERSPECTIVES IN CONSTRUCTING TEACHER KNOWLEDGE ABOUT HIV/AIDS

Ladislaus M. Semali

⊸

> What HIV/AIDS does to the human body, it also does to institutions.
> It undermines those institutions that protect us.
>
> —*Piot, 2000, p. 22*

Protecting the education system and its principal players—teachers—in the face of HIV/AIDS is the theme of this chapter. Not only will schools have to deal with aspects such as teacher absenteeism, but also with children who are affected, infected, and orphaned as a result of the HIV/AIDS pandemic. Unless we first understand teachers, we can hardly claim to understand teaching or the pedagogical constructs that form much of the teaching about HIV/AIDS that takes place in classrooms. To appreciate what teachers must do to protect themselves and the students in their classrooms, we need to develop a broad understanding of teacher knowledge and of the way in which teachers construct HIV/AIDS prevention education. To do this, we must ask: What pedagogical approaches can address students' social and health needs? What might influence teachers' intentions to teach students about HIV/AIDS? What informs teachers' beliefs, attitudes, subjective norms, and perceived behavioral control regarding AIDS education? Finding answers to these questions poses formidable challenges.

Two overarching assumptions surround the study of teacher knowledge in this area. First, the study of HIV risk and prevention behavior is clouded over by many contradictions and unconscious elements that motivate behavior, especially sexual behavior. To sort out these contradictions, one must consider how ideology, gender, race, ethnicity, and class shape people's understanding of their place in society and in their relationships with others. Ignoring these psychosocial and contextual factors will yield only partial understanding of what is happening. In postcolonial Africa, young people are well informed, for the most part, about HIV prevention, and some populations (particularly university students) have been so since the early 1990s. In sub-Saharan Africa, for example, most studies have shown high levels of understanding of the main methods of transmission and risk prevention. Nonetheless, the infection rates have not slowed down, nor has the knowledge seemed to result in adoption of condom use. In addition, young people in poor and rural communities have far less access to a wide range of sources of information on HIV/AIDS than do their urban and economically advantaged counterparts.

The second overarching assumption is that epidemiological strategies and policies are believed to be universal regardless of psychosocial contexts and therefore applicable to all situations as a response to the pandemic. The basis of prevention science as practiced in sub-Saharan Africa is based on knowledge and studies conducted outside Africa. While the health and economic sectors in many countries where HIV/AIDS has been prevalent seem to have been recognized and explored, the impact of this pandemic on education and social service sectors has remained peripheral to the debates until very recently and is beginning to shift only slowly (Johnson, 2000). The literature on education as a vehicle for combating HIV/AIDS shows that even though much has been written about the disease in the education sector, the focus has been driven largely by two sets of questions. One set focuses on the impact of the disease, and another set seeks to explore what knowledge, attitudes, and beliefs those teaching within this sector hold regarding HIV/AIDS (Johnson, 2000). In this literature, little attention has been given to how the pedagogy of HIV/AIDS education and prevention is constructed and much less to the research studies that inform such pedagogy.

Studies in postcolonial Tanzania suggest that knowledge about HIV/AIDS does not necessarily lead to actions that would curb the spread of the disease. Risk-taking among secondary and postsecondary graduates is part of the mystery or "unrelenting logic" of sexual behavior for which these studies have not accounted (Whyte, 1997).

Some anthropological research on AIDS conducted elsewhere in Africa has demonstrated the necessity of considering a range of factors that contribute to conditions of sexual risk, including gender relations, land tenure, poverty, and the global economy (Bond, Kreniske, Susser, and Vincent, 1997). In Tanzania and elsewhere in Africa, however, there has been little research on AIDS, schooling, and the political economy to see how they interact and affect young people in different regions of the country.

In this chapter, I pose the question *How is teacher knowledge about HIV/AIDS constructed, and what are the postcolonial forces that influence such construction?* First, using a "postcolonial" approach, I challenge the construction of teacher knowledge about health education and prevention with regard to HIV/AIDS. Second, I outline the ways in which cultural customs and traditions are imbedded in the values and behaviors surrounding academic achievement as well as personal and community health, particularly as they relate to HIV/AIDS. The medical and health conditions brought by HIV/AIDS are more than just biological phenomena. These conditions are accompanied by meanings shaped by cultural, political, and legal discourses as well as scientific ones. These meanings take on moral significance in the context of teachers' relationships with their students, the students' parents, and the teachers' colleagues. These human relationships produce a framework of a humanizing pedagogy about HIV and AIDS that goes beyond dealing with physical needs and begins to address the bigotry that surrounds the disease.

This chapter concludes with the recommendation that if teachers are to be prepared to respond to the full human significance of HIV/AIDS, then the cultural, moral, and political dimensions of the disease need to be addressed in teacher professional development curriculum. Gaps in teacher knowledge will be important considerations in curricula for teacher preparation colleges.

CONSTRUCTION OF TEACHER KNOWLEDGE IN THE ERA OF HIV/AIDS

The HIV/AIDS pandemic is ravaging sub-Saharan Africa, taking its toll throughout the population. Compounding the social impact of the epidemic, the ranks of teachers in this region of the world are being decimated by AIDS. The number of teachers dying from AIDS is estimated to be greater than the output of all training colleges (Kelly, 2000). According to the Global Health Council (2005), Zambia lost 1,300 teachers to AIDS in the first 10 months of 1998—the equivalent of two-thirds of all new teachers trained annually—and this trend has only slowed down slightly in recent years. In Kenya, 10 teachers on average die from the disease each week. And in South Africa, as many as 60,000 teachers are expected to die before the decade is out (McElroy, 2003). In Botswana, 38.8 percent of all adults are infected with HIV/AIDS (Global Health Council, 2005). In Namibia, the incidence of HIV infection among teachers is assumed to be well above that for the population as a whole, which is currently between 20 percent and 25 percent. Projections by the Joint United Nations Programme on HIV/AIDS (UNAIDS) indicate that by the end of this decade, at least 3,500 working teachers will have died in Namibia, but the figure could be higher (*The Namibian*, 2002; Coombe, 2000). In Tanzania, it is estimated that 27,000 teachers are likely to die from AIDS by 2020 (Vavrus, 2002). Data from Mozambique show a very rapid acceleration in deaths among working teachers. In 1999, throughout sub-Saharan Africa, 860,000 primary school students lost teachers to AIDS, and many more children can no longer attend school because they are needed at home to care for ailing relatives or for the children of deceased family members (UNAIDS, 2000). These data and projections provide only a limited view of the dimensions of this disease and the toll it has taken on the population.

The literature on education for HIV/AIDS prevention and care is largely surrounded by dominant discourses in the economics, medicine, and epidemiology sectors (Airhihenbuwa, 1995). Three types of research trends conducted in the past 10 years have influenced how teachers talk and think about HIV/AIDS: (a) projective or trajectory studies based on regression models, (b) knowledge-attitude-practice types of studies, and (c) impact studies. Airhihenbuwa argues that this way of framing the HIV/AIDS epidemic, although useful, neglects the situated context in which messages, knowledge, experience, and behavioral change practices are produced, reproduced, and publicly expressed. Little or no attention has been paid in the past 10 years to the discourse on everyday sexual practices among African teachers in such a way that their "cultural knowledge" is valued or used in a meaningful way in prevention literature on HIV/AIDS. Much less is visible in public announcements. The roles of leader, elder, and sage that the classroom teacher fills in educational circles is almost absent or unaccounted for when we look at that role in the community or outside the school. What has happened? What changes have precipitated this absence? This situation motivates me to examine how teachers produce and reproduce knowledge about HIV/AIDS in their roles as classroom teachers and community leaders to effect change among students and the general population.

In this exploration, I examine the postcolonial discourse on human health promotion. Constructing teacher knowledge in HIV/AIDS prevention lies at the heart of the postcolonial condition. According to Gupta, this condition describes "a specific set of locations articulated by the historical trajectories of European colonialism, developmentalism, and global capitalism" (1998, p. 10). The postcolonial condition draws attention to the lasting impact of the economic deprivations of colonialism as well as to cultural and ideological aspects of colonialism that continue to influence present conditions. Exploring the postcolonial condition in sub-Saharan Africa requires delving into the ideological and material legacies of German, British, and Portuguese colonialism. It demands attending to developmentalism—dominant representations in development discourse—to understand the appeal of educational programs in the era of HIV/AIDS, and it necessitates looking at the effects of global capitalism in a specific location.

Teacher knowledge in this postcolonial condition is complex, multifaceted, and difficult to pinpoint, primarily because of the situation in which these African teachers find themselves. Teacher knowledge is largely surrounded by complex sociocultural contexts that are at the crossroads of poverty, inadequate infrastructure, a school curriculum that teachers do not own, and a devastating deadly epidemic. The success of health promotion programs and the work of African teachers in this endeavor rest with the degree to which they are based on the sociocultural realities of Africans. Even when other histories, languages, and cultures are taught, the images and the instruments of learning are often rooted in the past rather than in the present. The borrowing of textbooks and content that reifies Western medicine, epidemiological constructs, and prevention techniques that ignore the African local context are bound to fail. This result is consistent with Airhihenbuwa's (1995) conclusion following his study of aspects of the health education domain for individuals, extended families, and neighborhoods and how these elements inform educational diagnoses of health behavior including perceptions, enablers, and nurturers of positive, negative, and existential beliefs about health.

As observed by theorists of postcolonialism, research is perhaps one of the most pervasive ways in which the underlying code of imperialism and colonialism is both regulated and realized (Smith, 1999; Memmi, 1965). It is regulated through the formal rules of individual scholarly disciplines and scientific paradigms and through certification of who can talk about the medical field and epidemiology, prevention, and cure of diseases, including the institutions that support these areas (e.g., governments). Edward Said (1978), for example, sees this process as a Western discourse about the *other*. The success of this discourse is supported by "institutions, vocabulary, scholarship, research grants, imagery, doctrines, even colonial bureaucracies and colonial styles" (Said, 1978, p. 2). In this debate, the way forward seems to be that we ought to ask different kinds of questions that interrogate the prevailing assumptions surrounding knowledge about HIV/AIDS.

According to Airhihenbuwa (1995), the overemphasis of health promotion and disease prevention practices in the medical model has failed to ground its professional (both philosophical and practical) praxis adequately in such areas of humanities as philosophy, history, and cultural studies. The result has been the absence of meaningful participation of people and their cultures in positive behavioral transformation where appropriate. "It has become common practice in the field of public health and in the social and behavioral sciences to pay lip service to the importance of culture in the study and understanding of health behaviors, but culture has yet to be inscribed at the root of health promotion and disease prevention programs, at least in any manner that legitimates its centrality in public health praxis" (Airhihenbuwa, 1995, p. x).

Airhihenbuwa (1995) insists that health promotion and disease prevention practices continue to operate under the strong and direct influence of the Westernized medical model of prevention. Although benefits are derived from such influence, it seems unconscionable, Airhihenbuwa would argue, that a profession that anchors its raison d'être in the ability to influence human behavior has consistently undermined and, in most cases, ignored the centrality of culture in health and education. "There continues to be strong reliance on medicine and individual psychology, even though such orientation has constantly been challenged for its limitations, which are driven by monocentricsm and often result in cultural inappropriateness" (Airhihenbuwa, 1995, p. x). Therefore, it is important to note how HIV/AIDS research, especially within the African context, can be limited in scope because the context as a discursive field, including social practices, cultural practices, and the like, is either absent or unaccounted for in many of the studies under scrutiny. Such scrutiny especially becomes apparent when viewed against three critical considerations: the changing nature of the disease, its increasing prevalence in heterosexual populations, and its major effect on sub-Saharan Africa, where prevalence is reported to be the highest in the world.

One of the central themes of the postcolonial literature and discourse is the recognition of the dialectic of the global and the local. Within this dialectic, tension persists around notions of native versus foreign, indigenous versus colonial/imposed, or simply what has been termed "subjugated" knowledge. In the past, educational theorists and curriculum specialists have warned about the possibilities of a collision between subjugated or *indigenous pedagogies* and the school curriculum, paralleling the silent struggle between indigenous beliefs and practices and the Western medical model of prevention and cure (Semali and Kincheloe, 1999). When I talk about indigenous pedagogies, I refer to ways of learning, teaching, and knowing that are enhanced by local knowledge and often are found among indigenous, rural, or remote area peoples. In the school context, these non-Western education traditions and thoughts consist of complex sets of processes or abilities that span a lifetime—from employing indigenous languages to relating to oral traditions, rites, and agrarian health practices and use of traditional therapies that have endured locally. These pedagogies are informed by a systematic body of knowledge acquired by local and indigenous communities through the accumulation of experiences, informal experiments, and intimate understanding of the local environment—skills and knowledge derived from many years of experience and usually communicated orally through family members across generations (Semali, 2000).

In a nutshell, teacher knowledge is surrounded by complex psychosocial contexts and postcolonial conditions. The process of decolonization explored in health education, for example, maps out the discursive terrain of indigenousness, histories, cultures, and traditions—and how collectively they influence common folk in indigenous communities in their ways of being, doing, talking, and thinking.

HOW DO TEACHERS CONSTRUCT AND TRANSFER KNOWLEDGE?

The construction and transfer of teacher knowledge in the African context is a complex matter. In the African context, *humanistic* teacher knowledge refers to culturally responsive education and teaching that respect and use the culture, history, and perspectives of teachers and students in educational practice (Kaunda, 1966). Humanistic educators believe that both feelings and knowledge are important to the learning process. Unlike traditional educators, humanistic teachers do not separate the cognitive and affective domains. In addition, they insist that schools provide students with a nonthreatening environment so that they will feel secure enough to learn. Once students feel secure, learning becomes easier and more meaningful.

Feeling secure and being sensitive to HIV/AIDS means being aware of the pandemic and of students' feelings, wishes, and values about the disease. But sensitivity requires more than awareness: It also requires actively engaging people and objects in the dynamics of education. Sensitivity also entails cultural selectivity because, in some instances, including all aspects of local culture in schooling is not possible or even desirable. To what extent, then, does this humanistic teacher knowledge reflect sensitivities to traditions, cultural heritage, and the cultural apparatus in school and society, particularly with respect to the HIV/AIDS pandemic, while also meeting challenging global changes that affect future education practice?

In the literature, Coombe and Kelly (2001) outline the implications of a humanist education in the African context. First, a humanist and caring education will ensure that those affected by the disease can work and learn in a caring environment that respects the safety and human rights of all. Of major concern here would be efforts to make the system fully and patently inclusive by challenging all forms of AIDS-related stigma and discrimination, providing for the most extensive possible participation by persons living with HIV/AIDS, and rooting all provisions in strong frameworks of human and children's rights.

Second, the construction of teacher knowledge is intimately connected with the institution in which the teacher works. As is often the case, each and every learning institution has its own unique institutional culture. For this reason, the institution must be a place of safety for all who are associated with it. Mitigation efforts should also be addressed to provide counseling services, make provision for voluntary counseling and testing, work with social welfare and health ministries to provide learner-friendly services, and ensure responsiveness to the special needs of infected or affected learners and educators. This effort would include such actions as prompt and trouble-free payment of sickness or death benefits and new provisions for treatment and/or retirement of educators who are sero-positive.

A third concern in the area of mitigation would be to provide HIV/AIDS education in the workplace for all categories of education employees, including teachers and lecturers, and in the school or college curriculum for all learners, from the time they enter school to the time they complete formal education and beyond.

Unfortunately, the capacity of teachers to provide instruction about AIDS and other related health problems with knowledge and comfort may be limited by academic, institutional, and cultural barriers (Carl-Hill, 2002). Such barriers are associated with the way teachers are trained on the African continent, the structure and administration of schools, and, most important, the cultural contexts in which schools and communities are immersed. Other barriers include postcolonial legacies, stigma, and conflicts between Western and non-Western approaches to disease prevention and science instruction.

Clearly, the teaching of comprehensive sexuality education from kindergarten through twelfth grade begins with the proper training of the teachers. Too often, teachers do not have the skills, knowledge, or inclination to teach such courses. Few have received training in sexuality education, and even fewer have received certification as sexuality educators, let alone teaching about the prevention and care of HIV/AIDS victims. Although studies have looked at school teachers' beliefs and attitudes toward AIDS and students with the disease, almost none have specifically addressed teachers' intentions, abilities, competence, and attitudes toward teaching HIV/AIDS education (Vavrus, 2002). In the next section, I will examine how a humanist education can address these barriers and support the needs of teachers infected with HIV/AIDS or working within an AIDS environment.

TEACHERS' VOICES FROM THE FIELD

The onslaught of the HIV/AIDS pandemic has altered the dimensions of indigenous structures. It has also revealed how ill-prepared social systems are to understand the seriousness of the epidemic or to handle its influence on communities in a region characterized by numerous cultural traditions, taboos, and secrecy. Further, the epidemic is eroding the region's traditional practice of caring by overloading its capacity with the sheer number of orphaned children needing support and care. More children have been orphaned by AIDS in Africa than anywhere else. While in former traditional or indigenous societies, sex education was offered by the community, this practice is no longer widespread or common, in part due to rapid urbanization and migration disrupting community networks (Aggleton and Rivers, 1998). The deep-rooted kinship systems that have existed in Africa for millennia—the extended family networks of aunts, uncles, cousins, and grandparents—are an age-old social safety net for children, and these systems have long proved themselves resilient to even major social upheavals. But capacity and resources are now stretched to the breaking point, and those providing the necessary care are in many cases already impoverished and elderly, and many have themselves depended financially and physically on the support of the very son or daughter who has died of AIDS.

Traditional safety nets and indigenous structures are unraveling as more young adults die of AIDS-related illnesses. Families and communities can barely fend for themselves, let alone take care of the orphans (USAID, 2003; Mhango, 2003). Typically, half of the people with HIV become infected before age 25, developing AIDS and dying by the time they are age 35, leaving behind a generation of children who must be raised by their grandparents or who are left on their own in child-headed households.

What is the role of schools—and of teachers—in dealing with these situations? Sociological studies tend to ignore the personal dimensions of teaching and often give an oddly inhuman account of this most human of jobs (Goodson, 1992). But unless we first understand teachers, we can hardly claim to understand teaching or the pedagogical constructs that form much of the teaching that takes place in classrooms.

To document educators' perspectives, I surveyed teachers in Tanzania and South Africa on their knowledge of HIV/AIDS-related beliefs, attitudes, and life skills. These teachers reported that their knowledge and life-skills curricula were constructed from a variety of sources, including government-sponsored publicity materials, such as posters, booklets, and newspaper advertisements; newspaper articles; public health announcements over the radio; television; and counseling from AIDS campaign agents. Teachers were asked to identify books or materials they know or have encountered that provide information about

HIV/AIDS (e.g., health-related textbooks, including those for biology and chemistry) used at the high school level. Teachers responded by circling the relevant statements from the following list:

1. Have used in classroom in group instruction.
2. Have recommended for recreational reading.
3. Have recommended for research, reference, or resource.
4. Have used as read-aloud.
5. Am familiar with but have not used the book (or materials) in my classroom.
6. Not aware of the book or materials.

In general, school administrators and teachers were knowledgeable about HIV/AIDS, the ways in which HIV is transmitted, and the means of protection against infection. The majority of the respondents attributed their knowledge about HIV/AIDS to mass media (radio, television, and newspapers), to public campaigns, and to training programs. In response to the question, "If you were to teach about HIV in class, do you feel well equipped to do so?" over 50 percent of teachers said, "No." Further analysis of the qualitative data from this ongoing study might reveal some of the reasons why so many teachers would feel uncomfortable teaching about HIV.

With regard to local and traditional knowledge, some of the teachers I met in schools, particularly in East Africa, explained to me that the Western systems of formalized school instruction take little account of local cultures. Some of these teachers argued that many African governments promote teaching methods used in non-Western schools within a model of curriculum based on a nationalist view of history and a universal interpretation of the sciences and mathematics. "Unfortunately, such curriculum does not take account of local culture, practices, and traditions," said one teacher. Sometimes, such models of school curriculum deliberately dismiss or eradicate local culture by excluding it completely from the classroom as if it were irrelevant to the concerns and lives of local populations. As Shiva cautioned (1993), local knowledge of any kind is compelled to disappear when the dominant system negates its very existence or when such systems erase or destroy the reality that the local knowledge represents.

Teachers, students, and administrators—and the communities they come from—must come to terms with the dilemmas and contradictions that undermine education about HIV/AIDS prevention and care. These dilemmas and contradictions became apparent during focus group interviews in Tanzania and South Africa. Teachers revealed three areas of concern: conflicts in constructing knowledge, in understanding the disease, and in willingness to teach sex education in schools. The following opinions surfaced during the interviews:

- HIV-infected teachers saw themselves as failures in society where they no longer can be a role model if they are known to be infected.
- Teachers continually face fears related to violating taboos, giving offense to parents, being accused of encouraging promiscuity and loose moral practices in the young, or being regarded as using their teaching in this area as a form of personal sexual outlet.
- Teachers said they do not feel empowered to teach about intimate relationships—matters they do not tackle even as parents to their own children. They questioned whether it is the teacher's responsibility to teach about sex, appropriate sexual attitudes, and very specific behavioral guidelines about the sex act when their training and orientation were directed toward what are essentially academic areas.
- Some teachers noted that they hear mixed messages and they are in turn likely to transmit similar messages to their students. On the academic side, they hear the educational program itself with its scientific messages about the cause of HIV/AIDS and how it is transmitted. This knowledge is received and stored for subsequent action within the context of the scientific, academic, modern, Western world; as it relates to personal behavior, such messages may be impractical or irrelevant. On a much deeper and more practical level, teachers hear stories about the disease from peers, through the grapevine, or from family members. Such stories are told when someone dies, or at funerals of infected people. These stories have an impact on what the teachers know about the disease, what they think, and what they talk about with reference to the causes and cure of the disease. The traditional view that interprets the disease and its causes in terms of the cultural world of taboos, obligations, and sorcery is very powerful. One teacher reminded me that sickness and disease are almost invariably considered to have external causes other than

the viruses, germs, and microbes identified by medical science. These remarks echoed much of the position that Airhihenbuwa (1995) maintained.

- Some teachers insisted that the disease is associated with external causes, attributing it to an ill-willed, malevolent human agent who uses the powers and forces that are at the disposal of a witch or sorcerer. The external cause also is associated with ancestral spirits who are offended by the violation of certain taboos. This can include having intercourse with a woman before she has been "cleansed" or with a woman who has had a miscarriage, or failing to observe certain rituals (such as the "cleansing" by a man of his brother's widow). Such rumors circulate widely and have achieved a strong following. The focus group noted that even people who believe in such causes are often willing to try Western medicine when available, undertaking a variety of therapies as economics allow.

The opinions expressed by the teachers in the focus groups simply show the complexity of how teachers construct knowledge about HIV/AIDS (see Figure 13.1). People's history is part of the rationalization of their ways of knowing. The deep-rooted view that sorcery and witchcraft are the root causes of HIV/AIDS manifests itself not just among teachers from rural settings but also among those from urban and well-to-do settings. It further shows that societies immersed in traditional practices will have a long way to go to combat the spread of the disease unless their history and belief systems are part of the prevention and care education.

WHAT DO TEACHERS KNOW ABOUT HIV/AIDS PREVENTION?

The empty classrooms and ailing teachers in many African schools make it relatively easy to track the effects of AIDS on children's education, but it is far more difficult to study the opposite: the impact of education on curbing the AIDS epidemic. The studies from Zambia and Uganda reviewed by Vandemoortele (2000) suggest that the more years a woman spends in school, the lower her likelihood of HIV infection. According to the author, the "education vaccine" works through the mechanism of empowerment: Women with more years of schooling have more equitable sexual relations, which allow them to put their knowledge of AIDS prevention into practice (Vandemoortele, 2000).

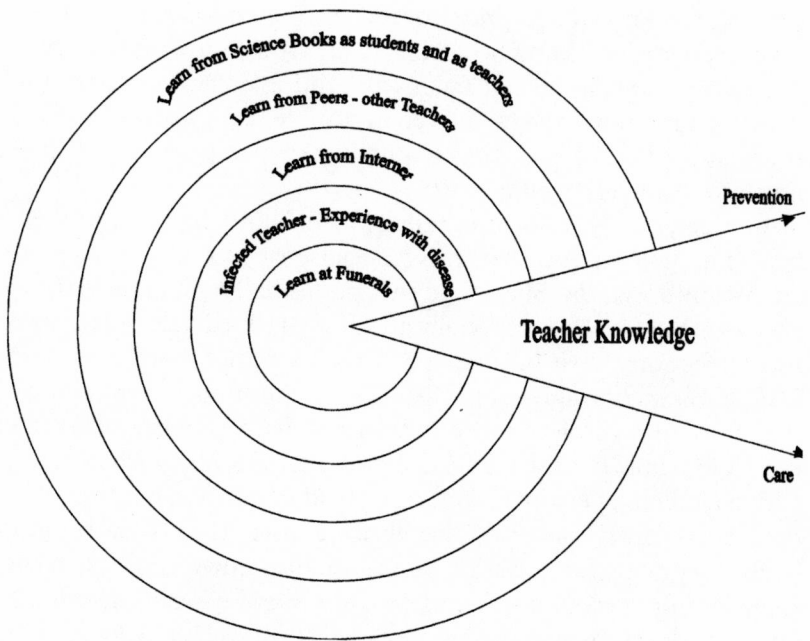

Figure 13.1 Construction of Teacher
Knowledge in Sub-Saharan Africa

In an attempt to shed light on teacher knowledge, Ross and Levine (2002) sought to examine what knowledge, attitudes, and practices teachers, youth, and adolescents have about HIV/AIDS. They found that two conditions seemed to influence youth's knowledge on HIV/AIDS: (a) knowledge on reproductive health and (b) socioeconomic and cultural constraints that affect youth decision-making regarding safe sex (Ross and Levine, 2002). Some studies in South Africa, for example, examined what youth know about reproductive health (UNAIDS, 2004), asking questions such as these: How do youth come to know reproductive health? How accurate is their knowledge? How is their knowledge influenced by teachers' knowledge? In general, youth are perceived to be particularly vulnerable to HIV infection as a result of their risky behavior patterns.

Harrison, Xaba, Kunene, and Ntuli (2001) found that girls in Kwa Zulu Natal had poor factual knowledge of sex. Teenagers had very little sexual knowledge prior to and during the first few months of sexual activity, including not being aware that intercourse can result in pregnancy. Circulating cultural myths reinforced beliefs that evil spirits would eat teens who were delayed in experiencing sex. The girls in the study also believed that boys would experience pain later if they did not have sex while young.

In a case study in Zambia, Malambo (2000) found that the risky behavior patterns seem to thrive because of lack of accurate or systematic information. She found that pupils had high knowledge levels about HIV and AIDS, especially about sex-related methods to prevent HIV infection. Most of the pupils also knew that there is no cure for HIV/AIDS, although many cited use of condoms. Overall, however, the knowledge displayed by pupils lacked detail. For example, according to Malambo, most pupils did not associate HIV/AIDS infection with an infected person, blood, razor blades, needles, or other infected objects. Malambo observed that although the HIV/AIDS subject has been integrated into science, social studies, environmental sciences, English, home economics, religious and moral education, geography, physical education, and the proposed psychosocial life skills, it has been given little emphasis because it appears as a topic in passing.

Malambo's findings are important in providing insights into teacher knowledge. Perhaps the lack of school discussions led to students' lack of factual details about the disease. Malambo noted that teachers and pupils were, in general, not satisfied with the extent to which HIV/AIDS is taught in schools. Pupils and teachers would also like to see an increase in the supply of teaching and learning materials in schools including audiovisual materials. In this study, pupils also pointed out that they would like to see teachers improve their approach and involvement in the teaching of HIV and AIDS in schools.

TEACHING PREVENTION AND CARE

The old adage "knowledge is power" is the mantra of the Ugandan AIDS Comprehensive Education program. Educators in Uganda believe that HIV/AIDS education must not merely make students aware of the need to protect themselves against infection but also bring about gradual changes in the wider social environment, making safer sex more acceptable. But what is the best way to introduce HIV/AIDS education to schools with scarce resources and a packed curriculum? Who will teach such a curriculum? Kinsman et al. (2001) found that teachers were reluctant to tackle these controversial and unfamiliar topics for fear of antagonizing parents, the wider community, or school principals. Also, teachers lacked sufficient classroom time to implement the package due to curriculum overload.

Bennell (2003) found that curriculum and delivery of HIV/AIDS and sexual reproductive health education are problematic; integration or infusion approaches to teaching, in which HIV/AIDS topics are included in carrier subjects, are not effective. He found that teachers lack both the competence and commitment to teach these topics in an already overcrowded and examination-driven curriculum. Little training has been provided, and guidance and counseling services and peer education are also seriously inadequate.

Overall, available research shows that there is not adequate teacher preparation to assume the teaching of HIV/AIDS prevention or care of HIV/AIDS victims. Teachers know little about the disease. Many teachers in sub-Saharan Africa learned about the disease from the public media and private conversations. Several factors make teacher preparation related to HIV/AIDS necessary and critical:

1. Children with HIV are living longer, and the number of children with the disease who are attending school is expected to grow. Teachers need an understanding of the special educational, social, psychological, and medical needs of these students.
2. Teachers may expect to confront educational and psychosocial issues among children whose parents have HIV or AIDS.
3. To prevent the spread of any disease, teachers must be knowledgeable and skilled in using correct infection-control guidelines in and around the classroom.
4. In some instances, a teacher may be entrusted with information about a student's, parent's, or staff member's HIV status and must understand ethical and legal requirements for respecting confidentiality.
5. Teachers may be expected to provide HIV/AIDS education and to answer students' questions about the disease in a manner that is developmentally and culturally appropriate.
6. Teachers' attitudes affect their comfort with and capacity to teach specific subject matter. The preservice setting offers an opportunity for future teachers to explore their own beliefs and biases toward the disease.

CONCLUDING COMMENTS

Experts agree that prevention through education is the best way to fight the transmission of HIV and that education must begin before young people initiate sexual activity and certainly no later than seventh grade (Hartell, 2005; Simbayi et al., 2005). Confronting teacher knowledge is critical, because schools in an AIDS-infected region cannot be the same as in an AIDS-free world. But unless we first understand teachers, we can hardly claim to understand teaching or the pedagogical constructs that form much of the teaching that takes place in classrooms. The ways in which schools and their stakeholders produce and reproduce knowledge about HIV/AIDS must be confronted.

In this chapter, I discussed postcolonial perspectives in constructing humanistic teacher knowledge about HIV/AIDS—how it is constructed, appropriated, and transferred to students. I suggested ways in which teachers can come to terms with their own knowledge about the disease before they can venture to teach others comfortably. From the vantage point of my recent work in Tanzania and South Africa, I acknowledge the complexity of education for prevention and care amidst teachers' dilemmas and contradictions in this region. I have also observed that strong ties and connections between peoples and their historical past exist; these historical legacies should be considered in prevention and care education. Postcolonial legacies continue to slow down the economy, education, and social services in these countries. To introduce a humanistic education and maintain it will require an investment of resources, both human and material. Family networks must be encouraged and strengthened to care for infected victims and orphaned children.

The most important lesson to take from this chapter, however, is that teacher knowledge continues to be contradicted by African epistemologies, local customs, taboos, and traditional beliefs and practices. Epidemiologists and educators must bridge this gap. Behavior change interventions should not neglect the development of life skills and positive attitudes. But deficiencies in these areas do not represent the core of the problem. Regardless of whether or not it imparts a given set of skills, if an intervention fails to produce among learners an accurate knowledge of the basic characteristics of HIV and its prevention, researchers are mistaken to expect that it will lead to significant positive behavior change. Finally, the extended family continues to be the major resource that most victims and orphaned children continue to rely on for knowledge, emotional support, and material resources.

REFERENCES

Aggleton, P., and Rivers, K. (1998). Behavioral interventions for adolescents. In L. Gibney, R. DiClemente, and S. Vermund, eds., *Preventing HIV infection in developing countries* (pp. 213–219). New York: Plenum.

Airhihenbuwa, C. (1995). *Health and culture: Beyond the Western paradigm.* Thousand Oaks, CA: Sage.

Bennell, P. (2003). The AIDS epidemic in sub-Saharan Africa: Are teachers a high-risk group? *Comparative Education* 39(4): 493–508.

Bond, G. C., Kreniske, J., Susser, I., and Vincent, J., eds. (1997). *The anthropology of AIDS in Africa and the Caribbean.* Boulder: Westview.

Carl-Hill, R. (2002). Practical and theoretical problems in training teachers to confront HIV/AIDS. In E. Thomas, ed., *Teaching education: Dilemmas and prospects* (pp. 193–204). London: Kogan Page.

Coombe, C. (2000). *Managing the impact of HIV/AIDS on the educational sector.* Briefing paper prepared for African Development Forum, UNECA, University of Pretoria, South Africa.

Coombe, M. J., and Kelly, C. (2001). Education as vehicle for combating AIDS. *Prospects* 31(3): 439–445.

Global Health Council. (2005). *Poverty and HIV/AIDS.* Washington, DC: Global Health Council.

Goodson, I. F. (1992). *Studying teachers' lives.* London: Routledge.

Gupta, A. (1998). *Postcolonial developments: Agriculture in the making of modern India.* Durham, NC and London: Duke University Press.

Harrison, A., Xaba, N., Kunene, P., and Ntuli, N. (2001). Understanding young women's risk for HIV/AIDS: Adolescent sexuality and vulnerability in rural Kwa Zulu/Natal. *Society in Transition* 32(1): 69–78.

Hartell, C. G. (2005). HIV/AIDS in South Africa: A review of sexual behavior among adolescents. *Adolescence* 40(157): 171–181.

Johnson, S. (2000). *The impact of AIDS on the education sector in South Africa.* Presentation at meeting of the International Institute for Educational Planning, Paris.

Joint United Nations Programme on HIV/AIDS. (2000). *Report on the global HIV/AIDS epidemic, June 2000.* Geneva: Author.

Joint United Nations Programme on HIV/AIDS. (2004). *2004 report on the global HIV/AIDS epidemic.* Retrieved October 9, 2005, from http://www.unaids.org/bangkok2004/report.html.

Kaunda, K. (1966). *A humanist in Africa: Letters to Colin M. Morris from Kenneth D. Kaunda.* London: Longmans.

Kelly, M. (2000). Standing education on its head: Aspects of schooling in a world with HIV/AIDS. *Current Issues in Comparative Education* 3(1): 1–10.

Kinsman, J., Nakiyingi, A., Kamali, L., Carpenter, M., Quigley, M., Pool, R., and Whitworth, J. (2001). Evaluation of a comprehensive school-based AIDS education programme in rural Masaka, Uganda. *Health Education Research* 16(1): 85–100.

Malambo, R. M. (2000). Teach them while they are young, they will live to remember. The views of teachers and pupils on the teaching of HIV/AIDS in basic education: A case study of Zambia's Lusaka and Southern Provinces. *Current Issues in Comparative Education* [Online], 3(1). Retrieved October 14, 2005, from http://www.tc.columbia.edu/cice/articles/rmm131.htm.

McElroy, E. (2003). *Expansion of AFT-Africa AIDS Campaign Programs in South Africa and Kenya*. Washington, DC: AFT-Africa AIDS Campaign.

Memmi, A. (1965). *The colonizer and the colonized*. Boston: Beacon Press.

Mhango, G. (2003, May 28). Orphan care assists 4000 children in Karonga. *Malawi standard* [Electronic version]. Retrieved October 9, 2005, from http://www.sahims.net/batchfiles_web/mlw/05/allAfrica_com percent-20percent20Malawi percent20Orphan percent20Care percent20Assists percent204000 percent20Children percent20in percent20Karonga.htm.

Namibian, The. (2002, December 16). Older AIDS caregivers face stigma. Retrieved October 7, 2005, from http://www.namibian.com.na/2002/December/national/02A107340E.html.

Piot, P. (2000). *Report on the global HIV/AIDS epidemic*. London: Oxford University Press.

Quinn, S. C., Thomas, S. B., and Smith, B. J. (1990). Are health educators being prepared to provide HIV/AIDS education? A survey of selected health educators' professional preparation programs. *Journal of School Health* 60(3): 92–95.

Ross, F., and Levine, S. (2002). Perceptions of and attitudes to HIV/AIDS among young adults at the University of Cape Town. *CSSR Working Paper No. 14.* Cape Town, South Africa: Centre for Social Science Research, University of Cape Town.

Said, E. (1978). *Orientalism*. London: Vintage Books.

Semali, L. (2000). Cultural perspectives and teacher education: Indigenous pedagogies in an African context. In E. Thomas, ed., *Teacher education: Dilemmas and prospects* (pp. 155–165). London: Kogan Page.

Semali, L., and Kincheloe, J. (1999). *What is indigenous knowledge? Voices from the academy*. New York: Garland.

Shiva, V. (1993). *Monocultures of the mind: Perspectives in biodiversity and biotechnology*. London: Zed Books.

Simbayi, L. C., Kalichman, S. C., Jooste, S., Cherry, C., Mfecane, S., and Cain, D. (2005). Risk factors for HIV/AIDS among youth in Cape Town, South Africa. *AIDS Behavior* 9(1): 53–61.

Smith, L. (1999). *Tuhiwai decolonizing methodologies: Research and indigenous peoples.* London: Zed Books.

USAID. (2003, May). *Building community-based partnerships to support AIDS orphans and vulnerable children.*

Vandemoortele, J. (2000). *Absorbing social shocks, protecting children, and reducing poverty: The role of basic human services.* New York: UNICEF.

Vavrus, F. (2002). *Desire and decline: Schooling amid crisis in Tanzania.* New York: Peter Lang.

Whyte, S. R. (1997). *Questioning misfortune: The pragmatics of uncertainty in Eastern Uganda.* Cambridge, England: Cambridge University Press.

14

AFRICAN TERTIARY INSTITUTIONS' RESPONSE TO THE HIV/AIDS EPIDEMIC: CURRENT PRACTICES AND THE WAY FORWARD

Barnabas Otaala

⤙

We know the statistics on the prevalence, distribution, and possible effects of the HIV epidemic in sub-Saharan Africa. Apart from Uganda, very few countries have yet succeeded in reversing the epidemic. Statistics show the disproportionate impact the epidemic has in sub-Saharan Africa compared to other continents and particularly on young women—the backbone, the heart, the soul of our communities—and on children, the future of our societies.

What has been the African response to this tragic epidemic, which is not merely a health issue but also a development problem? Specifically, what has been the response of African tertiary institutions, including colleges and universities? What policies and practices are currently in place, with particular reference to policy development; peer counseling, mentoring, and tutoring; curriculum integration; and voluntary counseling and testing?

To obtain information on the various innovative responses to the threat posed by HIV/AIDS, I requested that a number of selected universities supply information on their current HIV/AIDS activities.[1] This paper includes suggestions about what tertiary education leaders can do to further limit the spread of HIV/AIDS on their campuses, and it offers suggestions to other stakeholders and participants about how to make their HIV/AIDS-related work more effective in their respective institutions. I briefly examine these issues, in that order.[2]

WHY SHOULD TERTIARY INSTITUTIONS
BE CONCERNED WITH HIV/AIDS?

African tertiary institutions face a number of challenges, particularly related to globalization and communication technology development. Recently, the challenge posed by HIV/AIDS has become paramount in our thinking, actions, strategies, and programming. Tertiary institutions especially are obligated to respond decisively to the HIV/AIDS epidemic for a variety of reasons.

1. Given the magnitude of the HIV/AIDS crisis in the lives of individuals and countries, the education system—especially tertiary institutions—needs to cooperate with all other bodies in stemming the spread of this disease. As a major socializing force in society, the system has a profound obligation to educate the young on HIV/AIDS by providing knowledge, fostering awareness, and promoting life-asserting attitudes. It also has an obligation to those who work in the system, to heighten their awareness and strengthen their determination and efforts to remain uninfected. The education system has a further responsibility toward those who are already infected, to help them in a compassionate and unpatronizing manner to live positively. This latter responsibility is all the more grave and delicate in relation to school-age children who are affected and infected by HIV/AIDS. We recognize that the burden of fighting HIV/AIDS cannot rest only with our national governments. Together with our governments and external partners (including nongovernmental organizations, or NGOs), tertiary institutions can and must make a difference if we are to succeed.

2. In an HIV/AIDS–affected society, it is essential that universities produce AIDS-competent graduates who are sufficiently flexible to cope with covering for sick and dying colleagues; who are well informed about the ethical (human rights) as well as the practical implications of HIV/AIDS in the workplace (including precautions, support and care, and the budgetary implications thereof); who are sensitive to the gender issues; and who, above all, approach their academic discipline with HIV/AIDS in mind. Government departments, the teaching professions, and some specific industries are already aware to some extent that they must

produce graduates competent to plan and strategize for the needs of AIDS-affected industries and society. Much more open debate is required between the university and the public and private sectors, and also among disciplines within the university itself, so that everyone understands the implications of HIV/AIDS and the practical measures needed to address the epidemic. Similarly, much more research is required into the ramifications of HIV/AIDS within every discipline. For instance, what will be the impact on society of millions of AIDS orphans? What sort of housing should architects be planning for future communities of child-led households? HIV/AIDS is not only a serious intellectual issue in its own right, it is also a professional issue for every discipline (Association of Commonwealth Universities [ACU], 2001).

3. HIV/AIDS has clearly affected the core business of tertiary institutions: teaching and learning; research; and management and community engagement. HIV/AIDS is no respecter of institutions. In fact, tertiary institutions that have large numbers of sexually active young people between the ages of 19 and 25 are particularly vulnerable.

4. According to the World Bank, tertiary education is "a critical pillar of human development worldwide. In today's lifelong-learning framework, tertiary education provides not only the high-level skills necessary for every labor market but also the training essential for teachers, doctors, nurses, civil servants, engineers, humanists, entrepreneurs, scientists, social scientists, and a myriad personnel. It is these trained individuals who develop the capacity and analytical skills that drive local economies, support civil society, teach children, lead effective governments, and make important decisions which affect entire societies" (World Bank, 2002, p. ix).

Having briefly referred to some reasons why tertiary institutions should be concerned with issues related to HIV/AIDS, I now turn to an examination of what has been done as a response to the epidemic.

RESPONSES OF TERTIARY INSTITUTIONS IN AFRICA TO THE HIV/AIDS EPIDEMIC

Although the HIV/AIDS epidemic has been present for over two decades, we knew very little until recently about how various tertiary institutions were responding to the challenge and threat posed by the disease. Kelly (2001) synthesized seven surveys done in Benin, Ghana, Kenya, Namibia, South Africa, and Zambia. The work was supported by the Working Group on Higher Education (WGHE) of the Association for the Development of Education in Africa (ADEA). Otaala and Lutaaya (2004) undertook a survey, on behalf of the Association of African Universities (AAU), of over 140 tertiary institutions in Anglophone, Francophone, and Lusophone Africa to determine HIV/AIDS activities and the contributions of these institutions.

Gabriel (2003) synthesized the results of a study designed to collect information about how universities are responding to the HIV/AIDS epidemic through their administrative policies, academic programs, involvement with national policy, and involvement with community-level HIV/AIDS issues. Supported by the AAU and the African-American Institute, the project covered 12 Global AIDS Initiative countries supported by the U.S. Agency for International Development (USAID).[3]

In the following sections, I examine how tertiary institutions have responded (or not responded) to the HIV/AIDS epidemic. I then turn to examples of good practice, including what has been done in policy development.

THE PATTERN OF PRESENT RESPONSES BY AFRICAN TERTIARY INSTITUTIONS TO THE HIV/AIDS EPIDEMIC

The following conclusions were gleaned from the various surveys cited above and represent a picture of the current responses of tertiary institutions.

- Between countries (and within countries), universities are at different stages of their response to the HIV/AIDS epidemic.
- Systematic impact and risk assessments of the disease are absent.
- In many institutions, various indicators show considerable HIV/AIDS effects on universities including loss of staff and students; reduced productivity; direct and indirect costs; strain on facilities and services; and, eventually, diminished quality of services.
- In many instances, tertiary-education responses to the epidemic leave much to be desired:

- Many universities are doing practically nothing tangible;
- Many members of institutions fail to realize that universities should be at the forefront of the fight; and
- Institutional responses tend to be reactive rather than proactive, ad hoc rather than systematic.
- Most universities do not accord a high level of priority to the institutional response to HIV/AIDS. Integration of HIV/AIDS into tertiary curricula has been largely the domain of health/medical faculties; consequently, core programs have not adequately integrated HIV/AIDS.
- AIDS-related community and outreach programs are not being vigorously implemented in many institutions. Universities are not proactively selling themselves or manifesting their willingness to work with government or other external agencies.
- The involvement of staff (particularly academic staff) in HIV/AIDS response initiatives is indiscernible in many institutions; the little activity that does exist is performed by students. Academic staff have not sufficiently felt the urgency to act, and capacity-building programs have been driven by supply and constrained by resources.
- Current HIV/AIDS research in Africa is marked by the following characteristics:
  - It is accidental rather than systematic, individual rather than institutional, and externally induced rather than internally initiated.
  - It is largely undertaken in "silos" of disciplines and organizations. Thus, it is very difficult to find out who is doing what and where, whether on a regional, national, or international basis.
  - The emphasis remains primarily on research in the biomedical, social, and health sciences. Scant regard is paid to establishing multidisciplinary research projects.
  - Philosophy and medical-ethics departments must be engaged immediately in developing appropriate policies to guide research.
  - There is, however, perceivable growth in the use of systematic needs assessments (both internally and externally) to set direction.
  - Networks are beginning to emerge to support research activities.

One key element of a university's mandate is to extend and disseminate knowledge. With respect to HIV/AIDS, this charge means searching for the answers to questions that concern and affect society and imparting that knowledge to the principal actors both within and outside the university so they can make informed decisions about how to manage HIV/AIDS both institutionally and nationally.

One can sum up the present constraints by stating that lack of institutional support and inadequate leadership commitment are the major hindrances. Other writings and surveys have supported these findings (e.g., ACU, 2001; Katjavivi and Otaala, 2003, 2004a, 2004b; Khulisa Management Services, 2003; UNESCO/BREDA, 2002; UNESCO/Gamsberg MacMillan, 2004).

Despite the litany of inadequacies in the current responses of tertiary institutions, a number of examples of good practice do exist. These examples include policy development and management, peer counseling, tutoring and mentoring, curriculum integration, voluntary counseling and testing, and child-to-child programs.

POLICY DEVELOPMENT

For each undertaking, policies are needed to guide the vision and goals of the enterprise before strategic planning and implementation are begun. In the area of HIV/AIDS, institutional policy development has been slow, particularly within tertiary institutions where AIDS is often viewed as a private matter.

In 1997, the University of Namibia developed HIV/AIDS guidelines that were approved by the University Senate. But it was not until officials visited the University of Botswana, the University of Natal, and the University of Pretoria and engaged in numerous exchanges on HIV/AIDS issues with several universities that fall under the South African Vice Chancellors' Association (SAVCA) that our university began to actively develop its own policy, drawing heavily on its 1997 guidelines and on other HIV/AIDS policies that have been adopted since or were in draft form.

The University of Namibia's policy on HIV/AIDS articulates with and supports the National Strategic Plan on HIV/AIDS Medium Term Plan II (1999–2004) as well as the 2001 Namibia HIV/AIDS Charter of Rights. The policy is strongly shaped by normative considerations and the human rights provisions embodied in the constitution of the Republic of Namibia. The policy has four principal components:

- The rights and responsibilities of staff and students
- The integration of HIV/AIDS in teaching, research, and community service
- Preventive care and support services
- Policy implementation, monitoring, and review

MANAGEMENT

The university ensures that all staff members are familiar with the HIV/AIDS policy and the legislation that governs HIV/AIDS in the workplace. Most of the universities and technikons in South Africa have HIV/AIDS policies. The few that do not have them are in the process of developing them, often with financial support from the United Kingdom's Department for International Development. In other Anglophone countries, many tertiary institutions do not yet have HIV/AIDS policies. Recently, however, with ADEA-WGHE support, several universities have either developed or are in the process of developing such policies. These institutions include the Mombasa Polytechnic and Highridge Teachers Training College in Kenya; Nkumba University in Uganda; the University of Botswana, Gaborone; and the Kigali Institute of Science and Technology (KIST) in Rwanda.

At the time this chapter was written, there were no Francophone or Lusophone tertiary institutions with HIV/AIDS policies. Many of them, however, follow unwritten understandings with regard to HIV/AIDS patients. Those who are infected have equal opportunity for service and privileges as do those who are not infected as well as an equal chance for further training. Moreover, a number of these schools, such as KIST in Rwanda, are preparing institutional policy development proposals to submit to ADEA-WGHE for a competitive award available for institutions in Francophone countries.

In addition to policies, some tertiary institutions have established separate structures charged with carrying out these policies. Some institutions (for example, the University of Botswana, the University of Cape Town, the University of Natal, Kenyatta University, and the University of Namibia) have established HIV/AIDS units to coordinate activities across the institutions and to combat ad hocism, or the temptation to leave the work to a few passionate people. The University of Pretoria supports a Center for the Study of AIDS in Africa whose primary purpose is to mainstream HIV/AIDS instruction through all activities of the university to ensure that the university can plan for and cope with the impact of HIV/AIDS on the tertiary education sector in South Africa.

PEER COUNSELING, TUTORING, AND MENTORING

Several variations of youth engagement in counseling and interactions with fellow youth have proved very promising in Southern Africa. I cite a few illustrative examples: the University of Namibia Youth Radio Station, the My Future Is My Choice program, and the University of Cape Town's Students' Peer Education Project (SHARP).

Youth Radio Station

The University of Namibia established a radio station in 2001 (under the auspices of the United Nations and currently in partnership with Johns Hopkins University, Maryland), which uses music, jingles, drama, and talk shows as means of mainstreaming HIV/AIDS issues among youth. The radio program must be highly entertaining in order to attract young Namibians to listen to it and also engage in dialogue about its content. An interactive variety show with segments such as drama, music, discussion (with youth and "experts"), telephone call-ins, and contests enable the program to attract young people. Young, enthusiastic, and knowledgeable radio hosts add to the market appeal of the program. After the initial series is aired, it will be evaluated for impact, and the data will be incorporated into the redesign of the program and its expansion.

The goals of this program are to instill in the youth a sense of self and collective efficacy; provide the youth with information, motivation, and life skills to make informed choices; and link media to community health and social services. Each of these concepts will be explored in the radio program.

My Future Is My Choice

My Future Is My Choice (MFMC) is a University of Namibia initiative that aims to empower learners by giving them information and skills that will enable them to decide to change their behavior. Over the course of 10 sessions, the training covers topics such as reproductive health and HIV/AIDS, decision-making skills, saying "NO," relationships and values, and alcohol and drug use and abuse.

Over 100,000 school learners and out-of-school youth have been reached and more than 200 University of Namibia students instructed. So impressive has the program become that it not only won the Commonwealth Award for Actions on HIV/AIDS in 2001, but the Ministry of Basic Education, Sport, and Culture in Namibia declared it a compulsory extramural activity for all secondary schools.

SHARP (University of Cape Town)

SHARP started in 1994 to recruit and train 200 students per year to present interactive workshops for other students and pupils in the Cape Town metropolitan region. Training modules cover a range of topics similar to those of the MFMC program described above.

A number of other peer education programs run by other institutions are well developed and well utilized, though they may not necessarily be part of a coherent tertiary institution response to HIV/AIDS.

CURRICULUM INTEGRATION

A number of courses, both voluntary and compulsory, have been introduced in various institutions at different levels in an effort to integrate HIV/AIDS education in the curriculum.

University of Cape Town (UCT)

The HIV/AIDS unit is incorporating HIV and AIDS material into formal curricula at UCT. Drawing on staff from various departments, the unit develops, teaches, and evaluates courses to ensure that UCT students know how to respond to HIV personally, professionally, and as responsible members of the community, by the time they graduate. The unit offers training to UCT staff members through a series of three workshops conducted every term. Workshops cover topics such as basic information, communicating with children about AIDS, and living with HIV. UCT also focuses on workplace issues, looking at managerial responsibilities and the rights of employees with HIV, and understanding the UCT policy on HIV/AIDS. The unit has been presenting a module on HIV/AIDS in the Psychology I course since 2003 as well as a Commerce Faculty foundation course titled Thinking About Business.

University of Namibia

The University of Namibia has introduced a compulsory examinable module for all first-year students. The module, titled Social Issues, deals with gender, ethics, and HIV/AIDS. Various departments have also made efforts to incorporate aspects of HIV/AIDS, including the Faculty of Medical and Health Sciences; the Departments of Psychology and Sociology; the Department of Information and Communication Studies; and the Department of Fine Art.

Kenyatta University

Kenyatta University offers a wide variety of HIV/AIDS-related courses at the certificate, diploma, and postgraduate levels as well a compulsory core unit for all students. These courses are proving to be increasingly popular because of their reputation for helping graduates to secure good jobs (ACU, 2001).

In addition to the programs cited above, a number of universities currently offer master's degrees with a specialization in HIV/AIDS. At UCT, for instance, a master of philosophy in HIV/AIDS is being offered in the Faculty of Humanities. At the University of Botswana, master of education degrees in counseling and human services (with HIV/AIDS components) have been mounted.

In general, commendable efforts are being made to integrate HIV/AIDS into tertiary institutions' curricula. However, not many institutions have yet joined in this effort, and complete "mainstreaming" of HIV/AIDS into academic programs has not been achieved.

VOLUNTARY COUNSELING AND TESTING

Voluntary counseling and testing (VCT) is generally defined as a confidential dialogue between a client and a care provider aimed at enabling the client to cope with stress and make personal decisions related to HIV. People affected by HIV/AIDS want counseling and testing services to address future planning (including planning for marriage and children), emotional support, medical and other referral services, and insurance.

VCT has proven to be one of the early factors in behavioral change in countries such as Uganda, Senegal, Kenya, Tanzania, and Trinidad and Tobago. It is also efficacious and cost effective. Generally, people who want to know about their HIV status are willing to change their behavior. In Namibia, the number of persons demanding VCT is growing steadily. Private industry, in particular the mining industry, has played a decisive role in this regard, showing positive results in condom use and infection rate. VCT is in high demand in rural areas. However, VCT facilities have yet to be made available throughout the various countries.

At the University of Namibia, one of our objectives is to have a VCT center available to our students in short order. These students, the country's greatest resource for future development, are at extreme risk of infection; informed estimates now suggest that between 1 in 4 and 1 in 7 will be HIV-positive upon graduation. To look at these students' faces and imagine their apparent fates is heartbreaking. The campus VCT center project is not envisioned to simply be a counseling/test facility ruled by numbers in and numbers out. Rather, we envision a New Start on campus to have a multidimensional social marketing function. The center would be a salient reminder to students about their epidemic. Conveniently located on campus, it would promote thinking and conversation about the epidemic, the necessity for testing, and the imperative for healthier living. Ultimately, the center's function would be to counsel and test. I don't think any of us believe there would be an immediate rush to the center. Rather, we anticipate a gradual increase in usage as the social marketing messages increase in effectiveness.

The experience of the University of Zambia, which houses a functioning VCT center, confirms this trend. Students there were slow to use the center at first, but over time they came forward in increasing numbers. Moreover, a posttest counseling group of students there has attracted a large and active membership. This group has encouraged many more students to be tested. The slow adjustment to testing is often related to issues of shame, stigma, and discrimination, which are addressed later in this chapter.

Various universities sponsor active and functional VCT centers. These include the University of Botswana, the University of Durban–Westville, the University of Cape Town, the University of Pretoria, the University of Witwatersrand, the University of Natal, and the University of Stellenbosch. Others provide voluntary counseling without necessarily maintaining centers on campus, as actual testing is done on a referral basis.

An important element of any prevention and care strategy is access to information about one's HIV status. However, voluntary counseling and testing services are still rare in most African nations. More viable centers need to be set up so that universities and other tertiary institutions, as key agents in the response to HIV/AIDS, can encourage students and staff to obtain information about their HIV status and get the counseling that they need, as well as the support needed to maintain a negative HIV status or to live positively with HIV. In addition, it is only through voluntary counseling and testing that vertical transmission of HIV from parent to child can be reduced. Tertiary institutions can themselves set up VCT centers where feasible.

CHILD-TO-CHILD PROGRAMS

Child-to-child is an approach to health education and primary health care spread by a worldwide network of health and education workers in over 70 countries. Primary Health Care seeks to involve communities in making decisions and taking action to improve their own health. The child-to-child approach involves children in this task in three ways:

1. Through helping to care for their brothers and sisters and other young children in their family group, and working with parents to improve the health of the whole family;
2. Through assisting children in their own age group including those who have not gone to school; and
3. Through working together to spread health ideas and improve health practices in school, home, and community.

Child-to-child programs are designed for children who are often simultaneously caretakers of younger siblings; future parents; communicators of information to their parents and other caretakers; and community members capable of improving conditions affecting health and development. Various approaches and strategies, beginning during the International Year of the Child in 1979, have been used to implement the approach, including the following:

1. Child-to-child programs based in schools, as additions to the formal curriculum. For example, in Kenya's Health Scouts program, school children between 9 and 14 years teach their parents about disease prevention. Children are also encouraged to help the less fortunate in their communities.
2. Programs based at schools, with teachers and older pupils playing a key role. Volunteer teachers pass on health messages to older

children in their free time, and these in turn pass the messages to younger children. This is exemplified in the Botswana case, at least when the program was an outreach program from the schools to the community. That trend, however, has been reversed; now it is the older school children who take their brothers and sisters to school to acquaint them with the school environment in preparation for the smooth entry into school the following year.

3. Programs emphasizing health-training schemes.
4. Youth groups can undertake child-to-child activities. This is exemplified in the "Tirelo Setchaba" project in Botswana. This project stipulating that learners proceeding for further studies in tertiary institutions, including university, must provide a year of compulsory service to the nation, including teaching in remote areas of the country and engaging in child-to-child activities.
5. Countries seeking to introduce new programs of health education by incorporating aspects of a child-to-child program is an example of this approach. It is a school-based program directed specifically at improving the knowledge and caretaking practices of primary school learners, aged 9 to 12, and through them, the knowledge of parents or guardians, and their community. Begun in 1979 on an experimental basis in only one school by the Tropical Metabolism Research Unit (University of West Indies), the program was extended to 14 schools when an evaluation showed it to be well received. Now the child-to-child curriculum is incorporated into the regular primary school curriculum for the entire country, demonstrating its possibility of going to scale.
6. Variations of the above programs also exist; for instance, the Mobile Créches in India and Somalia areas of northeastern Kenya where nomadic pastoralism is practiced.

In all the situations described above, colleges of education have not played a very significant role. An effective and sustainable implementation of child-to-child approaches depends on an improved teacher education, which begins at the preservice level. It was this observation and realization that inspired the Namibia representatives at the British Council–sponsored workshop held in Swaziland in March 1994 to develop a concrete action plan on the Health Through the School Project.

As originally proposed, the project was to last for 3 years, but due to difficulty in locating the necessary funding, it was decided to restrict the project to 1 year; the University of Namibia's Research and Publications Committee gave a modest research grant for this purpose. But the basic ideas of the original project are still the same.

THE PILOT PROJECT

A pilot project has been set up to examine the workings of the child-to-child approach in a college of education and selected nearby primary schools. As a result of the operating and monitoring of this project over a period of time, it will be possible to assess better the potential of the child-to-child approach in health education; the potential of colleges of education in promoting such an approach; and the value of health education as a model for promoting more active, learner-centered, relevant, and community-related learning in other areas of the curriculum and within school programs as a whole.

Objectives of the Pilot Project

Through operation of a child-to-child approach to health education in a selected college of education and primary schools in one site, the pilot project has the following goals:

1. To gain insights into the use of the approach
   a. in the direct teaching of health care/life skills
   b. as a component within other subjects
   c. within the life and activity of the college of education or the primary schools
   d. within the outreach activities operated by colleges of education and primary schools in their communities
2. To explore the cooperation desirable and possible between the educational activity of a college of education and primary schools and the health activities organized by the Ministry of Health and Social Services
3. To examine the effects of the approach upon the knowledge, skills, and attitudes (on health) of a defined group of teacher trainers and students in a college of education, and teachers and learners in primary schools
4. Following the operation of the pilot project over 1 year, to produce an account of the project to aid others, particularly Ministry of Education and Culture, Ministry of Health and Social Science, and NGOs, which seek to involve colleges of education and satellite primary schools in child-to-child programs.

The first stage of the pilot project will be to hold a workshop for participants selected from Windhoek College of Education and schools in Katutura. The workshop will have the following objectives:

1. To familiarize participants with the child-to-child approach
2. To select certain health priorities through which the approach can be tried during the pilot stage
3. To agree on a plan of action
   a. in the selected college of education
   b. in the selected primary schools
   c. for the monitoring of all stages of the project during the year

Thus far, I have looked at some of the positive responses of the tertiary institutions in Africa to the HIV/AIDS epidemic. I turn now to a consideration of four effective strategies that, in addition to activities already cited, leaders could undertake to limit the spread of HIV/AIDS on their campuses as well as within their communities.

FOUR EFFECTIVE ACTIONS UNIVERSITY LEADERS CAN TAKE TO MOVE THE AGENDA FORWARD FOR HIV/AIDS PREVENTION

1. Provide Immediate Training, and Conduct Impact and Tracer Studies. Within tertiary institutions, capacity development is an immediate need. Key personnel require training to deal with AIDS in the workplace, and they also need staff to ensure that peer education and program support are implemented. Members of the Dean of Students' office and other student support services, the campus clinic, the library, and key members of the unions should all have some basic training on how to handle issues related to HIV/AIDS in the workplace.

Second and equally important is the need to develop an extensive research program, planned probably in collaboration with other tertiary institutions. One area to begin would be to assess the impact of HIV/AIDS on the particular tertiary institution. An excellent recent example of a serious attempt to bring together all available data for analysis of the AIDS situation at the University of Botswana is described by Chilisa and Bennell (2001). The main conclusion is that, at least up until 2000–2001, the university had been less affected by the epidemic than might be expected, given that the overall adult prevalence rate in Botswana was almost

40 percent in that year. However, the role of on-campus AIDS prevention activities in creating this unexpected variance is not investigated.

The results of such impact assessments should lead to concrete recommendations of what tertiary institutions could do to develop a comprehensive program on prevention, to care for and support those affected by HIV/AIDS, and to mitigate the impact on individuals and tertiary institutions as well as on communities. For tertiary institutions in existence for at least 10 years, it would be instructive to undertake tracer studies of past students. Information from such studies would, among other things, assist institutions to plan intakes more realistically, taking into account losses inflicted by the HIV/AIDS epidemic.

2. Tackle Shame, Discrimination, and Stigma: The Need for a Research Program. The most effective health interventions are worthless if they are not used. What is it about our culture that compels us to overlook a major barrier to improved health care: the entwined issues of stigma, discrimination, and shame (hereafter referred to as SDS)?[4]

SDS is such a powerful force that, if there is a chance their conditions would be revealed, people would suffer and die, and allow their children to suffer and die, rather than seek treatment that could improve their quality of life or save their lives. Currently, those with any number of illnesses are stigmatized and rejected, as are family members, if those illnesses are made public. People also hide their medical conditions because they fear, oftentimes justifiably, that they will lose friends, jobs, housing, or educational or other opportunities if their conditions are publicly known. The many conditions affected by SDS include forms of cancer, Hansen's Disease, mental illness, mental retardation, tuberculosis, domestic violence, substance abuse and dependence, sexual dysfunction, and sexually transmitted diseases, now most notably HIV disease.

Repeatedly, loudly, and for decades, experts at the international level and service providers at local levels have described the powerful forces of SDS. No less a personage than the late Jonathan Mann, then director of the WHO Global Program on AIDS, warned the world about SDS in regards to HIV. Speaking to the UN General Assembly in 1987, he identified three components of the HIV/AIDS epidemic: "the epidemic of HIV; the epidemic of AIDS; and the epidemic of stigma, discrimination, and denial." He noted that the third phase is "as central to the global AIDS challenge as the disease itself" (Mann, 1989).

"Each year, more and more people die from the [HIV] disease, and it is the stigma and misinformation around HIV that is killing people," said Juan Manuel Suarez del Toro, president of the International Federation of Red Cross and Red Crescent Societies, in a recent World Red Cross Day message. "People place themselves at high risk from infection or refuse to seek treatment rather than face the consequences of social stigma, such as losing their homes, businesses, and even their families," he said (cited in Olafsdottir, 2003).

Despite the insistent voices of warning, no concerted action has been initiated to understand and confront SDS across many cultures. I suspect that we may be ashamed of the existence of SDS. Studying these constructs would plumb our basest aspects, and would not be pleasant. Perhaps we don't want to know, so scholars, funders, and others have turned a blind eye to SDS. Alternatively, perhaps research institutions and funders find it difficult to embark on explorations into areas—psychological, social, and attitudinal—that cannot be neatly measured in laboratory values and that have many cultural complexities. Understandably, medical scientists may continue to believe a great biomedical intervention will be easily accepted, welcomed by all. Tragically, that may not be the case.

Some scholarship regarding shame and stigma suggest the topic is approachable. Kaufman (1996) has studied these factors in terms of Western psychological factors, but little Third World research is documented. Parker and Aggleton (2002) addressed stigmatization and discrimination regarding HIV and articulated a research agenda, including studies of social processes and aspects across cultural boundaries. Others have reviewed 21 interventions that explicitly attempted to decrease stigma associated with other diseases (Brown, Trujillo, and Macintyre, 2002). They concluded that the reviewed studies indicate something can be done about stigma through interventions such as information, counseling, coping skills acquisition, and contact. Underlining the scarcity of SDS interventions, the authors found only two national-level efforts to combat stigma and no documented studies on the effects of mass media campaigns.

Although these studies hint that something can be done, in fact we still know very little, and perhaps whatever we "know" is only culture-specific. The grand challenge is to understand and diminish SDS so that people and individuals are willing to access available and effective biomedical and psychosocial interventions. Basic questions remain: Do the constructs of SDS have commonality across cultures? Are these constructs indeed conceptually entwined? Is it useful to think of them in this way or do we need alternative, as yet unconceptualized, factors?

What are the bases for shame in different cultures—sexuality, pride versus weakness, inability to perform gender-based roles, illness, or issues that we cannot guess? What are the psychosocial bases in various cultures for stigmatization and discrimination? Interventions to reduce SDS, if there are to be any, require some theoretical underpinnings, even if these are different from culture to culture.

We then need to move to the issues of interventions regarding SDS. Funders need to support more scientifically based intervention studies. Researchers and communities will require encouragement for large- and small-scale interventions. In this regard, our African researchers may also need to note that the Ford Foundation recently awarded the Center on AIDS and Community Health of the Academy for Educational Development (AED) a grant to implement its HIV/AIDS Anti-Stigma Initiative. AED will examine the impact of HIV/AIDS–related stigma and will work with community-based organizations to create strategies to combat it. This suggested research agenda may be a tall order, but it is a direct challenge to tertiary institutions, particularly in Africa, because their role is critical in resolving some of Africa's problems.

3. Societal Standards: The Need for Moral Regeneration, Supported by Sexual Harassment Policies. Many people, especially among the young, are not given sufficient help by society in their efforts at HIV prevention. They find that double standards for sexual and other behaviors prevail for men and women, for old and young. Men and boys tend to have more sexual partners than women and girls. Males are expected to be knowledgeable about sexual matters, whereas females who show knowledge or interest in sexual issues may be regarded as immoral or promiscuous. Communication on sexual matters for boys and men may consist of little more than boastful accounts of "conquests," whereas women and girls discuss issues more sensitively and intimately among themselves and within their families. For the greater part, virginity is highly prized in a girl, whereas in some cultures it is viewed with suspicion and concern in a boy.

As they strive to adapt themselves to the gender norms that their culture prescribes for their biological sex, young people experience difficulties with these ambivalent attitudes of society. Their difficulties are increased when they see older people behaving and living in ways they would condemn in the young. Many societies create an almost impossible task for young people, expecting them to behave in certain ways but confronting them with social norms, expectations, and role models that point in a very different direction. The models placed before the young through advertisements, in the media, and through the entertainment industry glorify the physical aspects of sex, but say little about the arduous task of building enduring human relationships that support and are supported by sexual practice (Kelly and Otaala, 2002).

The horrific litany of abuse of women and children, the soaring level of criminal violence in many African countries, and the prevalence of corruption in public life have all helped us to see that moral values have been destroyed in many of our countries. We have found ourselves to be societies with very little private or public morality. It is not that there has been a moral vacuum; immoral practices have replaced our moral values, and our moral capital has vanished. We African societies are morally bankrupt. How can tertiary institutions contribute to a strengthened public morality?

Tertiary institutions need to be proactive and have gender-sensitive policies for staff and students as well as provide leadership in research on gender issues. Such policies include the anti–sexual harassment policies recently introduced by the University of Botswana and the University of Namibia. Sexual harassment policy and procedures should be available to assist any case where a member of the university community feels that he or she is being or has been sexually harassed and to designate penalties for those who are found guilty.

In the case of Namibia, and presumably in many other African countries, the Convention on the Elimination of All Forms of Discrimination Against Women is currently being implemented. Tertiary institutions should be at the forefront of those supporting the implementation of this and similar conventions designed to better the lot of African girls and women. Such institutions can help by providing moral leadership as well as by conducting research related to traditional African core values on sexuality.

In our work with the My Future Is My Choice program, we have found that the program teaches young men and women in a very dynamic and interactive way, so that the learners and out-of-school participants become part of the learning process. We make use of other young people to be facilitators. These facilitators are usually just a few years older than the target group.

Young people discuss the often-difficult issues that surround HIV/ AIDS. "Is it true that circumcised men are less likely to get HIV?" "Doesn't one get sick when one abstains for a long time?" These are just some of the questions posed by young people in their sessions. In a recent question-and-answer session, a young man asked, "If the condom does not fit, can I use cello-tape?" Perhaps the reader can come up with an appropriate answer!

Discussions such as these, encouraged for participants in the MFMC program, can be extended to public debate on HIV/AIDS issues. To undertake such debate, it would be crucially important to understand the political and social context within which one is working; the varying target and audiences' capacities to participate; and key ethical issues such as informed consent, confidentiality, and the use of information.

In many African contexts, people infected with AIDS and those around them are in great fear. As Doubleday (1986) wrote in his essay "Spiritual and Religious Issues of AIDS," "Many are talking about an even greater disease than AIDS, which is affecting the person infected, those who are suffering with him or her, and those who are the 'worried well.' It is the disease known as AFRAIDS, that is, Acute Fear Regarding AIDS." Tertiary institutions can provide leadership in promoting and participating in public debates to engage and eliminate such fears, including issues of SDS, as described earlier.

4. Effective, Committed Leadership in Mainstreaming HIV/AIDS. Effective, committed leadership in a number of countries (and institutions) has been a factor in the successful reduction of HIV prevalence. In Uganda, President Museveni's charismatic directness in addressing the threat placed HIV/AIDS on the development agenda and encouraged constant and candid national media coverage of all aspects of the epidemic. This early high-level support fostered a multisectoral response, prioritizing HIV/AIDS and enlisting a wide variety of national participants in the war against the decimating disease (Hogle, 2002). Leaders at other levels and in other domains of society learned from the example of their president. The outcome was a unified voice throughout the country for action against the disease, with strong NGO and community-based support leading to "flexible, creative, and culturally appropriate interventions that succeeded in changing behavior despite extreme levels of post–civil war household poverty" (Hogle, 2002, p. 4).

In Uganda, in 1987, a multisectoral, multidisciplinary approach was initiated to address the sociocultural and economic impacts of the epidemic. Uganda's HIV/AIDS control program integrates all sectors of society and has emphasized the involvement of people living with AIDS. Within sub-Saharan Africa, Uganda is a model for the successful reduction of rates of HIV prevalence, and President Museveni had demonstrated by example the importance of strong, consistent, high-level leadership in the fight against HIV/AIDS. Leaders at all levels in the countries of sub-Saharan Africa, including heads of tertiary institutions, should do no less.

One area of paramount importance and urgency is the mainstreaming of HIV/AIDS. "Mainstreaming" incorporates a pervasive HIV/AIDS perspective that transforms the existing institutional agenda so that all thinking or analytical processes, development directions, and activities reflect HIV concerns and vision at the policy, planning, and program levels (Kelly, 2003).

A FEW SUGGESTIONS

In responding to the issues of prevention, care, support, management, and mitigation of the impact of HIV/AIDS, individual countries and institutions have to take into account the different contexts in which they operate. Nevertheless, a couple of general lessons learned can be shared.

Collaboration and Partnership

Collaboration has become a buzzword in discussions on the fight against HIV/AIDS, referring to a variety of efforts to bring people together for shared goals, projects, or tasks. Funders and policy makers favor collaborative efforts among institutions or organizations to bring about synergy. But true collaboration requires a set of dispositions, beliefs, commitments, and skills. Even then, it is not easy to collaborate, especially across significant differences in geographical distances, cultural perspectives, experiences, and personal, institutional, or organizational histories. Collaboration is not a passive phenomenon; nor is it something one can check off one's strategic plan or assessment tool. It is an ongoing work in progress, with all the highs and lows of human frailty and experience.

According to Jones and Nimmo (1999), "Collaboration, on the surface, is about bringing together resources, both financial and intellectual, to work toward a common purpose. But true collaboration has an 'inside,' a deeper, more radical meaning. The inner life of collaboration is about states of mind and spirit that are open" (p. 5).

An illustration of effective collaboration in HIV/AIDS work could be two or three institutions (within a country or across borders) coming together for a 2- to 3-day meeting. The meeting might address the following purposes:

1. Advocacy to sensitize participants on the actual and potential impacts of HIV on the operations of their institutions.
2. Clarification of needs and responsibilities in the four domains of knowledge and understanding of the epidemic, teaching and preparation of students, research and dissemination of knowledge, and service to or engagement with society.
3. Reaching agreement on the need for institutional response and what this implies in terms of a way forward at the institutional and group level.
4. Considering a new mechanism that ties all the institutions together to fight the HIV/AIDS epidemic, with a view to institutionalizing the response throughout the respective institutions (in country or cross-border).

Learning From Exchanging Visits With Other Institutions

Our experience at the University of Namibia has taught us that much can be gained through personal visits to other institutions as well as inviting colleagues to visit us. When we developed our HIV/AIDS policy, we arranged for a number of our colleagues of the university's HIV/AIDS Task Force to visit the Universities of Botswana, Natal, and Pretoria to meet and interact with their colleagues in the various HIV/AIDS units. We followed this step by inviting those individuals to present papers at our workshops, and we held consultative meetings with them. From these experiences, and in the belief that there was no need to "reinvent the wheel," we developed our HIV/AIDS policy as well as our strategic plans.

Doing Activities at Zero Budget

Whenever a project must be undertaken, one main preoccupation we often think about is the financial cost. A number of activities, however, can be undertaken at very little cost, or at no cost at all. A couple of examples follow:

1. *The child-to-child approach.* The child-to-child approach to health education as elaborated earlier was introduced in 1979, following the Alma Alta Declaration on Primary Health Care (see descrip-

tion earlier in this chapter). The approach helps us to realize the potential of children to spread health ideas and practices to other children, to families, and to communities. The methodology has now spread all over the world and has the same central ideas developed in partnership between education and health. In our communities, this approach can be used effectively in sensitizing them since it has been indicated that "the answer to controlling HIV has remained and will remain, social action: responses by societies, communities, families and individuals to come to terms with the risk of infecting and becoming infected and vulnerability to exposure or exposing others to a formidable threat" (Brenzinger and Harms, as cited in Robins, Madzudzo, and Brenzinger, 2001).

2. *Free information and contact with others.* A creative search for information from the several agencies in our respective towns/cities will provide our institutions with material for use in our programs. In our capital cities, many development agencies provide libraries and free information sheets and booklets. Invitations can be given to various stakeholders:—faith-based persons, government ministries, or foreign embassies—to address our institutions on various issues related to HIV/AIDS. These are but a few of many creative but inexpensive methods to make our work more effective.

CONCLUDING REMARKS

It has been demonstrated that HIV prevention works. In the USA, prevention has helped to slow the rate of new infections from over 150,000 per year in the mid-1980s to around 40,000 in 2002. Prevention programs have been effective with a variety of populations: clinic visitors, heterosexual men and women, youth at high risk, prisoners, injection drug users, and men having sex with men. Intervention programs have been extended to individuals, groups, and communities in settings ranging from storefronts to gay bars, from health centers to public housing, and from schools to universities.

These prevention successes were accomplished by collaboration among the infected and affected communities, national agencies, local organizations, the private sector, and community-based groups. They demonstrate the power of a collective effort to fight HIV/AIDS (Centers for Disease Control and Prevention, 2003).

It is also pointed out that to succeed, HIV prevention efforts must be comprehensive and science-based. The following conditions must be fulfilled in order for HIV prevention to work:

- An effective community planning process.
- Epidemiological and behavioral surveillance; compilation of the health and demographic data relevant to HIV risks, incidence, or prevalence.
- HIV counseling, testing, and referral and partner counseling and referral, with strong linkages to medical care, treatment, and needed prevention services.
- Health education and risk reduction activities, including individual-, group-, and community-level interventions.
- Accessible diagnosis and treatment of other STDs.
- Public information and education programs.
- Comprehensive school health programs.
- Training and quality assurance.
- Capacity-building activities for HIV prevention.
- A technical assistance assessment and plan for HIV prevention.
- Monitoring and evaluation of major program activities, interventions, and services.

The magnitude of the fight against HIV/AIDS is enormous. Consequently, the responsibility taken by the community of tertiary institutions through present and future activities designed to arrest the spread of HIV/AIDS must be equally enormous. I believe that the message is not at all bleak, for the future does not have to be like the past. We know how to prevent the spread of HIV. We can deal with the consequences of AIDS. With strong and visible leadership from the administration of tertiary institutions, there will be resonance from below.

NOTES

1. I acknowledge with gratitude the help I received from the following colleagues who provided information used in this paper: Mary Crewe, University of Pretoria; Wendy Orr, University of Witwatersrand; Barbara Michel of the South African Vice Chancellors' Association; Mandy Govender, University of Cape Town; Mary Kabanyama-Zigira, Kigali Institute of Science and Technology; Philip Owino, Kenyatta University; Mosarwa Segwabe, University of Botswana; and Mark Winiarski, University of Namibia.

2. Portions of this chapter were previously presented at a World Bank–sponsored conference on tertiary education in Africa in Accra, Ghana, September 2003; see draft presentation at http://www.worldbank.org/afr/teia/conf_0903/barnabas_otaala.pdf. A later version of the paper was published in the December 2004 issue of *The African Symposium* 4(4), available at http://www2.ncsu.edu/ncsu/aern/afriaids.htm.

3. Those countries supported by the USAID include Botswana, Ivory Coast, Ethiopia, Kenya, Mozambique, Namibia, Nigeria, Rwanda, South Africa, Tanzania, Uganda, and Zambia.

4. I am grateful to my colleague, Mark Winiarski, Fulbright professor at the University of Namibia, for his contribution to this section.

REFERENCES

Association of Commonwealth Universities. (2001). *HIV/AIDS: Towards a strategy for Commonwealth universities: Report of the Lusaka Workshop.* London: Author.

Brown, L., Trujillo, L., and Macintyre, K. (2002). Interventions to reduce HIV/AIDS stigma: What have we learned? In *Findings from the field: A compilation to date of publications on HIV/AIDS from Horizons and partner organizations.* (CD-ROM). New York: Population Council.

Centers for Disease Control and Prevention. (2003). *HIV prevention strategic plan through 2005.* Retrieved October 12, 2005, from http://www.cdc.gov/hiv/partners/psp.htm.

Chilisa, B., and Bennell, P. (2001). *The impact of HIV/AIDS on the University of Botswana.* Unpublished manuscript.

Doubleday, W. A. (1986). Spiritual and religious issues of AIDS. In V. Gong and N. Rudnick, eds., *AIDS: Facts and issues.* New Brunswick, NJ: Rutgers University Press.

Gabriel, A. H. (2003). *African universities' response to HIV/AIDS in the Global AIDS Initiative countries: A synthesis of country reports.* Accra, Ghana: Association of African Universities.

Hogle, J. A., ed. (2002). *What happened in Uganda? Declining prevalence, behavior change, and the national response.* Washington, DC: The Synergy Project.

Jones, E., and Nimmo, J. (1999). Collaboration, conflict, change: Thoughts on education and provocation. *Young Children* 54(1): 5–10.

Katjavivi, P. H., and Otaala, B. (2003, March). *African universities responding to the HIV/AIDS pandemic.* Paper presented at the AAU Conference of Rectors, Vice Chancellors, and Presidents of African Universities (COREVIP). Mauritius.

Katjavivi, P. H., and Otaala, B. (2004a). African higher education institutions responding to the HIV/AIDS pandemic. In P. T. Zeleza and A. Olukoshi, eds., *African universities in the twenty-first century.* Dakar, Senegal: Council for the Development of Social Science Research in Africa.

Katjavivi, P. H., and Otaala, B. (2004b). African higher education institutions responding to the HIV/AIDS epidemic. In P. T. Zeleza and A. Olukoshi, eds., *African universities in the twenty-first century* (Volume II: *Knowledge and society*). Dakar, Senegal: Council for the Development of Social Science Research in Africa.

Kaufman, G. (1996). *The psychology of shame: Theory and treatment of shame-based syndromes.* 2nd ed. New York: Springer.

Kelly, M. J. (2001). *Challenging the challenger: Understanding and expanding the response of universities in Africa to HIV/AIDS.* Washington DC: World Bank, ADEA Working Group on Higher Education.

Kelly, M. J. (2003). *UNESCO Nairobi Cluster: Consultation on HIV/AIDS and Education,* MTT Report.

Kelly, M. J., and Otaala, B. (2002). *UNESCO regional strategic plan for HIV/AIDS education in sub-Saharan Africa.* Consultancy draft report submitted to UNESCO/BREDA, Dakar, Senegal.

Khulisa Management Services. (2003). *Audit and scan of HIV/AIDS in South Africa.* Final draft report submitted to the Higher Education Against HIV and AIDS (HEAIDS) Program.

Mann, J. M. (1989). AIDS: A worldwide pandemic. In M. S. Gottlieb, D. J. Jeffries, D. Mildvan, A. J. Pinching, and T. C. Quinn, eds., *Current topics in AIDS.* Vol. 2. John Wiley and Sons.

Olafsdottir, S. (2003, May 12). Red Cross at forefront of fighting stigma. *Herald.* Harare, Zimbabwe.

Otaala, B., and Lutaaya, E. (2004). *Survey of HIV/AIDS activities and contributions by African tertiary institutions.* Consultancy report prepared for the Working Group on Higher Education of the Association for the Development of Education in Africa, Accra, Ghana.

Parker, R., and Aggleton, P. (with Attawell, K., Pulerwitz, J., and Brown, L.). (2002). HIV/AIDS stigma and discrimination: Conceptual framework and an agenda for action. In *Findings from the field: A compilation to date of publications on HIV/AIDS from Horizons and partner organizations.* (CD-ROM). New York: Population Council.

Robins, S., Madzudzo, E., and Brenzinger, M. (2001). *An assessment of the status of the San in South Africa, Angola, Zambia, and Zimbabwe.* Windhoek: Legal Assistance Center.

UNESCO/BREDA. (2002). *Towards an African response: UNESCO's strategy for HIV/AIDS education in sub-Saharan Africa.* Dakar, Senegal: Author.

UNESCO/Gamsberg MacMillan. (2004). *HIV and AIDS preventive education: A training programme for teacher educators in sub-Saharan Africa.* Windhoek, Namibia: UNESCO.

World Bank. (2002). *Constructing knowledge societies: New challenges for tertiary education.* Washington, DC: Author.

15

HIV/AIDS AFFECTING POSTSECONDARY EDUCATION IN SOUTH ASIA

Neena Khanna

✤

The number of people with human immunodeficiency virus (HIV) and acquired immunodeficiency syndrome (AIDS) has increased to an alarming level in Asia, especially for youth between 15 and 24 years old. Because HIV/AIDS affects the younger generation, educators need to be aware of the current information and the latest statistics about the population infected with HIV/AIDS. With the appropriate tools and strategies identified, educators can develop effective school-based prevention programs and serve the educational and psychological needs of people with HIV/AIDS.

This chapter discusses the status of HIV/AIDS in South Asia. The central message is that the education of children and youth merits the highest priority in a world afflicted by HIV/AIDS; good basic education is an effective means of HIV prevention. Even policy makers and health workers in Asia have difficulty fully absorbing and responding to the reality that since the 1980s, when the disease was first recorded in the region, the epidemic has claimed the lives of more than 30 million people worldwide. Estimates indicate that at least another 37 million were infected as of 2003 (Joint United Nations Programme on HIV/AIDS [UNAIDS], 2004).

In the late 1980s, AIDS began to make an impact in Asia, initially being seen in Thailand and later spreading in epidemic numbers to Myanmar and Cambodia; it continues its deadly course today. Until recently, HIV and AIDS were seen as problems to be dealt with by health departments, doctors, and health workers alone. Estimates of the economic losses associated with the incidence of the disease in India and Indonesia are placed within the context of the present outlays on health as well as in the context of the development objectives of the countries. The challenge is to do everything possible to prevent a full-scale epidemic similar to that seen in other parts of the world. Such an epidemic would have devastating social and economic impact.

The governments in South Asia have intensified their fight against HIV/AIDS, but the spread of the virus exceeds their efforts. The sentinel data show that the epidemic has spread from urban to rural areas and from individuals practicing risky behavior to the general population. The social stigma attached to sexually transmitted infections (STIs) is greater for HIV/AIDS, and the effects of stigma are devastating. Discrimination hinders effective responses. Predictions indicate that India soon will emerge as the country with the largest HIV burden in the world. HIV/AIDS produces unprecedented global challenges that have already caused too much hardship, illness, and death.

This chapter examines the status of HIV/AIDS as it affects postsecondary education in two large democracies in South Asia: India and Indonesia. India is the largest democracy in the world. Although the prevalence of HIV remains low in the country (UNAIDS, 2004), India has the second largest number of estimated HIV-positive people in the world. Indonesia is the third largest democracy and, being close to Australia (which saw high HIV infection rates through the mid-1990s), is an important country for discussion.

HIV/AIDS IN INDIA

"The HIV/AIDS epidemic in India is extremely grave," said Richard Feachem, executive director of the Geneva-based Global Fund to Fight AIDS, Tuberculosis, and Malaria (Agence France-Presse, 2004). According to India's National AIDS Control Organization (NACO), India ranks second in terms of infection rates behind South Africa, which has 5.3 million people living with HIV/AIDS. India recorded 520,000 new HIV cases in 2003, down from 610,000 in 2002 (NACO, 2004a); NACO indicated that the drop in new infections in 2003 was proof that its anti-AIDS approach was working. But Feachem, whose Global Fund has approved $265 million since 2002 to combat AIDS in India, said the country still lacks effective AIDS detection and surveillance mechanisms.

Widespread poverty, illiteracy, poor nutritional and health status of the population, social inequalities based on caste and gender, poor health infrastructure, public perception of sex as a taboo subject, lack of strong political commitments, and a persistent denial about AIDS in many states are factors that make India especially vulnerable to the epidemic. If effective control measures are not implemented immediately and sustained over a long period of time, projections warn of an adult HIV-prevalence rate of 5 percent within the next 5 years.

According to the standard AIDS-case definition, 78,229 cumulative AIDS cases have been reported in India (NACO, 2004b). Epidemiological analysis of reported AIDS cases reveals that the majority of the HIV infections (87.7 percent) are among people in the age group of 15 to 44 years. The predominant mode of transmission of the HIV infection is heterosexual contact (85.7 percent), followed by injection drug use (2.2 percent), blood transfusion and blood product infusion (2.6 percent), perinatal transmission (2.7 percent), and others (6.8 percent). Men in India are infected with HIV at three times the rate of women. Given the number of people living with HIV/AIDS, preventive measures must be pursued to curtail further spread of the disease in the country. The common man must be made aware of the consequences of AIDS and how to avoid them. The most effective approach starts with education at the school level, particularly because youth remain most susceptible to the disease.

Prevention of HIV/AIDS in India

Knowledge about HIV/AIDS is scant and incomplete in India. Perceptions and beliefs about HIV/AIDS are very strongly entrenched; myths, misinformation, and misconceptions abound. The associations of HIV/AIDS with death and with dirty, bad, and wrong actions add to the barriers that make it difficult to change behavior. Taboos surrounding HIV/AIDS often prevent recognition, discussion, or acceptance and practice of safe and responsible behaviors. AIDS can be viewed as a disease of ignorance, indulgence, and intolerance (and work can be done to remedy all three perceptions). In the absence of a vaccine or a therapeutic cure, communication programming represents a key ingredient in the social vaccine against HIV/AIDS.

In India, about 40 million secondary school students are 15 to 18 years old. One-third of these students are girls. Encouraging them to adopt appropriate attitudes and values regarding various issues related to HIV/AIDS can help minimize the spread of HIV infection. The only way to move effectively and more quickly than the HIV/AIDS epidemic is to attack it from all angles. This means including appropriate education in the school-health curricula and encouraging heads of universities to get involved to break the silence and stigma. Past efforts have included projects that consist of HIV/AIDS training and prevention measures directed to transportation employees, as well as truck drivers and migrant workers. The police are sensitized to help prevent discrimination and harassment of highly vulnerable populations such as sex workers, the peers who deliver HIV/AIDS services, and those who are HIV-positive. When women are taught to read or start a savings account, they also should be given information about HIV/AIDS, its spread, and the preventive measures that can be taken against it.

The Need for Education

The government of India is taking several steps for the prevention of HIV/AIDS in the country. Every Indian state is affected by AIDS (UNAIDS, 2004), and the disease does not discriminate among classes, castes, or communities. AIDS control already accounts for about 10 percent of India's national health budget (Ukil, 2004). With the perception of AIDS as a major threat to the survival of humanity, education can be a catalytic agent in creating social conditions that can prevent the spread of HIV/AIDS (National Council of Educational Research and Training [NCERT] and NACO, 1994). NCERT, a premier educational research institution, plays an important role in the HIV/AIDS education of school personnel and students. In collaboration with NACO, NCERT has developed several publications for educators.

The publication *AIDS Education in Schools: A Training Package* is the outcome of the collaborative endeavor. A core group consisting of the experts from the NACO, the World Health Organization (WHO), the United Nations Children's Educational Fund (UNICEF), the United Nations Educational Social and Cultural Organization (UNESCO), the United Nations Population Fund (UNFPA), and faculty members of NCERT planned and developed the package. The package consists of content and enrichment materials for teachers on students' activities that may be organized in schools. There are plans to translate this NCERT-NACO package into regional languages as for adaptation by different states in India to promote AIDS education in their schools.

Young people are among those most exposed to the HIV virus. They are highly impressionable and require appropriate information about reproductive issues including safe sexual behavior. Different strategies are being adopted for young people; among those strategies, a school AIDS education program is very important. Another important publication that has been developed by the joint efforts of NCERT, NACO, UNICEF, and UNESCO is *Learning for Life: A Guide to Family Health and Life Skills Education for Teachers and Students.*

The schools AIDS education module has been developed keeping in mind the central role teachers have in influencing students. It is essential for the teachers to create an environment where free and frank discussions between teachers, peer educators, and students can take place. Integrating the issue of HIV/AIDS as part of the larger issue of family-life education in the schools will go a long way in bringing about change in socially acceptable values.

Experience from around the world has shown the benefits of educating children about the process of growing up and its implications. This education on sexual and reproductive health will enable children to develop a stable value system and adopt a responsible lifestyle. Young people also can be agents of change and spearhead advocacy for HIV/AIDS education among peers, community members, and parents. Information alone is not enough; rather, the skill and empowerment to make correct choices will prevent further spread of HIV/AIDS.

This comprehensive training package has been beneficial to adolescents' education and rewarding for the teachers and peer educators who participate in these activities. In collaboration with UNICEF and NACO, part of India's Ministry of Health and Family Welfare has developed this module for teachers as part of its program to implement AIDS education in the school system. The module will serve as a resource guide for teachers about adolescence, HIV/AIDS, and STIs.

The contents of the module are based on the observation that biomedical information on the disease is not enough to convince people, especially young people, to adopt healthy behavior that prevents HIV/AIDS. People need the motivation to act and the skills to translate knowledge into practice. Through the achievement of a set of learning objectives, the curriculum aims to help students (a) increase their knowledge of adolescence, HIV, and AIDS; (b) to develop skills in self-assertiveness; and (c) to develop positive attitudes toward sexuality and those living with HIV/AIDS.

Some parents and teachers fear that AIDS education will result in early or increased sexual activities among adolescents; however, studies have shown that fear is not supported by the evidence. Rather, the evidence indicates that educating students about various issues and problems relating to HIV/AIDS promotes positive attitudes and responsible behaviors that help them avoid infection (NCERT and NACO, 1994).

Information, Education, and Communication

It is increasingly believed that comprehensive preventive education must reach young people both in and out of school. In India, advocacy for AIDS education almost coincides with that of sex education. In recent years, many important national seminars and conferences have strongly recommended the introduction of sex education in schools to enable students to shape healthy and responsible sexual mores. When providing education about sex and sexuality, gender issues, responsible and safe sexual behavior, STIs and AIDS, family planning, and welfare, teachers must recognize the importance of the cultural sensitivities of Indian society.

The key components in preventive measures are information, education, and communication (IEC). A national IEC strategic framework is required for effective message design, delivery, and impact. More specifically, the need for a national IEC strategic framework (NACO, 2004c) has emerged for the following reasons:

1. Systematic and evidence-based IEC is perceived as more effective and accountable. Availability and access to data, findings, lessons, and experiences will add value and sharpness to the response.
2. The current message is failing to capture the required attention to how HIV/AIDS spreads or is contained and how to encourage more effective, sustainable behavior change.
3. The IEC operational guidelines focused mainly on mass media products and channels; many of the emerging issues and priorities were not reflected adequately.
4. The need to set basic standards of uniformity and consistency, gender sensitivity, cultural contextuality, and creativity in broader issues related to HIV/AIDS is strongly believed, although there is recognition that standards should be tailored locally.

Generating awareness about HIV/AIDS and about services for HIV prevention, care, treatment, and support of those infected is critical to efforts to stem growth and spread of infection. The strategy for awareness among the general population is implemented at both national and state levels. At the national level, NACO is responsible for policy and strategy formulation and for framing guidelines for IEC activities. At the state level, the AIDS-control societies conduct communication needs-assessment studies. The assessment studies enable the societies to evolve state-specific IEC strategies that address local priorities within the overall national strategy and framework.

Unmet needs exist for information on certain topics:

- The four known routes of HIV transmission (i.e., heterosexual contact, drug use, blood transfusion, and perinatal transmission).
- The veracity of the most common myths and misconceptions about the HIV infection.
- The modalities for avoiding susceptibility to HIV.
- The availability of services for HIV prevention and for care, treatment, and support of these who are affected by HIV.

The IEC strategy has been instrumental in the central effort of alleviating stigma and discrimination against individuals living with HIV. Information and communication on HIV/AIDS must motivate people to use services provided through the National AIDS Control Program, such as STI treatment, counseling, testing, medicines for opportunistic infections, and, most recently, antiretroviral treatment for people living with AIDS. The IEC initiatives should include society's help to integrate HIV/AIDS messages into existing activities, creating a supportive environment for the care and rehabilitation of people living with HIV/AIDS.

Media Awareness Activities

Mass media plays an important, active role in responding to HIV/AIDS. Several awareness-generating activities have been produced:

- Television spots run on the national news channel at prime time. Celebrities have endorsed messages on HIV/AIDS prevention.

- All India Radio has been broadcasting sponsored programs every week on various channels. A series of spots also has been produced and broadcast on events such as Voluntary Blood Donation Day (October 1) and World AIDS Day (December 1).
- The bulk of print advertising is done by AIDS-control societies in the form of materials such as posters, handbills, flip charts, flash cards, handouts, information booklets, stickers, and wall hangings. During 2004, NACO supported the Department of Posts and Telegraphs in printing 15 million postcards with messages on HIV/AIDS.
- Hoardings, wall writings, and kiosks also have been used appropriately to communicate messages about the disease. NACO also has disseminated key messages on HIV/AIDS inside two Delhi Metro trains.
- State AIDS-control societies and the Directorate of Field Publicity, a media unit of the Ministry of Information and Broadcasting, have been provided with mobile exhibition kits produced by NACO in the regional languages.
- Folk media is extensively used for disseminating messages at the grassroots level to complement other forms of IEC, mostly through the Song and Drama Division of the Ministry of Information and Broadcasting.
- Events such as World AIDS Day and the Voluntary Blood Donation Day mark high points each year in NACO's efforts to generate awareness and to motivate behavioral change. The events help to dispel myths and misconceptions surrounding the illness and reduce HIV-related stigma and discrimination.

Community mobilization is also a crucial strategy for HIV/AIDS prevention, management, and control. This effort requires collaboration between government and nongovernment stakeholders, while constantly involving individuals affected by HIV/AIDS. Ensuring the widespread availability of safe and clean blood is a critical component of the National AIDS Prevention and Control Program.

STIs and HIV are behaviorally and epidemiologically linked. Similar high-risk behavior patterns are responsible for spreading both ills. An individual with a STI is 8 to 10 times more vulnerable to contracting HIV than someone without an STI. Hence, controlling STIs is seen as a step toward reducing the incidence of HIV. Over 85 percent of

HIV infection in India is the result of sexual transmission. With the success of condom use in Thailand and Cambodia in slowing the spread of HIV, India also must augment resources for condoms and make condoms widely available. To help young adults resist peer pressure, NACO disseminates messages on abstinence and on the need to maintain single-partner fidelity through mutual monogamy between uninfected sexual partners, as well as information on correct and consistent condom use.

Counseling and testing services for HIV aim to help individuals come to terms with knowledge about the HIV virus. These services provide a key entry point for a range of interventions in HIV prevention and care, including preventing HIV transmission from mother to child during childbirth, referrals for STI treatment, condom promotion, care and support for treatment of opportunistic infections, management of the HIV-TB (tuberculosis) coinfection, and referrals to designated medical centers for antiretroviral therapy. NACO has supported the establishment of counseling centers in all states. These centers, which are located in medical colleges, district hospitals, civil hospitals, primary health centers, and village hospitals, are positioned as one-stop shops for prevention with referrals for care and support (NACO, 2004b).

Institutional strengthening, capacity building, and training of health care professionals at the state and the local level are key objectives of the second phase of NACO's National AIDS Control Program. Training is used as a sustained tool to strengthen the capacity of NACO and the state AIDS-control societies to respond to the long-term challenges posed by HIV/AIDS. Acquisition of knowledge on HIV helps health care providers in allaying fears and misconceptions regarding infection rates, and it sets the groundwork for the medical fraternity to reach out to communities to enable an environment free from discrimination.

Studies from around the world show that the majority of young people have little or no idea how HIV/AIDS is transmitted or how to protect themselves from HIV infection. Most young people become sexually active during adolescence and are more likely than other population groups to have sex with high-risk partners or multiple partners. Young women are biologically more vulnerable to HIV infection than young men. That vulnerability is heightened because young women are less likely to access information on HIV and have limited power to exercise control over their sexual lives. Early marriage also poses special risks to young people, particularly women. This factor is especially relevant for India, where a high percentage of girls are married by the age of 18.

The School AIDS Education Program is being carried out in India across secondary and higher-secondary schools using an extracurricular approach. It is being implemented through the AIDS-control societies along with the Department of Education, the Department of Health, and nongovernmental organizations.

The Family Health Awareness Campaign is an effort to use the existing health infrastructure to address the key issues related to reproductive health (including HIV/AIDS), especially among rural and marginalized populations (NACO and Ministry of Health and Family Welfare, 2004). The campaign sensitizes the target population (15 to 49 years old) to these issues and encourages early detection and prompt treatment by involving the community. The campaign is organized at the district level after detailed diagnostic microplanning. Camps are organized at strategic public venues to facilitate diagnosis, administration of free drugs, and referral for treatment if necessary.

Development of an AIDS vaccine for India has surged ahead on several fronts since its formal beginning in a tripartite Memorandum of Understanding among NACO, the Indian Council of Medical Research, and the not-for-profit International AIDS Vaccine Initiative. Substantial progress has been made in scientific inquiry, research, and development. Potential sites for clinical trials have been selected. Potential manufacturers for the AIDS vaccine have been meticulously reviewed, and the most appropriate among them identified.

Nearly 90 percent of the infections in India have been reported from the 15–49 age groups, the most productive segment of society. HIV has an intense negative impact on the workforce, businesses, individual workers and their families, and the economy at the macro level. Growing evidence from the world indicates that the challenge of HIV/AIDS is best met with a strategy that combines prevention and care.

The Teacher's Role as AIDS Educator

Nearly 50 percent of new HIV infections occur in young people between 15 and 24 years old (NCERT and NACO, 2004). This rate is partly because a large percentage of the world population is young (one-fifth of the world population is between 10 and 19 years of age). In addition, because AIDS is a sexually transmitted infection, it affects young, sexually active people the most. The fundamental risk for young people is their ignorance about sexuality, HIV/AIDS, and the dangers of unprotected sex. Therefore, targeting adolescents with early intervention information on HIV/AIDS, with self-confidence improvement skills, and with assertiveness skills may be effective in safeguarding their future health. Although traditionally psychologists, social workers, and doctors have served as counselors, teachers also have a role as AIDS educators with young students. To be effective, a teacher needs to gain the trust and confidence of students (NCERT and NACO, 1994).

For teachers, providing instruction on HIV/AIDS is both challenging and rewarding. Most young people have never had the opportunity to openly talk about sex and drug use with adults, and they might welcome an open and honest discussion on those topics. In AIDS education, the relationship of the teacher with students counts more than anything else. The success of the lessons depends on how knowledge is imparted to the students; hence, participatory teaching methods are important. Suitable methods include group work, brainstorming, discussion, question, role-play, and case study/situation. Studies show that counseling is not only part of good clinical management and care but also vital for preventing the transmission of HIV infection (NACO, 2004c).

The classroom atmosphere is an important dimension. Sexuality education should be conducted in an atmosphere that promotes openness and acceptance. The teacher should be careful about the reactions of students to discussions about sexuality and develop rules for controlling classroom atmosphere, dealing with special problems, and helping the student who might be anxious about HIV/AIDS. Teachers must function as resources for accurate information on the sensitive matters of sex and sexuality. Many teachers have difficulty getting over their own embarrassment and shyness about dealing with such issues. Teacher training can address these difficulties and help teachers be in a better position to communicate with the students in their own language and appreciate their problems and needs. A trusted teacher's advice is more acceptable to students and more likely to encourage behavior change than advice from someone else.

The HIV epidemic is not about denial, nor despondency. In the years 2002–2004, NACO and its partners produced several innovations. NACO has rallied its partners to provide hope, help, and confidence to people living with HIV and to those indirectly affected by it. NACO has identified the gaps in the HIV/AIDS prevention and smoothly ushered in new initiatives to implement a comprehensive national response.

HIV/AIDS IN INDONESIA

In rural Indonesia, the terms HIV and AIDS are not unfamiliar, but the government officially downplays the magnitude of both real and potential HIV/AIDS-related issues (Graham, 2003). The nation's first case of HIV infection was identified in 1987, when a foreign tourist died of AIDS in Bali (USAID, 2005b), but shortly thereafter cases were identified in the local population. On the basis of limited blood testing, HIV/AIDS has been confirmed in 14 provinces. In March 2004, 55 cases of AIDS and 213 HIV-positive cases were reported. The WHO, however, estimates the real numbers to be closer to 35,000 to 50,000 cases, an increase of extraordinary proportions (UNAIDS, 2002).

Indonesia, the largest Muslim country in the world (Kamil, 1997), is struggling with its response to the AIDS epidemic. Development of the disease in Indonesia has followed the pattern of other countries, appearing first in the homosexual community and later in a small number of people with high-risk behavior such as intravenous drug users and commercial sex workers and their clients. Ultimately, infection spread throughout the population, reaching both men and women, including female prostitutes and single-partner women infected by their husbands. The largest percentage of infected people (96 percent) is found in the 15–49 age group (Ministry of Health, 2001). Sexual transmission is the primary mode of infection (95.7 percent), with 62.6 percent heterosexual and 33.1 percent homosexual and bisexual (USAID, 2005a).

The total number of HIV/AIDS cases reported in Indonesia may be considered small. Nonetheless, one must consider the fast rate of transmission throughout the population (all provinces, all socioeconomic groups) and the faster rate of infection among women than men. The AIDS epidemic is a threat to Indonesian development and way of life. Crude death rates (especially among those of productive age) will rise, and life expectancy at birth will decline. The number and productiveness of the workforce will decline, producing a direct impact on national economic productivity and income. Health costs (both direct and indirect) and welfare budgets will explode to provide for families who lose their earning capacity and for children orphaned by AIDS-related death of their parents. The progress of the first quarter century of the nation's development could be wiped out, and the burden on the national budget could be so heavy that current efforts to reduce and eliminate poverty—as well as other development programs—would be retarded.

The infection rate in the countries around Indonesia (including Australia, the Philippines, and Singapore) is already high (USAID, 2005a). High personal mobility between Indonesia and these countries could contribute to an acceleration of HIV infection in Indonesia. Negative political, social, and cultural reaction in the form of deportation, stigmatizing, discrimination, isolation, and violence against those living with HIV/AIDS should be anticipated and steps taken to prevent such reaction.

The challenge is that HIV/AIDS is not just a health problem; it has major political, economic, social, ethical, religious, and legal consequences for all aspects of life. This challenge threatens the national effort to improve the quality of human resources. To protect the process of national development and the goals for human development, Indonesia needs to strengthen efforts for prevention and control of HIV/AIDS, involving all sectors of development in a focused, integrated, and comprehensive program.

Hugo (2001) states that HIV in Indonesia has entered an epidemic phase with some high-risk subpopulations having prevalence rates of more than 5 percent. One of the distinctive features of the epidemic in Indonesia is a high degree of spatial variation in the level of prevalence of the disease. The highest levels occur in Irian Jaya/Papua, Jakarta, Bali, Riau, and North Sulawesi provinces. In each of these cases, there is a clear element of population movement involved in the above-average incidence because of the significance of migrant workers and the substantial commercial sex industry in each province. Irian Jaya/Papua represents a particularly disturbing situation, with very high prevalence rates being recorded in parts of the province and among some high-risk populations. Hugo's study presents and discusses the findings of behavioral sentinel surveillance regarding the incidence of HIV among high-risk populations including commercial sex workers (CSWs), transport workers, and sailors. The study also shows a relatively high level of knowledge about how to prevent HIV/AIDS but a low rate of condom usage in sexual activity among CSWs.

Since the first case of HIV was reported in Indonesia in 1987, much has been done to anticipate the epidemic. A presidential statement outlined the National AIDS Prevention Strategy in 1994. A variety of nongovernmental organizations have been formed to address the issue. AIDS has been covered widely in the media, with both positive and negative effects. Although Indonesia has AIDS prevention committees at every level of the government, the effect in the field has been minimal. Government officials and public figures are still frequently quoted in the mass media as saying things contrary to the official AIDS strategy, as well as giving misinformation about AIDS.

Epidemiologists have struggled to map the epidemic, but with minimal resources for surveillance, the status of the disease across the provinces remains unclear. Without real information about sexual behavior, it is even more difficult to plan effective AIDS prevention strategies for both the government and nongovernmental organizations (Kamil, 1997). As a consequence, a national AIDS strategy has been developed for Indonesia. The objective of the national AIDS control program is to

1. Prevent transmission of HIV.
2. Minimize personal suffering, as well as the social and economic impact of HIV/AIDS throughout Indonesia.
3. Mobilize and unify national efforts to control and manage HIV/AIDS.

The national strategy (USAID, 2005a) provides the framework and guidelines for all efforts by the government, community, nongovernmental organizations, families, individuals, institutions of higher education or research, donors, and international agencies to address the challenge of HIV/AIDS in an effective, complementary manner while building on their respective expertise and interests. The responses to HIV/AIDS should be guided by Indonesia's strong religious/cultural values, and they should preserve family bonds and welfare and traditional community support systems. Although the national strategy does not mention sexual- and reproductive-health education in school settings, it names youth as a priority. The national strategy is organized as follows:

- The basic principles include the national effort to control HIV/AIDS by the community and by the government. The government has the responsibility to lead and guide the efforts and to help create a supportive environment.

- The national response to the HIV/AIDS epidemic is designed to protect human development efforts from the negative impact of HIV/AIDS; to promote widespread individual, family, and community action throughout Indonesia to eliminate causes of and opportunities for HIV transmission; and to ensure technically sound, humane, and dignified treatment, care, and other support services for those living with and dying from AIDS as well as for their families, coworkers, and friends.
- The program areas include information, education, and communication; prevention; blood testing and counseling; treatment, service, and care; research and study; and monitoring and evaluation.
- The effectiveness of the national effort to respond to the threat of HIV/AIDS in Indonesia will depend on cooperation and roles and responsibilities among all segments of Indonesian society.
- International cooperation is also important. As a member state of the WHO, Indonesia's national strategy has been conceived within the context of the global AIDS strategy. Experience in HIV/AIDS prevention and control among Indonesia's neighboring countries, the Association of Southeast Asian Nations, and Australia is broad and important.
- Financing for activities developed within the context of this national strategy will be derived from national and local budgets, contributions from the community, the private sector, and international Badan Perencanaan dan Pembangunan Nasional (BAPPENAS, Indonesia's central planning agency).

The national strategy, as a statement of national commitment, emphasizes that HIV/AIDS education should be delivered at all levels in Indonesian schools (primary, secondary, formal, and informal) through a range of methods. For school students, HIV/AIDS education should be incorporated into study material. It can also be incorporated in cooperation with community health centers. The national strategy stresses inclusion of activities that improve knowledge about HIV/AIDS and awareness about the importance of a healthy and responsible life.

Indonesia faces several barriers to implementing HIV/AIDS education in schools (UNESCO, n.d.). Teachers express strong resistance to discussing questions relating to sexual health, and they have no guidance about how to deliver reproductive health education; parents and religious organizations pressure schools not to deliver such education. Government and other institutions are reluctant to recognize young people as sexual beings, and sex is considered a private matter. As a result, sexual health remains a marginal concern within health and education, especially when it involves a public domain such as school.

Indonesia, as a member of the family of nations, shares the responsibility to join worldwide efforts to control HIV/AIDS. Much work needs to be done, especially in the dissemination of knowledge and the creation of awareness. The task is not easy, but Indonesia has a successful record of national mobilization for the common good.

CONCLUSION

Although India and Indonesia have alarmingly high levels of HIV/AIDS cases, the governments in both countries have done much to prevent and control the disease. In the absence of proper care and supportive measures, infected people will transmit the infection to others and die within a short time. The existing stigma, discrimination, and denial of services to affected people and the poor knowledge about HIV/AIDS, illiteracy, and associated poverty among the population form an atmosphere conducive to rapid spread of the epidemic. The spread of disease also is attributed to seasonal migration out of the area, the widespread use of prostitutes, and the trafficking women.

Because of these factors, HIV/AIDS will likely emerge as a major factor in determining mortality levels in India and Indonesia. Efforts must be made now to increase the life span of HIV-infected individuals and to improve quality of life for them. The issue of better access to education for people with HIV/AIDS needs to be reviewed. Communities need to identify HIV-prevention programs and strategically tailor the intensity of intervention in high- and low-risk villages. Communities need to create awareness about HIV/AIDS to change citizens' attitudes toward the infection and to minimize existing stigma, discrimination, and further spread of disease. Drugs must be available at affordable rates so poor people can receive treatment at earlier stages and live longer. AIDS education seems to be a viable option. The younger generation needs to be made aware of preventive practices and strategies. Mass media and communication play an important role. School teachers and college and university professors can play an important part in HIV/AIDS education.

Finally, the pressing issue of how best to care for the millions of HIV-infected people in these countries must not divert resources and efforts from prevention of new HIV infections. We must continue to push for widespread implementation of effective interventions, to work on developing new strategies for interruption of HIV transmission, and to intensify efforts to develop the HIV vaccine.

REFERENCES

Agence France-Presse. (2004, September 15). *India sitting on AIDS "time-bomb," says international funding agency chief.* AEGiS-AFP News [Electronic version]. Retrieved October 8, 2005, from http://www.aegis.com/news/afp/2004/AF040953.html

Graham, S. (2003). The government works with *waria* in South Sulawesi. *Inside Indonesia.* Retrieved October 6, 2005, from http://www.insideindonesia.org/edit75/p17–18graham.html.

Hugo, G. (2001). *Indonesia, internal and international population mobility: Implications for the spread of HIV/AIDS.* Retrieved October 6, 2005, from http://www.hiv-development.org/text/publications/hugo_Indonesia.pdf.

Joint United Nations Programme on HIV/AIDS. (2002). *Join the fight against AIDS in Indonesia.* Retrieved October 17, 2005, from http://www.weforum.org/pdf/Initiatives/Indo_menu1.pdf.

Joint United Nations Programme on HIV/AIDS. (2004). *2004 report on the global HIV/AIDS epidemic.* Retrieved October 14, 2005, from http://www.unaids.org/bangkok2004/report.html.

Kamil, O. (1997). Preventing AIDS. *Inside Indonesia.* Retrieved October 6, 2005, from http://www.insideindonesia.org/edit51/aids.htm.

Ministry of Health. (2001). *Cases of HIV/AIDS in Indonesia.* Indonesia: Directorate General CDC and EH, Republic of Indonesia.

National AIDS Control Organization. (2004a). *An overview of the spread and prevalence of HIV/AIDS in India.* Retrieved October 8, 2005, from http://www.nacoonline.org/facts_overview.htm.

National AIDS Control Organization. (2004b). *Annual report: 2002–2003, 2003–2004.* Retrieved October 6, 2005, from http://www.nacoonline.org/annualreport/annulareport.pdf.

National AIDS Control Organization. (2004c). *HIV/AIDS counseling training manual for trainers.* Retrieved October 6, 2005, from http://www.nacoonline.org/publication/8.pdf.

National AIDS Control Organization and Ministry of Health and Family Welfare. (2004). *National IEC/BCC strategic framework for HIV/AIDS programme*. Retrieved October 6, 2005, from http://www.nacoonline. org/guidelines/iec_strategy.pdf.

National Council of Educational Research and Training and National AIDS Control Organization. (1994). *AIDS education in schools: A training package*. Retrieved October 6, 2005, from http://www.nacoonline.org/ publication/aids_education.pdf.

National Council of Educational Research and Training and National AIDS Control Organization. (2004). *Learning for life*. Retrieved October 6, 2005, from http://www.nacoonline.org/publication/learningfrolife.pdf [sic].

Ukil, A. (2004, July 16). Sonia sees Bangkok bond in AIDS fight. *The Telegraph* [On-line]. Retrieved October 14, 2005, from http://www.telegraphindia. com/1040717/asp/nation/story_3506175.asp.

UNAIDS India. (2004). *HIV epidemic in India*. Retrieved October 8, 2005, from http://www.unaids.org.in/displaymore.asp?itemid=56andchkey=7 6andsubchkey=0andchname=HIV Epidemic in India.

UNESCO. (n.d.). *Country profile: Indonesia*. Retrieved October 6, 2005, from http://portal.unesco.org/education/en/file_download.php/ 86e6e17fdac25fda2cc4073e2d4695ccIndonesia.pdf.

USAID. (2005a). *Asia and the Near East*. Retrieved October 17, 2005, from http://www.usaid.gov/locations/asia_near_east/countries/indonesia/ indonesia.html.

USAID. (2005b). *Health profile: Indonesia*. Retrieved October 17, 2005, from http://www.usaid.gov/our_work/global_health/aids/Countries/ ane/indonesia_05.pdf.

PART V

TRANSFORMATIVE PRAXIS IN SCHOOL AND COMMUNITY

Overview, *Dirck Roosevelt*

᠊ᘓ᠊

This section comprises close-to-practice explorations of qualitative change in the relationship between learners and knowledge. Shifts in position with respect to HIV/AIDS as subject matter—from being nearly deaf to it, or speechless in the face of it, but in no sense in dialogue with it, to a stance of active critical inquiry, as conducted by one who has the need, right, and power to know—are the core focus and aim of the explorations. But shifts with respect to knowledge as such (e.g., recognition that its communication is human and fallible) and to personal experience as a source of knowledge are intimately entwined with and enabling of change in relationship to the specific subject matter of HIV/AIDS.

Clearly, these authors' overarching interest is in encouraging *action,* modes of action that are life-sustaining rather than life-threatening, in promoting movement from a posture of victim or bystander to one of agency. They all, however, understand action in the world and construction of knowledge as reciprocal. The contexts for their explorations, all in the United States, include a prevention program for alcohol- or drug-addicted women, an inner-city high school biology class, and teacher preparation classes in the pedagogy of mathematics and science. The learners of ultimate interest are, naturally, the women who are "at risk," the high school students (including the many actual or virtual dropouts among them), and the future teachers and *their* students. These chapters, however, address themselves substantially to an intermediate group of learners, those who teach the ultimate target group. This section of the volume considers the educational needs of this intermediate population to be significant, complex, and not easy to meet. These chapters are, then, in addition to all else they are, essays in teacher education—a topic they approach in variously heterodox ways.

Each one depicts the learner as an agent, an active knower; in each, the movement from knowing less to knowing more, often a transformation of invisible knowledge and disregarded experience into valued knowledge, is shown to be one in which acting and knowing are interdependent. Each shows learning as praxis. The learner—whether she is an HIV-infected, drug-addicted sex worker in Tucson; an alienated, disenfranchised high school sophomore; or an ordinarily committed, talented, overwhelmed prospective teacher—must become engaged in a sense of need *and* of possibility, become engaged in a voluntary endeavor and search to move out of the position of knowing little of worth, into that of one who knows and is seen to know and to be capable of knowing more. It is the job of the teacher educator, facilitator, outreach worker, and so forth—it is the justification of pedagogy—to create and sustain the conditions of engagement, a task that involves but does not reduce to making available and accessible the kinds of formal knowledge represented elsewhere in this volume. At issue, then, are transformations of location and relationship.

Teaching, in turn, has aptly been characterized as "working in relationships" (Lampert, 2001). Bearing in mind this perspective and the standing of the learner as active subject, this section is primarily intended to influence practice, in particular that of teacher educators and others active in or concerned with the "intermediate" audience of those who work with at-risk populations. The chapters distinctively seek to influence practice by contributing to the development of a conceptual framework that is pedagogically sound, morally and politically coherent, cognizant of structural inequities, practitioner oriented, and "learner centered" (Darling-Hammond, 1997). Such a framework is not an instrumentalist approach to influencing practice, nor does it simply serve to articulate a context in which techniques may be purposefully employed; rather, it addresses the generation and adaptation of technique. The research represented in these chapters is empirically grounded, spanning a range from a systematic scheme of quantitative and qualitative data collection and analysis of a program to a practitioner's retrospective inquiry into her own practice. In every case, the findings speak both to the development of a conceptual framework and to pedagogical and curricular decision-making of a concrete and local character.

In "Cultivating a Heartfelt Sense of Community: An Essential Teacher Competency for Preventing HIV and AIDS," Lisa Green-Derry and Mwangaza Michael-Bandele describe a teacher's self-education in a troubled urban high school and how she eventually catalyzes her students' study of biology and engagement in the community through a focus on HIV/AIDS, helping them come to "see learning as not only the science of living things, but the key to living life at a very different level." This is essentially a retrospective report and concluding analysis of a piece of action research that had been conducted without benefit of that framework. It contains numerous lessons, many implicit, for teacher educators and for school administrators with responsibility for mentoring and other forms of professional development. Perhaps most important, it is also a testament to a different and more potent vision of accountability than that now prevailing: accountability arising, without coercion, from the heart, as a reciprocal relationship among teachers, students, local community, and society.

In "A Conversation on HIV/AIDS Education and Teacher Education in Science and Mathematics," Bill Rosenthal and Elaine Howes present a model of curriculum development for HIV/AIDS prevention work in teacher education. They posit the teacher educator as a curriculum designer who aims to prepare teachers to themselves be conscious and deliberate cocreators of curriculum with the ultimate aim of educating K–12 students to be active, critical agents of their own learning. The subtext: Teaching is not implementing; learning is not consuming. Rosenthal and Howes offer two *Gedankenexperiments* (thought experiments) in curriculum development—one for secondary mathematics, involving categories and rates of change for AIDS in community contexts, the other for science at the elementary level, addressing viruses and myths about HIV/AIDS transmission. This study, with a strong conceptual–analytic component, draws upon the authors' substantial experience as teacher educators, their review of pertinent literatures (prevention literature as well as curriculum studies and mathematics and science education), and interviews they conducted with health care professionals, secondary school teachers, and teacher educators.

In "Establishing Ties: HIV Prevention Through Facilitation," Rosi Andrade and colleagues describe and analyze a community-based program to prevent HIV and other sexually transmitted diseases (STDs). Principles of liberatory pedagogy animate and structure the program; within that frame, "establishing ties" serves as an image for the approach to the construction of educative relationships. The authors describe with care the program's curriculum and the ways it approaches training the staff, in particular, how it engages them in reconsideration of their own views of teaching and tendency to position the women to be served as "other." They argue that the concept of risk must be addressed as an element in or descriptor of the entire constellation of social relationships in which a person is to be found; as they put it, "the process of risk reduction is a process of social transformation." The authors draw on data and report findings from an evaluation study of the program in question, itself shaped by the theory and practice of participatory action research. They also summarize quantitative descriptions of HIV/AIDS, STDs, and substance abuse patterns and trends, drawing on up-to-date primary and secondary sources.

A conceptual framework constructed in part from the knowledge—and wisdom—represented in these chapters would have as an essential plank the certain understanding that if HIV/AIDS prevention *education* is to occur, and tendencies toward life-sustaining rather than life-threatening modes of action are to flourish, persons deemed "at risk" must be positioned as active subjects whose questions, needs, and desires are vital content of the curriculum. Mere information about HIV/AIDS is mute, no matter how articulate the presentation; learners do not "acquire" such information, far less transform it into new ways of acting, simply by being in its presence. They must rather participate in educative relationships such that they come, in the well-chosen verb of Andrade and her colleagues, to *embrace* the new information. Those charged with playing some part in prevention education must be similarly positioned, for only an agent is capable of treating others as agents.[1]

As with all serious progressive or liberatory pedagogies, this approach demands of the educator not only considerable formal knowledge—such as that accessible elsewhere in this volume—and knowledge of larger social structures—including systemic inequities and closed discourses—both of which are demanding to acquire—but also a kind of devoted attention to the particular, an energy and integrity to "learn the learners," learn the context, elicit the learners' stores and powers of perception, curiosity, capacity for commitment, and knowledge. This quality of active attention, this sense of teaching *as* acts of attention (Roosevelt, 1998), this openness to participation in a reciprocally educative relationship, with attendant risks of uncertainty, is itself difficult to learn and to practice. Without it, however, the HIV/AIDS education efforts discussed in these chapters would have little prospect of success; indeed they would hardly come into being in the first place. Education is everywhere local and situated, and everywhere the same: It occurs when students become authors of their own lives.

This section recognizes HIV/AIDS as a ruinous presence in communities of particular importance to teachers and schools: youth, constituted in part by their sexuality; African Americans ages 25–44, for whom AIDS is now the leading cause of death (Consensus Panel, 2002); and the larger world community in which students must learn how to locate themselves. In considering how teachers might be better prepared to address this threat, however, it is important to note that every object worthy of study cannot have its own discrete home in the curriculum of either schools or teacher education—such a route would lead to fragmentation, superficiality, and a lack of resistance to fads, untoward political pressures, and sheer overwork (also see Pateman, 2003). If prospective teachers (likewise, teacher educators) are to take responsibility for addressing HIV/AIDS education within the terms of the conceptual framework sketched here, to envision such work as part of good practice and to make it part of their practice, they will need to possess the disposition and imagination as well as the knowledge and skills to do so. They will clearly need to feel that such content and purposes are compatible, at least, with other responsibilities they are not at liberty to ignore, specifically the responsibility for learning in the core academic areas. Ideally, teachers would be able to conceive of such aims as coexisting with rather than canceling out another honorable purpose of schools: to serve as places apart from pressing, often corrosive, daily realities; places dedicated in part to engagement with other realities and the reach of unfettered imagination.

All of this holds some implications for research and development in teacher education:

- There is a clear moral and practical imperative to continue learning, as a profession, how to teach teachers who have the knowledge, skills, and disposition to consistently treat their students as active knowers, as persons with intellectual and social agency.

Prospective teachers and teachers over the course of their careers must be taught to be "students of their students" and of their students' contexts, to elicit learners' stores and powers of perception, curiosity, capacity for commitment, and knowledge. This is much easier to state than to accomplish. As with risk reduction, this goal envisions less a set of curricular adjustments than "a process of social transformation." It is a call to make education a profoundly more democratic practice. There is, however, much work going on in this area. What reflection on the challenges of HIV/AIDS education could do is (a) make clearer that these are cardinal imperatives for teacher education, not subsidiary ones; (b) broaden the base of support for the endeavor; and (c) contribute powerful exemplars of such work.

- It is indeed both possible and necessary to build the knowledge base of practices consistent with the conceptual framework sketched by these chapters. The kinds of curriculum development proposed by Rosenthal and Howes, for example—critical study of HIV/AIDS matters within the core academic areas, designed and adapted by teachers and teacher educators who understand that they are and need to be "cocreators" of curriculum, especially if it is to be specific to learners and context—need to be documented and analyzed. Andrade and colleagues likewise are engaged in a kind of curriculum development that is at once highly particularized and guided by broadly relevant principles and skills.

- If imagination and hope are not engaged, knowledge remains inert, at best; at worst, destructive and self-destructive habits of action persist in ever more constricting rounds. Green-Derry's work gives an example of the kind of creativity and energy that must be widely released if democratic, life-sustaining education is to be a more than occasional reality. That releasing is a task for teacher educators, school administrators, and others to take up or renew commitment to. This is assuredly not a matter of converting the fruits of such creativity into static programs to be implemented by others—nor, in a just system, are individuals all on their own expected to educate and remake themselves in isolation without benefit of other voices, other experiences, or prior learning. Learning how to be an educator, like becoming educated in the broadest sense, is an adventure of the imagination eventuating in the improvement of some space for human life. That is at root and at end a social project—toward which, however, no individual contribution can ever be duplicated or replaced.

NOTE

1. This proposition necessarily entails the risk of reposing consequential trust in the judgment of the teachers and teacher educators (formally designated as such or not) encompassed by it. Although such judgment can arguably be said to inhere in the meaning of "teacher" (Richardson and Roosevelt, 2004), it is indeed a risk of a sort, not one well-favored in an era of top-down standards and standardization.

REFERENCES

Consensus Panel on HIV/AIDS Education and Teacher Preparation. (2002). *Consensus panel on HIV/AIDS and teacher education: A synthesis report.* Washington, DC: American Association of Colleges for Teacher Education and American Academy for the Advancement of Science.

Darling-Hammond, L. (1997). *The right to learn: A blueprint for creating schools that work.* San Francisco: Jossey-Bass.

Lampert, M. (2001). *Teaching problems and the problems of teaching.* New Haven: Yale University Press.

Pateman, B. (2003). *Linking national subject area standards with priority health-risk issues in PK–12 curricula and teacher education programs.* Washington, DC: American Association of Colleges for Teacher Education.

Richardson, V., and Roosevelt, D. (2004). Teacher preparation and the improvement of teacher education. In M. Smylie and D. Miretzky, eds., *Developing the teacher workforce—National Society for the Study of Education yearbook, 103, Part 1* (pp. 105–144). Chicago: University of Chicago Press.

Roosevelt, D. (1998). Teaching as an act of attention: An interview. *Changing Minds* 13: 29–30.

16

CULTIVATING A HEARTFELT SENSE OF COMMUNITY: AN ESSENTIAL TEACHER COMPETENCY FOR PREVENTING HIV AND AIDS

Lisa Green-Derry and Mwangaza Michael-Bandele

☙

Knowing how to cultivate community is an essential ability for educators desiring to effectively engage their students. It is particularly vital for teachers who will help reduce the growing incidence of HIV and AIDS. This chapter asserts that an educator who can harness the humanizing power inherent in community can interact with students as a transformational agent, one who conveys academic and life lessons, including HIV/AIDS prevention. These lessons, including but not limited to academic information, afford students greater access to knowledge, skills, and life opportunities. Such a transformational agent is grounded in a culture and practice of community that guides and inspires classroom instruction.

In this chapter, *cultivating community* refers to a teacher's ability to see each student as a full, complete human being who is connected to and affected by a network of people, circumstances, and experiences. The process of cultivating community involves the ability to understand, value, and access parts of each student's network and then to determine how and where to impart the academic information and skill that best serves the student. This process requires knowing the issues that affect students' learning and nurturing relationships with the people who most directly affect students' lives. Successful cultivation of community requires a genuine interest in the students' overall well-being, current and future, and understanding how it connects to the teacher's. The teacher proficient in cultivating community is adept at creating opportunities and identifying when, where, and how to effectively convey subject matter. Such an ability, involving attitudes and skills that can be developed during teacher preparation, is at the heart of creating and maintaining a teaching force sufficiently able and inspired to engage HIV and AIDS prevention.

This chapter explores the theoretical and practical application of cultivating community through two lenses: that of a researcher (Michael-Bandele) and that of a practitioner (Green-Derry). Both voices are blended in an effort to relay the value of one to the other and their joint value to cultivating community. The researcher's voice is printed in a Roman font, and italicized text distinguishes the practitioner's comments. This juxtaposition of thought and practice is intended to help spawn unconventional answers to the challenges of teacher education preparation. The unconventional demands of our children require nothing less.

Substantial research literature asserts the value of teachers' knowing the ethnic, social, historical, and other cultures of their students and the communities they represent (Breitborde, 2002; Delpit, 1996; Irvine, 1997; Ladson-Billings, 1994; Lane, Lacefield-Parachini, and Isken, 2003; Lieberman, 2000; Meier, 1995/2002; Michael-Bandele, 1998; Murrell, 2000; Nieto, 2000; Wenger, 1999). Such knowing allows educators to develop content, methods, communication styles, and other teaching tools that are effective because they are relevant and meaningful to students. The point is to foster an understanding that generates insights to support classroom instruction and interaction. Knowing community is foundational to such an understanding.

The value of preparing teachers competent in creating and sustaining a sense and practice of community is grounded in the theoretical framework of *situated cognition,* which posits that learning is naturally tied to authentic activity, context, and culture (Brown, Collins, and Duguid, 1989) and is situated in the context of the everyday world (Wilson, 1993). The relationship among learner, information, and environment determines how to learn and why. This process advances the learner's ability to store information and to link what is learned to other useful meanings (Gersten and Baker, 1998). Situated cognition encourages students to not only memorize information but also engage in higher-order thinking (Choi and Hannafin, 1995). It also asserts that "activities of person and environment that shape learning are parts of a mutually constructed whole" (Bredo, 1994, p. 4). Social interaction becomes a critical component of situated cognition because learners are actually involved in a community of practice that reflects the beliefs and behaviors to be acquired (Lave and Wenger, 1991).

This theory of knowledge acquisition values teachers' engagement with students, one human being to another, unencumbered by the blinders often imposed by teacher education doctrine that focuses on the teacher's ability to transfer academic information. Situated cognition empowers teachers to imagine, create, and explore the real-life worlds of their students in order to meet their real-life needs. This world is their community, and its context is their culture. The teacher can create a culture of community by knowing and valuing each student well enough to recognize where and when the academic content or skills can be taught in ways useful to the student. When that occurs, an arena becomes available where teachers can imagine and then create indigenous content and learning strategies that actually improve the academic skills of students in ways that resonate through, and are evident in, their lives. Situated cognition theory encourages real-world interactions between teachers and students within the context of the students' community. The teacher must have facility in that community in order to fashion useful teaching and learning.

How does this notion of preparing educators to cultivate community get out of the theoretical realm, off the textbook page, and into the classroom? The reflections of a practicing teacher who has successfully cultivated community on behalf of her students are provided here. Her thoughtful recollections express her personal perspective. Musing establishes its own order, committed only to mining the riches inherent in the contemplative voice. Her authentic voice conveys the relationship between the educator and effective teaching in the community and provides insight for moving theory to practice.

Teaching is a second career for Green-Derry, a 40-something-year-old African American woman who is a native of the southern United States. As she reflects upon the career transition that moved her into her teaching career, she remembers considering the many changes she would make.

CONCEPTUALIZING COMMUNITY

I began my teaching life after a career as a registered medical technologist. This transition required a change of mind, a change in direction, a change in knowledge base, and essentially a heart change. Evolving from a laboratory scientist to an educational practitioner required that I become a student.

My desire to learn how to teach, coupled with scientific skills honed during my previous career and a real sense of accountability to the students I encountered, helped me to learn instructional strategies quickly and to tap into my resources as a mother and a scientist. These characteristics also helped me to seek ways of extending lessons so that science would be for my students not just what was written in books, but also part of a process of joining the larger "community of learners." My professional experience as an ASCP (American Society of Clinical Pathologists) Registered Medical Laboratory Technologist positioned me to bring to the classroom scientific and clinical skills.

As the new practitioner conceptualizes changes that will occur because of her career move, she considers her emotional shift to be essential. Covello (1958), and more recently Noddings (2002), and others have written extensively about the impact of the affective domain on teaching and learning. The positive impact of caring teachers, informed and connected to the communities represented by their students, is well documented. What is less documented is the relationship between the notion of "teaching from the heart" and the transitioning teacher's capacity to "become a student" as she learns to teach.

The willingness of a teacher—the principal professional whose responsibility it is to know—to enter a classroom with a value in *not knowing* may appear contradictory. Teachers are trained and paid to convey what they know. Like parents, priests, doctors, and other people responsible for fortifying individual lives in some way, teachers who pause to know the human terrain become more likely to identify effective routes. These paths are ways to transfer and translate meaningful information, skills, and perspectives to the people they serve. By spending enough time "not knowing," teachers may cultivate relationships that facilitate greater access to students and to their communities; observation may then take on a greater meaning. Useful observations neither verify what the teacher already knows nor validate teaching strategies that worked well in the past. Instead, they increase the teacher's ability to accurately *describe* the students she is responsible to before attempting to *prescribe* which teaching practices are most effective. To be accurate, these descriptions should take into account the varied roles the student assumes outside of the school environment, including familial relationships and the students' own sense of efficacy. Student strengths may be veiled, buried, mislabeled, or unknown, but seeing them is an essential prerequisite to effective teaching. The teacher who can suspend "knowing" long enough to experience the observational and other data-gathering benefits of being a student herself may develop a greater appreciation of the varied, unscripted ways students do learn.

CHALLENGES TO COMMUNITY

How does a teacher teach students who seem as if they aren't interested in learning? What does a teacher do to pique the interest of teenage students whose lives require attention at a level usually reserved for adulthood? What kinds of lessons does a teacher design to get and keep the attention of students who are faced with homelessness, life-threatening occurrences and diseases, early parenthood, responsibility for younger siblings, and ailing parents or grandparents?

To which books does a teacher refer to find the "how to" of teaching in an inner city where the poverty level is comparable to that in underdeveloped countries, the murder rate within the school population reflects the murder rate in the larger community, life-threatening diseases such as HIV affect the students' immediate families and community, and single-parent or grandparent-headed households are the norm rather than the exception?

Which books give sufficient directions, examples, and instructional strategies to help a teacher make biology relevant to the students in a high school located in the heart of an aged, dilapidated, and neglected government housing development where drug sales, ensuing gun fights, crippling injuries, or deaths occur as regularly as in some war-torn places in the world?

Which universities include in their curriculum applicable information that not only accurately reflects the inner city classroom but assists the teacher with implementing meaningful lessons? Which education classes prepare teachers not only to learn the subject, but also to learn about the subjects so that the ability to design and deliver sound instruction is based on knowledge of social mores within specific communities; knowledge of ways to hook students on learning; techniques to relate to students in a positive and respectful, noncondescending, nonpatronizing manner; and methods to help students see the validity of education as it relates to their present circumstances and how attaining or neglecting education can affect their future?

These thoughts and many other challenges flooded my mind. As a new teacher with minimal formal teaching experience but maximum desire to make biology real for students, I was determined to involve, engage, instruct, expose, and help students see the subject not only as the science of living things but also as the key to living life at a level very different from their own.

Green-Derry grapples with many of the same issues that teacher educators, researchers, and policy makers investigate daily. How does a teacher maintain the attention of students preoccupied with adult issues that are sometimes life-and-death dilemmas? Where are the teaching strategies that really work? And when they don't, whom does the teacher call for support?

The literature on multicultural, diverse, and culturally responsive practice addresses the value of teacher education that prepares teachers to deal with a wide array of learners. Researchers such as Jordan-Irvine, Banks, Delpit, Dilworth, Grant, Ladson-Billings, and many others have written extensively over the last 40 years on the significance of responding to the cultural and other human needs of students. The enormous value in partnering with parents (Nieto and Rolon, 1997); the value of education for transforming not only the mind, but all aspects of a person, including body and spirit (Hilliard, 1997); and the value of gaining critical insights about a student by listening authentically and generating conversations about their lives (Pang, 1997) are all important factors. These strategies provide teachers information about their students that enhance teacher effectiveness.

Each of these strategies associated with preparing teachers to be effective with diverse learners involves basic issues of human interaction. Although these strategies deliberately recognize and treat students as whole and complete human beings, connected to a culture of community, they have not become the baseline for teacher education. It is ineffective to continue preparing teachers as conveyers of subject matter only, holding them and the institutions that train them accountable only for the academic enrichment of students. The real-life outcome of such limited thinking and practice is too often lethal. Life dreams, aspirations, personal and group efficacy, financial stability, expanded world view, and other life outcomes often tied to a quality education perish in the hearts and minds of students who have been dehumanized by the effect of underdeveloped teaching practices.

Teacher education might benefit tremendously by considering culturally responsive practice for all students because all students—indeed, all people—represent at least one identifiable culture. That culture is a product and reflection of community. Preparing teachers to cultivate the community to which their students belong can not only close achievement gaps but also raise the national standards of education for all.

CULTIVATING COMMUNITY

I began to ask myself questions. While learning how to work within the existing framework, what does a teacher do to validate—that is, give credence to, listen to, and respect—the students' concerns? How do you help school-site administrators to support a real need to think and work "outside the box" and to support instructional strategies that veer far from those traditionally employed in many schools? How does a teacher transform the learning process for students so that it is authentic, extends beyond the classroom and school building into the community, and has an impact on the lives of students? In other words, how do you teach in a manner that, as some of my students might say, has to do with their lives?

Parental skills that I had developed as a mother of three children enrolled in public schools, my personal experience as an alumna of the school district, and a keen sense of accountability to students who were historically denied consistent, viable, and meaningful learning experiences framed my instructional interactions with students.

The desire to teach in order for students—my students, my children—to learn stirred emotions and spawned questions about what needed to happen to transform their academic lives. Many of these questions remain unanswered; others are addressed in this text. How does a teacher remain accountable to students and the community? Help students take responsibility for their learning and for applying what they have learned? Pique the interest of the collective community?

Accountability, the buzzword for school districts around the country, was part of my concern, although not from the same perspective as educational administrators and policy makers. I was not fully aware of all the mandates and policy issues encompassed by accountability and standards. In my mind, accountability had to do with responsibility, reciprocity, and resourcefulness. My desire was to help students become more accountable to themselves for their academic success as well as to help students understand the connection of the community's accountability, or lack of accountability, to them as members of the larger community and of society as a whole. The communities where my students lived were disfranchised. Nevertheless, I wanted them to learn that they had a responsibility to be resourceful, and as they achieved academically, to give back, as an act of reciprocity and responsibility to themselves, to the community.

For me, the term accountable *also expresses my identification with the ethnicity of my students and includes what I perceive as a way of being with them. It also describes what I view as a spiritual responsibility to be the teacher that my students needed. For me, accountability was more than just educational jargon. It meant that I could not, in the vernacular of my elders, "teach any kinda way." I had to teach my students as if they were my own biological children. I truly had to teach them as my own.*

Traditionally, the ninth- through twelfth-grade students feared and displayed an intense disdain for science. I ascertained some of the reasons by observations and from informal conversations with students. Several students explicitly said, "I don't see what [learning biology] has to do with my life." Other barriers I was able to surmise include these:

- *Teachers routinely assigned vocabulary words to define and questions to answer without providing or creating a meaningful context for learning.*
- *Opportunities to perform laboratory experiments were minimal or nonexistent.*
- *Connection to their current and future experiences was not clear.*
- *Classes were boring.*

I began to validate students' concerns by respecting the fact that students' life experiences often shaped their response or lack of response to academic experiences. I knew that I had to do several things that would help them to trust me, believe me, and know that my role as their teacher extended beyond our encounters with textbook information. I had to let them know that they came to my class with a wealth of knowledge that in many instances would be applicable to our teaching and learning relationship, while also being clear that some of their knowledge and experiences would not be appropriate or applicable in our setting. By sharing these thoughts with my students, I helped them to reframe those experiences and I validated rather than dismissed them.

My idea of "reframing" is similar to what we do with a photograph and a frame. We choose the frame based on several features—the size of the photograph, the background color or background images, and the surrounding environment in which the framed photograph will be placed. While the sentimental value of the photograph doesn't change, the monetary value may. Nevertheless, the photograph and its intrinsic value remain.

I began designing and implementing lessons that became transformative for not only the students but for the community and me as well. My exploration was an experiment in a sense; more than that, it was an act of faith, an act in faith. It was also the result of necessity, or as some might say, "necessity is the mother of invention." Attributing the unknown or unseen to God while doing things not fully familiar to me is reflected in my phrases "of faith" and "in faith."

In addition to the evident physical deterioration, there was evidence of social, spiritual, and academic deterioration in and around the school. Social and academic deterioration manifested themselves in many ways, such as in the large number of students who chose not to begin school on the mandated date.

This daunting situation, which seemed to frustrate and drain many of my colleagues, challenged and inspired me. It caused me to seek creative ways of maintaining high expectations of students who chose to begin school during mandated days of August; design lessons that were generic, but specific enough to fulfill curricular constraints; and refrain from penalizing students who chose to operate within their own time frame instead of the district's. Implementing "generic lessons" responded to the curriculum requirements to start with concepts of the scientific method. Although I knew the students needed to learn or review this information, I realized that many who came later than the mandated opening of school would miss important principles in this concept. I chose to modify the curriculum.

How do you begin teaching at the start of the school year when many students arrive several weeks after it begins? To what extent can you begin addressing the concerns and needs of students who begin the school year promptly, without leaving the latecomers to fall farther and farther behind? You just start. The required curriculum becomes a proposal, something that can be revised as needed, infused with field experiences, field trips, video recordings, science-related movies, and real-life and community-inspired activities. It can also incorporate activities and actions about leadership training and other skills not necessarily included in the biology curriculum.

Green-Derry's description of the thinking and subsequent action she took to teach her students effectively reveals she is immersed in a process of cultivating community. She treats the students as if they were her own sons and daughters, validates their life experiences, and becomes what they need. Any one of these three practices can significantly advance a teacher's effectiveness (Delpit, 1996). Human beings welcome interaction that is kind, affirming, and responsive.

Becoming or *being* what her students need distinguishes her role from *doing* what is needed. *Being* asserts a willingness to transform oneself and alter some dimension of who one is to create and manifest beyond what would normally be required of a professional. *Being* positions Green-Derry to connect with students to determine their real-life needs. That stance corresponds with the same intent of cultivating community: to know the issues that influence students' learning and to be in relationship with the people who most directly affect students' lives. This knowing lays the groundwork for developing relevant classroom activities, like the reframing she describes. *Being* has the potential to liberate the classroom as a place where students are forged into the people teachers want to interact with, whether the student is willing to take on the characteristics of that person or not. The weight of becoming something other or different from one's authentic self can be lifted when the teacher welcomes the students and what they represent. The value of liberating pedagogy for both the student and teacher (Freire, 1970/2000) is well documented. More attention to what liberated learning environments provide teachers may encourage closer investigation of their merits.

CREATING AN HIV AND AIDS PREVENTION COMMUNITY

Another situation that affected my decision about content, structure, and timing of lessons was the annual fund-raising activity of the NOAIDS Task Force, a 5K walkathon, during the second week of September. Alarming statistics about sexually transmitted diseases (STDs) among teenagers also strongly influenced my thoughts. I saw this event as an opportunity to design lessons that would incorporate the science of viruses, specifically human immunodeficiency viruses, and a local community activity into the academic lives of students in attendance prior to the Labor Day holiday. Little did I know that this serendipitous opportunity would have such far-reaching consequences.

The lessons were neither very refined nor derived from my study of research-based strategies. They were practical and meaningful and became increasingly motivational to the students as years passed. Part of the instructional approach was adopted from classroom experiences I recalled as a high school student in a challenging, yet enjoyable, biology class. The teacher had lectured, required "daily recitations," and given us regular opportunities to learn biology with our hands. Dissecting small animals such as frogs and lizards had been included in many of our lessons. We also had developed and refined our scientific writing skills by making "books" of writings about our work, personalized illustrations of organisms, and comments from our teacher.

One lesson I developed helped students learn by comparing bacterial infections to viral infections and by participating in the NOAIDS walkathon. This series of lessons became a part of a mini unit that also counted students' participation in a walkathon as a test grade.

My students had some rudimentary knowledge of cellular biology. They could state that all living things were made of cells and that human cells consist of a nucleus (the center of genetic information) and other organelles that could become infected with HIV and other pathogens. But they did not indicate a level of understanding about other things they read in the textbook that described changes that were actually occurring in their bodies. Although students had completed written assignments and constructed cell models, there were still gaps in their ability to make the connection to real-life situations (colds, younger siblings' asthma attacks, parents' high blood pressure episodes, and the like) with textbook content about human cells. The lessons I described, along with activities that occurred outside of the classroom, were designed to help them make the connections.

The classroom activities included a hands-on, minilab session with Styrofoam packing peanuts injected with food coloring to represent human cells infected with HIV. Students worked in cooperative groups to brainstorm ways to determine whether or not a "cell" had been "infected" with HIV.

Watching the movie Outbreak *stimulated students' questions about whether or not HIV and other STDs were purposely prepared and given to specific people, including people of color and poor people. The students also responded to questions such as "Can you determine if someone is infected with HIV by their outward appearance? What comparison can be made between the Styrofoam peanuts and the cells of humans exposed to HIV or other pathogens? How does a bacterial infection, such as the type referred to in the movie* Outbreak, *compare to viral infections?" The students, including many who started the school year late and displayed lackadaisical attitudes toward science, had thoughts, concerns, beliefs, and questions that were substantive. At first, they were not inclined to bring these ideas up in class.*

Vividly and fondly, I recall the Sunday morning in early September 1995 when 25 freshmen, sophomores, and juniors greeted me on the front steps of the high school. They were anxiously waiting to board the bus provided by the local sheriff that would take us to the NOAIDS walkathon. Many of the students had arrived long before I did with my own son, a freshman at another high school in town.

My students—many of whom misbehaved, rarely arrived at school on time, and had not shown much academic promise—were present, prompt, and prepared not only to get a grade but also to fulfill a responsibility to the community. Yes, my students, whose encounters with the sheriff's department would have been less than positive in other situations, boarded the bus in anticipation of walking with others in solidarity with the fight against HIV and AIDS.

These 25 students, accompanied only by me and a student teacher, took their place in the crowd of walkers and runners who had gathered at a local park to raise funds. The crowd included individuals who had lost loved ones to AIDS, concerned citizens, politicians, families with children, researchers who were trying to find answers, and clinicians who were trying to treat persons with AIDS.

These students, many of whom had never been in this park located less than 10 miles from their homes, had solicited funds from classmates, teachers, and family members, completed prerequisite academic assignments, requested permission from parents and guardians, awakened early, arrived at the school promptly, then proudly and respectfully demonstrated what they were learning in class as they walked with thousands on that Sunday morning.

The students returned to school weary but proud, tired yet triumphant. They returned asking, "When are we going to do this again?" Students who had often been discounted by some teachers, peers, parents, and administrators reported to school the next day with an enthusiasm that was observed by some of those who had previously criticized them. Other students who had not participated asked about being included the next time.

The research findings of Murrell (2000, 2001), Hilliard (1997), Shujaa (1992, 1994), and other teacher education scholars have suggested an urgent need for schools of education to reexamine and refigure themselves to address the varied needs of the students their graduates serve. Too often, the teachers not only fail to met the needs of their students, but they also often seem ignorant of what they need to offer, and how.

The call for teachers trained with facility in building community relationships grows stronger. Murrell (2001) asserts that serious conversations about the renewal of teacher preparation may benefit from a program that is "community dedicated, research focused, [and] collaboration oriented" (p. 3). Such a program, in partnership with urban communities, would provide schools of education the opportunity to "draw on locally derived practical knowledge in order to develop vital, urban-focused, and community-committed teaching practices" (Murrell, 2001, p. 2). Murrell further states, "The success of urban school reform will depend, in part, on how the new national agenda makes good on its enthusiasm for creating new 'communities of learning,' embracing diversity, and preparing teachers through community and collaborative partnership" (Murrell, 2001, p. 2).

The kind of preparation proposed here situates prospective teachers in a learning environment where identified communities within schools of education—professional cohorts—collaborate with community-based organizations to learn the culture of the community represented by the pupils the preservice educators intend to teach. This preparation model recognizes the benefit of providing teachers with skill and knowledge to cultivate community at the onset of their careers. When teachers are trained to attend to the myriad of human issues their students inevitably bring into the classroom, including housing, health, and law, then they can transcend barriers to educating a student. When teachers genuinely listen to a student, create an environment where students express themselves freely, learn enough about a particular ethnic nuance to sincerely value it, seek insight from community members about the context in which students live, and routinely engage in other humane interactions, they can make subject matter relevant, select the most effective methodology for delivery, and develop other aspects of good teaching. Teachers prepared to cultivate community are likely to attend to HIV and AIDS prevention as a normal part of what they do.

CONNECTING AND EXPANDING COMMUNITY

Out of this unforgettable experience grew a project that resulted in students' being recognized for their leadership and participation in the NOAIDS walkathon. A group of civic leaders heard about what the students had done and saw an opportunity for a meaningful lesson not only in biology but also in civic responsibility.

The civic leaders met with the students and me to establish a framework for increasing the level of HIV/AIDS awareness. They discussed specific needs in the community related to HIV/AIDS. They decided to learn more together and to begin raising funds for infants and babies infected with HIV.

The ninth- through eleventh-grade students were becoming leaders in philanthropy and biology. Working with the civic leaders and with a representative from a local philanthropic agency, my students and I began fund-raising activities that included bake sales and school dances. The civic leaders and philanthropic representative agreed to match whatever funds the students raised.

I used every opportunity I saw as a teachable moment. Students worked after school, during lunch, and even several Friday nights to raise money and reinforce what they had learned in the classroom, from the textbooks, from field trips to pediatric wards for patients with HIV or AIDS, and from participation in walkathons. They had learned from observation, discussions, and reading that the little they knew about HIV/AIDS could begin to have a huge impact.

MY RECOMMENDATIONS AND SUGGESTIONS

My experiences as a teacher lead me to suggest some guidelines to help others cultivate community. First, teach students, not the subject. Share the information that students need to know in ways that are respectful, meaningful, useful, and sometimes fun. Approach teaching as if the students are your own children or grandchildren, your own siblings, your nieces or nephews, your next door neighbors—members of your community. This approach tranforms the teacher, student, and larger community.

Teach students from what I like to think of as a global perspective. We are not as far away from others geographically, culturally, or educationally as we sometimes think. The children we teach are as close to us as the next room, wherever the computer is in our homes.

Approach and teach students—the difficult, not so easily engaged, angry students—as if they might knock on your door someday asking, "Can your daughter come out and play with me?" That student who is easily distracted and misbehaves could possibly become the parent of your grandchild. What if his teacher, maybe you, had dismissed him and responded to him with minimal expectations, minimal positive exposure to the world of teaching and learning, and maximum negative remarks? What if he had missed the opportunity to be transformed by a great teacher? What then?

Teach outside the box (the classroom, the traditional expectations, and political, economic, and social constraints). Bring science to students and students to science. Expand students' knowledge base by bringing them to clinical laboratories, research facilities, and universities. Give students opportunities to participate in community-based fund-raising activities, such as AIDS Awareness Day and events sponsored by the March of Dimes, Heart Association of America, and others that have relevance to science.

Respect the mandates of educational policy, but remain mindful that policy is often decided outside of the actual classroom, outside of the day-to-day experiences of students and teachers most affected by it. Be a risk taker.

Review and become intimately familiar with science standards and strategies for teaching. Always seek opportunities to learn, develop professionally, and collaborate with colleagues, as well as others, outside of the classroom and school community. These activities will help us remember that although we are teachers, we don't know it all. Although we might know a lot, there is always something or some other way to do, learn, or experience that can benefit the teaching and learning process.

Reject the idea that students come to us as "empty vessels to be filled." They come already filled with experiences, knowledge, and skills that may require some refining, reframing, or reworking in order to be useful and productive in the larger society. They come to us with assets that can enhance and transform our lives as educators.

Consider that students "must be allowed the resource of the teacher's expert knowledge while being helped to acknowledge their own 'expertness' as well" (Delpit, 1988, p. 296).

Seek creative means to help students make the connections between theoretical science and applicable science. If action research is the route you choose, remember that the final action should reflect sound, meaningful, passionate, and compassionate teaching. Action research should not only convey numbers, statistical data, and raw data; it should also view students not as research subjects but as important people whose academic, social, and spiritual successes and failures will shape our future. Pursue action research not for the sake of your learning alone but toward the goal of improving teaching and learning.

The heart of the matter is not biology, nor human immunodeficiency virus, nor insufficient funds to study or treat diseases such as AIDS. The heart of the matter is the responsibility that university professors, scientists, teachers of teachers, educational policy makers, school district administrators, and classroom teachers have to students who are our children, our youth, our young adults, the parents of our grandchildren. We are responsible for teaching from our hearts to reach the hearts and minds of students so that their lives and the lives of future generations will be transformed.

We are responsible for teaching so that science becomes more than molecules, atoms, deoxyribonucleic acid, viral load, bacterial infection, or Gram stains. We are responsible for teaching so that science, specifically science about how HIV/AIDS is transmitted and affects families and communities, becomes relevant and related to other subjects as well. We are responsible for teaching so that a world without AIDS becomes the focus not only of research scientists but also of the classroom science teacher and of science students.

The heart of the matter is to make science real by teaching, informing, modeling, learning, and sharing in ways that transform students, even if only a few at a time. The heart of the matter is to teach so that school communities and the geographical areas in which they exist are transformed because of students' transformations. Ultimately, we are to teach so that a world without AIDS becomes a foreseeable reality, not merely a futuristic thought.

Green-Derry's passionate assertions prompt a very basic question: Why would a teacher want to take on HIV and AIDS prevention? Aren't the academic challenges of the classroom enough? And under what conditions could schools of education be compelled to infuse HIV and AIDS prevention into their curricula?

There is one sure way to prevent transmission of HIV: Practice safe behavior. One group of professionals has the reoccurring opportunity to influence most people's behavior: teachers. When teachers, at every opportunity, promote safe behaviors to students, they are influencing behavior. When students are informed in varied subject areas, on many grade levels, throughout their years of schooling, the likelihood that they will take the requisite action to stay safe may increase significantly. Teachers who work to prevent HIV and AIDS harness a power to transform the lives of students and the communities to which they belong.

Teacher educators who are principally responsible for cultivating the minds of young people have the unique opportunity to directly shape the future. They may consider this publication a personal invitation to do so.

REFERENCES

Bredo, E. (1994). *Situated cognition and Deweyian pragmatism.* Champaign, IL: Philosophy of Education Society. Retrieved October 17, 2005, from http://www.ed.uiuc.edu/EPS/PES-Yearbook/94_docs/bredo.htm.

Breitborde, M. (2002). Lessons learned in an urban school: Preparing teachers for the educational village. *The Teacher Educator* 38(1): 34–47.

Brown, S., Collins, A., and Duguid, P. (1989). Situated cognition and the culture of learning. *Educational Researcher* 18: 32–42.

Choi, J., and Hannafin, M. (1995). Situated cognition and learning environments: Roles, structures, and implications for design. *Educational Technology Research and Design* 43(2): 3–69.

Covello, L. (1958). *The heart is the teacher.* New York: McGraw-Hill.

Delpit, L. D. (1988). The silenced dialogue: Power and pedagogy in educating other people's children. *Harvard Educational Review* 58(3): 280–298.

Delpit, L. D. (1996). *Other people's children: Cultural conflict in the classroom.* Toronto: University of Toronto Press.

Freire, P. (2000 [1970]). *Pedagogy of the oppressed.* Trans. M. B. Ramos. New York: Continuum.

Gersten, R., and Baker, S. (1998). Real world use of scientific concepts: Integrating situated cognition with explicit instruction. *Exceptional Children* 65(1): 23–35.

Hilliard, A. G., III. (1997). Teacher education from an African American perspective. In J. J. Irvine, ed., *Critical knowledge for diverse teachers and learners* (pp. 125–148). Washington, DC: American Association of Colleges for Teacher Education.

Irvine, J. J. (1997). Location, location, location: A synthesis perspective on the knowledge base for urban teacher education. In J. J. Irvine, ed., *Critical knowledge for diverse teachers and learners* (pp. 217–222). Washington, DC: American Association of Colleges for Teacher Education.

Ladson-Billings, G. (1994). *The dreamkeepers: Successful teachers of African American children.* San Francisco: Jossey-Bass.

Lane, S., Lacefield-Parachini, N., and Isken, J. (2003). Developing novice teachers as change agents: Student teacher placements "against the grain." *Teacher Education Quarterly* 30(2): 55–68.

Lave, J., and Wenger, E. (1991). *Situated learnings: Legitimate peripheral participation.* Cambridge, England: Cambridge University Press.

Lieberman, A. (2000). Networks as learning communities: Shaping the future of teacher development. *Journal of Teacher Education* 51(3): 221–233.

Meier, D. (2002). *The power of their ideas: Lessons for America from a small school in Harlem.* Boston: Beacon (original work published in 1995).

Michael-Bandele, M. (1998). The African advantage: Using African culture to enhance culturally responsive comprehensive teacher education. In M. Dilworth, ed., *Being responsive to cultural differences: How teachers learn* (pp. 78–93). Thousand Oaks, CA: Corwin.

Murrell, P. C., Jr. (2000). Community teachers: A conceptual framework for preparing exemplary urban teachers. *Journal of Negro Education* 69(4): 338–348.

Murrell, P. C., Jr. (2001). *The community teacher: A new framework for effective urban teaching.* New York: Teachers College Press.

Nieto, S. (2000). Placing equity front and center: Some thoughts on transforming teacher education for a new century. *Journal of Teacher Education* 51(3): 180–187.

Nieto, S., and Rolon, C. (1997). Preparation and professional development of teachers: A perspective from two Latinas. In J. J. Irvine, ed., *Critical knowledge for diverse teachers and learners* (pp. 89–124). Washington, DC: American Association of Colleges for Teacher Education.

Noddings, N. (2002). *Educating moral people: A caring alternative to character education.* New York: Teachers College Press.

Pang, V. O. (1997). Caring for the whole child: Asian Pacific American students. In J. J. Irvine, ed., *Critical knowledge for diverse teachers and learners* (pp. 149–188). Washington, DC: American Association of Colleges for Teacher Education.

Shujaa, M. J. (1992). Afrocentric transformation and parental choice in African American Independent Schools. *Journal of Negro Education* 61(2): 148–159.

Shujaa, M. J. (1994). Education and schooling: Can you have one without the other? In M. J. Shujaa, ed., *Too much schooling, too little education: A paradox in Black life in White societies* (pp. 13–36). Trenton, NJ: African World Press.

Wenger, E. (1999). *Communities of practice: Learning, meaning, and identity.* Cambridge, England: Cambridge University Press.

Wilson, A. L. (1993). The promise of situated cognition. *New Directions for Adults and Continuing Education* 57: 71–79.

17

A CONVERSATION ON HIV/AIDS EDUCATION AND TEACHER EDUCATION IN SCIENCE AND MATHEMATICS

Bill Rosenthal and Elaine V. Howes

✑

To say that we, the authors, are neophytes in the field of HIV/AIDS prevention is to understate the case. Neither of us has scholarly expertise in the field. Howes, a biologist, has created and taught courses in science teacher education, and Rosenthal, a mathematician, has done the same in mathematics. While we have both made efforts to address sociopolitical issues in these courses, we have never devoted attention specifically to HIV/AIDS. We avidly keep current on developments in science, and we are comfortable with such terms as *retroviral, immunodeficient, T-cells,* and *logistic growth curve and the resultant steady-state population.* We anticipate that our readers are also teacher educators who have limited contact with HIV/AIDS issues in their professional practices.

Because we believe that the writer–reader relationship is pedagogical, that all pedagogy is dialogic, and that a dialogue with a text ensues when a reader is engaged, we hope to initiate a conversation with our readers. (Even if we had the technical expertise to write a how-to treatise on addressing HIV/AIDS-related issues in science and mathematics teacher education classrooms, we would be disinclined to outline a definitive program for readers to follow.) We shall engage in conversation on teaching teachers to teach mathematics and science—fields in which we claim a critical mass of professional knowledge—and on the realm of HIV/AIDS prevention, with which we are less familiar. As we begin, we hold ourselves to a principle that we impose on our students. As elegantly stated by one of Rosenthal's students a decade ago, this concept reads, "Questions before answers." We pose, therefore, a central question: *How can teachers create curriculum so that they and their students will learn symbiotically about HIV/AIDS, about important science and mathematics concepts and skills, and about their local communities?*

Please notice the phrasing, *How can teachers create* .... In this chapter, we do not include ready-made lessons, units, activities, exercises, or "tasks" for teacher educators or for practicing teachers. We have never done curriculum production on behalf of others absent the participation of those others. Instead, in a manner similar to the way we guide our students in their instructional planning, we will generate ideas meant for your use in developing specific answers to our central question. We will offer experiments, principles, and reflections concerning science and mathematics education courses as sites in which teachers can create curriculum through which the teaching and learning of HIV/AIDS, subject matter, and the local community are intertwined and mutually supported. We will end our cross-disciplinary conversation with a set of principles to guide science and mathematics teacher educators in creating community-sensitive curriculum that addresses HIV/AIDS. In the next section, we reveal the tenets that undergird our own practice and that structure and shape this chapter.

WORKING TENETS FOR OUR PEDAGOGY AND THIS CHAPTER

Neither of us specializes in curriculum theory or curriculum studies. Nevertheless, as educators of teachers, we adhere to a strong set of beliefs about curriculum (and related matters) as we discuss issues concerning the intersection of (a) HIV/AIDS-related consciousness raising, (b) learning about communities, and (c) educating teachers to teach science and mathematics. We offer the following enumeration of ideas most germane to this chapter.

1. We subscribe fully to the maxim, "Curriculum is that which students have the opportunity to learn" (McCutcheon, 1988).
2. No matter how "teacher-proof" purveyors of mass-market curriculum materials attempt to render their wares, classroom teachers are cocreators of the curricula they enact. In particular, teachers are always "instructional curriculum gatekeepers" (Thornton, 2004).

3. Mathematics and science teacher education classrooms should be sites for learning about society, culture, politics, economics, and philosophy.

4. Practicing teachers should take the lead in creating that which their students learn (Clandinin and Connelly, 1992; Schubert, 1986).

5. Mathematics and science teacher education classrooms should be sites for learning mathematics and science content.

6. Lessons, activities, experiments, and tasks are too narrow to be the basic elements of curriculum. The material to which students are exposed should be larger in scope, and more time should be allotted (e.g., units and long-term investigations can be undertaken, or a topic can be threaded through the entire year). Lessons, activities, experiments, and tasks should be developed within larger curricular structures, and learning objectives should pertain to the larger elements, not to individual lessons.

7. Many of the contexts presented as real-life situations in mathematics and science are fabricated—potentially realistic yet not real to students. Although we find value in such situations and often create them ourselves, we insist on distinguishing them from what we term *actual real-life situations* involving actual settings and data, often drawn from students' own lives.

8. Because learning happens (for better or for worse) in the present tense, we think of objectives as that which students are working on learning, not what students should have learned by the end of a curricular element. Although it is productive (and necessary) to plan and teach in terms of desired learning, it is artificial to insist that learning be manifested by a particular date. Such insistence is contraindicated for human cognitive development.

9. Practicing teachers are de facto teacher educators who typically contribute as much to teacher candidates' learning as do their higher education counterparts. Thus, when we speak of teacher educators in this chapter, we embrace school-based as well as college- and university-based personnel.

10. Controversy is pedagogically generative.

A SAMPLER OF EXTANT WORK PERTINENT TO OUR CENTRAL QUESTION

Rather than offering a comprehensive literature review, we will consider examples of scholarship that has informed our thinking. Before specifically discussing HIV/AIDS education, we will temporarily broaden the playing field to consider sources for teacher educators seeking to link sociopolitical issues to teaching and teacher education in mathematics and science. Work in this field near the end of the twentieth century typically used the terms *critical, radical,* and *democratic;* over the past 5 years, much of the scholarship has been collected under the heading *social justice.*[1] The voluminous literature on equity and diversity in science and mathematics education incorporates much relevant material as well. Prominent works relating teacher education in general to societal matters include Cochran-Smith (1999), *Radical Teacher* (2002; 2002–2003), and Michelli and Keiser (2005; this reference contains a chapter on science but none on mathematics).

In mathematics education, Gutstein and Peterson (2005) offer a state-of-the-art compilation of prospects for connecting mathematics teaching and learning to contemporary societal, political, and economic concerns. In science education, Barton and colleagues (2003) relate accounts and analyze after-school programs in which children and adults create science knowledge and practices that pertain to their lives in urban settings. Broad strands of science education studies under the headings of science-technology-society (Aikenhead, 2000, 2003; Bybee, 1993) and science-technology-society-environment (Pedretti, 2003) address connections between science and society as they are or could be taught in schools. More specifically, the use of "socioscientific issues" in the science classroom allows students to learn content as well as to examine the connections between contemporary scientific issues and society (Zeidler, 2003). Such socioscientific issues provide an ideal setting for the discussion of communicative diseases. Turner and Strawhun (2004–2005) formulate a sterling example of putting actual real-life issues to work in promoting brand-new subject matter rather than applying concepts and skills already studied in other contexts, as is much more common. This curricular use of the real world is precisely what we promote for teaching teachers.

Although none of these works is explicitly directed toward teacher education, many of the authors use the materials and instructional strategies explicated in their chapters to educate teachers. We are unaware of any full-length published books or monographs wholly dedicated to the use of actual real-life issues in mathematics/science teacher education. Rodriguez and Kitchen (2005) present a series of essays in which teacher educators discuss their efforts to address students' resistance to learning to teach for diversity; although a valuable resource and theoretical background text, this volume does not include the teaching of specific science or mathematics content within such contexts. The many articles and chapters in this area include Vithal (2003) and our own modest experiments and reflections (Howes, 2005; Rosenthal, 2005). Other wonderful work draws on the intersection of everyday contexts and sociopolitical issues with science and mathematics curricula. Mistrik and Thul (1993) and Thul (1997) are delightful compilations of mathematics problems set in contexts no commercial publisher would go near. There are curricula designed to support teaching about the environment and globalization—areas most likely to lend themselves to teaching about epidemics and diseases and their relationships to social conditions such as war and famine (see also Ballin, 1993; Bigelow and Peterson, 2002; Grant and Littlejohn, 2001).

Many of the materials cited speak to linking mathematics and science teachers and their curricula with the specific urban neighborhoods, rural expanses, and indigenous lands they serve. Vithal (2003) shows a splendid recent example in mathematics-teacher education. We also are most impressed by the work that has emerged in connection with the *funds of knowledge* paradigm (Gruenewald, 2003; Moje et al., 2004; Moll, Amanti, Neff, and González, 1992; Warren, Ballenger, Ogonowski, Rosebery, and Hudicourt-Barnes, 2001).

One of our key intentions is to use science and mathematics methods classes to broaden and deepen students' subject-matter knowledge. We must note, however, that although there are countless published studies on teachers' content knowledge, particularly pedagogical content knowledge, we have found little empirical work on the deliberate use of mathematics and science methods as venues for subject-matter learning, either in elementary or in secondary schools.

Our search of the main journals in science education research indicates that if teacher educators are teaching about HIV/AIDS, they are not writing about it. More likely, HIV/AIDS education is considered the purview of health education and, thus, is not on the minds of most science teacher educators. Nonetheless, recommendations for teaching about HIV/AIDS at the high school level are put forth by the National Science Teachers Association (NSTA) under the aegis of sexuality and human reproduction in a position statement, which states, "Methods to prevent the acquisition of HIV, herpes, and other STIs (sexually transmitted infections) must also be included in the instruction and information made available to students" (NSTA, 2000). Because nothing similar appears in the many position statements on the association's Web site, the following sentence in NSTA's position statement becomes notable: "It is important that this instruction be ... conducted by qualified teachers" (NSTA, 2000). If that isn't a broad hint aimed at teacher educators, it is certainly an indication that we should play some role in preparing "qualified teachers" to teach appropriately about HIV/AIDS.

We close this section with attention to the three groups with the most influence on issues pertinent to our central question: writers of standards, creators of commercial curricula for schools, and authors of textbooks for science and mathematics teacher education. Although standards documents pertaining to science and mathematics inevitably stress the value of authentically joining these disciplines with societal issues, this honorable rhetoric has yet to become visible in the materials used in schools and schools of education. It is no surprise that major publishers who wish to avoid controversy do not introduce such matters as skyrocketing child-poverty rates and sexually transmitted diseases into mathematics and science curricula unless absolutely necessary. Overall, the creators of mass-market materials in our fields appear to be averse to actual real-life situations, preferring instead simulations, hypotheticals, and contrivances. Some late-model project-based curriculum programs in both mathematics and science are an exception to such avoidance, although controversial matters are hard to come by even there. One notable exception to this rule is a prescribed HIV/AIDS high school curriculum (DiSpezio, 2000). Given its attention to the issue in its position statement, it is not surprising that NSTA published this curriculum.

The song remains the same with textbooks in science and mathematics education. It is rare to find a mathematics methods book that mentions incorporating examples with sociopolitical content, much less one that advocates and teaches how to use mathematics as a vehicle for learning about society. Because science content often is unavoidably entangled with the outside world, the situation is marginally better in that subject area. Overall, however, the massive force exerted by mainstream materials on science and mathematics leaves us more than a bit discouraged.

REAL PEOPLE WITH REAL PROPOSALS:
THE VOICES OF PRACTITIONERS

The experience and wisdom of numerous constituencies should be solicited to create HIV/AIDS curriculum for teacher education courses. Primary among these constituents are (a) secondary school science, mathematics, and health teachers; (b) elementary school teachers; (c) teacher educators involved in HIV/AIDS education; (d) higher-education–based health care professionals involved in HIV/AIDS education, prevention, and care; (e) community-based health care providers involved in HIV/AIDS education, prevention, and care; and (f) individuals living with HIV/AIDS. For this chapter, we contacted secondary school science teachers, higher-education–based health care professionals, and community-based health care providers. The most immediate and enthusiastic responses came from the higher–education-based health care professionals; they are, therefore, best represented here. Secondary school science teachers and one elementary school teacher provided their impressions of and concerns about teaching HIV/AIDS. We summarize what we found from these two groups below.

Higher-Education-Based Health Care Professionals

We contacted 12 infectious-disease specialists, and we received responses from five. All of the contacted health care professionals were supportive of our effort. We posed three questions to them:

1. What do you think it is important for teachers to know about HIV/AIDS?
2. If you were to teach these teachers about HIV/AIDS, how would you go about doing so?
3. In what ways do you believe it is appropriate and/or useful for teachers and their students to engage in their local community concerning HIV/AIDS?

The second question yielded little of interest; we summarize responses to questions 1 and 3 below.

All health professionals agreed on the importance of having teachers learn the biology of HIV/AIDS: how it is transmitted, its viral life cycle, and its epidemic proportions. They also agreed that teachers must be prepared to "bust myths" about HIV/AIDS. Tightly connected to these biological themes is a strong recommendation that teachers be able to teach HIV/AIDS prevention methods. The "ABC" strategy was mentioned twice, with a minor disagreement: The first respondent believed that the A for *abstinence* and the B for *be faithful to one partner* should be stressed and that educators should "reserve the C [for *condoms*] when the A and B is not accepted or adhered to." His colleague responded, "I agree ... that the ABCs of HIV are basic—teaching how not to get infected. But I think he underweighs the potential benefits of C. The problem is that none of these or any other behavioral interventions is likely to be followed as rigorously as needed to prevent HIV, so all are needed."

Concerns surfaced about restrictions on discussing sexuality; these health professionals stated that teachers who are comfortable with the topic, as well as morally nonjudgmental, are best suited to teaching about HIV/AIDS. However, these professionals recognize, as do teachers, that prevailing political attitudes do not welcome discussing sexuality in public school classrooms. Nonetheless, the issue remains vitally important; as one respondent said, "It's critical to have an open discussion about what SEX is: any penetration (oral or anal as well as vaginal) by anyone of either sex!"

The professionals' recommendations for working with the community included sending students into the community as well as bringing community experts into the classroom. Specifically, Dr. Sandra G. Gompf, section chief of the Division of Infectious Diseases and Tropical Medicine at the University of South Florida's College of Medicine, suggested that having students "meet infected individuals of varied backgrounds, who are willing, who can describe their personal experiences upon learning of their infection, and of living with HIV" and/or "having them 'shadow' a physician or nurse in an HIV clinic and have an opportunity to ask questions ... may be an eye-opener for those who believe the stereotypes." She added that "personalizing and humanizing this topic is very important because no one ever expects to get HIV." Other respondents recommended that community representatives come into the classroom (including fund raisers for HIV work) as another way to "raise awareness" and inspire discussion.

We find these suggestions enormously useful, particularly those that get the students out into the community. Even more useful is our new understanding that professionals working in HIV/AIDS treatment and research would welcome partnerships that work to educate teachers and children.

Secondary School Science Teachers

Our secondary school educator informants believed that HIV/AIDS could provide an intriguing context within which to teach about the immune system, about viruses, and about human reproduction and sexuality. They did not feel, however, that teaching about HIV/AIDS would be welcome in their mandated local science curriculum. Teaching about HIV/AIDS is generally the responsibility of the school's health educator or of a visiting teacher who delivers short-term HIV/AIDS instruction. In one large county, the science teachers in schools whose budgets disallow this luxury use a premade curriculum. The foci of this curriculum are risk reduction, abstinence, and factual information that addresses misconceptions about the disease.

One middle school teacher gave the following account: "I really don't teach HIV/AIDS education in the classroom. It comes up once during our unit on bacteria and viruses, but only if a student picks it for their research project. We did have an all-school play this year on the topic of HIV/AIDS. A local thespian group came and did a play for our middle school students and then it was discussed in the classrooms following the play."

Thus, for reasons ranging from lack of time in the mandated curriculum to parental and political disincentives toward discussing sexuality in the classroom (including direct restrictions on such) to the use of drop-in programs, the teaching of HIV/AIDS in the science classroom seems rarely to be approached directly.

However, these teachers are sensitive to their students' interests, including their sexual activity and their concerns about pregnancy and disease. When learning an HIV/AIDS curriculum, as with learning anything related to human sexuality, students' personal concerns about their own sexuality arise. When we asked another middle school teacher what she would want preservice teachers to learn about teaching HIV/AIDS, she stated that "knowing your kids" was most important because in the context of HIV/AIDS instruction, students will "bring their real lives in." The teacher needs to be ready to support her students emotionally and socially, as well as intellectually; within the context of teaching about possible risks associated with sexuality, this support or lack thereof can make a serious difference in an adolescent's life.

In agreement with the health professional cited above, a teacher of eighth-grade science stated, "If you throw [HIV/AIDS education] in with all the science stuff it's going to get lost ... they tune out." She said that she might use HIV as an example in a unit on viruses. This insertion seemed like a stretch to her, however; she argued that "these kids need a health class" because they are "in transition," physically, socially, and emotionally. This statement implies that health class is a more sensible place to teach about HIV/AIDS than is a science class.

None of this feedback should suggest that preservice teachers for elementary and secondary school should not learn about HIV/AIDS. They undoubtedly will encounter students who are living with HIV/AIDS or who have someone close to them who is. For this reason alone—aside from education's role in helping young people avoid contagion in the first place—"it is necessary for educators to have a working knowledge of the disease, its course, and the various modes of transmission, as well as the ... needs of children and youth with the disease" (Stinnett, Cruce, and Choate, 2004, p. 211). Arguably, knowledge will allow understanding and reduce prejudice; teachers, as do adults in the general population, have varying attitudes toward people with HIV/AIDS. Not all of these attitudes are positive. Some stem from moralistic judgments concerning sexual behaviors and drug use, which "suggests that information and objectivity about course of infection in teacher education students might need to be targeted to decrease depreciatory judgments about these children and youth" (Stinnett, et al., 2004, p. 217).

Part of our role as teacher educators is to help our students know their students and to set up classroom communities in which open discussion is possible. Science and mathematics classrooms are not advertised as caring places, but as one teacher stated, they must be. In the trenchant words of another health care professional, "Trying to do anything about HIV without the intellectual freedom to discuss sexual issues is useless, sterile intellectualism."

EXPERIMENTS WE WOULD LOVE TO TRY

Neither author has practiced a concrete response to our central question; that is, we have not used mathematics- and science-teacher education as a laboratory for developing curriculum that fosters the symbiotic learning of HIV/AIDS prevention, subject matter, and the local community. Nor are we acquainted with scholarship that responds directly to the central question. To make our abstract ideas concrete, therefore, we have devised some *Gedankenexperiments* (thought experiments), a term popularized by Albert Einstein. These experiments provide the foundation for the hard work we anticipate doing with our students in addressing the central question.

Change and Community in High School Mathematics

From the counting sequence itself to advanced calculus and beyond, the quantification of change is at the heart of mathematics. One of the welcome developments in present-day mathematics education is concerted attention to describing changing quantities in a variety of discursive modes. This approach contrasts with traditional modes such as formulas (e.g., the formula $h = -16t^2 + 400$ tells us the height "*h*" after "*t*" seconds of a ball dropped from a height of 400 feet under the absurd assumption of no air resistance and the even more absurd assumption that the ball is zero-dimensional). Graphs and tables also are traditionally used. Verbal descriptions also express change (i.e., "the changes in the height continue, but they go up by 32 each time"). The ubiquitous presence of changing quantities both in and outside school mathematics lends this broad topic unlimited potential as a wellspring for curricular experimentation of the sort we are considering.

In high school mathematics, and sometimes earlier, students are taught to quantify change by classifying changes into various categories. The simplest category of change is usually called *linear* change (in everyday language, *constant* change). This category comprises quantities that change at a steady rate. For example, "If I stash a $20 bill under my mattress every Friday night and the mattress pays me no interest, each week the amount stashed under the mattress goes up by $20," or "The circumference of this circular string increases by a little more than 3.14 inches each time I increase the circle's diameter by an inch." The name *linear* comes from the fact that the graphs of quantities that change in this fashion are straight lines.

After linear change, the next level of complexity may be either *quadratic* change or *exponential* change. The most common example of quadratic change is probably the hackneyed one just mentioned about a ball being dropped at a specific time and height. Quadratic change is a good match for some HIV/AIDS-related circumstances (see Winter,

2003, which considers the number of deaths attributed to AIDS in the United States between 1981 and 2001 as a case of quadratic change). So is the category called exponential change. In arenas outside of mathematics, we frequently hear "exponential growth" used as a synonym for explosive or uncontrollable growth—"That exurban region has grown exponentially over the past few years." As used more technically, however, the term *exponential* need not refer to rapid change; rather, the term is a twist on the category of linear change. A quantity grows linearly when it is *added to* (or subtracted from) at a steady amount—for example, $20 each week; 789 new cases of AIDS every year; or 500,000 fewer barrels of oil each day. A quantity grows exponentially when it gets *multiplied by* a steady amount—for example, twice as much each week, 2.3 times as many new cases of AIDS every year, half as much Carbon-14 each 8 minutes. *Linear* is a label for growth that steadily adds, *exponential* a descriptor for growth that steadily multiplies. In particular, when a quantity changes over time at a set percentage, that's exponential change. Ever since the doomsayer Malthus projected that unconstrained human population would increase exponentially while resources would grow only linearly, demographers and epidemiologists have found the exponential-growth category to be a good match for many population- and disease-related phenomena. They also know (as did Malthus, and as many mathematics curriculum writers have yet to learn) that populations don't grow and diseases don't spread in an unconstrained fashion. Often, populations grow—and the number of individuals infected with a disease increases—exponentially at first. Then, however, the limits on growth (e.g., food supply, improved drugs) kick in. Instead of continuing to multiply by the same amount over the same time period, the population or infection rate will begin to grow at a slower rate, eventually leveling off. These actual real-life situations make for a category of change generally called *logistic*.

We have, then, four categories of change: linear, quadratic, exponential, and logistic. The first three are staples of school mathematics. Until recently, logistic growth was absent from school curriculum, with the probable exception of enrichment questions and honors projects. Recently, the logistic category has made inroads into high school curricula. As a result, it no longer makes sense to study the category of exponential change without considering in tandem logistic change (in addition to linear and quadratic change). Any of these categories of change is rightly related to HIV/AIDS.

Here, then, is the *Gedankenexperiment* we would love to upgrade from pure *Gedanken* to applied experiment. Teacher education students would create units on the mathematical topic of different categories of change. All of our actual real-life data would come from HIV/AIDS-associated circumstances such as changes in the total number of HIV-positive individuals over time, changes in the month-to-month rates of new HIV infections and full-blown AIDS cases, and changes in the yearly and cumulative number of deaths from AIDS. In terms of our central question concerning the mutual learning of subject matter, HIV/AIDS, and the local community, the mathematical potential of this *Gedankenexperiment* is significant. Few if any secondary school mathematics teachers and teacher candidates have been exposed to logistic change. Considering this underconsidered category alongside the other three categories of change, teacher candidates can explore fresh conceptual and mechanical learning that can be related directly to the mathematics they will have to teach.

How would the teacher educator formulate objectives, goals, aims, and purposes toward learning about HIV/AIDS through this unit planning? Such planning cannot be undertaken successfully without connecting with and listening to the teacher education constituencies from whom we heard in the previous section.

The possibilities for learning about local communities are somewhat clearer. The logistic-change category is being introduced into high school mathematics, and it is usually taught together with exponential and other types of change. Many such curricular innovations entail HIV/AIDS (see Wheat Ridge [Colorado] High School, n.d.). The examples we have located draw on large-scale data such as statewide, nationwide, and global statistics, models, and projections. Perhaps secondary school mathematics students could embed their units in a particular local community (or in more than one, for productive contrast). To determine what work those students would undertake with respect to the community, we would have to consult and coplan with its representatives.

This *Gedankenexperiment* affords one subtle, revelatory opportunity to learn. When we file a particular situation into a general category of change, we must simplify or ignore many of the situation's details. This process of simplification-ignoration is deeply woven into the hidden curriculum of school mathematics. For instance, to decide into which category to place the change in the total number of HIV-positive individuals living in the United States since 1981, students would be given (or told to look up) a table of these numbers as they changed over the years. No other data or factors would be considered admissible. Furthermore, it is unlikely that the stripped-down quality of the allowable information would be brought to the surface.

Secondary school mathematics students often are willing to accept mowing down a complex context to a single number. Real people in real local communities might not be so sanguine about having their circumstances thus reduced. A nurse could insist that a needle-reduction program be factored into the calculations; a community elder might be adamant that attention must be paid to gentrification that pushes long-time residents out of the neighborhood. In addition to learning about a community itself, students who collect and make sense of data from actual persons become uniquely knowledgeable about their communities and broaden their horizons on the use of mathematics outside of the Platonic realm.

Community members' mathematical thinking is much closer to that of secondary students than to that of their teachers. When teachers hear firsthand that these persons value more than a single raw set of numbers, the teacher candidates and the teachers are potentially enlightened by these cognitive and epistemological differences.

Through teaching classes in elementary school mathematics education, Rosenthal became aware of the predilection of most people to consider contextual factors washed (and wished) away by quantification. This realization resulted from an investigation in an elementary mathematics content course that arose from the central question, "How can we predict the U.S. population 100 years from now?" (One of the purposes of this investigation is to contrast the linear- and exponential-change categories.) This investigation, however, should be replaced by one whose driving question is, "How can we predict the number of HIV-positive individuals in East Harlem 20 years from now?"

HIV Transmission and Science Teacher Education

Curriculum planning, in some form, is included in Howes's elementary and secondary methods courses. Students begin the process of curriculum planning with a concept that they want their students to learn, rather than with a topic. The distinction is that a concept is explanatory; this being science, concepts are ideas that explain natural phenomena.

Topics are areas of study that could include or allow the teaching of varied concepts. For example, the topic of apples might help students learn about plant life cycles, fermentation, gravity, and color.

Just as with the topic of apples, there are myriad scientific concepts one could teach through the model or example of HIV/AIDS, including the workings of the immune system; the properties, genetics, and transmission of viruses in and among human and nonhuman populations; and the biology of sexuality. In addition, the health professionals with whom we consulted believed that the science of HIV/AIDS *is* important to teach. Their focus was on the transmission of the disease; this focus, in turn, is linked to HIV/AIDS educators' desire to dispel myths (particularly about its transmission) and to induce behavior change.

As a biology teacher, Howes wanted to help students learn the science that would help them understand HIV/AIDS. What science would be most appropriate for this effort? There is no simple answer. But responses we received from health professionals indicate that transmission of the virus is an important aspect of HIV/AIDS education. If behavior change is the goal (along with dispelling myths), then HIV/AIDS transmission appears to be a good focus for teaching the science of HIV/AIDS. Perhaps learning the science will make transmission more believable and thus reinforce behavior changes and dispel misinformation. In addition, learning about HIV/AIDS may help preservice students to treat any HIV-positive students they encounter with respect and understanding and to help their students learn to do the same.

According to the Centers for Disease Control and Prevention, "The ways in which HIV can be transmitted have been clearly identified. Unfortunately, false information or statements that are not supported by scientific findings continue to be shared widely through the Internet or popular press" (2003, para. 1). Preservice teachers are as likely as anyone to be exposed to, and possibly concerned or puzzled by, these myths about transmission. Teaching about the transmission of HIV from a scientific perspective that focuses specifically upon how viruses pass from one person to another may help to address these myths. Such a perspective also supports the teachers' development of a nonprejudicial attitude toward those they encounter who are living with HIV/AIDS.

Because teacher education students will be familiar with the effects of the cold virus and because they will be working with children—the population that contracts more colds a year than any other—it makes sense to begin with a study of how the cold virus is transmitted. The transmission of a virus is related to what the virus needs to survive between hosts, as well as to where it multiplies within the host. Cold viruses and HIV are different in this way; cold viruses can remain contagious outside of their host, while HIV is destroyed by exposure to air and can multiply only within its host. Hand-to-hand contact, kissing, and other close contact can transmit the cold virus, but this immediate physical contact between people is not necessary for transmission. The cold virus can be transmitted, therefore, through casual as well as noncasual contact. For example, cold viruses are spread through coughing and sneezing because they live in the mucous of the nose of the person who is carrying them; some of these particles are expelled through coughing and sneezing. One can also pick up a cold from sharing a drink or by touching a doorknob or other surface and then touching one's mouth or eyes. The virus also can also be transmitted through hand-to-hand contact (especially among children, as they are more likely to touch their noses, mouths, and eyes than are adults). Thus, we teach children to cover their mouths when they sneeze, avoid sharing drinks with sick people, and wash their hands regularly. In fact, since Lister figured out that women who went to midwives rather than to hospitals died less often of childbed fever because midwives washed their hands, regular hand washing has been shown to be the very best way to avoid contracting viruses that cause colds.

The HIV virus is not as easy to transmit as are cold viruses. It loses its contagious abilities when it meets air or water. It lives[2] best in body fluids such as blood, semen, and vaginal excretions; although it may be present in other body fluids, it reaches high enough concentrations to infect another person in these three fluids. Thus, HIV can be transmitted through sex (vaginal, anal, and oral sex), through the sharing of infected needles, and through blood transfusions. It also can be passed from a pregnant woman to her fetus. HIV can be transmitted from one person to another if an open wound encounters the blood of an infected person. Health care workers (those who would be most likely to encounter such a situation) take precautions that disallow the transmission of HIV from one person to another through nonsexual contact; however, unbroken skin provides a very good barrier to infection, including to HIV. In addition, in the United States, the blood supply is now tested for HIV; therefore, its transmission through transfusions is vanishingly unlikely.

As mentioned earlier, students should also be supported in explicitly addressing myths regarding transmission—those to which they themselves subscribe, as well as those maintained and multiplied via tabloids and the Internet. We would certainly include the following myths:

Myth 1: Mosquitoes carry HIV.

Scientific Refutation of Myth 1: When mosquitoes bite, they leave behind a chemical that coagulates the blood. Then, they go off to digest their meals; they do not immediately go on to bite another person. Mosquitoes, in addition, are not good hosts for HIV. There is no evidence of anyone's contracting HIV from a mosquito.

Myth 2: You can get HIV from a toilet seat.

Scientific Refutation of Myth 2: HIV does not survive exposure to air and water. It cannot multiply outside a living host. There is no evidence of anyone's contracting HIV from the environment. Noncasual contact with an infected person through sex or sharing needles is the most common way that HIV is transmitted.

Myth 3: You can get HIV from saliva (e.g., if someone spits on you).

Scientific Refutation of Myth 3: It is very unlikely that HIV will be transmitted through saliva. Saliva contains chemicals that destroy HIV; thus, there are very few viral particles in saliva. In addition, there is no evidence that "HIV is spread through sweat, tears, urine, or feces" (National Institute of Allergy and Infectious Diseases, 2005).

Elementary School Science Teacher Education and Learning About HIV/AIDS

How would we create a curriculum in which science teacher candidates have the opportunity to learn about the transmission of HIV? First, students could be asked to write privately about their knowledge, experiences, and questions concerning HIV/AIDS. They then could be required to contact local health workers to find answers to their questions. An initial goal would be to help students avoid embarrassment through representing common myths concerning HIV/AIDS. Many Web sites address common myths and provide straightforward information on the transmission of HIV. Finally, a community expert could share her or his knowledge and experience with the class. One very useful recommendation from a survey respondent was that we have students shadow a doctor, nurse, or other healthcare professional during a day of working with HIV/AIDS patients. This shadowing would have to include reflection and ideally should include multiple experiences (more than one day, more than one health care site), as mere exposure without challenging one's own initial beliefs could lead to the reinforcement of prejudices. In addition, a health care professional recommends spending time as a volunteer with people living with HIV/AIDS; fear and prejudice may be ameliorated by personalizing the disease. Then, armed with accurate knowledge and the ability to recognize common myths and how to refute them, students would consult with teachers in the elementary schools concerning their positions on treating (or not) the topic of HIV/AIDS in their classrooms.

Most likely, elementary school teachers will suggest that we not teach about HIV/AIDS directly with children. In fact, two of our health professional respondents said that middle school would be the earliest that they would teach about HIV/AIDS. This attitude, however, does not mean that elementary school teachers will not encounter HIV/AIDS in some form or another. Sending the topic of HIV/AIDS underground when it arises in their students' lives or questions will only support the repression of knowledge that fosters the spread of the disease. Open discussion can help children to adopt nonblaming attitudes toward those (in their lives and otherwise) living with HIV/AIDS. As related to us by an elementary teacher respondent, "It's most important that the child feels his or her feelings are heard and feelings are validated" and to know that "kids have learned that you got AIDS because you were bad." Myths and prejudices are picked up early in life. It's wise to address them just as early.

PRINCIPLES FOR SCIENCE AND MATHEMATICS TEACHER EDUCATORS

Teach Ourselves

Because no two communities are the same, teachers and teacher educators should get to know their communities.[3] We are always telling our students this. We need to put our actions where our mouths are. The higher-education-based health care professionals with whom we consulted work together in the same community. Therefore, their knowledge and experiences pertain to that community; it is likely that other communities would share different concepts and approaches. This example stresses the importance of teacher educators getting to know their community representatives and their shared knowledge and experiences in the course of planning community-based (or at least community-linked) curriculum.

The authors have benefited from teaching themselves more science and mathematics. Rosenthal didn't know about logistic change until after completing a Ph.D. in mathematics, and until recently, he held the misconception that the quadratic change category could never fit with HIV/AIDS. Howes "went to school" on viral transmission in the course of writing this chapter. Each author has more mathematics and science to study before braving the classroom with their *Gedankenexperiments*.

Recruit Allies

In general, the inability of teacher educators to work in a thorough and ongoing fashion with community-based workers is an indication of our larger struggle to break out of the academy and recruit nonacademicians as co-teacher educators. Our first contacts were fellow college-based health care professionals; this was a comfortable place for us to begin. Our university colleagues turned out to have educational concerns and experiences that we, as educators ourselves, recognized. These experts can serve as connections to community HIV/AIDS educators and community-health groups farther from our familiar surroundings in the academy. This experience of collaboration has helped us to recognize that we may expect too much of our students too soon. We would do well to support them in beginning with the familiar before reaching out to the unknown in their work communities. In addition, we know that our *Gedankenexperiments* will not work well without both the local knowledge of community-based workers and the curricular knowledge of practicing teachers.

Personalize the Disease

Although it seems logical, we would not have developed this principle without the help of our health care respondents. Over time and using ongoing individual and group reflection, teachers can develop situations in which students get to know people living with HIV/AIDS, as well as encountering the medical and social workers who support them. Such interaction can help students move beyond their fears and prejudices. As Dr. Gompf argued, "Having them meet infected individuals of varied backgrounds, who are willing, who can describe their personal experiences upon learning of their infection, and of living with HIV ... may be an eye-opener for those who believe the stereotypes." Because moving beyond the stereotypes is central to educating teachers to care for *all* of their children, this aspect of HIV/AIDS teacher education appears particularly pertinent.

Don't Let Teaching and Learning About HIV/AIDS Get Lost

Teachers could employ HIV/AIDS to teach numerous scientific and mathematical concepts; however, these concepts could be taught with other models as well. It is not necessary to use HIV/AIDS to teach about the immune system, about viruses, about change, or about population dynamics. Teaching about HIV/AIDS, however, can best be accomplished by teaching about HIV/AIDS. Perhaps because the epidemic is so immediate, our concern for our students overwhelms concerns for learning traditional content. As one of our health-professional respondents said, "Of course students should know what a virus is, what RNA is, etc. But in addition to having an 'HIV training lecture' that lasts an hour and then ends, HIV education could be a continuous process involving lots of exposures ... as much as I find the mechanisms of RNA self-cleavage and chain termination by thymidine analogs fascinating, [students must] put scientific/techni-cal knowledge into a social, 'everyday' context. And this context can facilitate behavior change."

We are indeed informed (and taken aback) by these caveats from our informants. The danger that HIV/AIDS could become superseded by scientific or mathematics content had not occurred to us; now, the practice of not integrating our disciplines with HIV/AIDS education makes some sense. We believe, however, that conceptual mathematics and science knowledge can and should be used in the service of learning about HIV/AIDS, and vice versa. This position recapitulates the call for symbiotic opportunities to learn subject matter and HIV/AIDS (along with the local community) that we issue in our central question and strive to make concrete in the *Gedankenexperiments*. The pedagogical and ethical error occurs when we use HIV/AIDS as a device to teach something that has nothing to do with HIV/AIDS. For instance, Rosenthal once taught secondary mathematics teacher candidates to toss a question such as the following into a problem set on rate of change: "In 1990, there were 100,000 HIV+ individuals in the fictional nation of Freedonia. By 2002, this number had risen to 134,000. Calculate the average yearly rate of increase of HIV+ individuals in Freedonia from 1990 to 2002."

Such an example does not represent symbiosis. The setting is simply a wrapping for the mathematics, no door has been opened to learn about HIV/AIDS, and the local community isn't invited into the problem. As Senator John Kerry urged throughout 2004, we can do better—and we must.

NOTES

1. Our effort is one that we see as connected to "teaching for social justice" in at least two ways: As preservice teachers learn more about society through mathematics and science, they may learn to take more progressive views toward teaching. Also, science and math have been used for centuries, and are still used, as tools of oppression (Harding, 1998; Powell and Frankenstein, 1997). In the spirit of the late Stephen Jay Gould, we hope to use our chosen disciplinary fields to do the opposite.

2. The debate concerning whether viruses are "alive" has not been thoroughly resolved. In the documents we read concerning its transmission, the words "live" and "survive" were used in reference to HIV.

3. University of Alaska teacher educators have developed strong relationships, over time, with Alaskan Native elders. Through this work, they have developed curricula that directly involve community elders in teaching K–12 students indigenous knowledge (Denali Foundation and Alaska Rural Systemic Initiative, n.d.). In this way, they are able to make connections between indigenous knowledge and academic science knowledge.

REFERENCES

Aikenhead, G. (2000). STS science in Canada: From policy to student evaluation. In R. Millar, J. Leach, and J. Osborne, eds., *Improving science education: The contribution of research* (pp. 245–264). Milton Keynes, UK: Open University Press.

Aikenhead, G. (2003). STS education: A rose by any other name. In R. T. Cross, ed., *A vision for science education: Responding to the work of Peter J. Fensham* (pp. 59–75). New York: Routledge.

Ballin, A. (with Benson, J., and Burt, L.). (1993). *Trash conflicts: An integrated science and social studies curriculum on the ethics of disposal.* Cambridge, MA: Educators for Social Responsibility.

Barton, A. C. (with Ermer, J. L., Burkett, T. A., and Osborne, M. D.). (2003). *Teaching science for social justice.* New York: Teachers College Press.

Bigelow, B., and Peterson, B., eds. (2002). *Rethinking globalization: Teaching for justice in an unjust world.* Milwaukee: Rethinking Schools.

Bybee, R. W. (1993). *Reforming science education.* New York: Teachers College Press.

Centers for Disease Control and Prevention. (2003). *Fact sheet: HIV and its transmission.* Retrieved October 7, 2005, from http://www.cdc.gov/hiv/pubs/facts/transmission.htm.

Clandinin, D. J., and Connelly, F. M. (1992). Teacher as curriculum maker. In P. W. Jackson, ed., *Handbook of research on curriculum* (pp. 363–401). New York: Macmillan.

Cochran-Smith, M. (1999). Learning to teach for social justice. In G. A. Griffin, ed., *98th yearbook of NSSE: Teacher education for a new century: Emerging perspectives, promising practices, and future possibilities* (pp. 114–145). Chicago: University of Chicago Press.

Denali Foundation and Alaska Rural Systemic Initiative. (n.d.). *Observing snow.* Retrieved October 6, 2005, from http://www.ankn.uaf.edu/ObservingSnow.

DiSpezio, M. (2000). *The science of HIV.* Arlington, VA: National Science Teachers Association.

Grant, T., and Littlejohn, G. (2001). *Teaching about climate change: Cool schools tackle global warming.* Gabriola Island, BC: New Society Publishers.

Gruenewald, D. A. (2003). The best of both worlds: A critical pedagogy of place. *Educational Researcher* 32(4): 3–12.

Gutstein, E., and Peterson, B., eds. (2005). *Rethinking mathematics: Teaching social justice by the numbers.* Milwaukee, WI: Rethinking Schools.

Harding, S. (1998). *Is science multicultural? Postcolonialisms, feminisms, and epistemologies.* Bloomington: Indiana University Press.

Howes, E. V. (2005). Environmental education: Sense of place and social justice. In C. Kershaw, ed., *Voices and reflections: An urban education handbook* (pp. 49–54). Milwaukee, WI: Urban Network to Improve Teacher Education.

McCutcheon, G. (1988). Curriculum and the work of teachers. In L. E. Beyer and M. W. Apple, eds., *The curriculum: Problems, politics, and possibilities* (pp. 191–203). Albany, NY: SUNY Press.

Michelli, N. M., and Keiser, D. L., eds. (2005). *Teacher education for democracy and social justice.* New York: Routledge.

Mistrik, K. J., and Thul, R. C. (1993). *Math for a change.* Chicago: Mathematics Teachers' Association of Chicago and Vicinity.

Moje, E. B., Ciechanowski, K. M., Kramer, K., Ellis, L., Carrillo, R., and Collazo, T. (2004). Working toward third space in content area literacy: An examination of everyday funds of knowledge and discourse. *Reading Research Quarterly* 39(1): 38–70.

Moll, L. C., Amanti, C., Neff, D., and González, N. (1992). Funds of knowledge for teaching: Using a qualitative approach to connect homes and classrooms. *Theory into Practice* 31(2): 132–141.

National Institute of Allergy and Infectious Diseases. (2005). *HIV infection and AIDS: An overview.* Bethesda, MD: National Institutes of Health. Retrieved October 6, 2005, from http://www.niaid.nih.gov/factsheets/hivinf.htm.

National Science Teachers Association. (2000, July). NSTA position statement: The teaching of sexuality and human reproduction. Retrieved October 6, 2005, from http://www.nsta.org/positionstatementandpsid=33.

Pedretti, E. G. (2003). Teaching science, technology, society, and environment (STSE) education: Preservice teachers' philosophical and pedagogical landscapes. In D. L. Zeidler, ed., *The role of moral reasoning on socioscientific issues and discourse in science education* (pp. 219–239). Dordrecht, Netherlands: Kluwer Academic Press.

Powell, A. B., and Frankenstein, M., eds. (1997). *Ethnomathematics: Challenging Eurocentrism in mathematics education.* Albany, NY: SUNY Press.

Radical Teacher 64 (2002, Fall).

Radical Teacher 65 (2002–2003, Winter).

Rodriguez, A. J., and Kitchen, R. S., eds. (2005). *Preparing mathematics and science teachers for diverse classrooms: Promising strategies for transformative pedagogy.* Mahwah, NJ: Erlbaum.

Rosenthal, B. (2005). Two vignettes about mathematics and science education for social justice, followed by a question intended to provoke and disturb. In C. Kershaw, ed., *Voices and reflections: An urban education handbook* (pp. 71–78). Milwaukee, WI: Urban Network to Improve Teacher Education.

Schubert, W. H. (1986). *Curriculum: Perspective, paradigm, and possibility.* New York: Macmillan.

Stinnett, T. A., Cruce, M. K., and Choate, K. T. (2004). Influences on teacher education student attitudes toward youth who are HIV+. *Psychology in the Schools* 42(2): 211–219.

Thornton, S. J. (2004). *Teaching social studies that matters: Curriculum for active learning.* New York: Teachers College Press.

Thul, R. C., ed. (1997). *Math for a world that rocks: Twenty-three math-justice investigations for grades eight through twelve.* Chicago: St. Ignatius College Prep.

Turner, E. E., and Strawhun, B. T. F. (2004–2005, Winter). With math, it's like you have more defense. *Rethinking Schools* 19(2): 38–42.

Vithal, R. (2003). Teachers and 'street children': On becoming a teacher of mathematics. *Journal of Mathematics Teacher Education* 19(2): 165–183.

Warren, B., Ballenger, C., Ogonowski, M., Rosebery, A. S., and Hudicourt-Barnes, J. (2001). Rethinking diversity in learning science: The logic of everyday sense-making. *Journal of Research in Science Teaching* 38(5): 529–552.

Wheat Ridge (Colorado) High School. (n.d.). *Exponential growth and decay.* Retrieved October 6, 2005, from http://www.ncsec.org/cadre2/team17_2/precalc/timeline.htm.

Winter, D. (2003, Fall). *Solving quadratic equations I: Factoring.* Retrieved October 7, 2005, from http://www-math.bgsu.edu/~dalew/math112/m112_f03_notes/m112_f03_ne10_1.pdf.

Zeidler, D. L., ed. (2003). *The role of moral reasoning on socioscientific issues and discourse in science education.* Dordrecht, Netherlands: Kluwer Academic Press.

18

ESTABLISHING TIES: HIV PREVENTION THROUGH FACILITATION
The Case of Mujer Sana—"Healthy Woman"

*Rosi Andrade, Luis Moll, Sally Stevens,
and Karen Spear-Ellinwood*

᳜

In general, efforts to prevent the spread of human immunodeficiency virus (HIV) and sexually transmitted diseases (STDs) intend, through information and awareness, to reduce high-risk behaviors leading to HIV and other STDs. HIV prevention efforts generally target one of four populations: injection drug users, heterosexual adult men and women, men who have sex with men, and youth. The efforts also target specific groups within those populations such as members of particular racial and ethnic groups, genders, and rural or urban populations. The prevention and risk-reduction messages (e.g., practice safe sex, use condoms, avoid contact with the four bodily fluids through which HIV can be transmitted, and get tested) are relatively the same. The behavioral-based prevention approaches, however, are varied. Approaches used include the transtheoretical or *stages of change* model (Prochaska, DiClemente, and Norcross, 1992; Stevens and Estrada, 1996); social learning principles (Des Jarlais, Casriel, Friedman, and Rosenblum, 1992); problem-solving therapy (Magura, Kang, and Shapiro, 1994); social cognitive theory, relapse prevention, and concepts from the health belief model and theory of reasoned action (McCusker et al., 1992); and theories of peer influence and diffusion of innovations (Kegeles, Hays, and Coates, 1996).

This chapter focuses on a unique approach to the prevention of HIV and STD, developed and delivered by Mujer Sana—"Healthy

337

Woman"—a program of the Southwest Institute for Research on Women in Tucson, AZ.[1] This chapter draws on data collected as part of the program evaluation including baseline information, sexual health history of traumatic life events, and 6- and 12-month follow-up interviews. The Mujer Sana program educates women addicted to drugs or alcohol (hereafter called substances) who are in recovery through treatment and women who are still actively using substances. These two populations are separate, as women enroll from a treatment program or through street outreach to study the Mujer Sana curriculum and receive services. Theories of liberatory teaching and participatory action research inform Mujer Sana.

Attention to teaching as facilitation guided the development of curriculum and training of staff. Mujer Sana's success raises the questions of how and when discussions on the underlying beliefs and understandings about learning, teaching, and the population served take place, within discourse about HIV/AIDS prevention. Clarity about such assumptions is considered consequential, not merely incidental, for developing effective strategies.

We begin this chapter by reaffirming that change is a very difficult process, that recovery and risk-reduction are lifelong processes, and that the information that we do not embrace personally does not readily become part of our respective knowledge base. The process of risk-reduction involves transformation, a process of reflection that allows information to cast a different light on individual risks and behaviors. Facilitation, a key concept in the work described here, creates opportunities for transformations around the subjects of HIV and STDs. "Facilitation" means that teaching and learning play a pivotal role as they call attention to the process by which learners engage with information and establish it as their own. Facilitation accepts that all individuals come with complex experiences and systems for making sense of the world and that hindered access to accurate information and new experiences exacerbates risks. However, "access" is a more complicated matter than simply being presented with information. Teaching and learning through facilitation requires participants to be responsible for the process by asking, "Have I engaged everyone? How have I been inclusive of learning needs and styles? Have I promoted equity while soliciting active participation in sharing information and other resources?" In framing opportunities for learning, especially for at-risk populations, pedagogy becomes fundamental to engaging and interacting with others.

How are we to behave with others when our objective is to facilitate transformations? Facilitators, like educators, are not simply experts. Experts may be well versed in a subject, but their abilities to teach others and share information in ways that suit learners' needs may be limited. Without a pedagogical foundation, individuals entrusted with leading the prevention activity can reduce teaching and learning to presenting facts that students memorize and regurgitate. Such practices have their roots in theories of learning (e.g., deficit model and/or transmission model) that have only minimally served the needs of minority and disenfranchised communities, the very communities placed at greater risk for HIV and other diseases because of systematic exclusion from economic and other resources. Without some foundation in pedagogy, programs for HIV prevention may overlook the significance of a theory of learning in program development, staff training, and curriculum delivery.

Besides the importance of the role of education in HIV prevention, attention must be paid to the historical contexts of equity issues and alienation of learners. These ideas of equity or social justice are not novel, and many come from adult education, participatory action research, and liberatory teachings in the work of Paulo Freire and many other colleagues who have propelled these concepts beyond theory to practical applications.

BACKGROUND

The Context for HIV and STD Prevention

The health and well-being of individuals and communities depends on the success of HIV and STD prevention efforts. HIV prevention calls attention to the trends and needs of the local cultural and social contexts because local variables, not just national trends, influence epidemics. The following section offers context on local and national trends.

Women and drug use. The number of women who use drugs, relative to men, has been increasing over the past two decades. While men (7.7 percent) still report illicit drug use more than women (5.0 percent), and men (53.6 percent) report high alcohol use more than women (40.2 percent), rates for nonmedical use of psychoactive drugs for men (1.7 percent) and women are similar (1.8 percent) (Substance Abuse and Mental Health Services Administration, 2001). According to the Treatment Episode Data Set, Caucasian, American Indian/Alaska Native, and Asian/Pacific Islander women most often enter treatment for alcohol use, while African American women are more likely to enter treatment for crack cocaine use, and Hispanic/Latina women for heroin use (Office of Applied Studies, 2000). Their particularly high rates cause much concern about the transmission of HIV and other communicable diseases. Because drug use trends vary by region and community (Stevens, Estrada, and Estrada, 2000), agencies providing services must understand local trends.

At the inception of Mujer Sana, data from a women's and children's program in Pima County (Tucson, AZ) indicated that women entering treatment reported their primary drug problem as cocaine (40 percent), alcohol (23 percent), heroin (14 percent), amphetamine (10 percent), or all other drugs (12 percent; Stevens and Patton, 1998). In a program for young pregnant women and women with children, primary drug use was reported as cocaine/crack (46 percent), amphetamine (16 percent), heroin (13 percent), alcohol (12 percent), marijuana (7 percent), or no problem (6 percent; Wexler, Cuadrado, and Stevens, 1998). Use differs by ethnicity and whether women are in treatment or using and living in the wider community (Stevens, Estrada, Glider, and McGrath, 1998). Ethnographic data also indicate that reasons for drug use and views of substance use differ between men and women (Andrade and Estrada, 2003). Bogart, Stevens, Hill, and Estrada (2005) report more recent drug use trends.

Women and HIV/AIDS. Women are at risk for HIV/AIDS through unprotected sex and injection drug use. The Centers for Disease Control and Prevention (CDC, 2005c) reports that in the United States as of 2003, more than 44,000 women ages 15 to 44 were living with HIV, and more than 52,000 women in the same age group were living with AIDS. According to CDC estimates, more than half of the 902,223 cumulative AIDS cases reported in this country have been in racial minorities; from 1981 through 2003, 59 percent of the women and children reported with AIDS were African American, and another 19 percent of the women and 23 percent of the children were Hispanic (CDC, 2005b). As of the end of 2003, it was estimated that 349,000 adults and adolescents were living with HIV/AIDS, 25 percent of whom were females (CDC, 2005a). The majority (79 percent) of the HIV/AIDS cases diagnosed among female adults and adolescents were attributed to heterosexual transmission; 19 percent to injection drug use; and 2 percent to the transmission category of other/not identified (CDC, 2005a).

In Arizona, nearly 10,000 cases of HIV were diagnosed in the years 1995 to 2001. Minorities were disproportionately represented, accounting for 42 percent of the cases but only 36 percent of the population. Young women (ages 13 to 19) featured notably, with 107 testing positive for HIV between 1990 and 2001 (DeStephens, 2002). Sexually active women may have contracted HIV but not sought diagnosis or treatment due to lack of symptoms. In 2000, the CDC reported 464 HIV infection and 233 AIDS cases in women between the ages of 15 and 44 in Arizona, resulting in an AIDS rate of 3.1 per 100,000 women, compared to the national rate of 8.7 per 100,000 (CDC, 2000).

Full data are not available for Pima County, but between 1995 and 2001, 97 percent of women diagnosed with HIV were between the ages of 13 and 39. Minority women (African American, Hispanic, and Native American) comprised 61.7 percent of those cases (B. Johnson, personal communication, June 13, 2002), although the population of Pima County is 61.5 percent Caucasian, 29.3 percent Hispanic, 2.9 percent African American, 2.6 percent American Indian, and 1.8 percent other (Census Data, 2001).

Sexually transmitted diseases (STDs). In the 1990s, the Arizona Department of Health Services (ADHS, 2001a, 2001b) focused on reducing sexually transmitted and vaccine-preventable diseases. Special efforts were made to reduce gonorrhea infections to no more than 100 per 100,000, and gonorrhea infection rates declined from 149.0 in 1990 to 85.9 in 2000. However, while rates among females ages 15 to 24 declined from 490.6 in 1990 to 304.3 in 2000, they continued to be more than triple the rates for the general population. ADHS efforts also helped reduce the rate of gonorrhea infections among African Americans to no more than 1,300 per 100,000 people. This incidence fell from 1,734.5 in 1990 to 630.8 in 2000, but rates continue to be high, at six times the goal for the general population. Little progress has been made to reduce the rate of chlamydia among females 15 to 24 years by 10 percent. Incidence was reduced by little more than 1 percent between 1990 and 2000, from 2,105 to 2,045 per 100,000. Rates for women in Arizona are well above the national average (CDC, 2000) and especially high among minority women.

Hepatitis B (HBV) easily spreads from person to person through the exchange of bodily fluids including blood, semen, vaginal fluid, and saliva. While there is no cure for HBV, an available vaccine can protect from infection. ADHS (2002) reports that Pima County's HBV rates fluctuated between 1990 and 2000. In 1990, 488 cases were reported, but only 91 in 1993, followed by an upward trend to 215 in 2000. Until recently, in Arizona, only elementary school children were required to receive vaccinations for HBV. Vaccinations were not required for adolescents in school or adults, who were left vulnerable to infection.

In the United States, some 170,000 new cases of hepatitis C (HCV) are reported each year. Of these, 42 percent involve injection drug use (Fisher, Fenaughty, Paschane, Cagle, and Orr, 1997). HCV is transmitted through infected blood and blood products, but its epidemiology and relationship to HIV infection in injection drug users is not well understood (CDC, 1999; Hagan, 1998). The possibility of the heterosexual transmission of HCV remains controversial. Some researchers suggest that HCV is only rarely transmitted sexually (Wyld et al., 1997), but the relative risk appears to increase with a larger number of sex partners (Salleras et al., 1997). In addition, viral cofactors, such as herpes simplex virus-2 and HIV, appear to increase the risk of sexual transmission of HCV (Bresters et al., 1993; Shev et al., 1995; Soto et al., 1994).

Since Arizona began reporting HCV rates in 1994, they have fluctuated; the 2000 rate was 21 per 100,000 (ADHS, 2002). Because the Pima County Health Department and other local county health departments do not directly provide testing for HCV, the data are incomplete. However, ADHS is providing testing and collecting epidemiological data (J. Norton, personal communication, February 5, 2004). Preliminary data analyses indicate that HCV rates may be much higher, judging from the residue of 1,000 used needles collected from injection drug users (through a needle exchange program in the same geographic area as Mujer Sana). Explains A. L. Estrada, "based on the preliminary serology testing, we estimated that 35 percent of syringes were used by individuals actively infected with hepatitis C, and that 55 percent to 100 percent of syringes were used by an individual who, at some point in their life, had been infected with hepatitis B" (personal communication, July 2002).

PEDAGOGICAL ACTIVITY

This section relates the challenges and dilemmas of Mujer Sana's efforts to engage in facilitation beginning with staff who would be facilitating the curriculum. The trainings themselves have been an exercise in facilitation as role-playing has helped create social contexts for teaching and learning.

The Little Prince

In Antoine de Saint Exupéry's *The Little Prince* (1971), the title character navigates a series of encounters on other planets that are a veiled critique of human behaviors. The little prince and the fox share one such exchange:

> "Come play with me," proposed the little prince.
> "I cannot play with you," the fox said. "I am not tamed." ...
> "What does that mean—'tame'?"
> "It is an act too often neglected," said the fox. "It means to establish ties."

Using such excerpts, Mujer Sana incorporates literature, poetry, and music to enrich its content, serve as teaching tools, and establish ties. *The Little Prince,* for example, indicates the role of social relationships, the context for high-risk behaviors that may lead to HIV and sexually transmitted diseases. In training, staff learned that risk reduction means more than avoiding contact with four bodily fluids (blood, semen, vaginal secretions, breast milk) and that considerations must be given to reciprocity and negotiation of relationships and social and economic situations. At the same time, the fox's definition of "tame" speaks to the training of staff as facilitators, because "establishing ties" with self and with the other suggests becoming a learner of other life contexts and needs through mutual acknowledgement.

Staff might come to prevention work intending to help or improve lives but without checking for bias in their own beliefs. Directly addressing "the other" is useful to examine some value bias (e.g., "us versus them," poor women, women as victims), to frame the interaction differently (e.g., we come together with varied experiences and resources; in this opportunity to learn from one another, everyone has something to teach and the opportunity to learn). This approach builds on the fluidity of the roles of teacher and learner in facilitation.

The theoretical underpinnings of participatory action research in adult education (Fingeret and Jurmo, 1989; Geissler, 1994; Hohn,

1998; Horsman, 1990; Kaplan and Alsup, 1995) and Paulo Freire's liberatory action research (e.g., Freire and Macedo, 1987) have informed the pedagogical preparation of project staff and curriculum development. These theories and research practices call for respecting adults as learners with experience and understanding what is important in their lives. These theoretical underpinnings also suggest that the content must challenge learners while raising their consciousness. Unfamiliar information or topics can be broken down in relevant parts (not watered down) to be accessible. Pedagogy is the daily practice of teaching and learning. Teaching and learning, in turn, are about the shared interactions among and between staff and women enrolled in Mujer Sana.

Programmatic Details

The curriculum for Mujer Sana's five group sessions centers around the topics of reproductive anatomy; female-specific risks; HIV, STD, TB, and Hepatitis A, B, and C education and prevention; HIV transmission and prevention; and social relationships and their impact on women's health.

Mujer Sana is incorporated within three existing women and women-with-children treatment programs and also has an outreach site for active substance-involved women not in treatment. The program collaborates with the University of Arizona, Southwest Institute for Research on Women, and the local county health department's HIV and STD clinic.

The Curriculum

The Mujer Sana curriculum is a 12-week course involving five 2-hour interactive group sessions about HIV, STDs, TB, and Hepatitis A, B, and C, including attention to issues of sexuality, social relationships, and women-specific risks (see Figure 18.1). In five 45-minute sessions, participants address personal risks, develop and monitor an individualized risk-reduction plan, and receive appropriate referrals. The group and individual sessions take place on alternating weeks. Within the curriculum, over a 2-week period, the women are offered voluntary disease counseling, testing, results, treatment/vaccinations, and referral. They may also volunteer to receive a pelvic exam and other services at the health department's STD clinic. The grant covers costs for these services. Upon completion of the course, participants can continue to participate at weekly drop-in social support sessions. As part of the program evaluation, women participate in a baseline 1– 1 ½-hour interview at enrollment in the program and in follow-up interviews of 45 minutes to 1 hour at 6 and 12 months. They receive $20 for each of the two follow-up interviews.

Each group session encourages participation through activities including brainstorming, discussions, review of participants' questions, games, and role-plays. Information and data are presented formally.

Seven key elements summarize these activities of the project (see Table 18.1).

Learning community (elements 1, 2, 3, 4, 5, 6, 7). Mujer Sana staff brainstormed respectful interactions for one another, what they would practice with participants, and what they would encourage participants to practice with one another. Ground rules were agreed upon and framed as essential to share with Mujer Sana participants and one another in the creation and pursuit of learning communities. Previous work with community women influenced the decision to establish ground rules (Andrade, González LeDenmat, and Moll, 2000). Group norms developed as cohorts adapted and internalized their sessions to develop a new vision of community. This vision was established and framed with the rationale that in the curriculum sessions all are teachers and learners, and that mutual respect must be the guiding principle.

Brainstorming and discussion activities (elements 2, 3, 4, 5, 6, 7). During the group sessions, the facilitator poses questions that elicit what learners know or believe. These responses are simultaneously recorded on a large sheet of paper for all to see and discuss following the brainstorming. For example, women are asked: "What is sex? And where did we learn about it? What is sexuality? And where did we learn about it?" The brainstorming activities prepare the way for sharing information and resources with women, while also challenging the influence of experiences that are disconnected from who each woman is or might want to become.

Women's questions (elements 3, 4, 5, 6, 7). The questions and informal knowledge women generate in group activities are reintegrated into the

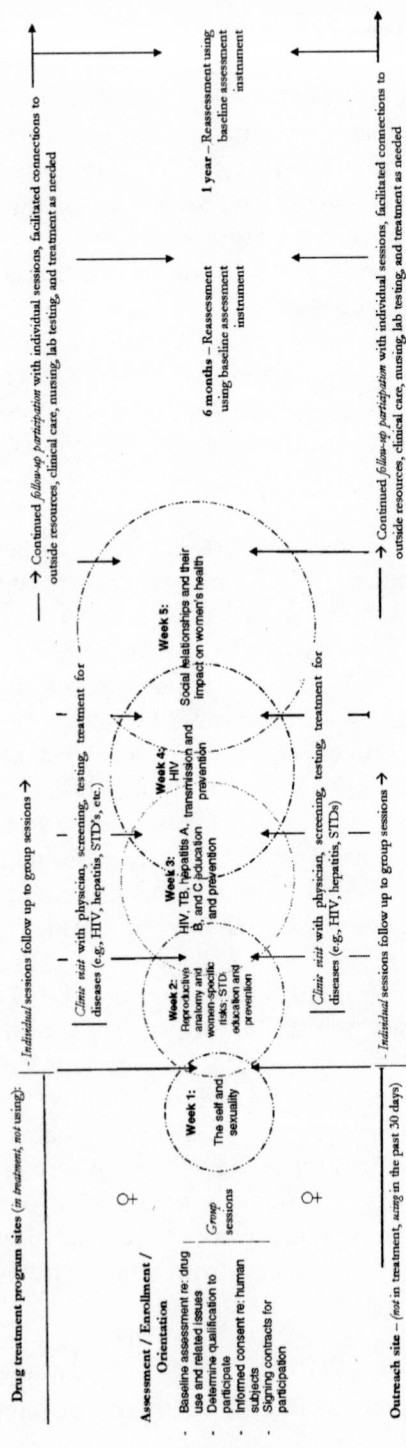

Drug treatment program sites (*in treatment, not using*):

→ Continued *follow-up participation* with individual sessions, facilitated connections to outside resources, clinical care, nursing, lab testing, and treatment as needed

→ *Individual* sessions follow up to group sessions →

| *Clinic visit* with physician, screening, testing, treatment for diseases (e.g., HIV, hepatitis, STD's, etc.)

Assessment / Enrollment / Orientation

· Baseline assessment re: drug use and related issues
· Determine qualification to participate
· Informed consent re: human subjects
· Signing contracts for participation

Group sessions

♀

Week 1:
The self and sexuality

Week 2:
Reproductive anatomy and women-specific risks; STD education and prevention

Week 3:
HIV, TB, hepatitis A, B, and C education and prevention

Week 4:
HIV transmission and prevention

Week 5:
Social relationships and their impact on women's health

→ *Individual* sessions follow up to group sessions →

| *Clinic visit* with physician, screening, testing, treatment for diseases (e.g., HIV, hepatitis, STDs)

Outreach site – (*not* in treatment, *using* in the past 30 days)

♀

→ Continued *follow-up participation* with individual sessions, facilitated connections to outside resources, clinical care, nursing, lab testing, and treatment as needed

6 months – Reassessment using baseline assessment instrument

1 year – Reassessment using baseline assessment instrument

Figure 18.1 Mujer Sana Curriculum

346

Table 18.1. Key Elements of Project Activities

Key element	Activity description
1	Formation of a learning community through established ground rules and group norms that facilitate community building
2	Presentation of formal knowledge coupled with the introduction of informal knowledge as generated through brainstorming and discussion activities
3	Documentation, research, and response to women's questions, such as development of *Mujer Sana I would like to know* ... informational pamphlets
4	Disease testing as a learning opportunity integrated into the curriculum
5	Elicitation and use of questions to broaden each individual's knowledge base
6	Examination of social relationships
7	Encouragement of new forms of wisdom and informed action

curriculum. Women generate new questions by developing curiosity about new information and by reflecting on their beliefs. Responses to women's questions are shared in the group sessions. Women are encouraged to write down their questions so the project director and the staff nurse can research answers. Together, the project director and staff nurse work to formalize responses in the *Mujer Sana I would like to know* ... pamphlets. This activity reinforces the development of a healthy learning community, specifically the reciprocal role of all participants as teachers and learners.

Disease testing as a learning opportunity (elements 4, 5, 6, 7). Disease testing is treated as yet another opportunity for learning. The individual disease testing sessions incorporate pre- and posttest HIV counseling with the staff nurse, followed by a visit to the health department's STD clinic on another day for additional testing (e.g., pelvic exam, cultures, etc.). The cohort's trip to the clinic encourages pursuing new forms of knowledge and experiences. Following the clinic visit, the staff and clients debrief about the clinic experiences and talk about the present and future impact of the various HIV and STD tests received. Disease testing follows group sessions 1 (self and sexuality) and 2 (women-specific risks), where it is almost natural to talk about assessing one's own health status and risks for HIV, STDs, and hepatitis. Often the women in the cohort begin that conversation with questions and concerns about getting tested.

Taken together, the sessions flow and enhance each other. The examination of social relationships takes place in context and is woven throughout the group sessions beginning with session 1 (self and sexuality) and coming full circle with session 5 (social relationships and their impact on women's health).

Sessions and Lessons

Group session 1, on self and sexuality, starts with a necessary research element: the pretest evaluation instrument. The pretest is not a tool to measure individual's knowledge but a means to capture the impact of the curriculum on participants. Following the pretest, the session officially begins with a greeting in the form of a colorfully decorated, laminated bookmark developed by the staff: "Do not confuse sex, love, and intimacy. One does not necessarily imply the other. Experiencing one does not necessarily satisfy our need for the other.... And finally, do not forsake one for the other. You can have them all" (Dr. Aaron Hass, 1983).

A review of the syllabus and discussion follow this presentation. Then staff and participants play the "telephone game" as an ice-breaking activity. One staff person begins by whispering to a neighbor, "Latex condoms are 99 percent effective when used properly to prevent pregnancy and diseases." In turn, one by one, women in the group whisper what they have heard from one neighbor to the next. The information can be whispered only once. The last person on the "telephone" then shares aloud the message she has received. Inevitably, the last message is nothing like the original and evokes a roar of laughter from everyone because it is often nonsensical. The staff talks about how health information and resources are similar to the telephone game, and they underscore that direct access to information is important because second-hand information presents few, if any, opportunities to confirm or question it. Second-hand information is exposed as unreliable.

Table 18.2 lists brainstorming responses generated by a cohort during group session 1. The lists reveal the experiences and origins of women's conceptions of sex and sexuality. Group dialogue broadens the conversation to address items any particular individual might not have thought of, but that could be important to her life. For example, responses to "What is sex?" range from intimacy to violence. The learners' experiences also indicate the normalization of exploitative sexual

Table 18.2. Brainstorming Responses

What is sex?	Where did we learn about sex?	What is sexuality?	How do people develop their notion of what sexuality means?
Sex is:	We learned about sex from:	Sexuality is:	People develop this through:
• physical	• school	• bodies	• experience
• penetration	• mother	• individuality	• environment
• oral	• pornos/	• feeling	• reading
• touching	magazines	• mentality	materials
• intimacy	• books	• beauty	• media
• income/job	• men	• emotion	• temperament
• confusing	• TV	• preference	• being told
• feel good	• movies	• frame of mind	• friends/peers
• comforting	• older siblings	• personality	• exposure
• condition	• abuse	• aura	• parents
• perverted	• boyfriend/	• appearance/	• role models
• workout	partner	physical	• observation
• fix	• sex hotline	• choice	• acts
• substitution/		• attitude	• parties
drugs		• confusing	• addiction
• validation/		• scary	• abuse
proving your			
worth			
• enjoyable			
• violent			
• responsibility/			
duty			
• submission			

behavior, and while some experiences are mundane, others are inherently dangerous. The order of the list is important, because it reveals a flow of experiences in which some feed off one another, then move on to a vastly different experience/interpretation. The list also reveals the many manifestations and offshoots of sex, which speak to the social construction of sex spanning its material dimensions to issues of power and control. The social context for sex as a voluntary expression of intimacy is not a universally shared experience.

Sources of knowledge, or experiences of sex, suggest that formal opportunities to learn about sex are limited. More informal contexts for learning about sex appear randomly through pornography and magazines (likely belonging to males) and experientially through men, boyfriends, older siblings, and partners. These sources of experience suggest exploitation is common, and therefore the stakes are high for teaching about sex. School and books appear as the only formal sources for learning about sex. The inclusion of mother on the list may complement formal learning or may not (e.g., a "birds and bees" talk).

Responses to "What is sexuality? And how do people develop their notion of what sexuality means?" reveal a number of things. Sexuality has its confines, whether imposed or expressed, "physical" or "confusing." In discussions, these two brainstorming activities often generate concern Instead of suggesting that these may be "above" individuals' levels, many facilitators believe they push individuals to examine another facet of their being, which has often been denied, shamed, or exploited as suggested by the discussion of how people develop their notions of what sexuality means.

There is no use of "you." Participants in the brainstorming and discussion speak in general terms, defining without revealing. Dialogues can include general questions one may encounter, as well as questions specific to settings. The discussion offers the group opportunities to reflect on those experiences, to examine how one reads those expressions, and to raise issues based on one's own experiences. Anticipated outcomes of this activity include that women (a) learn about sexuality as part of human identity, including the emotional (desire) and spiritual aspects, (b) understand that sexuality is not solely about engaging in the physical act of sex, and (c) know that sexuality is an expression of the self.

Women participating in Mujer Sana appear to connect both sex and sexuality with their physical and emotive selves. These connections between body and mind (or in some cases between disease and abuse, or drug addiction and sex addiction) contradict the unhealthy approach to social situations that present opportunities for sexual behavior. When discussed overtly, however, these connections represent an opportunity to reflect and reconstruct identity and identifications with notions of sexuality and sex that might provide a healthier, sustainable approach to life.

The nature of women's questions in context of discussion and inclusion of formal and informal knowledge is presented in the following examples from Table 18.3, listed in the order generated. The two sets of discussion-generated questions address STDs and HIV/hepatitis.

Table 18.3. Discussion-Generated Questions

On STDs:

1. How often would a man have to be tested for STDs?
2. How can we tell if they [men] have any STDs without being tested?
3. How can you get a man tested without offending the man?
4. What STDs can be transmitted orally?
5. Is cervical cancer an STD?
6. What signs or symptoms do you get when you have an STD?

On HIV/hepatitis:

1. If you are tested for HIV and the test turns out positive, when do you start taking medications? Can the medications make the symptoms come sooner?
2. Why is there a disproportion of HIV/AIDS infection between men and women?
3. Why do HIV cocktails work for some and not for others?
4. Is strain 1 worse or better than 2?
5. How can HIV be fought when the virus is constantly mutating? Can the mutating be arrested?
6. If a person has HIV and hepatitis C, do you treat both? Which one is more likely to kill?
7. How do they decide which disease to treat first (if you have both HIV and hepatitis C)?
8. What's the difference in the symptoms of HIV and hepatitis C? How will it affect me and my body?

There is an elegance to this exchange between participants, as one question begs another, and yet another. Each additional layer of information leads to even further inquiry, not only related to personal experience but also on a broader scale. Questions related to a discussion on STDs begin with a focus on testing in social context related to women's negotiation strategies with male sexual partners and express interest in details about exposure and progression of disease. It is impossible to overstate the seriousness related to the social context of women's health when it becomes secondary to men's sensibility, ego, or pride. Facilitators should notice how the questions on HIV begin with interest in specifics and include queries about health disparities but also lead to curiosity about coinfection and HCV.

These are examples of the curriculum moving far beyond the presentation of facts and information, as participants digest new information and think about practical and other implications of their new understanding and learning. One participant reported, "I truly enjoyed this first session. It's a great way to educate us about sexuality, and safeness." Another wrote, "I feel that this class will be a wonderful learning experience for myself and all the other people taking this class. I thank you for taking the time to come here to teach us." The questions raised by participants are formalized in the *Mujer Sana I would like to know* ... informational pamphlets, which maintain the integrity of the question and pair each question with researched responses and detailed resources. This method emphasizes the importance of direct access to information and resources. Mujer Sana distributes the pamphlet to all cohorts of women enrolled in the program. Thus, women in the program contribute to the curriculum by participating in group sessions and by generating brainstorming discussions that contribute to the development of the pamphlet content.

The closing activity includes specific music for each session. Group session 1 concludes with music and lyrics of "You Gotta Be" by singer Des'ree (1994). Women can read and sing along or listen. The song is relevant because it reinforces many of the session topics and allows everyone to participate in the way they feel most comfortable.

According to a staff nurse, the inclusion of disease testing within the Mujer Sana curriculum has been fruitful in creating opportunities for women to recognize their risks and subsequently follow through with testing. "Getting women into clinic [is] getting smoother with time. [We] had several (3) women from outreach who wanted no testing services. [They were] very adamant to not have a pelvic exam. Without any additional message, after they were midway into the curriculum [sessions] they decided they wanted everything. The level of trust increased as they went through the sessions (B. Cole, personal communication, March 2004).

The pedagogy of Mujer Sana, with its insistence on creating trust and on helping the women to articulate their own questions and circumstances, has (a) enabled the women to recognize their risks; (b) encouraged or inspired and even provoked women to follow through and to take a more affirmative relationship to their own bodies, selves, and well-being; and (c) given women the means to follow through by including testing in the curriculum and positioning it carefully so that when women are ready to take advantage of it, it is an identifiable and accessible resource. This process is significant to the women enrolled in Mujer Sana because they can make important strides in their respective decision-making to be tested and receive treatment when indicated. The curriculum allows for self-reflection and examination of past behaviors and individual risks. The cohort trips to the clinic often result in the diagnosis of disease, but these visits are a positive experience—an opportunity to take charge of health conditions and a means to debrief about the experience and findings in general. Participants have reported, "This wasn't so bad," "I didn't know where the clinic was," "The staff at the clinic made me feel comfortable," "I'm glad I didn't come alone," "I'm shocked about the results," "I had no idea, I didn't have any symptoms," and "I knew something was wrong, but I was afraid to find out." Cohort participants respect confidentiality. Taking these factors together, it is evident that respect and trust in these social relationships led to self-reflection and positive behaviors.

CONCLUSION

Those working directly with Mujer Sana have been challenged to find novel ways of presenting formal facts and information while validating informal knowledge. Within the structured format of the curriculum sessions, for example, brainstorming and discussion activities get at women's informal knowledge and beliefs by raising questions about the nature of that knowledge ("Where did we learn it from?"). The women are also introduced to formal facts and information. This technique creates ongoing opportunities for women to reexamine previous situations or beliefs in relation to new knowledge. This reexamination creates the potential for broadening individual understandings and clears a path for behavioral and other changes; as suggested by Cole (1990), "Insofar as the content of the curriculum allows them more broadly to understand their particular historical circumstances, it will lead students to be more effective problem solvers when they are not in school" (p. 106).

A fundamental aspect of the work is engaging in dialogue through facilitation, both with staff and with women participating in the project. This dynamic, inclusive approach frames interactions as those of a shared community of teachers and learners. For example, the importance of asking questions was encouraged early in the staff development trainings and subsequently in the group curriculum sessions with clients.

Asking questions is an essential pedagogical activity that also facilitates opportunities for making meaning that can lead to enhanced learning and transformations. Understanding the dynamics of learning and teaching were as important as the content or curriculum. Engaging in dialogue created opportunities for formal and informal sharing, which came out of the structure of the curriculum. Women enrolled in Mujer Sana drove the curriculum through the informal sharing and discussion of formal texts as they engaged with the content and its relevance to personal life contexts.

This approach to prevention draws upon educational strategies that include adult education and consciousness-raising and promotes the concept of lifelong learning through facilitation. The methodology shows what impact the presentation of formal knowledge, coupled with the inclusion of informal knowledge as generated through group activities, can have. The Mujer Sana program demonstrates that the process of documenting, researching, and responding to women's questions, as in the development of informational pamphlets, reinforced the fluidity of the roles of learner and teacher. Testing for HIV, STD, and hepatitis and integrating that testing became yet another learning opportunity for women. The examination of social context and relationships encourages new forms of wisdom.

The pedagogy that underlies staff training (intermediary learners) also sets the foundation for working with clients (ultimate learners). In that spirit, the pedagogy consists of a questioning of assumptions and beliefs about the teacher/learner relationship and a questioning of assumptions and beliefs about "the other" in establishing ties and fostering the conditions for establishing further ties.

Central features of the pedagogy include (a) the creation of a climate of trust and a shared sense of a community of learners; (b) dialogue and questioning in all directions; (c) the elicitation of informal knowledge and beliefs; and (d) the presentation of formal knowledge and new information in the context of learners' informal knowledge and own burgeoning questions. Taken together, these are the curriculum. And while they may appear as discrete activities, each of these features can be described as related acts in "establishing ties."

What is the intent of this pedagogy? The Mujer Sana program aims to foster a practice of examination of existing beliefs and received knowledge (critique) leading to changed behavior related to health (care, assessment of risk, and personal action through testing) and relationships with others through wisdom.

At least three messages seem important for anyone attempting education aimed at HIV/AIDS prevention:

First, for the ultimate population of learners, formal knowledge is "inert," not accessible, until the learners themselves have a felt need and desire for that knowledge.

Second, various elements of liberatory pedagogy can help to generate that felt need and desire. One very important element is education of the intermediary population of learners—that is, the staff/teachers who will do the bulk of the educative work with the ultimate intended population.

Third, in both cases, the creation of "ties" was essential. Both facilitators and participants had to critically examine their existing ways of thinking about, and being with, other persons. This examination included the power dimensions of relationships. Facilitators also had to carefully design and incorporate measures to build trust.

NOTE

1. Mujer Sana is funded by the Substance Abuse and Mental Health Services Administration's Center for Substance Abuse Treatment under Grant No. TI14452. The opinions offered in this chapter reflect the expressed views of its authors and do not necessarily reflect the views of the funding agency.

REFERENCES

Andrade, R., and Estrada, E. (2003). Are Hispana IDUs tecatas? Reconsidering gender and culture in Hispana injection drug use. *Substance Use and Misuse* 38: 1133–1158.

Andrade, R., González LeDenmat, H., and Moll, L. C. (2000). El Grupo de las Señoras: Creating consciousness within a literature club. In M. A. Gallego and S. Hollingsworth, eds., *What counts as literacy: Challenging the school standard* (pp. 271–284). New York: Teachers College Press.

Arizona Department of Health Services. (2001a). *Differences in the health status among ethnic groups: Arizona, 1999.* Phoenix, AZ: Public Health Services, Bureau of Public Health Statistics, Office of Epidemiology and Statistics. Retrieved October 13, 2005, from http://www.azdhs.gov/plan/report/dhsag/dhsag99/ethnic99.pdf.

Arizona Department of Health Services. (2001b). *Vital statistics trends: Reportable diseases, 1990–2000.* Phoenix: Author.

Arizona Department of Health Services. (2002). *Vital statistics trends: Reportable diseases, 1999–2001.* Phoenix: Author.

Bogart, J. G., Stevens, S. J., Hill, R., and Estrada, B .D. (2005). Criminally involved drug-using mothers: The need for system change. *Prison Journal* 85(1): 65–82.

Bresters, D., Mauser-Bunschoten, E. P., Reesink, H. W., Roosendaal, G., van der Poel, C. L., Chamuleau, R. A., et al. (1993). Sexual transmission of hepatitis virus. *Lancet* 342(8865): 210–211.

Census Data 2000. (2001). *The Arizona Daily Star,* p. A8.

Centers for Disease Control and Prevention. (1999). *The deadly intersection between TB and HIV.* Retrieved October 12, 2005, from http://www.cdc.gov/hiv/pubs/facts/hivtb.htm.

Centers for Disease Control and Prevention. (2000). *STD surveillance 2000: National profile.* Atlanta, GA: Author. Retrieved October 13, 2005, from http://www.cdc.gov/std/stats00/TOC2000.htm.

Centers for Disease Control and Prevention. (2005a). *HIV/AIDS surveillance—L179 slide series: General epidemiology (through 2003).* Atlanta, GA: Author. Retrieved October 18, 2005, from http://www.cdc.gov/hiv/graphics/L179.htm.

Centers for Disease Control and Prevention. (2005b). *HIV/AIDS surveillance by race/ethnicity—L238 slide series (through 2003).* Atlanta, GA: Author. Retrieved October 18, 2005, from http://www.cdc.gov/hiv/graphics/minority.htm.

Centers for Disease Control and Prevention. (2005c). *HIV/AIDS surveillance in women—L264 slide series (through 2003).* Atlanta, GA: Author. Retrieved October 17, 2005, from http://www.cdc.gov/hiv/graphics/women.htm.

Cole, M. (1990). Cognitive development and formal schooling: The evidence from cross-cultural research. In L. C. Moll, ed., *Vygotsky and education: Instructional implications and applications of sociohistorical psychology* (pp. 89–110). New York: Cambridge University Press.

Des Jarlais, D. C., Casriel, C., Friedman, S. R., and Rosenblum, A. (1992). AIDS and the transition to illicit drug injection: Results of a randomized trial prevention program. *British Journal of Addiction* 87(3): 493–498.

Des'ree. (1994). You gotta be. On *I ain't movin* [CD]. Sony Records.

DeStephens, R., ed. (2002). *HIV rates for Arizona 1990–2001.* Phoenix: Arizona Department of Health Services, Bureau of Epidemiology and Disease Control Services, Office of HIV/STD/Hepatitis C Services.

Fingeret, A., and Jurmo, P. (1989). *Participatory literacy education: New directions for literacy education.* San Francisco: Jossey-Bass.

Fisher, D. G., Fenaughty, A. F., Paschane, D. M., Cagle, H. H., and Orr, S. M. (1997). Hepatitis C virus infection among Alaskan drug users. *American Journal of Public Health* 87(10): 1722–1724.

Freire, P., and Macedo, D. (1987). *Literacy: Reading the word and the world.* South Hadley, MA: Bergin and Garvey.

Geissler, B. (1994). Literacy-health partnerships that work. *Adult Learning* 5(6): 21, 22, 26.

Hagan, H. (1998). Hepatitis C virus transmission dynamics in injection drug users. *Substance Use and Misuse* 33(5): 197–212.

Hass, A. (1983). *Love, sex, and the single man.* Franklin Watts.

Hohn, M. D. (1998). *Empowerment health education in adult literacy: A guide for public health and adult literacy practitioners, policy makers, and funders* (Vol. III, No. 4, Part A). Washington, DC: National Institute for Literacy.

Horsman, J. (1990). *Something in my mind besides the everyday: Women and literacy.* Toronto, Ontario, Canada: Women's Press.

Kaplan, S. J., and Alsup, R. (1995). Participatory action research: A creative response to AIDS prevention in diverse communities. *Convergence* 28(1): 38–56.

Kegeles, S. M., Hays, R. B., and Coates, T. J. (1996). The Mpowerment Project: A community-level HIV prevention intervention for young gay men. *American Journal of Public Health* 86(8): 1129–1136.

Magura, S., Kang, S., and Shapiro, J. L. (1994). Outcomes of intensive AIDS education for male adolescent drug users in jail. *Journal of Adolescent Health* 15(6): 457–463.

McCusker, J., Stoddard, A. M., Zapka, J. G., Morrison, C. S., Zorn, M., and Lewis, B. F. (1992). AIDS education for drug abusers: Evaluation of short-term effectiveness. *American Journal of Public Health* 82(4): 533–540.

Office of Applied Studies. (2000). *Treatment Episode Data Set (TEDS): 1993–1998.* Rockville, MD: Substance Abuse and Mental Health Services Administration.

Prochaska, J. O., DiClemente, C. C., and Norcross, J. C. (1992). In search of how people change: Applications to addictive behaviors. *American Psychologist* 47(9): 1102–1114.

Saint Exupéry, A. (1971). *The little prince.* San Diego, CA: Harcourt Brace Jovanovich.

Salleras, L., Bruguera, M., Vidal, J., Plans, P., Dominquez, A., Salleras, M., et al. (1997). Importance of sexual transmission of hepatitis C virus in seropositive pregnant women: A case-control study. *Journal of Medical Virology* 52(2): 164–167.

Shev, V., Widell, A., Bergstrom, T., Hemondson, S., Lindholm, A., and Norkrans, G. (1995). Herpes simplex virus-2 may increase susceptibility of the sexual transmission of hepatitis C. *Sexually Transmitted Diseases* 22: 210–216.

Soto, B., Rodrigo, L., Garcia-Bengoechea, M., Sanchez-Quijano, A., Riestra, S., Arenas, J. I., et al. (1994). Heterosexual transmission of hepatitis C virus and the possible role of coexistent human immunodeficiency virus infection in the index case. A multicenter study of 423 pairings. *Journal of Internal Medicine* 236(5): 515–519.

Stevens, S. J., and Estrada, A. L. (1996). Reducing HIV risk behaviors: Perceptions of HIV risk and stage of change. *Journal of Drug Issues* 26(3): 607–618.

Stevens, S. J., Estrada, A. L., and Estrada, B. D. (2000). HIV drug and sex risk behaviors among Native American drug users: Gender and site differences. *Journal of American Indian and Alaska Native Mental Health Research* 9(1): 33–46.

Stevens, S. J., Estrada, A. L., Glider, P. J., and McGrath, R. (1998). Ethnic and cultural differences in drug using women who are in and out of treatment. *Drugs and Society* 13(1/2): 81–96.

Stevens, S. J., and Patton, T. (1998). Residential treatment for drug addicted women and their children: Effective treatment strategies. *Drugs and Society* 13(1/2): 235–250.

Substance Abuse and Mental Health Services Administration. (2001). *The national household survey on drug abuse report*. Rockville, MD: Author.

Wexler, H. K., Cuadrado, M., and Stevens, S. J. (1998). Residential treatment for women: Behavioral and psychological outcomes. *Drugs and Society* 13(1/2): 213–234.

Wyld, R., Roberson, J. R., Brettle, R. P., Mellor, J., Prescott, L., and Simmonds, P. (1997). Absence of hepatitis C virus transmission but frequent transmission of HIV-1 from sexual contact with doubly-infected individuals. *Journal of Infection* 35(2): 163–166.

ADDITIONAL RESOURCES

᪣

GENERAL HIV/AIDS RESOURCES—UNITED STATES

Centers for Disease Control and
Prevention (CDC)
http://www.cdc.gov

CDC National Prevention
Information Network
http://www.cdcnpin.org

CDC National Center for Health
Statistics
http://www.cdc.gov/nchs/

CDC *Morbidity and Mortality Weekly
Report*
http://www.cdc.gov/mmwr/

CDC National Center for HIV, STD,
and TB Prevention, Divisions of HIV/
AIDS Prevention
http://www.cdc.gov/hiv/dhap.htm

Black AIDS Institute
http://www.blackaids.org

National Minority AIDS Council
http://www.nmac.org

U.S. Department of Health and
Human Services, Office of HIV/AIDS
Policy
http://www.osophs.dhhs.gov/aids/

GENERAL HIV/AIDS RESOURCES— FOREIGN/INTERNATIONAL

Afro AIDS Info Portal
http://www.afroaidsinfo.org

AIDS Education Global Information
System
http://www.aegis.com

Center for HIV/AIDS Networking
(South Africa)
http://www.hivan.org.za

Child-to-Child Trust
http://www.child-to-child.org/

International AIDS Economic Network	http://www.iaen.org
International Community of Women Living With HIV/AIDS	http://www.icw.org
Joint United Nations Programme on HIV/AIDS (UNAIDS)	http://www.unaids.org
UNAIDS resources on education in schools	http://www.unaids.org/Unaids/EN/In+focus/Topic+areas/Education+in+schools.asp
Monitoring the AIDS Pandemic (MAP) Network	http://www.mapnetwork.org
Teaching Aids at Low Cost (U.K.), Health Development CD-ROM; HIV/AIDS-specific products also available	http://www.talcuk.org
UNESCO Regional Office in Dakar, Database on HIV/AIDS Prevention Education	http://www.dakar.unesco.org/bsida/index_en.shtml
USAID Global Health, HIV/AIDS programs	http://www.usaid.gov/our_work/global_health/aids/
World Health Organization	http://www.who.org

HIV/AIDS EDUCATION—UNITED STATES

American Association for Health Education, HIV/AIDS Project	http://www.aahperd.org/AAHE/template.cfm?template=programs_hivoverview.html
American Association of Colleges for Teacher Education (AACTE), Build a Future Without AIDS project	http://www.aacte.org/Programs/Research/without_aids.htm
AACTE, *Everything You Wanted to Know About HIV/AIDS in the Classroom but Were Afraid to Ask* (interactive CD-ROM)	Contact AACTE, 1307 New York Avenue, NW, Suite 300, Washington, DC 20005, telephone: (202) 293-2450
American Red Cross, Health and Safety Services, HIV/AIDS Education	http://www.redcross.org/services/hss/hivaids/
American School Health Association	http://www.asha.org

CDC National Center for Chronic Disease Prevention and Health Promotion, Division of Adolescent and School Health

http://www.cdc.gov/HealthyYouth/index.htm

Council of Chief State School Officers, *State Profiles of HIV, STD, and Teen Pregnancy*

http://www.ccsso.org/Projects/school_health_project/state_profiles/6479.cfm

ETR Resource Center for Adolescent Pregnancy Prevention, Evidence-Based Programs, *Get Real About AIDS*

http://www.etr.org/recapp/programs/getreal.htm

Guilford Publications, *AIDS Education and Prevention: An Interdisciplinary Journal,* edited by Francisco S. Sy

Contact Guilford Publications, 72 Spring St., New York, NY 10012. ISSN 0899-9546. $245.00 institutions; $65.00 individuals.

National Association of County and City Health Officials, HIV/AIDS Prevention project

http://www.naccho.org/topics/infectious/hiv.cfm

National Association of State Boards of Education, "Someone at School Has AIDS: A Complete Guide to Education Policies Concerning HIV Infection"

http://www.nasbe.org/healthy_schools/sasha.htm

SCIENCE OF HIV/AIDS

Johns Hopkins University, "Life Cycle of HIV Infection" (Flash movie)

http://www.hopkins-aids.edu/hiv_lifecycle/hivcycle_flsh.html

Manbir Online, overview of DNA

http://www.manbir-online.com/diseases/dna.htm

National Institutes of Health, National Human Genome Research Institute

http://www.genome.gov

National Institutes of Health, National Institute of Allergy and Infectious Diseases, AIDS-related publications

http://www.niaid.nih.gov/publications/aids.htm

University of Arizona Biology Project, HIV/AIDS Tutorial

http://www.biology.arizona.edu/immunology/tutorials/AIDS/main.html

University of California–San Francisco, HIV InSite Knowledge Base	http://hivinsite.ucsf.edu
University of Maryland Biotechnology Institute, Institute of Human Virology Information Guides	http://www.ihv.org/guides/index.html
Western Kentucky University course on microbiology of HIV	http://bioweb.wku.edu/courses/BIOL115/Wyatt/HIV/HIV.htm

INDEX

✦

ABOUT THE AUTHORS

⋄

Note: Names marked with an asterisk designate contributors who also served on the Consensus Panel.

Rosi Andrade, Ph.D., is a research associate with the Southwest Institute for Research on Women in the College of Social and Behavioral Sciences at the University of Arizona. She holds a terminal degree in reading with a minor in Chicana literature.

Francesca A. Armmer, Ph.D., RN, currently serves as chairperson of the Department of Nursing at Bradley University, Illinois. She has been a nursing educator for more than 25 years. Her research emphasizes access to health care for vulnerable populations and leadership styles.

*Wanda J. Blanchett, Ph.D., is associate professor of urban education and associate dean for academic affairs in the School of Education at the University of Wisconsin–Milwaukee. Her research focuses on urban teacher preparation; issues of race, class, culture, and gender; overrepresentation of African American students in special education; and issues of sexuality and disability.

Nirmala Erevelles, Ph.D., is associate professor of social foundations of education in the Department of Educational Leadership, Policy, and Technology Studies at the University of Alabama. Her research and teaching are in the areas of sociology of education, disability studies, multicultural education, Third World/postcolonial feminist theory, and qualitative research methodologies.

Reginald Fennell, Ph.D., is professor of health education in the Department of Physical Education, Health, and Sports Studies at Miami University (OH). His scholarly interests include health education and human sexuality with an emphasis on HIV/AIDS education and research as these relate to knowledge, attitudes, and behaviors of individuals; Black Americans and health issues as these relate to disparities; international health; and men's health.

Paulo Freire, Ph.D., one of the most influential education theorists of the twentieth century, was a Brazilian educator dedicated to educational practices that advanced liberty and humanity, with a particular interest in empowering the oppressed. His most famous publication is *Pedagogy of the Oppressed.* Freire died in 1997.

Matthew George, Jr., Ph.D., is associate professor and chairman of the Department of Biochemistry and Molecular Biology at Howard University, College of Medicine (DC). His research centers on molecular genetics, molecular evolution, and mitochondrial DNA.

*Yolanda S. George, M.S., is deputy director of the Directorate for Education and Human Resources Programs at the American Association for the Advancement of Science. Her responsibilities include developing and implementing projects and studies designed to increase the participation of minorities, women, and disabled persons in science, math, and engineering.

*Carl A. Grant, Ph.D., is Hoefs-Bascom Professor and chair of the Department of Curriculum and Instruction at the University of Wisconsin, Madison. His research interests include multicultural education, preservice and in-service teacher education, and urban education.

*Lisa Green-Derry, M.A., is currently employed as a teacher of seventh-grade science in the Dallas (TX) Independent School District. She is a doctoral student in the School of Urban and Public Affairs at the University of Texas at Arlington. Much of her work focuses on curriculum and instruction, staff development, and culturally responsive educational practices.

*Mose Yvonne Brooks Hooks, Ed.D., professor of education and director of teacher education at Langston University (OK), is a member of AACTE's Committee on Global and International Teacher Education. Her research in Europe, Africa, and Asia has focused on HIV/AIDS issues in teacher education. She also has served as dean and as vice president in higher education.

Elaine V. Howes, Ph.D., is in the Department of Secondary Education in the College of Education at the University of South Florida, Tampa. Her research is focused on teachers (preservice and practicing) learning to teach science well to all children, particularly to those who are underserved by our schools.

Neena Khanna, Ph.D., is a researcher for the Interdisciplinary Human Development Institute at the University of Kentucky. She previously taught graduate school in India at Kurukshetra University and worked at the Rehabilitation Council of India.

*Beverly Lindsay, Ph.D., Ed.D., the first American to become a Senior Fulbright Specialist in South Korea and Zimbabwe, is professor and senior scientist of higher education and international policy studies at Pennsylvania State University. She is a former American Council on Education governmental fellow and former international affairs dean at Hampton University (VA) and Penn State.

*Donaldo Macedo, Ph.D., is professor of English and distinguished professor of liberal arts and education at the University of Massachusetts, Boston. He is also the university's graduate program director of the applied linguistics M.A. program. He has published extensively in the areas of linguistics, critical literacy, and bilingual and multicultural education.

Valerie L. Mazzotti, M.A., teaches exceptional children in an inclusive classroom setting for the Charlotte Mecklenburg School District (NC). Her research interests include multicultural education and HIV/AIDS prevention.

*Mwangaza Michael-Bandele, M.A., is director of the Build A Future Without AIDS project at AACTE and guided the work of the Association's Consensus Panel on HIV/AIDS and Teacher Education. She is a doctoral candidate at Morgan State University (MD) whose research interests include translating the value of indigenous knowledge into teacher education.

*James M. Mitchell, Ph.D., is assistant professor of teacher education at California State University, East Bay. He has worked in the HIV/AIDS education field since 1995, beginning when he was a doctoral student at the University of Minnesota.

Luis C. Moll, Ph.D., is associate dean for academic affairs and professor of language, reading, and culture at the College of Education of the University of Arizona. His main research interest is the connection among culture, psychology, and education, especially as it relates to the education of Latino children in the United States.

Barnabas Otaala, Ed.D., is professor in the College of Education at the University of Namibia. He is currently chairperson of the university's HIV/AIDS task force as well as director of its HIV/AIDS unit. He has previously taught at Makerere University, Kampala, Uganda; Kenyatta University, Nairobi, Kenya; the University of Botswana, Gaborone, Botswana; and the National Teachers College, Maseru, Lesotho.

Mary Anne Prater, Ph.D., is professor and chair of the Counseling Psychology and Special Education Department at Brigham Young University (UT). Her research interests include portrayal of disabilities in children's literature, effective instruction for students with mild disabilities, and special education teacher preparation. She earned her doctorate in special education from Utah University.

*Farah A. Ramirez-Marrero, Ph.D., is associate professor in the Department of Physical Education and Recreation at the College of Education, University of Puerto Rico, Rio Piedras. She directs one of AACTE's three Build a Future Without AIDS demonstration sites. Her research focuses on physical activity and health of people living with HIV in Puerto Rico.

*Dirck Roosevelt, Ph.D., is director of the Master of Arts in Teaching Program and associate professor of education at Brandeis University (MA). His current scholarship and practice address teachers' earning of intellectual and moral authority for their work as teachers in the context of education for democracy.

Bill Rosenthal, Ph.D., is director of the El Barrio–Hunter College Professional Development School Partnership in New York City and adjunct instructor in the Department of Secondary Education at the University of South Florida in Tampa. His principal professional interests are school-university collaborations, feminist critiques of mathematics, and mathematics teacher education for societal awareness and social activism.

*Jerry Rosiek, Ph.D., is associate professor of educational research at the University of Oregon, where he teaches cultural foundations of education and qualitative research methodology. His current research focuses on the intersection of discursive structures that enable or disable teachers' practice and the type of preparation teachers need if they are to navigate those contexts constructively. His articles have appeared in leading journals such as *Harvard Educational Review, Educational Researcher,* the *Journal of Teacher Education, Curriculum Theory,* and *Educational Theory.*

Joan L. Sattler, Ed.D., is dean and professor of education at the College of Education and Health Sciences at Bradley University (IL). Her research and publications are in the fields of teacher education and special education. She currently serves on the Specialty Areas Studies Board of the National Council for Accreditation of Teacher Education.

Ladislaus M. Semali, Ph.D., is associate professor in the Department of Curriculum and Instruction at Pennsylvania State University. He is a media analyst and director of the Interinstitutional Consortium on Indigenous Knowledge. His research interests explore the comparative study and analysis of media languages, contexts of cross-cultural literacy curricula, and critical media literacy across the curriculum.

Nancy M. Sileo, Ed.D., is associate professor in the Department of Special Education at the University of Nevada at Las Vegas. She is currently assistant chair and graduate coordinator for the department. Her areas of expertise and professional focus include early childhood special education, teacher education, and HIV/AIDS prevention education.

*Thomas W. Sileo, Ed.D., is professor in the Department of Special Education at the University of Hawaii at Manoa. His research and professional interests focus on multicultural considerations for HIV/AIDS prevention education.

Karen C. Spear-Ellinwood, Ed.S., JD, is a doctoral student in language, reading, and culture at the College of Education, University of Arizona. She is currently studying post-Vygotskian activity theory, cultural mediation of learning and development, and issues concerning language ideologies and language policy.

Sally Stevens, Ph.D., is executive director of the Southwest Institute for Research on Women at the University of Arizona. She has conducted large-scale process and outcome research studies in the areas of education, health disparities, substance use, HIV and other infectious diseases, and mental health issues. Much of her work has focused on at-risk Mexican-origin Hispanics and American Indians living in the southwestern United States and on cultural and gender issues specifically applicable to these groups.

*Liane M. Summerfield, Ph.D., is associate dean in the School of Health Professions at Marymount University in Arlington, VA, where she is also professor of health promotion. Summerfield teaches and writes in the areas of health promotion and nutrition education and was principal investigator for AACTE's Build a Future Without AIDS project.

ADDITIONAL CONSENSUS PANEL MEMBERS

Michael G. Caruso, Ph.D., serves as assistant superintendent for secondary schools and government relations for the Archdiocese of Washington. He has served as dean of education at Trinity College (DC) and as lead author of the first two reports to Congress on the Child Care and Development Block Grant program.

Gwendolyn H. Middlebrooks, Ph.D., is associate professor of education at Spelman College (GA). Her research, publications, and professional presentations focus on instructional methods and on teaching and learning in urban settings.

Wil Parker, M.Ed., is manager of diversity initiatives and minority recruitment for the National Board for Professional Teaching Standards. He serves as a professional development specialist for teacher education leaders and has worked in HIV/AIDS education since 1987.

Marcia Rubin, Ph.D., is director of research and sponsored programs for the American School Health Association and has represented the Association on the AACTE Advisory Board for a number of years. She earned a terminal degree in health education from the University of Illinois at Urbana-Champaign and a master's degree in public health from the University of Minnesota.

David Scanlon, Ph.D., is associate professor of special education in the Lynch College of Education at Boston College (MA). His scholarship focuses on learning disabilities and content-area teaching and learning.

Maria Sosa, M.A., is senior project director at the American Association for the Advancement of Science. She is co-principal investigator of the Healthy People 2010 Library Initiative, funded by the National Institutes of Health, and editor-in-chief of the review journal *Science Books & Films*.

Build a Future Without AIDS Project Support Staff

Catherine Anyaso, M.A., program associate, recently completed her graduate degree in literature from Johns Hopkins University.

Bonita Walker, administrative assistant, is a senior at Howard University who is dedicated to preventing HIV and AIDS in underserved communities.